MW00666916

A NATION **RISING**

NARRATING NATIVE HISTORIES

YANKEE
GO
HO

A NATION RISING

Hawaiian Movements for Life, Land, and Sovereignty

Noelani Goodyear-Ka'ōpua, Ikaika Hussey
& Erin Kahunawaika'ala Wright, EDITORS

PHOTOGRAPHS BY *Edward W. Greevy*

Duke University Press Durham and London 2014

Printed in the United States of America on acid-free paper ∞
Text designed by Chris Crochetière, BW&A Books, Inc.
Typeset in Arno and Fette Engschrift DIN 1451 by BW&A Books, Inc.

Library of Congress Cataloging-in-Publication Data
A nation rising : Hawaiian movements for life, land, and sovereignty /
Noelani Goodyear-Ka'ōpua, Ikaika Hussey, and Erin Kahunawaika'ala Wright, editors ; photographs by Edward W. Greevy.
pages cm—(Narrating Native histories)
Includes bibliographical references and index.
ISBN 978-0-8223-5683-7 (cloth : alk. paper)
ISBN 978-0-8223-5695-0 (pbk. : alk. paper)
1. Hawaiians—Government relations. 2. Sovereignty. I. Goodyear-Ka'ōpua, Noelani. II. Hussey, Ikaika. III. Wright, Erin Kahunawaika'ala IV. Series: Narrating Native histories.
DU624.65.N358 2014
323.1199'42—dc23
2014006868

Duke University Press gratefully acknowledges the support of The Kohala Center, which provided funds toward the publication of this book.

Cover photo: Kumu Hina Wong-Kalu and students of Hālau Lōkahi, 2007.
Frontispiece: "Yankee, Go Home!," Kalani 'Ohelo, Kalama Valley, May 1971.

No ka po'e aloha 'āina

Contents

Illustrations

About the Series

Narrating Native Histories aims to foster a rethinking of the ethical, methodological, and conceptual frameworks within which we locate our work on Native histories and cultures. We seek to create a space for effective and ongoing conversations between North and South, Natives and non-Natives, academics and activists, throughout the Americas and the Pacific region.

This series encourages analyses that contribute to an understanding of Native peoples' relationships with nation-states, including histories of expropriation and exclusion as well as projects for autonomy and sovereignty. We encourage collaborative work that recognizes Native intellectuals, cultural interpreters, and alternative knowledge producers, as well as projects that question the relationship between orality and literacy.

Acknowledgments

We first recognize the kūpuna of generations past who have guided and sustained us; these include all our lands and waters, as well as the beings who reside in all places around us. While this book features the names and stories of many individuals and communities who have enacted and fought for ea—life, breath, land, and sovereignty—there are thousands who have engaged in and inspired Hawaiian movements. This book honors the collective efforts of all those who have pushed Hawaiian movements forward. Mai ka pi'ina a ka lā i Kumukahi ā ka welo 'ana i Hōlanikū, mai ke kumuhonua i luna a'e i ka lewa lani, mahalo i nā po'e ā pau.

Like the movements explored in this collection, the book itself has also been a collective effort. Several people read drafts of key portions of this book. Mahalo nui to Noenoe Silva, Terri Keko'olani, Joan Lander, Candace Fujikane, Dean Saranillio, Judy Rohrer, Vince Diaz, and an anonymous reviewer secured by Duke University Press. Great thanks go to Iokepa Casumbal-Salazar for his work on the bibliography and to Bryan Kamaoli Kuwada for his assistance on the index. We extend our mahalo to Tsianina Lomawaima for her support of this project from very early on in the process. Many thanks go to Valerie Millholland and Gisela Fosado at Duke for their assistance in seeing this project through to completion.

Mahalo nui to Kate Bell and Tom Blackburn of the Deviants from the Norm Fund for their generous donation supporting the printing of this book. Mahalo also to Matt Hamabata and The Kohala Center for helping to make and facilitate this connection. A fellowship funded by the Andrew W. Mellon Foundation, Kamehameha Schools, Kahiau Foundation, and The Kohala Center allowed Noelani to work on this book. Hawai'inuiākea School for Hawaiian Knowledge also provided support for some of the photo printing costs.

Ed Greevy would particularly like to thank the following individuals for the ideas and assistance they provided: Ho'ala Greevy, Haunani-Kay Trask, David Stannard, John and Lucy Witeck, Ha'aheo Mansfield, John Dominis Holt, Joni Bagood of Mokauea, John and Marion Kelly, Kathleen Kelly, Barry Nakamura, Soli Nīheu, Kalama Nīheu, Ke'ala Kelly, Neil Sananikone, Masako Ikeda, P. F. Bently, Hadi Salehi, Bennett Hymer of Mutual Publishing, Lopaka Mansfield, Donna Green, Kathryn Joiner, Antonio Andres, Nancy Aleck, Setsu Okubo, Kitty Bartel, and Bob Stauffer.

Mahalo nui to the additional photographers who donated their photos to this book: Kalei Nuʻuhiwa, Franco Salmoiraghi, Michael Puleloa, and Bryna Storch.

Mahalo me ke aloha to Kumu Hina Wong-Kalu and Hālau Lōkahi Public Charter School for gracing the cover of this book and for your steadfast commitment to aloha ʻāina and ea.

Introduction

Noelani Goodyear-Kaʻōpua

> Free the waters and the land you stole from me.
> I don't wanna wait for anotha' minamina century,
> Because you owe it all, from the mountains to the reef.
> We gonna carry on, til our liberty—sweet sovereignty.
> Yeah, sweet sovereignty.
>
> —KAPALI KEAHI OF LAHAINA GROWN

A constellation of land struggles, peoples' initiatives, and grassroots organizations gave rise to what has become known as the Hawaiian movement or the Hawaiian sovereignty movement. These Hawaiian movements for life, land, and sovereignty changed the face of contemporary Hawaiʻi. Through battles waged in courtrooms, on the streets, at the capitol building, in front of landowners' and developers' homes and offices, on bombed-out sacred lands, in classrooms and from tents on the beaches, Kanaka Maoli pushed against the ongoing forces of U.S. occupation and settler colonialism that still work to eliminate or assimilate us. Such movements established recognition of and funding for Hawaiian language instruction in public schools. They got the largest military in the world to stop bombing and begin the cleanup of Kahoʻolawe Island. They preserved, even if sometimes temporarily, entire coastlines or sections of various islands from being turned into suburban and commercial hubs. Because of Hawaiian movements like those documented in this book, water in Hawaiʻi is protected as a public trust; Indigenous cultural practitioners can continue to access necessary natural resources and sacred sites; white supremacy cannot go unchecked; and the unadjudicated claims of the Hawaiian Kingdom's descendants to our national lands and sovereignty still remain intact. There have, of course, been major losses too: highways built over burials and religious temples, the eviction of families from their ancestral homelands, and the alienation of communities from once-productive fishponds and taro fields. The stories gathered in this collection chronicle some of these gains and losses, and, in so doing, emphasize the active role Kanaka Maoli have played in the making of our own histories.

Our usage of the term "Kanaka Maoli" is itself a result of the movements discussed in this book. In the late 1980s and 1990s, this way of self-identifying became more and more frequent, as the Native Hawaiian people asserted our distinctive identity in our own language. The reemergence of ancestral ways of describing ourselves also disrupts the racialized, U.S. legal definition of "native Hawaiian," which uses blood quantum measurements that do not emerge from Hawaiian culture. In this introduction and the larger collection, the authors use the terms "Kanaka Maoli," "Kanaka 'Ōiwi," or simply "Kanaka," "Maoli," or "'Ōiwi," to refer to the autochthonous people of the Hawaiian archipelago—the original people who emerged from this place.[1] These terms indicate our genealogical relationship to the lands and waters of our islands and distinguish us from other residents.

What are the struggles, relationships, and strategies that gave rise to what has come to be known as the Hawaiian movement? What key tensions have formed its contours? Who are the people who have shaped Kanaka Maoli movements? What values, demands, strategies, and networks have they articulated, thus defining late twentieth- and early twenty-first-century Hawaiian politics? What lessons can we learn from their stories? In addressing these questions, this book brings together the voices of scholars, community organizers, journalists, and filmmakers who have led, participated in, or closely studied Hawaiian social movements. Most but not all of the writers are 'Ōiwi. The text is complemented by images primarily captured by Ed Greevy, a non-Hawaiian photographer who has worked in support of grassroots peoples' movements in Hawai'i by documenting various communities in struggle since the 1970s.

This volume includes a range of issues, communities, and individuals from across the archipelago. However, this book is not intended to be a comprehensive accounting of all the people, lands, and events that have composed the contemporary Hawaiian movement. There are many more stories to be told. We hope this book will catalyze new opportunities for retelling and reflecting upon the countless mo'olelo, or narratives, of Hawaiian movement during this period and beyond.

The essays and images in this book work toward two broad aims. First, this collection allows readers to see a multiplicity of claims and strategies that have emerged from Hawaiian movements to protect and revitalize lands, histories, language, and spiritual and economic practices. While the term "Hawaiian movement" is sometimes used, this dynamic force should not be seen monolithically. This book gathers a range of voices from the movement, recognizing the common commitment to restoring the collective well-being of the lāhui 'Ōiwi Hawai'i while also honoring the fact that a diversity of positions and perspectives is a mark of a healthy nation. In that regard, this collection resists knee-jerk criticisms that suggest Hawaiians cannot or should not have land and sovereignty because "they just cannot agree or get together." As a political goal and praxis, ea (see explanation below) is unifying while also open enough to allow for a robust expression of differences. This diversity should be celebrated. This book does not seek to romanticize late twentieth- and early twenty-first-century Hawaiian movements. A number of the essays take up the productive and sometimes paralyzing tensions that emerged within different conjunctures of people and agendas. In this way, the contributors present our words and images as evidence that Hawaiian life, land, and sovereignty persists.

Given the significant influence political, cultural, and intellectual Hawaiian movements have had on contemporary life in Hawai'i as well as in international Indigenous arenas, it is stunning that more books have not been written about the late twentieth- and early twenty-first-century movements for Hawaiian land and sovereignty.[2] Haunani-Kay Trask's *From a Native Daughter* (first published in 1993 and revised and republished in 1999) still remains the most widely known book on contemporary Hawaiian political movements even though the bulk of it was written about twenty-five years ago. More recent books, such as Ty Kāwika Tengan's *Native Men Remade* and J. Kēhaulani Kauanui's *Hawaiian Blood*, provide important, in-depth studies of particular aspects of Native Hawaiian cultural nationalist and political independence movements.[3] However, there remains a clear and dire need for Kanaka to narrate the fullness of our histories of twentieth-century resistance and resurgence, lest they be told by others or lost with time. Like the Hawaiian scholars, political leaders, and composers of the late 1800s and early 1900s, the contributors to this book intend to document the resistance of our generations for those to come, so that these histories may ground and inspire future decisions, actions, and identifications.

Second, this volume collectively explores the political philosophy and driving ethic of ea. Taiaiake Alfred, Kanien'kehaka (Mohawk) scholar and activist, has asked Indigenous people to consider, "How do we create a political philosophy to guide our people that is neither derived from the Western model nor a simple reaction against it?"[4] Ea can be seen as both a concept and a diverse set of practices that make land primary over government, while not dismissing the importance of autonomous governing structures to a people's health and well-being. In that vein, this book is divided into three parts—life, land, and sovereignty—each exploring and elaborating a different aspect of ea. Ea confounds arbitrary distinctions between politics and culture. It is a principle that includes both independence and interdependence. Most importantly, it is a way of living that has deep roots in Kanaka Maoli understandings of the nature of creation.

Ea: Life, Breath, Sovereignty

The word "ea" has several meanings. As Hawaiian language and political scholar Leilani Basham argues, each utterance of the word carries all these meanings at once even when one meaning may be emphasized. Ea refers to political independence and is often translated as "sovereignty." It also carries the meanings "life" and "breath," among other things. A shared characteristic in each of these translations is that ea is an active state of being. Like breathing, ea cannot be achieved or possessed; it requires constant action day after day, generation after generation.

Unlike Euro-American philosophical notions of sovereignty, ea is based on the experiences of people on the land, relationships forged through the process of remembering and caring for wahi pana, storied places.[5] In that vein, the essays in this book trace a genealogy of the contemporary Hawaiian sovereignty movement through the vigorous efforts of people trying to maintain or restore their relationships with specific lands.

Ea, in fact, extends back to the birth of the land itself. Basham writes, "'O ke ea nō ho'i ka hua 'ōlelo no ka puka 'ana mai o kekahi mea mai loko mai o ka moana, e la'a me ka mokupuni."[6] Indeed, ea is a word that describes emergence, such as volcanic islands from the depths of the ocean. In looking to mele Hawai'i—Hawaiian songs and poetry—Basham points out that the term "ea" is foregrounded within a prominent mele ko'ihonua, or creation and genealogical chant for Hawai'i: "*Ea* mai Hawaiinuiakea / *Ea* mai loko mai o ka po."[7] The islands emerge from the depths, from the darkness that precedes their birth. Basham argues that, similarly, political autonomy is a beginning of life.

While "ea" has long referred to political independence as well as to life itself, the term first became associated with state-based forms of sovereignty in the 1840s following the promulgation of the first constitution of the Hawaiian Kingdom. In an era of increasing European and American imperialism, nineteenth-century Hawaiian leaders took domestic and diplomatic measures to stave off foreign encroachment by securing recognition of Hawaiian sovereignty under the dominant international system of nation-states, sometimes referred to as the Westphalian system.[8] After a rogue British captain claimed the islands for Great Britain in 1843, Hawaiian emissaries secured the restoration of sovereign government. King Kamehameha III famously proclaimed, "Ua mau ke ea o ka 'āina i ka pono." Roughly translated: "The sovereignty of the land continues through justice and proper acts."[9] Hawaiian language and politics scholars such as Basham and Kaleikoa Ka'eo have called our attention to the fact that the king did not reaffirm the sovereignty of the government (ke ea o ke aupuni) but rather the sovereignty and life of the land itself (ke ea o ka 'āina), to which Kanaka are inextricably connected.[10]

Following this historic proclamation, the Hawaiian nation celebrated Ka Lā Ho'iho'i Ea as a national holiday annually beginning July 31, 1843. The first celebration, honoring Hawaiian independence, lasted over a week. That same year, British, French, and U.S. governments became the first Western powers to formally recognize Hawai'i's independence, and numerous treaties between the Hawaiian Kingdom and other states followed.[11] While these historical events and legal documents plainly demonstrate the centrality of Western notions of sovereignty to the changing definitions of ea, nineteenth-century Hawaiian writers also emphasized that the meanings of ea exceeded Westphalian notions of the sovereignty of a government.

In 1871, the organizers of Ka Lā Hoʻihoʻi Ea turned toward educating a new generation about the meanings of ea and of this significant national holiday. In a public speech, Davida Kahalemaile asked, "Heaha la ke ano o ia hopunaolelo, 'Ka la i hoihoiia mai ai ke Ea o ko Hawaii Pae Aina'?" ("What is the meaning of this phrase, 'the day the ea of the Hawaiian archipelago was returned'?")[12] He answered this rhetorical question with the following list:

> 1. Ke ea o na i-a, he wai. 2. Ke ea o ke kanaka, he makani. 3. O ke ea o ka honua, he kanaka. . . . 4. Ke ea o ka moku, he hoeuli. . . . 5. Ke ea o ko Hawaii Pae Aina . . . Oia no ka noho Aupuni ana.

> 1. The ea of fish is water. 2. The ea of humans is wind. 3. The ea of the earth is the people. . . . 4. The ea of a boat is the steering blade. . . . 5. The ea of the Hawaiian archipelago, it is the government.

The fullness of meaning in Kahalemaile's words cannot be captured in English, but we can begin to see some of the ideas he was suggesting to his audience. Ea referred to the environment that sustains life for creatures such as fish or humans. Water and air provide the media in which we absorb the oxygen that gives us life. Ea, then, is essential for survival. It is the environment in which we thrive. In exchange, people help to make the earth healthy and productive. In that sense, ea refers to the mutual interdependence of all life forms and forces. Additionally, Basham observes that Kahalemaile shows how ea is like the tool that allows us to navigate and guide ourselves—the large steering paddle of a canoe or the rudder of a boat. The list culminates with the statement that the ea of Hawaiʻi is its independent government. The holiday celebrates the return of life to that government in the wake of a threat to its very survival. In this list, then, Kahalemaile emphasizes that ea is necessary for life and that political independence is necessary for the well-being of the Hawaiian people. Yet he also shows how the meanings of ea surpass state-based forms of sovereignty.

The onset of prolonged U.S. occupation beginning in 1898 brought an abrupt halt to the growth of Hawaiian national life. After a generation under the occupier's regime, the Hawaiian nationalist press was largely extinguished. Control of the national land base was wrested from the Hawaiian Kingdom. The Hawaiian language was banned. For most of the twentieth century Hawaiʻi did not have a single school in the islands that made the Indigenous Hawaiian language or culture central to its curriculum. Stories of Hawaiian resistance to American takeover were hidden, overwritten by American historical narratives fabricated to make people believe there was a legal merger between the Hawaiian Kingdom and the United States.

But in the wake of the 1893 coup d'état by sugar businessmen backed by the U.S. Marines, Kanaka Maoli contested U.S. empire and called for the continuance of ea. In 1895, the *Buke Mele Lāhui* (book of Hawaiian national songs) was published shortly after a failed armed counterrevolution waged by Hawaiian loyalists against the white oligarchy that had claimed the government. One mele took the earlier proclamation by King Kamehameha III and framed it as a command: "E mau ke Ea o Hawaii i ka Pono."[13] The life and sovereignty of Hawai'i must continue in pono (justice, balance, goodness).

Almost five decades later, in 1941, Alvin Kaleolani Isaacs wrote a song that echoed the same sentiment. Like Kahalemauna's 1895 composition, "E Mau" ("Let's strive" or "Persevere") transforms Kauikeaouli's famous saying to future imperative tense:

E mau ko kākou lāhui, e ho'omau
E mau ko kākou 'ōlelo, e ho'omau
E mau ka hana pono o ka 'āina
I mau ka ea o ka 'āina i ka pono
I ka pono o ka 'āina

Let's strive to keep our nation alive, let's strive
Let's strive to keep our language alive, let's strive
Let's strive to preserve the good of the islands
so that righteousness may continue to be with us
all that's good in the islands[14]

The song was a favorite of George Jarrett Helm Jr., a Hawaiian musician, public intellectual, and activist who became a leader of the movement to stop the U.S. Navy's use of the island of Kaho'olawe as a bombing target.

Helm—a child of Moloka'i Island who grew up on Hawaiian homestead land in Kalama'ula—became a passionate community organizer in the mid-1970s, using his music as an organizing tool. Many elders first perceived him as a radical, until they heard him sing and speak to them in person. An eloquent orator and writer, Helm often sang and quoted "E Mau" as he talked to others about the importance of aloha 'āina, loving the land, and the need to defend Kaho'olawe and Hawaiian culture against further destruction by the U.S. military.[15] He and a handful of others from the Protect Kaho'olawe 'Ohana (PKO) put aloha 'āina into living practice when they landed on the island, placing their lives between the bombs and their 'āina. These landings were acts of ea, and they are retold in this volume by Jonathan Osorio, another Hawaiian musician-scholar-leader.

Helm and other members of the PKO emphasized the need to make not only an anti-imperialist political stand but also to honor and use the places our kūpuna recognized as sacred and to protect a way of life based on sustenance from the land and ocean.

Rally in the Valley, June 5, 1976. George Helm, a leader in the Protect Kaho'olawe 'Ohana, sings at a rally in Waiāhole in support of residents protesting eviction.

During the fourth occupation of the island in January 1977, Helm wrote, "The breath in man is the breath of Papa (the earth). Man is merely the caretaker of the land that maintains his life and nourishes his soul."[16] Here ea, both breath and sovereignty, reflects not a supreme authority over territory but a sacred connection to the land requiring dutiful, nurturing care. It was this connection that moved Helm and others to action.[17]

The remainder of this chapter provides some historical context for the essays presented in this collection, while also giving the reader a glimpse of what can be found in them. In so doing, it also attends to some of the rhythms of late twentieth- and early twenty-first-century Hawaiian movements.

Land Struggles: From Kalama to Kaho'olawe

In post-1959 Hawai'i, hotels and resorts were becoming the new plantations. Newly built luxury homes and suburban sprawl accommodated the rush of U.S. American settlers in the years after the U.S. Congress declared Hawai'i a state within its union. These "developments" displaced people who continued to live "Hawaiian style," relying on land-based subsistence practices like fishing, gathering, and farming. Multiethnic

Kōkua Hawai'i activists sit atop one of the last unbulldozed houses in Kalama Valley. Plainclothed police officers climb the ladder to remove them. On May 11, 1971, after a long standoff with the landowner, Honolulu police ended nearly a year of resistance that is often seen as the catalyst of twentieth-century Hawaiian movements. Photo courtesy of Edward W. Greevy.

working-class communities began to challenge the unfulfilled commitments of a post–World War II, local political establishment that had risen to power on promises of land reform.[18] Out of those land struggles, a Hawaiian nationalist consciousness reemerged, sometimes in tension with those who saw these contestations over land, culture, and power only through the lens of class struggle.

At Kalama Valley, for the first time in the twentieth century the landless who had been pushed around from place to place decided that they would stand up to the largest private landowner in Hawai'i, the Bishop Estate. Kalama Valley evictees like Moose Lui and George Santos were supported by Kānaka like Kīhei "Soli" Niheu, Kehau Lee, Kalani 'Ohelo, Larry Kamakawiwo'ole, Joy Ahn, and Pete Thompson of the Kōkua Kalama Committee. Together they pointed out the irony that an institution founded for Native Hawaiian students by a Hawaiian ali'i (chief) was evicting Hawaiians and other local farmers in order to build high-priced suburban homes that most Kanaka could not afford. Their occupation of the valley, against bulldozers and snipers, taught other communities that they could similarly organize.

The activists in Kalama broadened their analysis beyond that specific battle to larger trends of alienation and structural violence that were happening throughout the islands. Taking a broader view, they transformed the Kōkua Kalama Committee into Kōkua Hawai'i to support land struggles around the islands.[19] Over the next several years, the founders of Kōkua Hawai'i stood in many of the struggles discussed in this book—Waiāhole-Waikāne, Niumalu-Nāwiliwili, Kaho'olawe, Mākua, and Sand Island—as well as other antieviction struggles such as in Chinatown and Waimānalo. Davianna McGregor and Ibrahim Aoudé (chapter 2, this volume) describe the ways ethnic studies students and faculty from the University of Hawai'i at Mānoa organized to support many of these antieviction movements of the 1970s. The emergence of ethnic studies was intimately tied to the community organizing work of groups like Kōkua Hawai'i and others.

In her landmark article "The Birth of the Modern Hawaiian Movement: Kalama Valley, O'ahu," Haunani-Kay Trask describes the ways the discourse shifted through the 1970s, from land struggles in Kalama to Kaho'olawe:

> The Hawaiian Movement began as a battle for land rights but would evolve, by 1980, into a larger struggle for native Hawaiian autonomy. Land claims first appeared, as in Kalama Valley, as community-based assertions for the preservation of agricultural land against resort and subdivision use. By the mid 1970s, these claims had broadened to cover military-controlled lands and trust lands specifically set aside for Hawaiians by the U.S. Congress but used by non-beneficiaries.
>
> Justification for these claims had also expanded. In the beginning of the decade, the rallying cry was "land for local people, not tourists." By 1976, the language of protest had changed from English to Hawaiian, with emphasis on the native relationship to land. The cultural value of Aloha 'Āina (love of the land) was to characterize the demands of protesters into the 1980s. By then, the Movement had branched out politically to link up with American Indian activists on the mainland, anti-nuclear independence struggles throughout the South Pacific, and international networks in Asia and at the United Nations.[20]

In some cases, this shift from focusing on class-based land struggle to Indigenous cultural resurgence happened quite organically. For instance, Jacqueline Lasky documents the ways an antieviction movement in Waiāhole-Waikāne morphed into a struggle for the water necessary to farm kalo, the elder sibling and traditional staple food of Kanaka Maoli (chapter 1). After the victory of a multiethnic coalition of tenant farmers and other residents against eviction by a wealthy landowner, Waiāhole taro farmers shifted toward remedying the taking of tens of millions of gallons of water per day from streams that could feed lo'i kalo. This protracted movement inspired and connected with efforts on other islands to maintain or restore lo'i and to revitalize ecological health by replenishing streams with the water that had been taken for industrial sugar production. The

George Santos was a pig farmer who became one of the most vocal residents resisting eviction from Kalama Valley. He warned of two problems that would change Hawaiʻi: a flood of affluent settlers from the U.S. mainland seeking high-cost homes, and a resulting loss of agricultural lands. 1970.

battles over water on Maui Island, discussed in chapter 9 by D. Kapuaʻala Sproat and chapter 10 by Pauahi Hoʻokano, were informed and inspired by the Waiāhole water struggle. As Sproat argues, it was ultimately these movements that helped protect water as a public trust for all people in Hawaiʻi.

However, there were also times when the shift in focus from class struggle to Hawaiian nationalism was painful. For Kōkua Hawaiʻi, tension developed between hard-line Marxists, who emphasized the need to build a working-class, proletarian movement, and emergent Hawaiian nationalists, who were asserting the need for Native Hawaiian leadership, for cultural revitalization, and for recognition of the distinctive genealogical relationship that Native Hawaiians have to the islands. Kīhei "Soli" Niheu writes that during the PKO's early occupations of the island in protest of U.S. Navy bombing, he initiated communication "inviting PKO to come to Kōkua Hawaiʻi if they needed

"People Not Profits." In the 1970s, Michael McCormack announced plans for a massive condominium and marina project that would have destroyed the He'eia wetlands and fishpond. In August 1975, He'eia residents and supporters occupied Honolulu city and county offices for three days and nights. This photo was taken shortly after they were successful in gaining a conversation with the city planning director. Activists pictured include (from left to right): Lorna Omori, Mike Kido, Antonio Andres, Susan Wagner, Kitty Bartel, Jo Patacsil, Tony Bartel, and Joy Ahn.

to get information out." When the PKO responded with requests to disseminate their material, some Kōkua Hawai'i members were opposed. According to Niheu, "We did not print some of their requests in our newsletter, *Kōkua Hawai'i*. The collective that was printing the paper decide[d] against providing technical support. They condemned PKO's material as 'cultural nationalistic.' I was so angry. That was a conflict between the cultural and Marxist perspectives, and we were too dogmatic."[21] The efforts to stop the bombing of Kaho'olawe Island were organized explicitly around the assertion of distinctively aboriginal relations to land, which other "locals" do not have. This was an important change from the earlier ways the Kalama Valley struggle had been waged.

As Jonathan Osorio suggests in chapter 6, the PKO's longevity can be seen as a triumph of an "indigenous movement devoted to the realization of what are, essentially, non-western aims" over Western liberal ideologies.[22] More than just a challenge to Western liberalism, Kīhei Soli Niheu's analysis also reminds us that the PKO and other Kanaka Maoli cultural resurgence initiatives pushed against the Western radical tradition as well. Still, such ideological engagements have been and continue to be necessary. As Anne Keala Kelly's portrait of two houseless Hawaiian women warriors that opens this collection reminds us, in no uncertain terms: an Indigenous movement without a class analysis can be vapid in terms of its ability to produce meaningful change.

Culture Is Political, Politics Are Cultural

Hawaiian social movements have been, at their core, about protecting and energizing 'Ōiwi ways of life: growing and eating ancestral foods, speaking the native language, renewing relationships through ceremonies, making collective decisions, and simply remaining on the land. As "life," ea encompasses the cultural, the political, the economic. In observing the rhythms of Hawaiian movement over time, one sees peaks—or catalytic events—when the arbitrary boundaries between activities represented as merely cultural (such as hula or voyaging) and those cast as political (such as land rights protests or sovereignty rallies) are blurred. When people explicitly assert the ways cultural practice is political, and political movement is cultural, Hawaiian social movements leap forward.

In 1976, the same year that a boat holding nine people made its first landing on Kaho'olawe, the double-hulled wa'a (canoe) named Hōkūle'a made its first voyage from Hawai'i to Tahiti, led by Satawalese master navigator Mau Piailug. More than just a successful scientific experiment or an exercise in cultural wayfinding, Hōkūle'a became an icon for the renewal of Indigenous Oceanic pride and faith in ancestral knowledges. For Kanaka 'Ōiwi, the canoe's success was an in-your-face redemption against dominant narratives framing Hawaiians as incapable and inconsequential. Loretta Ritte connected her own involvement in the movement to stop the bombing of Kaho'olawe to the symbolic power of Hōkūle'a's travels: "Everybody told me Hawaiians were stupid, Hawaiians were lazy, Hawaiians were good for not'in'. That's how I grew up, raised on Kaua'i. That's what they told us Hawaiians." It was against this backdrop of racism that the vision of the Hōkūle'a approaching the island of Moloka'i, to which Loretta had moved in her young adulthood, refreshed and inspired her. "When the Hōkūle'a came and you see this magnificent ship coming in and [*her voice slowed and dropped to a hush*] there's no engine, there's no noise, only Hawaiians—hoooooh [*she shook her fist above her head then opened her palm over her heart, patting it several times*]—it was awesome. . . . [It was] a strong opening of the eyes of who we were as people."[23] Within months, Loretta became one of four individuals who crossed the channel between Moloka'i and

Kahoʻolawe to make the second landing in protest of the U.S. Navy's desecration of the island. What "opened people's eyes," she said, was the synergy of ostensibly purely cultural initiatives, like the Hōkūleʻa's voyages, with movements viewed from the outside as simply political, such as the PKO.

Both Kapā Oliveira (chapter 3) and Kekailoa Perry (chapter 12) similarly demonstrate the direct connection between the sovereignty of an Indigenous people and the health of their language. "Our identity, culture, and worldview pour forth from our Native language," Oliveira writes. She describes the multipronged approach that Hawaiian language educators have taken over several decades to build comprehensive educational systems and family support networks to revitalize the Native language, showing the ways that political organizing was necessary to establish these programs. Perry focuses on the specific tactics employed by a group of university students who sought to normalize the use of the Hawaiian language, against both blatant and subtle forms of institutional racism. The efforts to revitalize the Hawaiian language have been an indispensable part of Hawaiian movements of ea.

Following the spread of Hawaiian language immersion schools across the archipelago in the late 1980s and early 1990s, another group of Hawaiian cultural educators became explicitly politicized. In "Kū i ka Pono: The Movement Continues" (chapter 5), Manu Kaʻiama narrates the story of ʻĪlioʻulaokalani, the coalition of hālau hula (schools of Hawaiian chant, dance, and associated knowledges) that came together amid state efforts to regulate Hawaiian customary gathering practices out of existence. When ʻĪlioʻulaokalani held its first vigil at the capitol building in 1997, hundreds of trained dancers and chanters used their cultural skills as forms of political critique and opposition. Thousands more learned and voiced a small repertoire of basic oli (Hawaiian chants) as part of the Kū i ka Pono marches through downtown Honolulu that Kaʻiama describes. Comparing the early 1970s antieviction struggles, as at Kalama Valley, to the early twenty-first-century mobilizations of Hawaiian communities, one notices a growing sophistication in Hawaiian cultural-political expressions.

Tengan's essay closes part I by offering a *kiʻi* (image, likeness) of Sam Kahaʻi Kaʻai. Kaʻai, who learned the art of wood carving from his kūpuna before the Hawaiian cultural renaissance of the 1970s, crafted the kiʻi that sat upon the Hōkūleʻa on its first voyage. As Tengan describes, Kaʻai has purposefully used Hawaiian cultural arts—both material and martial—as a means to unify and move the lāhui (nation, people) forward. In pursuing excellence in ancestral arts, Tengan suggests, "the ancestors came into our world, [and] we too stepped into theirs." This intergenerational exchange has given potency to ʻŌiwi cultural-political practice.

Sovereign Visions: Independence or Nation within a Nation?

By the late 1970s and 1980s many Hawaiian movement leaders who had emerged from earlier land struggles and cultural revitalization initiatives were articulating an explicitly nationalist agenda and calling for sovereign control of a national land base. Over the next few decades two parallel streams developed within the Hawaiian sovereignty movement. One sought some measure of justice within existing structures of the U.S. government. This has included a nation-within-a-nation approach, which seeks U.S. federal recognition of a domestic-dependent, reorganized, and ethnically defined Hawaiian nation. The other stream fundamentally questions the jurisdiction and authority of the United States in Hawaiʻi and has emphasized the independence of Hawaiʻi as a country unto itself. Over the last twenty years, proponents of Hawaiian independence have further refined this position by proposing at least two possible avenues within international law: (1) decolonization through reinscription on the United Nations list of non-self-governing territories, and (2) deoccupation through protocols governed by international laws regarding occupation. To better appreciate the differences between the nation-within-a-nation and independence approaches, one needs a basic understanding of the history of the Hawaiian Kingdom's national lands.

The vast majority of the lands controlled by the state of Hawaiʻi and the U.S. Department of Defense in the islands are the Hawaiian Kingdom's Crown and Government lands that were seized at the start of the U.S. occupation in the 1890s.[24] Of the 4 million acres that make up the islands, 1.8 million comprise these two classes of seized Hawaiian national lands. The two separate inventories of lands became commingled. Just over twenty years later, the U.S. government threw a crumb to benefit "native Hawaiians." In 1921, the U.S. Congress set aside 200,000 acres—a tiny fraction of the 1.8 million acres of seized Hawaiian national lands—for a beneficiary class defined by a 50 percent blood quantum. Thus the statute came to define "native Hawaiian" in those fractionalizing terms.[25] In 1959, the U.S. federal government transferred the remainder of lands that did not get reserved for U.S. military usage or for the Hawaiian Homelands trust to the newly formed state of Hawaiʻi. Under the 1959 Admissions Act, section 5(f) designated these lands as a public trust that should serve five purposes.[26] One of these purposes was "the betterment of the conditions of native Hawaiians." The national lands of the Hawaiian Kingdom, which remain under the control of the United States and the state of Hawaiʻi, continue to be sites of contestation.

In the late 1970s, building on the momentum of earlier community-level struggles, the Council of Hawaiian Organizations and Alu Like sponsored several "Pūwalu sessions" that brought together hundreds of individuals and representatives of different Hawaiian associations. Many ideas about how to improve the collective conditions of the Hawaiian people came out of these sessions. One strand emphasized holding the state government accountable to its legal mandate to use the public lands under its control to benefit Hawaiians. A fiery leader from Wai'anae, Adelaide "Frenchy" DeSoto represented her district in the 1978 Hawai'i State Constitutional Convention and rose to chair the Hawaiian Affairs Committee. She championed the initiative to create an office within the state system that is intended to receive 20 percent of the revenues from the Public Lands Trust (since the betterment of native Hawaiians is one of five purposes laid out in the Admissions Act). As a result, the Office of Hawaiian Affairs (OHA) was established in 1978 to utilize the income derived from the Public Lands for the benefit of native Hawaiians and to hold title to any property conveyed to that entity.[27]

At the same time though, many Kānaka were concerned to push further than simply holding the settler government responsible for its historical neglect of trust responsibilities under its own laws. People began to challenge the very legitimacy of U.S. and Hawaiian state governments on Hawaiian soil in the first place. Vogeler's essay traces contemporary legal challenges to U.S. legitimacy back to attorney Pōkā's 1978 motion to dismiss a case brought by the state of Hawai'i against Wilford "Nappy" Pulawa (chapter 11). The same year that OHA was founded to work within the settler state system, Laenui was arguing: "We are not American citizens, we are citizens of the nation of Hawai'i, and we refuse to dignify the court by entering a plea." Outside the courts, protests at places like Sand Island on O'ahu brought to light the buried history of the Hawaiian Kingdom lands. Puhipau's self-portrait, "The Ice Man Looks Back at the Sand Island Eviction," recounts the way Sand Island was both a place for him to rediscover an ancestral relationship with the ocean and a means to discover the history of his country's suppressed independence. After their arrest for resisting the state's eviction of Sand Island residents in 1980, Puhipau and his two brothers, Bobby Henriques and Walter Paulo, retained Pōkā Laenui to represent them based on the argument that the United States had no jurisdiction over these lands.

Like Puhipau, more and more people began to remember the Hawaiian Kingdom lands as such and to refer to them as sovereign lands or simply Hawaiian lands. Building consciousness about the history, status, and health of these lands provided a critical piece in the development of Hawaiian sovereignty discourse. Hawaiian homesteaders pushed for the right to sue the settler state government for breach of trust obligations, and this initiative developed into one of the largest Hawaiian sovereignty organizations—Ka Lāhui Hawai'i (KLH)—which in 1987 established its own constitution, government structure, and master plan for reviving the nation.[28] Mililani Trask served as the Kia'āina or head of KLH for eight years during its heyday. Ka Lāhui Hawai'i was composed of individual citizens, Kānaka who supported working within a U.S. federal recognition framework as well as those supporting independence from the United States. However, the dominant approach within the organization was to first seek U.S. recognition and then to gain control of the public trust lands.

Beyond KLH, independence leaders that rose to prominence throughout the 1980s and into the early 1990s, such as Skippy Ioane and Kekuni Akana Blaisdell, rejected reconciliation approaches and argued for nothing less than full autonomy and the reestablishment of Kanaka ties to ʻāina. Perry, in "Makeʻe Pono Lāhui Hawaiʻi: A Student Liberation Movement" (chapter 12), discusses the ways a student-led organization theorized and operationalized an independence-inflected Hawaiian nationalist discourse. According to Perry, an active participant in that student movement, "Makeʻe's manifesto defined sovereignty as having 'complete independence and self-government. No sub-status or affiliation with the United States.'" Perry traces a genealogy of their revolutionary praxis not only to Hawaiian mentors but also to public intellectuals and activists such as Edward Said, Frantz Fanon, Malcolm X, and Black Panther Party leaders like Kwame Ture and Assata Shakur. He reflects on some of the ways Makeʻe Pono tried to prevent and deal with the kinds of internal challenges that underresourced, radical activist organizations often face, and in so doing he shows how the praxis of ea can be enriched by an international exchange of ideas and explicit group commitment to self-reflection.

One thing that both independence and nation-within-a-nation advocates agreed upon was the need to build a broad, popular movement of educated Kanaka who could exercise their right to informed self-determination. The massive organization of the lāhui in the 1990s required popular education and consciousness-raising based on sound research. Not only academics but people of all vocations were striving to remedy a century of historical miseducation. In 1992, a year before the centennial remembrance of the 1893 armed invasion and coup against the Hawaiian Kingdom government, forty Hawaiian organizations joined together with the goal of reeducating themselves and the broader public about the historical basis for Hawaiian claims for sovereignty. Taking the name Hui Naʻauao, a "group seeking wisdom or enlightenment," they led hundreds of educational workshops on Hawaiian history, self-determination, and different models of sovereignty.[29]

Then in 1993 several key events and texts brought popular consciousness and politically engaged Hawaiian scholarship to new heights.[30] In January, Kānaka from across the archipelago gathered to honor Queen Liliʻuokalani and the Hawaiian nation in a series of events taking its name from the queen's motto, "ʻOnipaʻa," to remain steadfast. A five-act dramatization over three days reenacted the events of 1893 at or near the actual sites. The ʻOnipaʻa observance culminated with the largest known march in Honolulu's history. An estimated 20,000 people converged at ʻIolani Palace, the Hawaiian Kingdom's seat of government. During a series of speeches on the palace grounds, Professor Haunani-Kay Trask urged the audience to remember, "We are not American! We are not American! We will die as Hawaiians! We will never be Americans."

In building momentum toward 1993, Trask and her colleagues at the University of

On January 17, 1993, in the largest known protest of Kānaka Maoli and supporters in history, roughly twenty thousand marched through Honolulu to ʻIolani Palace. Thousands remained at the palace bandstand for speeches and music throughout the day.

Hawaiʻi at Mānoa's Center for Hawaiian Studies had also worked in conjunction with the activist-filmmaker duo, Puhipau and Joan Lander of Nā Maka o ka ʻĀina to produce the documentary film *Act of War: The Overthrow of the Hawaiian Nation.*[31] The film debuted that year, and it chronicled the historical events surrounding the 1893 overthrow and 1898 annexation, making the findings of Hawaiian historians and political scholars like Trask, Jonathan Osorio, and Lilikalā Kameʻeleihiwa available to a broad audience. The year 1993 also saw the release of Trask's internationally renowned book, *From a Native Daughter: Colonialism and Sovereignty in Hawaiʻi,* which powerfully critiqued various aspects of life and politics in Hawaiʻi including corporate tourism, academic exploitation, the suppression of Native epistemologies and histories, and contract archaeology that has allowed the destruction of significant Hawaiian burials and other sites.[32]

Later in the summer of 1993 Nā Maka o ka ʻĀina documented the ten-day People's International Tribunal, Ka Hoʻokolokolonui Kānaka Maoli, which traveled to five islands

At the January 17, 1993, 'Onipa'a events, Haunani-Kay Trask roused the crowd that gathered to remember the 1893 invasion of the Hawaiian Kingdom and to protest its ongoing effects.

in the archipelago gathering testimony from people on their own lands.[33] The story of the tribunal is told in this volume by its convenor and members of the organizing committee, Kekuni Blaisdell, Nalani Minton, and Ulla Hasager. Additionally in 1993, Hawaiian independence leader Pu'uhonua "Bumpy" Kanahele organized a fifteen-month occupation of Kaupō beach in Waimānalo, O'ahu. The occupation not only emphasized the historical and legal bases for an independent Hawaiian nation, but also underscored the real, material needs of Kanaka Maoli for homes and for 'āina. Kanahele also spoke in numerous communities about the need for an economic foundation for meaningful Hawaiian sovereignty. In 1993, even the U.S. government recognized that "the indigenous Hawaiian people never directly relinquished their claims to their inherent sovereignty as a people over their national lands to the United States, either through their monarchy or through a plebiscite or referendum." Popularly known as the *Apology Resolution*, U.S. Public Law 103-150 did not, however, return any lands or powers of government to the Hawaiian people.

In the years following 1993, advances were made in shifting the terms of popular debate in Hawai'i, in peeling back decades of misinformation, and in winning some localized struggles. By the time Noenoe K. Silva published her 2004 book *Aloha Betrayed: Native Hawaiian Resistance to American Colonialism*, Kanaka could confidently assert that our ancestors had never relinquished their sovereign claims and had in fact urged, "E kue loa aku i ka hoohui ia o Hawaii me Amerika a hiki i ke aloha aina hope loa" (Protest forever the annexation of Hawai'i until the very last aloha 'āina).[34] Silva's reflective memoir in this volume (chapter 14) recounts the journey of the 1897 anti-annexation petitions back home to Hawai'i from Washington, DC. Nicknamed the "Kū'ē petitions," the stacks of paper moved many Kānaka toward the independence side of the sovereignty movement spectrum, as individuals came forward to look at and touch the signatures of their ancestors who expressed their absolute opposition to Hawai'i's incorporation into the United States. The petitions were successful in their own time, as the U.S. Congress never ratified a treaty of annexation of Hawai'i. And they catalyzed Hawaiian independence discourse at the turn of the twenty-first century.

Kūhiō Vogeler asserts in "Outside Shangri La" (chapter 11) that as Hawaiian independence discourse evolved into the early 2000s, "occupation theory" began to shed light on the specific legal status of Hawai'i as a country under prolonged, belligerent occupation. Scholars could now provide a detailed evidentiary basis for the legal arguments that Laenui had made twenty-five years earlier.[35] Vogeler further argues that occupation discourse has begun to supplant analyses that describe the Hawaiian situation in terms of colonialism and indigeneity. In a biographical style, he tracks Hawaiian historian Kanalu Young's journey toward deoccupation discourse.

In the last ten years, some scholarship utilizing occupation theory to analyze Hawaiian sovereignty has proposed throwing out the language of colonialism altogether, arguing that prolonged occupation and colonization are two mutually exclusive statuses under international law.[36] The legal clarifications made by Sai, Vogeler, and others may not require dispensing with an analysis of colonialism, however, which is more than just a legal status but a set of social relations. Consider: it is important to name an incident of harmful force by one individual against another as assault and battery in a court of law. But that does not preclude using other language to describe, heal from, and analyze the manifold repercussions of that beating. Likewise, one might consider that a prolonged U.S. occupation of Hawai'i enables the ongoing hegemony of a settler society—settler colonialism—with varying aspects and effects.

Kanaka Maoli continue to assert both national and Indigenous identities. In "Resisting the Akaka Bill" (chapter 15), J. Kēhaulani Kauanui illustrates the complex terrains Kanaka Maoli must face when asserting both a national independence claim and an Indigenous, genealogical rootedness in the national lands of the Hawaiian Kingdom. She illustrates what is at stake when notions of indigeneity are hemmed within U.S.

domestic law and politics. Kauanui provides a critical analysis of the Native Hawaiian Government Reorganization Act, commonly known as the Akaka Bill, which would give Native Hawaiians U.S. federally recognized status similar to Indian tribes and would fundamentally weaken Hawaiian claims to national independence, which have never been relinquished. Whereas a domestic dependent "reorganized governing entity" would consist only of registered Native Hawaiians, the Hawaiian Kingdom was historically composed of a multiethnic citizenry, with Kanaka 'Ōiwi having particular protections. The activists about whom she writes clearly state that Kanaka Maoli are not "an indigenous people of the United States." Rather, they assert both Hawaiian national identity as citizens of the Hawaiian Kingdom and a distinctively Native identity as the original people of this land. These independence advocates realize that a future, functioning independent Hawai'i would be a multiethnic nation that would have to reckon with the fact that Kanaka 'Ōiwi have become a numerical minority in our own country.

Le'a Kanehe describes biological dimensions of colonial practices in "Kū'ē Mana Māhele: The Hawaiian Movement to Resist Biocolonialism" (chapter 16). She argues that Indigenous people are dealing with invasion at the level of not only governing apparatuses but also cells, the building blocks of life. Explaining different types of incursion into the biological makeup of our bodies and lands, Kanehe argues that "biocolonialism in Hawai'i is an extension of the United States' invasion of our Kingdom in 1893." Indeed, "Hawai'i has had more plantings of experimental biocrops than anywhere in the United States or the world, truly making our islands an international and national sacrifice zone." Kanehe weaves her own analysis with critiques and narratives of active resistance from Kanaka attorneys, farmers, and educators, positing Ea 'Āina, or food sovereignty, as perhaps one of the most important aspects of Hawaiian movements in the present.

Complicity and Guarding Against It: Remaining on the Land

Debates over both U.S. federal recognition and the planting of genetically modified crops on Hawaiian lands are different iterations of a recurring question in Hawaiian movements: When and to what extent does one work within the very power structures that oppress us? Where is the line between pragmatism and complicity? As many of the chapters demonstrate, people engaged in various struggles for life, land, and sovereignty have had to decide when to negotiate with and when to stand in direct opposition to settler state and corporate authorities that benefit from the denial of Hawaiian rights. The authors show us how different individuals and communities have dealt with these difficult questions.

Anne Keala Kelly's essay features two women, Marie Beltran and Annie Pau, and their incisive views on the conditions of their own houselessness through a politicized

Hawaiian lens. Each lives on the beaches of O'ahu for different reasons, but both women display a kind of courage against state removal that, Kelly asserts, permitted marches do not. Her words call us to ask whether working within state institutions benefits or marginalizes those 'Ōiwi who are the most vulnerable (but also sometimes the strongest) among us. Simply by staying on the land, Marie and Annie provide examples of how powerful, and how dangerous, it can be to resist settler colonial logics of elimination and removal. For Kelly, the master's tools can never fully dismantle the master's house.

The portraits (and self-portraits) of Hawaiian elders Puhipau, Nani Rogers, and Puanani Burgess each take up this question of how to negotiate with the system without being completely changed by it. Puhipau writes of how he and other Sand Island residents made every attempt to work with state officials. And yet state forces turned people's homes to "smoking rubble." They went to court and then to the legislature to try and establish recognition of Hawaiian rights to be on the land, but to no avail. At that point he stopped letting his life's work be about negotiating with or reacting to the state. Instead he has spent the last three decades changing popular consciousness through film. Similarly, Nani Rogers has used radio to build networks and spread awareness. When 'āina is threatened, such as the desecration of iwi kupuna (ancestral bones) in Naue, Kaua'i, by a haole landowner with permission from the state, she will kū'ē, stand in direct opposition.

Puanani Burgess reflects on the physical and emotional threats of negotiating with state and corporate interests. Her early involvement in trying to minimize the "West Beach development"—known today as Ko Olina and, most recently, the site of Disney's Aulani resort—drew ire from those who wanted to preserve the coastline and those who wanted to build over it. However, the settlement reduced the allowable development size and resulted in funding community programs such as Ka'ala Farms. The experience of the controversies turned her life toward peace-building initiatives.

Several of the chapters also show that when communities put land at the center, they have been willing to use an array of nonviolent strategies to protect 'āina and 'Ōiwi relationships to lands: lobbying government officials, picketing landowners, blockades, lawsuits, and negotiated contracts for usage. In chapters 9 and 10, "A Question of Wai" and "Aia i Hea ka Wai a Kāne?," Sproat and Ho'okano each describe water struggles as active efforts to restore streams and kalo (taro) cultivation. Sproat provides a historical and legal framing for understanding water struggles in Hawai'i, charting connections between the cases of Waiāhole and Nā Wai 'Ehā (literally "the four waters" of central Maui). Her chapter demonstrates the importance of working through the existing legal system both to restore specific streams and to protect the broader Hawaiian principle that the common people and the natural watersheds need free-flowing water. Ho'okano's chapter on struggles in East Maui also demonstrates that even when favorable decisions have been made by state authorities to restore some water to streams, that water is not always released and is still diverted to the benefit of corporate interests. Kalo farmers have been forced to physically ensure that water is released on a consistent basis. Legal battles within the settler state system, while important, cannot be seen as the sole or ultimate answer. Communities must exert vigorous measures of accountability upon state and corporate powers, and this often requires being on the land so as to attend to any changes in the quality and quantity of various resources.

Jonathan Osorio (chapter 6) and Kalamaokaʻāina Niheu (chapter 7) illustrate the importance of building ʻŌiwi structures, even when working within or against the occupying state's systems. Both describe community struggles against the myriad violences caused by the militarization of Hawaiian lands. Both underscore that the demilitarization movements centered on each of these places have been about restoring ʻohana (extended family) relationships and processes. Each of these communities grounded their decision-making processes about when and how to negotiate with the settler state by putting the health of the ʻāina and the ʻohana at the center. Niheu argues that U.S. military occupation has worked to destroy the Hawaiian ʻohana system, which is fundamental to Hawaiian health. She details the ways the formation of the Mākua Village Council, comprising those living on the beach, helped bring families together. Similarly, Osorio suggests that the self-identification and purposeful structuring of the Protect Kahoʻolawe movement as an ʻohana, rather than an association, has contributed to its longevity and success.

Another core aspect of Hawaiian demilitarization efforts at Mākua and Kahoʻolawe has been the restoration of these ʻāina as puʻuhonua, or places of refuge and respite. While a puʻuhonua welcomes anyone, it is stewarded by a purposefully constructed extended ʻohana, or community, that can include but is not limited to blood relations. Organizations such as the PKO and the Mākua Village Council are examples of contemporary, nonstatist, ʻŌiwi forms of governance. When the PKO negotiated the 1980 Consent Decree with the U.S. Navy, it did so only after tremendous time, energy, consultation, and prayer had been put toward building the land-based, Indigenous governance structure of the ʻohana. Thus we see how ea is distinct from Western iterations of sovereignty specifically because of the continuous renewal of land-based, familial relationships requiring mutual care.

Expanding upon genealogical relationships between Kanaka Maoli and land, Noʻeau Peralto's portrait of Mauna a Wākea (more commonly known as Mauna Kea) grounds current controversies over construction on the highest peak in the Hawaiian archipelago. Recent struggles have been waged over the proposed expansion of University of Hawaiʻi–affiliated and corporate-funded astronomical observatories, such as the massive Thirty Meter Telescope complex. Peralto has stood firmly against any further industrial development of the mauna (mountain), yet he focuses here on sharing stories that will ground the reader in the cultural and historical significance of the ʻāina, so that people can make informed decisions about whether or not to be complicit with the construction of more telescopes on this sacred land and watershed. His essay draws on mele—a Hawaiian poetic form of mapping, storytelling, and honoring—to illustrate the long, genealogical relationship between Hawaiian chiefs and specific wahi pana (storied places) on this mountain. Ultimately, his portrait reminds us that our lands are in fact living ancestors.

The Photography of Ed Greevy and the Politics of a Non-Indigenous Ally

Another persistent question that this book explores is the relationship between Kanaka ʻŌiwi and non-Hawaiians in these movements. People of different ethnic backgrounds have asked, "What should my role be in Hawaiian movements? If Hawaiian sovereign government became functional again, where would I fit in?" Given this concern, it is helpful and necessary to tell a little of Ed Greevy's story. Ed's photographs are featured throughout this collection. A settler and ally of peoples' movements in these islands, Ed visited Hawaiʻi for the first time in 1960. He was among the many U.S. tourists, students, and settlers who flowed into the islands after U.S. President Eisenhower declared Hawaiʻi the fiftieth state in August 1959. A young adventurer from a working-class background in Southern California, Ed spent most of the winter and spring of 1960 in the waves on Oʻahu's shores, and he was hooked. He returned to finish college in Long Beach but dreamed of returning to Hawaiʻi to surf and perhaps become a surf photographer. When he graduated in 1962 he wanted only two things: to buy a high-quality camera and an airplane ticket back to the islands. Within a year or two, he was able to purchase a Nikon thirty-five millimeter camera. But the search for work led him in the opposite direction from Hawaiʻi to New York, where his sister lived. Ed turned his kitchen into a darkroom and became the editor and chief photographer for *Competition Surf* magazine, taking advantage of the spread of surfing to the northeast and Florida shores from Hawaiʻi via the U.S. West Coast.

By the 1960s, the launch of jet travel had made it significantly easier and less expensive for American tourists and settlers to get to Hawaiʻi, and so Ed finally made his way back to the islands in 1967, this time to stay. He spent a year and a half doing some freelance photography for a California-based surf magazine, as well as a few other commercial projects. Then one of Ed's editors asked him to find out about an activist group called Save Our Surf (SOS), which had been making waves even beyond the islands. The group had gained a reputation for organizing to protect surfbreaks from environmental damage by urban and suburban expansion.

By chance the next day, while buying film in a Waikīkī photography store, Ed saw a hand-drawn poster about the state of Hawaiʻi's planned Kūhiō Beach widening project. Save Our Surf was calling people to come out and oppose the state's plan, which

Ed Greevy making an adjustment to a Linhof 4 × 5 camera in 1967. Photo courtesy of Edward W. Greevy.

threatened the area known as Queen's Surf, Canoes, and Baby Queen's. Additionally, the poster highlighted the way rapid development plans were poised to impact sites all along the coast: "Of 143 surfing sites from Koko Head to Pearl Harbor, 110 are scheduled to be destroyed under present State plans . . . Speak up now—or wipeout forever!"[37] At the bottom of the poster was a name, John Kelly, and a phone number. Ed called John that night, and his life's course changed.

Within the week, Ed was sitting at an SOS meeting at the home of John and his wife, Marion Kelly. A group of surfers in their teens and early twenties was there planning for a protest at the state capitol against the beach widening project, which would have particularly impacted an area known as a safe training ground for kids learning to surf. Ed was taken aback by their energy and political awareness:

> All these young kids were spending a lot of time and energy on this particular project, and then they were also talking about other issues: The Kalihi community had no public parks whatsoever. . . . They were talking about the sewage pipe that runs two miles out from Sand Island, concerned about effluent washing back on beaches. This group at the Kellys' house was just amazing! About fifteen or twenty kids . . . full of enthusiasm! When their treasurer read the treasury report, they had less than ten dollars in their bank account! I'm thinking, any group whose treasury only has ten dollars and is planning a big event where they need a

John Kelly raises a fist at an antievictions rally at the Hawaiʻi state capitol building on March 31, 1971. His organization, Save Our Surf, organized for public beach access from the Honolulu airport to Portlock and for an end to the dumping of raw sewage into the ocean off Sand Island, where many surfed and fished. Kōkua Hawaiʻi members stand in the background. Their slogan "Huli!" means to overturn.

> lot of leaflets printed is not going very far . . . but they didn't seem worried about the money. They knew how to raise the money they needed, and they knew how to organize.[38]

Ed began attending weekly SOS meetings at the Kaimukī Public Library, thinking to himself, "I wanna see how far these folks can go." Within a few months he started helping to document SOS events, taking photographs so that organizers could focus on other responsibilities.

Through these early collaborations with SOS and the related land struggles, Ed's approach to photography fundamentally changed. He came to realize how his skills and the resources to which he had access could be of strategic use to people whom he saw as simply fighting to survive and to maintain a good way of life on their own lands. In terms of photographic technologies, the early 1970s was a qualitatively different time than the 2000s. Very few people had access to high-quality cameras, photo paper, or darkrooms. The relatively low-cost Kodak Instamatic series, introduced in 1963, had made cameras more accessible but the images were still nowhere near the quality of professionally produced prints. Because Ed had been doing some commercial jobs, he could print black and white photos of exceptional clarity at various sizes up to four by eight feet. Such images—the kind that typically only corporations or wealthy individuals could afford—could be powerful organizing tools. Ed began to see how he, as a haole settler, could help grassroots community groups with few financial resources have the kind of representational power that only developers and other wealthy interests had previously enjoyed.

Ed remembers one particular case when this realization came into sharp focus. Plans had been put forward to develop a tourist resort at Kaimū Beach on Hawai'i Island. Developers had publicly asserted that there were no surf spots at Kaimū, in hopes of avoiding widespread opposition to the development by those on O'ahu who were not familiar with the remote rural area on the archipelago's easternmost island. However, John Kelly and other SOS members had been to Kaimū and had taken photos at the beach there. Ed took John's negatives and blew up one of the images. Ed recalls, "At the next hearing on O'ahu, when the developers tried to say there was no surf at Kaimū, SOS members held up a huge print of three young residents having a great old time on a wave there." From that time on, Ed found much deeper satisfaction in supporting community groups and families seeking to maintain their own ways of life than he knew he ever would have found as a commercial surf photographer. Instead of taking photos of "underpaid Hawaiian women dressed in hula costumes for the tourist industry," he could capture the strength and dignity of the men, women, and children who were being ousted from their homes by that very industry and the waves of settlers, of which he too was a part.

Ed learned from John and Marion Kelly, among others, that there was a different way to be haole in Hawai'i.[39] He began going on volunteer jobs for a handful of progressive and radical presses on O'ahu. His goal was to capture "the people's perspective" for the people themselves, in ways they could use for their own political struggles. In describing his approach, Ed says that he "never went cold into a community." Rather, he always accompanied an organizer or resident who already had an established relationship of trust within the communities where he was invited to shoot, and he was often connected to these folks through the Kellys.

One of Ed's early assignments with SOS was to help with a neighborhood survey in Kahalu'u and Waiāhole, rural communities in Windward Coast valleys on O'ahu. The photos were to be used as part of a community-developed report that could counter the slick, proposed plans for suburban and commercial development that wealthy investors were putting forward. Shortly thereafter, he photographed for a similar people's counterstudy of land use in Niumalu, Kaua'i. Through such projects, Ed came to know Native Hawaiian leaders of community-based struggles, such as Stanford Achi of the Niumalu-Nāwiliwili Tenants Association or Emile Makuakane of the People against

Chinatown Evictions. He befriended Kānaka Maoli who started at the university and branched out to support multiple antieviction and anti-imperialism struggles, such as Pete Thompson, Terri Keko'olani, Joy Ahn, Kīhei "Soli" Niheu, and Haunani-Kay Trask. Ed also worked with non-Hawaiian organizers, some of whom were residents practicing subsistence ways of life—such as George Santos in Kalama Valley—and others who advocated a broader agenda of leftist politics—such as printer Ray Catania, and writer George Cooper.[40] His relationship with the Kellys was perhaps the most central influence on his photography, and he recalls learning as much from Marion's scholarly interests in Indigenous Hawaiian subsistence traditions as from John Kelly's deep involvement in on-the-ground organizing.

From these friendships and the injustices he witnessed firsthand, Ed developed a lasting commitment to supporting Hawaiian people and culture. Photographing communities in struggle, he reflects, "was a way for [him] to learn and develop [his] own understanding." In capturing images of people clinging to subsistence livelihoods or fighting for their ancestral homes, surf breaks, streams, and farming and fishing lands, Ed emphasizes that his photographs are not meant to capture "a people or way of life passing into oblivion." Rather, he hopes his images illustrate the persistence of people remaining firmly in the present against powerful forces of dispossession and erasure. He also intends these images to show that there are alternatives to what he describes as the "insane greed and destructiveness of capitalism and mainstream Euro-American culture":

> Hawaiian culture has a lot of important lessons to teach the rest of the world about how to get along with nature so as not to destroy the natural surroundings for the future; how to have a different attitude about land that is not about making it a commodity, making money by exploiting it. Instead, take care of it and it will take care of you. . . . Hawaiians are not the only ones to have that understanding, but it is mostly Indigenous cultures that can teach that lesson to a world that has been dominated by Western thinking about land and riches, and getting ahead with no real concern about what is being damaged and destroyed in the process.

In short, Ed still believes that "capitalism is the engine that is destroying the world," and he believes that the ancestral wisdom gifted to Kanaka Maoli and other Indigenous peoples may help humankind think about how to create economic and social systems that can carry us all into the future.

In keeping with this anticapitalist philosophy, Ed has given an inestimable number of hours of his time and countless prints of his art freely over the last four decades.[41] He has developed a reputation in the Hawaiian community for his generosity. The photographs contained in this book are only a tiny fraction of the tens of thousands of images

Joy Aulani Ahn, a Kanaka Maoli demilitarization and anti-imperialism activist, hands out fliers about the Stryker Brigade in Waikīkī, March 19, 2005. At the time, the U.S. Army had announced a land grab for training these light-armored vehicles built for urban warfare. Joy began her activism when the Kalama Valley struggle erupted in 1970 and remained an ardent supporter of revolutionary movements in Hawai'i and beyond throughout her seventy-four years.

in his full collection. This book also benefits from the generous sharing of images by professional and amateur photographers Franco Salmoiraghi, Kalei Nu'uhiwa, Bryna Storch, and Michael J. Puleloa. In looking at the written texts and the images together, we hope that the reader will see and feel some of the ea—the life, the breath, the independent and interdependent spirit—of Hawaiian movements and the people who have lived them.

Conclusion

In the last two decades there has been a backlash against Hawaiian movements. Some settlers have pushed further to eliminate Native difference through the courts. In her book *Haoles in Hawai'i*, Judy Rohrer describes this flurry of lawsuits "attacking native programs, entitlements, and preferences wherever they are found, including targeting OHA directly, the Department of Hawaiian Homelands, and the Kamehameha Schools admission policy giving preference to Hawaiian students."[42] In one of the most significant cases, Harold F. Rice, descendant of a white American missionary settler family, challenged the constitutionality of Hawaiian-only voting in OHA elections.[43] The plaintiff framed Hawaiians as a racial minority, rather than an Indigenous people or a national group with collective rights, and he argued that the voting provisions were racially discriminatory under the U.S. Constitution. The U.S. Supreme Court found in Rice's favor and opened elections for OHA trustees to all Hawai'i residents.[44]

In the introduction to *Asian Settler Colonialism: From Local Governance to the Habits of Everyday Life,* Candace Fujikane describes how *Rice* and the cases that followed it operate according to what Patrick Wolfe has described as a settler logic of elimination that erases Native difference, so as to further extend settler access to land, rights, and power: "Settler lawsuits claim that in an American democracy Hawaiians' indigenous rights to land and resources jeopardize democratic ideals. . . . In the most egregious of ironies, settlers proclaim that Native Hawaiians are depriving them of their civil rights, but they do so in order to use the argument of equal rights to take from Natives their rights and resources as indigenous peoples."[45] For instance, with the *Rice* decision, the small measure of electoral control over resources Kanaka Maoli could collectively exercise within the settler state system was immediately dissolved. The decision powerfully demonstrated the limits of asserting ea within settler state frameworks.

In light of the failure of the Akaka Bill to make it through the U.S. Congress thus far, the Hawai'i state government passed in 2011 its own version of a recognition bill—Act 195 "First Nation Government Bill"—which set up a process to create a roll of eligible Native Hawaiians who could then form a governing entity subordinate to the state of Hawai'i and U.S. sovereignty.[46] Like its federal-level counterpart, the act makes no provision for the return of land nor would it impact the U.S. military's use of Hawaiian lands.

Moreover, given the state of Hawai'i's efforts to exert sovereign authority over the Public Lands Trust, it seems unlikely that any significant amount of those lands would be transferred to a new "First Nation governing entity." For instance, in 1994 OHA and four private individuals filed suit against the state of Hawai'i, asking for an injunction against the state's sale or swap of any lands within the Public Lands Trust until the issues of sovereignty and title over the Hawaiian national lands could be resolved.[47] The case went all the way to the U.S. Supreme Court, which took on the question of "whether the Joint Resolution to Acknowledge the 100th Anniversary of the January 17, 1893, Overthrow of the Kingdom of Hawaii strips the State of Hawaii of its authority to sell lands ceded to it by the federal government until it reaches a political settlement with Native Hawaiians about the status of those lands."[48] In essence, the Court's decision stated that despite U.S. Public Law 103-150—the 1993 resolution in which the United States apologized to the Hawaiian people and acknowledged that the Hawaiian people and government never relinquished their sovereignty or national lands to the United States—the United States and state of Hawai'i still had sovereign authority and absolute title to those stolen lands. Adding insult to injury, when plaintiff Jonathan Kamakawiwo'ole Osorio, a Hawaiian historian and contributor to this volume, refused to settle the case, the state moved to disqualify him on the basis of blood quantum. The state attorney general's official position was that Osorio has no standing because he has "less than 50 percent blood quantum"—and therefore is not legally native Hawaiian.

Given these attempts to further entrench the settler state's claim to and power over lands in the archipelago, to exclude Kānaka who have asserted the collective political rights of Hawaiian nationals to these 'āina, and to contain and co-opt movements of Hawaiian sovereignty within a U.S. frame, it seems as important as ever to remember the legacies of struggle that recent generations of Kānaka have undertaken for life, land, and sovereignty. In looking to the past, we inform the decisions and commitments that will shape our futures. The contributors to this volume believe that the need for Hawaiian movements of ea is as great as ever.

The trajectory of the Hawaiian movement, as told by this collection, shows that it continues to be necessary to work on multiple fronts—to build highly localized land-based struggles and to articulate these grounded movements in a larger call for national resources. The mo'olelo also tell us that political autonomy may be a baseline minimum for the restoration of functional ea, but it is also only one piece of the puzzle. As many of the chapters in this volume suggest, the scope and complexity of the issues require 'Ōiwi and settlers to continuously and constructively engage in conversations and decision-making processes because the problems cannot be solved or swept under the rug even if full sovereignty, pseudo-sovereign government reorganization, or some other state-initiated settlement is achieved. Like breathing, the work of ea will continue on and on.

NOTE ON LANGUAGE: All glosses and translations included in this collection have been generously provided by the authors of individual essays. Translations never completely convey the richness of cultural meanings. Additionally, the interpretive nature of translation has at times had damaging effects on Hawaiian communities, as in other Native communities around the world. Thus, we suggest you take each gloss and translation as an opportunity to do further research or approach other Hawaiian-language specialists to supplement the interpretations provided in this book.

Following Hawaiian and Indigenous studies scholars, we chose not to italicize Hawaiian words because that marks them as foreign. In a book by and about Hawaiian people, the Hawaiian language is essential, and we avoid "other-ing" the language. This may require a bit of extra work on the part of those unfamiliar with the Hawaiian language. But we hope this additional effort reminds readers that the Hawaiian struggle cannot be easily known and understood through reading alone.

Throughout this text, we use the kahakō (macron) and the 'okina (glottal stop) when using the Hawaiian language, except when quoting text that was originally printed without these markings. Additionally, in a few instances, the authors or photographers have specifically preferred not to use these markings so as to allow for a more open reading of the possible meanings denoted by a word.

Notes

Epigraph: Lahaina Grown, "2000 Years," on *Lahaina Grown* (musical recording), 3:05–3:48.

1. In our usage of Kanaka/Kānaka, "Kānaka" is a countable plural form. It is not used for an indefinite plural, but rather when the actual number can be estimated. "Kanaka," the singular-generic form, refers to an individual person or to the whole class of people. It is also the form that is used when the word is employed as an adjective, such as "Kanaka scholars." Our usage in this text is guided by Hawaiian language experts No'eau Warner and Noenoe K. Silva, but the editors take full responsibility for any mistakes.

2. Some important texts on late twentieth-century Hawaiian sovereignty movements by Native authors include Sai, "American Occupation of the Hawaiian State"; Sai, "Slippery Path towards Hawaiian Indigeneity"; Beamer, "Na Wai Ka Mana?"

3. Tengan, *Native Men Remade*; Kauanui, *Hawaiian Blood.*

4. Alfred, *Peace, Power, Righteousness*, xvii.

5. For further reading in Hawaiian and Indigenous studies on the relationships between place, power, and Indigenous conceptions of sovereignty, see Basso, *Wisdom Sits in Places*; Deloria, *The World We Used to Live In*; Barker, *Sovereignty Matters*; Andrade, *Hā'ena*; Beamer and Duarte, "I Palapala No Ia Aina"; Basham, "Ka Lāhui Hawai'i"; Kikiloi, "Rebirth of an Archipelago"; Bacchilega, *Legendary Hawai'i and the Politics of Place*; Moreton-Robinson, "I Still Call Australia Home"; Moreton-Robinson, *Sovereign Subjects*; Somerville, *Once Were Pacific.*

6. Basham, "Ka Lāhui Hawai'i," 50.

7. Basham, "Ka Lāhui Hawai'i," 51, emphasis added.

8. The Westphalian system of states is often traced to 1648, when the major European powers of the time signed a treaty called the Peace of Westphalia. The nation-state emerged as the primary political institution for negotiating international relations, with the idea that one state would not intervene in another's internal affairs and that the interests of the state supersede the interests of any individual citizen or group within that state. The notion of Westphalian sovereignty is marked by these ideas of exclusive, territorial integrity, the centrality of the state form, and the principle that states should recognize one another's autonomy.

9. This translation disrupts the more popularly known version, adopted as the state government's motto in 1959: "The life of the land is perpetuated in righteousness." That translation empties out the historical context of Hawaiian Kingdom sovereignty and the longer lineage of 'Ōiwi autonomy in these islands.

10. Basham, "Ka Lāhui Hawai'i," 54.

11. The Hawaiian Kingdom entered into international treaties with countries such as Belgium, Denmark, Russia, Samoa, and Spain, as well as the United States, France, and the United Kingdom. For a fuller listing and discussion, see Sai, "American Occupation of the Hawaiian State."

12. D. K. Kahalemaile's speech was printed in *Ka Nupepa Kuokoa*, August 12, 1871, 2, and is quoted in Basham, "Ka Lāhui Hawai'i," 60.

13. Kahalemauna, "Mau Hawaii i ka lanakila," in *Buke Mele Lahui*, ed. F. J. Testa (1895), 15; quoted in Basham, "Mele Lāhui," 161.

14. While we might translate the lyrics differently, we include here the translation as it appears in two sources: at Huapala, an online Hawaiian music and hula archive compiled by Kaiulani Kanoa Martin, http://www.huapala.org/E/E_Mau.html (accessed June 10, 2011), and in Morales, *Ho'iho'i Hou.*

15. Morales, *Ho'iho'i Hou.*

16. Morales, *Ho'iho'i Hou*, 55.

17. See, for example, Walter Ritte's description of the motivations behind the 1970s landings on Kaho'olawe in "The Essence Was Aloha 'Aina" (video), Mo'olelo Aloha 'Āina, November 9, 2010, http://moolelo.manainfo.com/2010/11/the-essence-was-aloha-aina/. In this interview he states that the essence of the whole movement was love for the land, aloha 'āina.

18. Cooper and Daws, *Land and Power in Hawaii.*

19. Trask, "The Birth of the Modern Hawaiian Movement"; Niheu, "Huli"; Kido, "Becoming Local."

20. Trask, "Birth of the Modern Hawaiian Movement," 126–127.

21. Niheu, "Huli," 49.

22. For examples of other Indigenous social movements that have challenged Western liberal ideologies and settler colonial states, see Smith and Warrior, *Like a Hurricane*; Swain, *Oka*; Alfred, *Peace, Power, Righteousness*; Alfred, *Wasáse*; Moreton-Robinson, *Sovereign Subjects*; Harris, *Hikoi*; Allen, *Blood Narrative*; Walker, *Ka Whawhai Tonu Matou*; Marcos, *Our Word Is Our Weapon*; Marcos, *Ya Basta!*

23. Loretta Ritte, interview by the author, June 2009. Video clips of this and other oral history interviews with early Kaho'olawe activists can be found at the Mo'olelo Aloha 'Āina project website, http://moolelo.manainfo.com/.

24. Van Dyke, *Who Owns the Crown Lands of Hawai'i?*

25. Kauanui provides a detailed historical analysis of this fractionalizing 50 percent blood rule and the 1921 Hawaiian Homes Commission Act. Through a detailed analysis of the congressional hearings at which various versions of this measure were debated, she argues that the colonial project of racializing Hawaiians in the name of "rehabilitation" marginalized Kanaka Maoli entitlements to land and sovereignty. Kauanui, *Hawaiian Blood.*

26. These lands are frequently referred to as the "ceded lands," a moniker which many Kanaka Maoli oppose since the lands were illegally taken from, not given or legally transferred by, the Hawaiian Kingdom.

27. For many years, the state of Hawai'i did not follow its own law and failed to contribute the 20 percent in public land trust revenues to OHA. In 2008, the state negotiated a proposal to settle past due revenues through a package of cash and land, valued in total at approximately $200 million. The deal was completed in April 2012, when Governor Neil Abercrombie approved the conveyance of ten parcels in Kaka'ako (just outside downtown Honolulu) to OHA.

28. Trask, *From a Native Daughter.*

29. Nā Maka o ka 'Āina, *Hui Na'auao*; Vance, *Hui Na'auao*; Hawaii Sovereignty Advisory Council, *Preliminary Report of the Sovereignty Advisory Council.*

30. Nā Maka o ka 'Āina, *Hui Na'auao*; Nā Maka o ka 'Āina, *The Tribunal*; Nā Maka o ka 'Āina, *Act of War*; Osorio, *Dismembering Lāhui*; Trask, *From a Native Daughter*; Kame'eleihiwa, *Native Land and Foreign Desires*; Silva, *Aloha Betrayed*; Young, *Rethinking the Native Hawaiian Past*; Dudley and Agard, *A Call for Hawaiian Sovereignty*; American Friends Service Committee, *He Alo ā He Alo.*

31. Nā Maka o ka 'Āina, *Act of War.*

32. Trask, *From a Native Daughter.*

33. Nā Maka o ka 'Āina, *The Tribunal.*

34. This quote comes from Kaulia's speech in 1897 at the 'Iolani Palace. See Silva, *Aloha Betrayed*, 147.

35. Sai, "American Occupation of the Hawaiian Kingdom"; Vogeler, "'For Your Freedom and Ours.'"

36. See Sai, "American Occupation of the Hawaiian State"; Sai, "Slippery Path towards Hawaiian Indigeneity"; Beamer, "Na Wai Ka Mana?"

37. A digital copy of this flier, as well as numerous other posters, pamphlets, and other SOS organizing materials, can be found at the SOS digital archive: http://digicoll.manoa.hawaii.edu/sos/.

38. Ed Greevy, interview by Noelani Goodyear-Ka'ōpua, Mānoa, O'ahu, April 15, 2012.

39. Judy Rohrer has taken up this question extensively in her book *Haoles in Hawai'i*. She argues for a vigorous understanding of Hawaiian history so as to "begin to imagine how we might become haole in different, and hopefully better, ways. We have to know where we have been to know where we are going" (10).

40. George Cooper is particularly well known for his book *Land and Power in Hawaii: The Democratic Years*, coauthored with Gavan Daws. The book exposed the ways "the Democratic Revolution" in post-1959 Hawai'i did not lead to the kind of redistribution of land and wealth for which many supporters of that movement had hoped. Rather, there was a transfer of power and wealth from a predominantly white, Republican oligarchy during the territorial era to a new Democratic political establishment. The book documents the ways public officials used their offices to reap personal financial benefit.

41. Ed donated a large number of his photos to an open-source Hawaiian resource website, Ulukau. This collection can be accessed at Ed Greevy's Photograph Collection, Ulukau: The Hawaiian Electronic Library, http://ulukau.org/apo/cgi-bin/edgreevy.

42. Rohrer, *Haoles in Hawai'i*, 87.

43. Participation in OHA elections had previously been restricted to anyone who could trace their ancestry to the Indigenous people who resided in Hawai'i prior to 1778, the first recorded date of European arrival in the islands.

44. *Rice v. Cayetano* (98-818) (146 F3d 1075, reversed). Kauanui points out that "Hawaiians were in a fraught position, with no direct voice in the case, even though it was central to Hawaiian concerns." See Kauanui, "Precarious Positions," 7.

45. Fujikane, "Introduction," 15.

46. For text of the bill and its legislative history, see the 2011 session archive at Hawaii State Legislature, http://www.capitol.hawaii.gov/.

47. Initially, when the state had proposed a land swap of the Leiali'i tract on Maui Island, OHA asked that a disclaimer that would preserve any Native Hawaiian claims to this land be included. This request was made on the basis that the tract is part of the Crown lands of the Hawaiian Kingdom and the political and legal questions over the cession of these lands to the United States remains in question. Thus OHA and the other parties sought to preserve Native Hawaiian interests in these lands until final determination of the larger issue of sovereignty and the status of the Hawaiian Kingdom's national lands.

48. *State of Hawaii v. OHA, et al.*, no. 07-1372. Argued February 25, 2009. Decided March 31, 2009.

PART I *Life*

Men cleaning kalo in preparation for a community lūʻau in Kahana, Oʻahu, June 16, 1979.

Marie Beltran sits at a picnic table at Mokulēʻia, her ancestral home, where she and her family have asserted their right to remain even after several evictions by police. August 23, 1997.

Portrait. Marie Beltran and Annie Pau

RESISTANCE TO EMPIRE, ERASURE, AND SELLING OUT

Anne Keala Kelly

Homeless at home, Marie Beltran and Annie Pau assert their rights to ea under the direst circumstances. They, and other Hawaiians who live off the legal and economic grid, represent a profound manifestation of kū'ē—resistance—against the U.S. occupation of Hawai'i. But because that resistance derives as much from the culture of poverty as it does from the politics of Hawaiian culture, their stories get lost in a media world that won't accommodate such fine distinctions. In highly competitive corporate media where space typically goes to the highest bidder, the nuances of complicated lives are too inconvenient to unpack. On a good day, claims of Hawaiian independence, if acknowledged at all, are typically perceived by most people as too esoteric to take seriously. When coupled with the tendency to shame or to fear impoverished Hawaiians, it's simpler to portray people like Marie and Annie as being preoccupied with the specter of a lost kingdom, rather than as citizens of an occupied country.

The dearth of Hawaiian representation in media is one measure of the success of the U.S. takeover of Hawai'i. That absence of Hawaiian stories is what motivated me to produce journalism and documentary film. And when I say stories, I'm referring to narratives about dissent. The danger of Hawaiian resistance not appearing in forms of media where most people get the story of Hawai'i is that our absence codes as consent to being American; we appear to want to assimilate, to like being ignored and relegated to the detritus of listservs, YouTube, and public access. Being indiscernible amid a sea of non-Hawaiian people and media, we're inundated with their issues and values, which renders us invisible to, and easily removed by, the dominant, settler society.

The now normalized American social order and economy requires Hawaiians to assimilate or disappear. One common form of the vanishing Hawaiian is evidenced by the ongoing mass desecrations of Hawaiian graves. In my documentary film *Noho Hewa,* Kaleikoa Ka'eo refers to these exhumations as evictions, saying, "Hawaiians, we can get evicted from our own homeland even when we're under the ground." And these kūpuna (elders, ancestors) are typically removed to make way for golf courses, resorts, vacation homes, or military expansion. Another example is the disproportionate number of homeless or, as some say, houseless Hawaiians, also linked to the real estate industry and military expansion.

Hawaiians constitute a little over 20 percent of the population, not counting the eight million tourists who pass through each year, or the thousands of itinerant military personnel. But about 70 percent of the people who live in the margins—along the shores, in cars and vans, in parks, and in the bushes that line highways—are Kānaka ʻŌiwi, Hawaiian people. Homeless Hawaiians: unwitting warriors, conscripted and thrown onto the front line (possibly the only line) of resistance to the occupation.

Homeless Hawaiians like Marie and Annie exist in nomadic border towns that shift geographically to avoid capture by the occupying force, a.k.a. law enforcement. Their lives are a brutal paradox: they have a genetic and cultural knowledge of belonging, but foreign peoples and institutions have been coveting, undermining, and criminalizing that belonging for two centuries.

Marie Beltran: Ancestral Connections and Settler Removals

Marie Beltran and her ʻohana have recently gone to live with one of her grown children in the Nānākuli homesteads. Prior to that, three generations of Beltrans lived for many years at the beach park in Mokulēʻia, an area on Oʻahu that is their ancestral ahupuaʻa (traditional land division). Marie's tie to that place is so strong that even now she goes to Mokulēʻia and camps regularly, without asking for a permit from the state.

Like every Hawaiian living out in the open, the Beltrans previously lived in a house. They were renters, struggling to get by on what they earned and occasional support from state programs. But at a certain point it became easier to forgo the struggles of that existence and reach for something else that doesn't involve the occupying government, beyond the law enforcement arm of it.

To understand why people like Marie choose resistance over assimilation, it's useful to look at the social, political, and economic milieu through which she and her ʻohana developed their political consciousness.

Several major historical shifts occurred simultaneously between the mid-1980s and 1990s: the modern Hawaiian sovereignty movement, heavily influenced by postcolonial Pacific movements and the American civil rights movement, spilled into every corner of the Hawaiian community; the state and federal governments were actively seeking ways to co-opt and weaken the movement, one example being the 1993 Apology Resolution (and later, its offspring, the Akaka Bill); and Japanese and U.S. investments in real estate were quickly pricing average working Hawaiians out of the market.

Even as Hawaiians protested tourism and real estate expansion, and the resulting mass desecrations of Hawaiian burials, many who had previously been able to keep a roof while living below the poverty line were going homeless. Although the rhetoric from the Hawaiian intelligentsia was about rights for all Hawaiians, the impact of the psychological and material oppression informing that discourse was nowhere close to being equally distributed. Neither was the need for true self-determination.

Hawaiians like Marie had a choice: assimiliate, like the middle-class Hawaiians who were translating the threat of the sovereignty movement into professional and economic power within the U.S. system; or make the radical decision to insist on their rights to the land and to live as Hawaiians without asking for permission from the occupiers.

There are certain events in our history that we know have been bad for the ʻāina (land) and the ʻŌiwi, the most obvious being the arrival of Captain Cook and his syphilitic merry men, Christianity, and the overthrow. But on that list should also be the plantation era and the Great Māhele. These are just two systematic processes that were visited upon the makaʻāinana (common people of the land) by haole Christians and Hawaiian converts of the aliʻi (chiefly) and privileged classes. Whether they intended to dispossess Hawaiians or not, the privatization of the land has proven to be the most powerful mechanism for Hawaiian removal.

Even though Hawaiians, as a people, have yet to recover from the changes in land use and valuation, many individual Hawaiians obscure the fallout of that history by straddling the fence between being American citizens with class privilege and Hawaiian nationals. Some strut about as if capitalism has improved the quality of Hawaiian life, deploying concepts of aliʻi infallibility that could rival the papacy in Rome. And these disingenuous Hawaiians mask their privilege by giving the false impression that it derives from Hawaiian culture and genealogy, when in reality their positions of power and prosperity are granted to them through American values and state institutions.

When Marie and her ʻohana lived at the beach and on the side of the road near the park, she never wavered from her personal commitment to her rights as a subject of the Hawaiian Kingdom. It was a position she raised consistently in the courtroom, whether or not she had legal counsel, often invoking Kānāwai Māmalahoe. Known as the Law of the Splintered Paddle, established by King Kamehameha the Great, it originally protected noncombatants during war, but also gave women, children, and elders the right to sleep near a road if they need to.

Marie's life without a house was somewhat different than Annie Pau's, in that members of sovereignty groups became involved with the Beltrans on a number of occasions and more than once were present with Marie in and out of court. But that political support evaporated because, as Marie explained it, she wasn't willing to agree to one party line of sovereignty politics. While being homeless may be a result of the occupation, it didn't lead Marie to seek membership in any of the many competing sovereignty groups.

Life for Marie and her ʻohana at Mokulēʻia was simple: they collected recyclable cans and bottles; her husband John had the occasional job as a laborer or in construction;

Marie Beltran, her husband, John Keawemauhili, and their ʻohana at their home on Mokulēʻia Beach, August 10, 1997. They flew their Hawaiian flag upside down as a sign of distress and protest against U.S. occupation.

Marie made shell necklaces to sell to tourists who visited the beach. It was a day-to-day existence, but for Marie it was as close to a tradtional Hawaiian life as she could get, actually living on the land and limiting the degree to which she and her ʻohana had to assimilate.

Yet even without "normal" housing, the Beltrans' daily life wasn't that different than that of most people. On a weekday, she woke up her moʻopuna (grandchildren) and got them ready for school. She then showered herself with a hose that was connected to a series of hoses hooking up to a faucet some distance from her camp. She wore a *pareu* and soaped up and rinsed off. The kids collected their homework and books into their backpacks as the school bus pulled into the parking lot. The bus driver stopped first at Marie's van, then at the half-dozen cars scattered throughout the rest of the lot, picking up kids the way he would pick up any child waiting outside a home.

The day I filmed Marie, John, and two of their grown children being arrested for trespassing, they were living on the side of the road about a mile from the beach park entrance. This was about two weeks after they and all the others were evicted from the parking lot and a chain was installed to block the entrance after 7 p.m. Anyone found in the park after that time would be subject to arrest. Marie's family had already been threatened and she talked to me about her fear that cops would come in the middle of the night and kill her. She had a genuine concern about this. The frustration and anxiety Marie and her family suffered was juxtaposed with a clear understanding of ancestral, aboriginal rights to live in Mokulēʻia , and their right as Hawaiians under Hawaiian Kingdom law to live in a public area.

On the day of the arrest I witnessed, as they were handcuffing her husband and son, and then herself and her daughter, Marie's mind was clear about what the state was doing to her and exactly what she was standing for. She said, "They want me to be afraid of them, but I'm not gonna be afraid of them no more, for who I am and for who my ancestors are."

After they were carted off to jail, it took the police and the tow truck operators about ten minutes to confiscate all of Marie's belongings. All that was left behind was a cooler, a plastic chair, some odds and ends, and a bicycle. The removal happened so quickly that when it was over it was as if Marie and her family had never been there. (This scene appears in *Noho Hewa.*) Now when I see what looks like an abandoned bike or ice chest on the side of a road, I imagine that moments before I drove past a family was living there that was either evicted or arrested.

Annie Pau was living in the Haleʻiwa Boat Harbor parking lot at the time this photo was taken in 2011. Months later, she died of a stroke during one of the Honolulu Police Department's sweeps of homeless people from public parks and streets, in preparation for the Asia Pacific Economic Cooperation leaders' conference on Oʻahu in November 2011.

Annie Pau: Military Expansion and Ethnic Cleansing

In Hawaiʻi, military and nonmilitary are partners in the theft and decimation of Hawaiian land and resources. Every single day the occupiers' housing and material needs are met as countless Hawaiians go homeless, and even larger numbers of Hawaiians live their lives on the verge of becoming homeless. Hawaiians are terrified of ending up under a blue tarp on the beach or pushing a shopping cart down King Street. That fear, itself a form of oppression, keeps Hawaiians from taking on the system that causes Hawaiian homelessness in the first place. It's humiliating because it silences us to such an extent that we don't even talk about it with each other. It's this silence that makes us cowards, though, not the violence of the oppressor. And as we agree to remain silent, we are further divided as a people into Hawaiians living in squalor and those striving to achieve assimilated glory.

Annie Pau was living in a tent on the Waiʻanae Coast with her husband, John, and their two dogs in August 2008 when we first met. I was looking for an interview subject for an Al Jazeera show and she was kind enough to agree. Our first introduction took place at Starbucks on Farrington Highway, which felt like meeting at colonizer central, but we had to meet someplace and it was the easiest thing to do at 6 a.m. on a Sunday. Annie's camp was across the road and about half a mile down at a place called Sewers. It's actually Lualualei Beach Park, nicknamed Sewers because it stinks from the nearby sewage treatment facility.

Having resided in a rental unit nearby for years, and admittedly not having sympathy for the homeless people she saw on the beach, Annie and John were evicted after their landlord raised the rent. By 2003, the largest military expansion in Hawai'i since World War II was underway, which included a huge influx of new military personnel, even though the existing military housing was not enough to accommodate them. To compensate for the housing shortfall, the Department of Defense took over the rental market by allocating rental stipends of up to $1,300 per month to personnel willing to live off base (that number is $2,000 and higher now). That meant that apartments that were $700 a month, already very competitive in a tiny housing market, skyrocketed to $1,300 overnight. Annie and others were literally shaken loose from their homes. In Wai'anae, where the poverty rate is already higher than on the rest of O'ahu, the alternative was to live on the beach. My friend Jamaican filmmaker Esther Figueroa calls it "ethnic cleansing by real estate."

Indeed, the high cost to rent on O'ahu is subsidized, and the poverty of people like Annie is manufactured, by the American system of economy, policies, laws, and weaponry. And the military's foray into the real estate market took place simultaneously with a new wave of Americans buying or building second homes in Hawai'i. In the span of just a few years, former tourists who would ordinarily stay in hotels, and military personnel who customarily lived on base, were creating an ugly and permanent spike in Hawai'i's property values reminiscent of what transpired in the 1980s.

Although it's an unpopular and inconvenient reality check, occupiers aren't just military personnel or haole people we hesitate to consider as locals because we hold their whiteness against them. Every non-Hawaiian in Hawai'i is an occupier and a settler, and many have profited for generations from the U.S.-backed overthrow and what followed. That event developed into the fraudulent annexation to accommodate the American war and genocide in the Philippines and every war the United States has waged or threatened to wage since.

In a place where the finite supply of land and water is visible to the naked eye, the U.S. takeover enabled subsequent settler policies and laws that are designed to stabalize the military occupation and commercial exploitation of these resources. So the entrenched military presence is in partnership with the settler-occupier population. It's a lovely, symbiotic relationship—send in the cavalry to secure a perimeter and after that it's all real estate, pilgrim. Add to that a willing class of Hawaiian gatekeepers and sellouts and the demise of anything that even resembles Hawaiian self-determination is inevitable no matter how many as-yet unenforceable international laws of occupation we invoke.

Like Marie, Annie's choice was born out of economic necessity and a deep sense of political and cultural agency. But Annie's resistance was also about choosing between sanity and insanity and organizing her life between degrees of oppression.

One of Annie's strongest character traits was her pride. But she did talk once about how a sibling forced her out of the Nānākuli homestead house that had belonged to her mother, and that she had expected to live there with John. It sounded like typical pilikia (trouble, problem), the kind that lots of us have likely experienced. Thing is, when the trouble happens inside an ʻohana where some members are barely getting by, the damage can be irreparable.

And while the journalist part of me wanted to press her about other means, such as financial support, whether from her or her husband's siblings, or their adult children, I would have been ashamed; it would be like framing her life through the standard, cherry-picked "Hawaiian value" of ʻohana, just one in a series of magic-native culture-screws thrown at downtrodden Hawaiians.

Annie and John could have entered a shelter, but they would have had to give up their dogs, and as she put it, "They aren't just dogs—they're like my children." For Annie, going into a shelter would have constituted another form of misery, and why trade one misery for another that would hurt more than the one she already knew intimately? Another matter was that she would not have passed the drug test imposed as a condition of entrance to some programs and shelters. Her husband was a medical marijuana user and she said, "Sometimes he asks me to smoke with him. . . . I'm not gonna say no."

To an indifferent observer these seem like small things to forfeit, and the expectation is that an indigent person has no right to prioritize emotional wellness and mental clarity ahead of material needs. On the day Ed Greevy shot the photo of Annie that appears here, Annie told me what, in addition to the matter of her dogs and the occasional toke, kept her out of the system: "I was born Hawaiian, but that was taken away by America. As an American I have my rights, whether the police do things legally or illegally. Civil rights, I don't have. Only ones who have freedom are politicians and companies. They can rewrite laws for their clans, the corporations. We [homeless Hawaiians] are discriminated against. They label us homeless, not disabled [both John and Annie have serious medical conditions]. I don't have food stamps. I have SSI $225 a month. John has Social Security, $412 a month." Her understanding about class structure included the belief (or fact) that laws exist to further oppress people like her, while helping people who already have the advantage.

> Why is it everybody that's rich getting richer, richer, richer? And look at that cop who had the DUI, all he got was a slap on the wrists. Only the poor pay. John got

> a ticket and because he has Social Security income he had to pay the ticket. If every government official, like, stand there in front of me and take the drug test, I will. But in the [homeless shelter] system you go into lockdown. They not giving us help. They gotta lock us up to help us? It's like a concentration camp. Where is OHA? Where is Hawaiian Homes? They should step in and help Hawaiians like us. I don't believe in nonprofits—they all profiting.

I said, "Okay, Annie, you've established that the system is corrupt. How do you move past that realization and get your needs met?" Her answer: "I can't. I won't. I stay right here. That way I have my sanity."

Annie equated government corruption with the individuals who participate in the running of it, and her choice not to enter the government's system was how she kept her sanity. She referred to it several times and I realized that for her, no matter how challenging it was to stay healthy and safe living on the edge, this was the most dignified way she could be, given the economic constraints. Being personally self-determining, with or without international recognition, was something Annie needed more than a roof or a flag.

Courage, Class, and Consistent Resistance

Like many Hawaiians, Marie and Annie chose to exercise their right to self-determination without permission from the state apparatus that steals full time from Hawaiians. Organized Hawaiian political events and marches, on the other hand, never take place without first being sanctioned by the state with a permit. There was more law enforcement on hand to arrest Marie and her family than I've ever seen at any rally or march, even when those events were attended by thousands of Hawaiians. Which begs the question: Why are four homeless Hawaiians who live in an isolated part of Oʻahu more of a threat to the state than thousands of Hawaiians marching, chanting, and speechifying for their rights?

Although ea is something Marie and Annie strived for in their lives, the poverty that forced them to take a stand is just hard, ugly, and despairing. Yet many people are confused by the dignity and political consciousness of Hawaiians like them and are eager to view homelessness as a lifestyle choice rather than resistance to empire.

The respective struggles of these women to survive without housing span many years, and their refusal to enter into the poverty industrial complex has meant having to challenge and subvert the occupier daily. In so doing they make the state give up the one thing the state truly cares about: money. It's expensive to monitor, harass, evict, and arrest Hawaiians. When Hawaiians deprive the state of money, while exercising their rights as Hawaiians, that's an act of ea.

Conversely, a self-proclaimed pro-independence Hawaiian professor, whose middle-class life is funded by the state, once said to me that paying taxes to the government is the right thing to do because even if the kingdom were the governing entity, taxes would still be required for roads and other infrastructure. To use that economic, class advantage to subvert the state never enters into the minds of privileged Hawaiians. They'll talk sovereignty as long as it doesn't interrupt their lives.

Frantz Fanon says, in *The Wretched of the Earth*, "The unpreparedness of the educated classes, the lack of practical links between them and the mass of the people, their laziness, and, let it be said, their cowardice at the decisive moment of the struggle will give rise to tragic mishaps."[1] It's an apt statement that applies to us.

By any standard of economic power, be it global or local, one group of Hawaiians is living in the first world, while the other lives in the third. Whether they already are, or are standing in line to be, CEOs, politicians, directors in the nonprofit industrial complex, or members of the academic elite, many in the Hawaiian intelligentsia identify more with the occupiers than they do with Hawaiians like Marie and Annie.

Ea means sovereignty. But isn't working for the entity whose first order of business has always been to contain, subvert, and end Hawaiian sovereignty the opposite? Hawaiians can't indigenize state institutions, but the state can certainly institutionalize Hawaiians, because rather than build the infrastructure of a sovereignty movement, first-world Hawaiians are busy shoring up the institutions of the occupier. Audre Lorde was right: the master's tools will never dismantle the master's house.

Too many Hawaiian academics and nonprofit industrialists benefit from the occupation, so they're not inclined to do more than talk about international laws and nationhood. Or they preach a philosophical alignment with indigeneity, but back it up with no political action even though throughout the world indigenous peoples are putting their lives on the line to save their respective homelands and cultures daily. Politely coifed discourse about our rights instead of demands for a liberation generations in the making; published words on paper that lead to paychecks from the state instead of inspiring a resistance movement. Doctorates and law degrees have academicized Hawaiian sovereignty, pressed it like a flower between the pages of a book written by the state. Twenty years ago, the Hawaiian sovereignty movement was palpable. Today, any actual physical resistance to the occupiers is left to the most vulnerable Hawaiians, the most impoverished, those who have no choice but to hold their ground.

There's a scene in a play called *The Lion in Winter* where Geoffrey and Richard believe they're about to be executed by their father, King Henry II. Richard stands up, pulls himself together and says, "He's not going to see me beg," and Geoffrey says, "You fool, as if it matters how a man falls down." Richard's reply is, "When the fall's all that's left, it matters a great deal."

Courage isn't showing up to a staged protest for a few hours, or parading down

Kalākaua Avenue wearing uniform red shirts, chanting "I Kū Mau Mau." Courage is standing up for what's right even when you're broke and afraid. Hawaiians like Marie and Annie live in that space of courage. Every time they confront the American system, they knowingly, intentionally, and unapologetically risk everything. They put themselves on the line, and by doing that they, not their oppressors, define themselves. Theirs is the most consistent resistance to the occupation and the most unambiguous manifestation of ea I've witnessed as a journalist in more than a decade.

Notes

Annie Pau died on August 6, 2011. She had suffered a stroke and collapsed in the dirt outside her van the night before. Annie was koa wahine (a woman warrior), a strong voice of the disenfranchised maka'āinana, and a soulful resister of empire and complicity. She is missed, loved, and forever appreciated, and she was honored to be included in this book.

1. Fanon, *The Wretched of the Earth*, 148.

CHAPTER 1. Waiāhole-Waikāne

Jacqueline Lasky

> Da night was still, da moon was by da mountain. It was like a little cloudy over da moon but it's still there, it's shining brightly. Da night is still. When dat horn wen blow, people wen know already "It's time; they coming in."
>
> —PAT ROYOS

When the people of Waiāhole and Waikāne heard the warning horn blowing from a treetop on the night of January 4, 1977, they knew that it signaled that the police were coming to enforce their evictions. Hundreds of supporters from all over the Hawaiian Islands were camped out to occupy and defend the valleys. The residents had fought their evictions in the courthouse, at the state capitol, in the media, in front of business and labor offices, at neighborhood and church meetings, and in alliance with other communities facing similar evictions during the turbulent decade. This night was the culmination of three years of struggle to stay in their rural homes and fend off the encroachment of suburban and tourism development.

A vehicular and human barricade was formed across one mile of the two-lane Kamehameha Highway on windward Oʻahu. Island-wide supporters converged on the valleys, and traffic was effectively stopped for hours on the only road along the thirty-mile coastline. Only a handful of police officers arrived on the scene, and it was unclear if there was sufficient backup waiting to come in and enforce the eviction decrees. Members of the Waiāhole-Waikāne Community Association (WWCA) were canvassing the waiting cars, handing out information pamphlets and explaining the reasons for the roadblock with mostly sympathetic drivers and passengers. The police appeared uncertain of how to proceed. An officer threatened to arrest Bobby Fernandez, the president of WWCA, who describes the scene:

> Dat's why I'm suppose to tell you, officer, dis is my attorney right here. I'm standing on private property. I didn't park any of dese cars, but, you know, I'm in charge of da people who did.
>
> *What you like me do, call da mayor?!*
>
> Yeah, dat's exactly what I want you to do!

A resident and Waiāhole-Waikāne Community Association member, October 21, 1974.

The mayor of Honolulu was called. The governor of Hawai'i was called. Ultimately, the chief of the Honolulu Police Department gave his personal assurance that there would be no evictions that night and promised to notify WWCA in advance of any future actions. Thus ended the historic roadblock. A few days later the governor announced a deal with the large landowner, McCandless heir Elizabeth Loy Marks, in which the state would purchase six hundred acres of Waiāhole Valley and issue long-term leases at fair and reasonable rents to all the valley's tenants. The antieviction struggle was a resounding success.

Nearly two decades later, another historic blockade was staged in Waiāhole Valley. In mid-1995, valley residents, farmers, and allies converged on the road leading to the Waiāhole Ditch irrigation system at the gate privately owned by Amfac JMB (Waiāhole Irrigation Company). For over seven decades, tens of millions of gallons of water each day had been diverted from the lush windward valleys to the dry leeward plains in service of the thirsty sugar plantations. With the closure of the last sugar plantation on Oʻahu in the early 1990s, Waiāhole taro farmers and allies sought to have the long-diverted waters returned to windward streams. This resulted in the decade-long Waiāhole Ditch Combined Contested Case at the State Commission of Water Resource Management, with the Waiāhole taro farmers as one of the primary petitioners (see chapter 9, this volume for further discussion of this case). In 1994 it was discovered that Amfac was dumping unused diverted water. A public outcry spurred by the taro farmers and allies forced the temporary return of the dumped water to the windward streams. However, Amfac was dissatisfied and threatened to reclaim the water. In resistance, the Waiāhole-Waikāne community and allies mobilized and staged the blockade, effectively dissuading Amfac from retaking the stream waters. Rather than a culmination, this was only the beginning of the Waiāhole taro farmers' water struggle, which was rooted in the earlier antieviction struggle.

The farmers and activists themselves best describe this dynamic:

> Like the original struggle against evictions, [the water struggle] was supported by a broad group of people all around the island and the islands in general. And one of the things that came out of the fight over water . . . was an attempt to help people get back to growing taro. In general, there was a revived interest in growing taro.—Liko Hoe

> Our first thought was we need more water for our taro. But as we got more into the issue, we began to realize that the issue was bigger than just water for *our* taro. The issue was if you want to revive taro planting, you need lots of water in the streams, and then stream life itself needs water to support stream life, particularly things like endemic [species]. . . . Then at the same time, the water flowing to the ocean was important to the health of the estuary. . . . So it became a real broad issue that kind of encompassed all the issues of development, population growth, water conservation, reuse of sewage. . . . We were well aware [of these issues before], overdevelopment and that kind of thing, but we didn't put it together as a strategy to fight for water.—Calvin Hoe

> Just being in the Waiāhole-Waikāne [antieviction] struggle and rooting ourselves in the community, it became natural to go with the kalo [taro] fight. . . . In this modern time, the struggle for the water became representative of that issue that resonates with people, like how the development issue in Waiāhole was at one time.—Gwen Kim

Unlike the three intense drama-filled years of the antieviction struggle, the water struggle was a relatively low-key movement for nearly three decades. From their beginning in the early 1970s, the Waiāhole farmers and their supporters continually expanded kalo (taro) cultivation, helped enact the 1978 Hawai'i State Constitution changes that protect traditional and customary Hawaiian rights such as taro farming (article 12, section 7) and created a water commission (article 11, section 7), engaged in lawsuits throughout the 1980s to enforce the new constitutional protections, actively contributed to writing the State Water Code in 1987 that defined Native Hawaiian rights to water in terms of customary practices reliant on free-flowing water, and were leaders in the formation of a statewide taro farming association in the early 1990s that focuses on restoring and expanding lo'i (taro fields). All of this laid the groundwork for the Waiāhole taro farmers' success in the 2000 Hawai'i State Supreme Court landmark ruling (repeatedly reaffirmed), which returned significant amounts of long-diverted water to the windward side for taro growing, stream and estuary restoration, and other public trust interests.

Both the land and water struggles of Waiāhole-Waikāne are seminal in Hawai'i—with significant relevance beyond the islands—for several reasons. Both struggles were among the first, largest, and most sustained community-based movements to garner widespread public and political support and effectively challenge the islands' prevailing land and water oligarchy.[1] In the antieviction struggle, diverse working-class people with little power or legal standing effectively shifted the issue from a singular private property dispute to broader matters of public land-use policies and disenfranchised citizenship rights.[2] Drawing upon this success in the water struggle, multiethnic taro farmers rooted in Hawaiian tradition and culture effectively reinserted Native customary laws combined with America's public trust doctrine into Hawai'i's constitution and political practices.[3] Finally, both of the struggles effectively mobilized a unique mix of multiethnic local, Native Hawaiian, and American identities and practices.[4] Focusing on lessons learned from these seminal struggles, this chapter outlines the 1970s land struggle in Waiāhole and Waikāne valleys and provides an overview of the subsequent 1990s water struggle in Waiāhole, thus demonstrating the possibilities for—and practices of—local and Native control and use of land and water resources.

Background

American businessman Lincoln Loy McCandless came to own hundreds of acres—the majority of privately owned land—in the Waiāhole and Waikāne valleys following the 1893 American overthrow of the Hawaiian Kingdom. While his attempts to purchase the valleys from the Native government prior to the overthrow were unsuccessful, he and his family's participation in the illegal coup d'état and subsequent regime allowed for McCandless's land and water acquisitions in Waiāhole, Waikāne, and throughout the islands in the following decades.[5] Not only was Lincoln McCandless among the top ten landowners in Hawai'i at the time, but he was also one of the most powerful water barons in the islands due to his family's artesian well digging operations and his construction of the Waiāhole Ditch.[6]

The Waiāhole Ditch, completed in 1917, siphoned tens of millions of gallons of water each day from the mountain springs and streams of the east side to the dry 'Ewa plains of central O'ahu's expansive sugar plantations. Native Hawaiian farmers and the growing multiethnic local communities of the windward valleys were deprived of the fresh waters they relied upon for growing taro and other subsistence and commercial crops. In the early 1920s, at least one windward farmer who relied on stream water that was diverted by McCandless's ditch petitioned the U.S. territorial government for redress: "I woke up this morning and had no water in my lo'i [taro patch]. How am I supposed to feed my children?!"[7] This taking of water—without permission or compensation—hastened the debilitating transformations that began in the nineteenth century when the majority of Hawaiians began losing their lands and livelihoods.[8] Moreover, this pattern of land acquisition and water diversion was evident throughout the Hawaiian Islands: in pursuit of personal profit, American businessmen associated with the haole (foreigner; white Euro-American) sugar plantation elite usurped land and water from Native Hawaiians and local communities.

As a result, Hawaiian traditional and customary practices and the islands' ecosystem were negatively altered. The Native system centered on the ahupua'a, a land division (often comprising a watershed with a valley topography) that encompasses mountainous forests, upland and lowland fields, and an ocean fishery. The collective use of water was integral to the functioning of this system, wherein mountain streams flowed through taro patches, watered other crops, and continued down to the near-shore fishponds.[9] The ahupua'a's resources were primarily produced and consumed within the extended family networks of 'ohana, and shared with the ruling chiefs. As the staple crop of Native Hawaiians, taro also has spiritual significance as Hawaiians' elder sibling: the taro plant was the first offspring of the mating gods who created the Hawaiian Islands and Hawaiian people.[10] Taro cultivation thus involves practices of sustenance, sustainability, and spirituality. The taking of water by McCandless and his contemporaries not only severely limited kalo cultivation and its corresponding communal and familial function, but also contributed to the diminishment of Hawaiians' integrative social economy within the collective resource management system and the degradation of plant and animal life reliant on free-flowing water.

Nevertheless, Hawaiians and their multiethnic neighbors in rural communities like Waiāhole and Waikāne persevered on the land. In addition to cattle ranching and goat grazing by Euro-Americans in the two valleys, an influx of Asian laborers in the late nineteenth and early twentieth centuries brought Asian farmers to the valleys and the growth of diversified crops such as rice, sweet potatoes, bananas, and so forth.[11] Despite

Kana Teruya tends her Waiāhole field, April 28, 1973.

these changes and the substantial decrease in available water, Waiāhole and Waikāne were among the most active taro cultivation areas of the islands throughout the twentieth century.[12] Asians also farmed taro, and it was common for Chinese, Okinawan, and Hawaiian farmers to share their skills and labor. This reflected a continuity of Native ways of life combined with introduced multiethnic lifeways, which was further evidenced in extensive intermarriages. In addition to the full-time commercial farmers, most of the valley residents also farmed and fished for subsistence use and commercial exchange. As was common practice in Hawaiian ʻohana, and similarly in Asian kin relations, some family members worked in urban employment and there was a general sharing of cash and crops (or catch) among them. Significantly, these shared social and economic experiences cut across ethnic and cultural differences in Waiāhole-Waikāne.

While some Hawaiians still retained ownership of their ancestral lands, the majority of valley residents lived on and farmed lands leased from McCandless at rates that were well below market value. McCandless engaged in exchange relations akin to America's post–Civil War Southern sharecropping system: he would pay cash advances, provide equipment, or process farm produce in exchange for a portion of the goods produced by his tenants in lieu of full rent payments.[13] These practices continued after Lincoln McCandless's death in 1940 when his daughter and primary heir, Elizabeth Marks, became the landlord.

However, following the 1959 Statehood Act Hawai'i was in the midst of an "economic takeoff" within a prevailing political "development" consensus of the islands' new power elite,[14] and Marks sought to cash in on Waiāhole-Waikāne. Many observers ironically joked that the state bird was the construction crane, with mainland Americans flocking to fill newly built hotels, houses, and military bases. Marks partnered with prolific local developer Joe Pao to develop the rural valleys with suburban housing. They met fierce opposition from the residents of Waiāhole-Waikāne and their allies.

The Antieviction Struggle

At the beginning of 1974 there were several hundred residents in the two valleys, making up about a hundred families, most of whom were at least second- or third-generation families on the land.[15] For many Hawaiian families, their genealogy in the place extended much further back. Almost half the residents were Hawaiian, 20 percent Japanese, 17 percent Filipino, 12 percent haole, and the remaining residents were of other ethnicities.[16] Among the residents, there were Hawaiian kuleana landowners, tenants who worked in the city and varyingly participated in subsistence farming, tenants who lived and farmed commercially in the valleys, and tenants who lived elsewhere and farmed commercially in the valleys.[17] Almost everyone in this multiethnic and economically diverse community referred to themselves as country folks or as living a country life, and this was a sufficient basis for community identification (among many other identifications).

This concept of country lifestyle—"keeping the country country"—served as a rallying point for the residents of Waiāhole-Waikāne and was incorporated into their four-point platform that proved salient for the rest of the island people:

1. Long-term leases at fair and reasonable rents.
2. Expand agriculture.
3. Preserve the integrity of the community and its lifestyle.
4. Provide for community involvement in regional planning.

Drawing upon the islands' rural traditions of Hawaiian culture and multiethnic plantation cultures—which coalesced in the place they shared—was a deliberate or-

The WWCA resisted evictions by their landlord, the Marks family, for several years in the mid-1970s. On April 21, 1976, the residents and their supporters marched up the driveway to the front door of Mrs. Marks's Nuʻuanu home to declare, "Hell no, we ain't moving!" Ray Catania (center) raises his fist and leads a protest chant. This was the first time in the 1970s eviction struggles in Hawaiʻi that protesting residents went on private land to take their message to landlords.

ganizational strategy to unite the community and avoid potential ethnic divisions.[18] The WWCA actively refused several efforts by outside groups who wanted to support various ethnic-specific constituencies within the valleys. Bobby Fernandez explains:

> We had several groups coming to us to tell us dat, you know, we should do it dis way and—one guy just pissed me off. His ting was, "Eh, I don't mind da Japanese, but we gotta take care of da Hawaiians." You believe him?! "You know what, good-bye" [*laughter and hand-waving gesture*]. . . . There were other, several factions dat wanted to tell, "Oh, you know, we got good rapport wit da governor [who was Japanese American], we can get you guys in. . . ." [We said,] "No, we gonna do 'em wit us. Through us, not through anybody else, but through us." Started dis ting, goin' see it through, as a community.

It is here where country lifestyle, and its shared socioeconomic experiences, functioned to unite what might otherwise have been ethnically divided interests. When under threat of displacement, these shared multiethnic traditions were politicized into action.

The WWCA arrive at the front door of the landlord, Elizabeth McCandless Marks, April 21, 1976. Organizer Pete Thompson remembers that the group marched for so long on her front lawn that they left a circular dirt path in the well-manicured grass.

Instrumental in this political mobilization were outside allies from the University of Hawai'i's fledgling ethnic studies program, Kokua Hawai'i, and other groups in the islands' loosely formed grassroots coalition that coalesced around the earlier Kalama Valley antieviction and related struggles.[19] Tracing their roots to the 1960s Marxist study groups of Save Our Surf in Hawai'i and influenced by continental U.S. groups such as the Black Panthers, Young Lords, Students for a Democratic Society, and anti–Vietnam War activists, a core group of island activists formed a Marx-Lenin-Mao collective. As activist Pete Thompson put it, their focus was on "raising the level of political awareness and consciousness so that people are not naive, you know, about what it is that they're up against. And once they understand the terms of the struggle then you can move accordingly." With designated point persons dispersed in different community struggles such as Waiāhole-Waikāne, the core activists regularly met to update each other, work out individual tactics and joint strategies, and mobilize a larger activist body as needed. Deploying a Marx-Lenin-Mao praxis enabled the various antieviction and antidevelopment struggles to be articulated as widespread system failings and not simply grievances between individuals and landlords or developers.

This proved to be crucial in the state Land-Use Commission (LUC) hearings of October 1974. The LUC was created in 1961 to implement statewide zoning of land for urbanization, agriculture, or conservation, with a mandated five-year boundary review for proposed changes to land-use designation. Before Marks and Pao could develop Waiāhole-Waikāne into suburban housing, the LUC had to approve a change in land designation from agricultural to urban. Bobby Fernandez describes the situation: "We couldn't fight it with money 'cause we didn't have money. Couldn't fight it with legality 'cause the law was quite clear: landlord has the right to evict people and do whatever they like with their property. But like everybody else, they had to go through the correct process—through the government. So that, we thought, 'We might have a fighting chance at that,' by fighting in da political forum." This strong sense of American democratic participation was evident in the public space of the LUC hearing. Hundreds of valley residents, allied activists, and sympathetic supporters presented powerful and moving testimonies overwhelmingly opposed to the "few guys showing up in suits who were paid by Marks and Pao." All the testimonies underscored how the people of the two valleys belonged there because of their enduring investments in the place and how the proposed development was misplaced. Moreover, they emphasized how the people of Hawai'i in general would continue to benefit from the significant agricultural productivity of the two valleys and the few remaining rural open spaces that brought relief from Honolulu's ever-expanding concrete jungle. To further emphasize this point, and as part of Hawaiian protocol, flowers, plants, fruits, and vegetables from the valleys were brought to the hearing and offered as gifts to the commissioners.

Prior to (and following) the LUC hearing, the WWCA engaged in widespread outreach to solicit support from the broader island residents and communities. This included slideshow presentations to the city and county neighborhood boards, churches, civic organizations, various schools, and community groups; sign-waving on high-traffic streets; door-to-door conversations in different neighborhoods; petition drives collecting tens of thousands of signatures; educational fund-raising events; demonstration marches at the state capitol building and other high-profile places; sustained boycott of the bank funding the development project; and alliance building with other community struggles, environmental groups, Hawaiian rights advocates, farming organizations, and so forth. The WWCA received widespread support from broader island residents and communities, many of whom were moderate and middle class.[20]

In December 1974 the LUC ruled against the Marks-Pao rezoning request. The notion of preserving the community's agricultural integrity and rural lifestyle was ambiguous and thereby flexible, making it a salient concept that many people in Hawai'i—including the LUC decision makers—could grasp and adopt as their own. The ability of WWCA to make their antieviction struggle resonate is reflected in a newspaper article at the time: "It's easy to romanticize Waiāhole[-Waikāne], but it isn't a fairytale. It is simply a place endowed with the natural splendor that blesses many similar settings in Hawai'i, populated with residents whose lifestyle is both fading fast on O'ahu and demands an expansive environment which is increasingly out of place and time with urbanized society. Thus, Waiāhole[-Waikāne] becomes *a symbol that stands for a goal,* supported by those that aren't personally connected nor share a common lifestyle, but have a similar moral conviction."[21] The goal that Waiāhole-Waikāne symbolized for the rest of the islands was to slow down Hawai'i's post-statehood development frenzy and reprioritize in favor of local community empowerment.

Despite a clear victory for WWCA, Joe Pao and Elizabeth Marks proceeded with their development plans. Pao's development group, Windward Partners, purchased part of Waikāne Valley and announced the immediate eviction of nine families to make room for 130 two-acre house lots (that required city approval and bypassed the state LUC). Marks substantially increased rents on all remaining tenants in both valleys in an effort to either evict them or subdue their resistance, specifically targeting community leaders with rent increases of as much as 700 percent. The community association decided to collectively negotiate all tenants' leases under the auspices of their pro bono attorney. The few small landowners who were not threatened with eviction but nonetheless faced displacement by development pressures stood firmly by them in WWCA. After several months of stalemate, in a bold move the WWCA decided to collectively withhold paying the higher rent to Marks and Pao, and instead deposited their prior, lower rent amounts into an escrow account, until a mutually satisfactory resolution was reached.

As the antieviction struggle moved into the courtroom to resolve the matter of rent increases and targeted eviction of community leaders, WWCA increased the frequency and militancy of their protest demonstrations at venues targeting Marks, Pao, their political supporters, and their financial backers. Residents even formed their own security force called Up in Arms, made up primarily of women. Members of Up in Arms wore helmets, boots, and armbands during demonstrations and courtroom proceedings. Their role was twofold: to counteract the intimidation residents felt because of significant police presence at such venues, and to maintain the discipline of WWCA so that the community was not misrepresented to the media and public. Other, increasingly militant, tactics included an aggressive public relations campaign of writing and distributing their own reports (self-described as propaganda), regularly inviting media reporters and personalities into the valleys, staging a mock eviction drill for TV cameras, and general showmanship in "a series of stuff that the media just ate up." Additionally, WWCA and its allies persistently researched the political and business connections of Pao and Marks and publicly confronted them. As the 1976 elections approached, legislators, city council members, the mayor, and the governor were all targeted with persistent telephone calls, intense meetings, protest demonstrations, biting newspaper editorials, and so forth. Pete Thompson describes WWCA's tactics:

Matriarch Tūtū Kawelo, here in her nineties, rests from working on her family's kuleana lands. Tūtū Kawelo was the grandmother of noted Hawaiian sovereignty advocates Randy and Mel Kalahiki. Both were active in establishing the Kahalu'u KEY Project as a politicized and safe space for Windward O'ahu youth. December 16, 1972.

> We pressured them [all] on almost every conceivable level, and then at the same time, we also went out and got petitions and support from other communities, etc. The key to winning these things is that it has to be built real broad and real big, and the bigger and broader it gets built, the harder it is for them to win. And for them to win, they're gonna have to pay a very high political price for winning. . . . You had to almost fight them with a guerrilla warfare. You have to let them know that, you know, you're everywhere, you're not gonna let go, you're gonna keep on reminding them. You know, we're gonna hit the financing; we're gonna hit the investors; we're gonna hit the union leaders; we're gonna hit the politicians; you know. For them, we tried to keep it raining every day, as much as possible, relentlessly.

None of these actions, however, were able to change the law in which a landlord can evict a tenant with twenty-eight days' notice. Ignoring the vast political and public sentiment favoring Waiāhole-Waikāne residents' continued tenancy, Marks and Pao proceeded with the evictions. By late 1976, WWCA exhausted its legal maneuvering through the courts and imminent evictions were looming. The residents' only recourse was to stand in the road and defend their homes, which they did on the night of the historic roadblock. In doing so, a genuine power of the people was demonstrated and Hawai'i's power elite had little choice but to comply with their demands.

The legacies of the WWCA antieviction struggle are many. Not only were large sections of northeast Oʻahu spared from (sub)urban and tourist development and kept country, but also precedent was set for establishing community participation in government land-use policies. For Hawaiʻi's people, one of the lasting legacies of Waiāhole-Waikāne is the knowledge and experience of resistance and empowerment—the capacity to resist the juggernaut of progress and empower themselves (as persons and communities) through such resistance. Perhaps the most important legacy for the residents is their continued ability to live in the homes most of them built, among the same neighbors they grew up with for generations, in the lifestyles of their choosing amid the beautiful green valleys and sparkling blue ocean, and, for the majority of tenants, the security of long-term leases at fair and reasonable rents.

The Water Struggle and Taro Movement

While the residents and tenants of Waiāhole-Waikāne were resisting what they didn't want—rampant sub/urbanization and tourist development—taro farmers in Waiāhole were concurrently working toward what they did want: reinvigorated Native Hawaiian cultural practices in a sustainable and just Hawaiʻi. The farmers understood the displacement threats experienced by valley residents in the mid-1970s as part of the larger forces of displacement directly implicated in the American occupation of Hawaiʻi and colonization of Hawaiians. Waiāhole taro farmers continued to mobilize long after the antieviction struggle ended. Their water struggle was an ongoing resistance to the oligarchic allocation of resources that sustains the islands' ceaseless development—not just for their local community but also for the islands' Native people. Reestablishing traditional relations of persons to place is one means by which to do so, as described by taro farmer Liko Hoe: "Displacement is probably one of the main [problems or issues]. It starts with the Māhele [1840s land division] and doesn't end until—well, it doesn't end actually. . . . This has had profound effects on families. I think that the effect of it has been separation from ʻāina [land] and for people whose culture that is directly connected to the ʻāina that is devastating. . . . [We try to meet this challenge] by reconnecting ourselves, our famil[ies], to the place, to the ahupuaʻa."

A small group of Hawaiians and non-Hawaiians (haoles, Asians, Portuguese) in Waiāhole and adjacent ahupuaʻa (Waiheʻe, Kahaluʻu, Hakipuʻu) joined together in the mid-1970s to grow taro as a means of reestablishing and living Hawaiian culture in contemporary Hawaiʻi. They consciously sought to bring Hawaiian tradition back to life. They organized as families, both in terms of their nuclear families and as ʻohana. All of them had long-standing ties to the area, either as kuleana holders dating back to at least the mid-nineteenth century or as immigrant settlers from the early twentieth century. They were all a part of, and highly influenced by, the stirring social, political, and cultural climate in the United States in the 1960s and in Hawaiʻi in the 1970s. Moreover, many Waiāhole taro farmers were involved in what is often called the Hawaiian Renaissance or the revitalization of Hawaiian culture and politics. As the islands' postwar and post-statehood tourist economy brought Hawaiian culture to the forefront in order to commodify and sell it for corporate profit and state tax coffers, Hawaiians began mobilizing against their economic and political marginalization as well as to reclaim their culture from its bastardization by the prevailing political economy. Once a source of shame, Hawaiians increasingly embraced their culture as a source of strength.

The emergent Hawaiian movement readily exploited openings in the islands' governance system forged by several groundbreaking cases and rulings of a receptive judiciary.[22] Seeking to halt the century-plus of Western legalism imposed on the islands, and reverting back to more ancient Hawaiian customary law practices, substantive changes were made to the Hawai'i State Constitution in 1978 through a statewide convention process (Con-Con), in which the Waiāhole taro farmers actively participated. In their water struggle, Waiāhole taro farmers mobilized this mix of Hawaiian and American legal traditions to initiate their own legal case in *Reppun v. Board of Water Supply*.[23] Through this legal case, and their aforementioned work during the Con-Con and writing of the 1987 State Water Code, Waiāhole taro farmers were laying the politico-legal groundwork step by step for the expansion of kalo cultivation in their taro patches. Farmer Calvin Hoe explains:

> I think we were very lucky nobody saw what we were doing. Water is [such] a huge issue that it is kind of mind-boggling to me that we have been able to do what we have been able to do. . . . This competition for water is a forever thing. . . . I think we were very fortunate to get the constitution amended so that we can rely on that to always go back to—"It's in the constitution!" All the rights and stuff like that were in place already [for the 2000 Waiāhole Ditch Contested Case]—it was just kind of a reaffirmation.

Concurrently, Waiāhole taro farmers were cultivating a taro-roots movement throughout the islands. Taro is propagated by planting the cuttings from a taro root, which then grows into a new plant. Through a similar process, Waiāhole taro farmers propagated kalo cultivation in the 1980s: bringing in farmers, school groups, and other interested persons to their Waiāhole taro patches to learn, appreciate, and share knowledge of kalo cultivation; or taking their experiences and expertise and sharing it with farmers in other ahupua'a and helping them in their taro patches. At first, this dissemination was done informally. The islands-wide network of taro farmers consisted of overlapping extended family networks and friendships. They cultivated kalo in their own lo'i on lands they either owned or leased. Through repeated trial and error, an expanding body of collective knowledge and information on taro developed. Fourth graders who were learning Hawaiian culture and history (as mandated by the state curriculum the farmers had helped push through) were invited to the Waiāhole taro patches to experience this culture and history firsthand. This educational outreach offered an alternative frame of reference for schoolchildren only familiar with American consumerism and fast-food culture. Hundreds, if not thousands, of children and adults from diverse backgrounds came through the Waiāhole taro patches or were otherwise touched by the Waiāhole taro farmers' outreach efforts in other taro patches during the 1980s and 1990s.

Most people experience the tactile sensations of mud in their toes and between their fingers while working in the lo'i, which provides a very physical connection with the earth, the 'āina, "that which feeds." In the lo'i, one is refreshed by cool waters of flowing streams that feed the taro patches and flow back into the streams and to the ocean. All persons who worked in the Waiāhole taro patches were quite literally feeling the vitality of water. In this way, many people throughout the islands came to understand water as an issue—not just for the Waiāhole taro farmers, but also for the ever-expanding taro-roots movement. Allied attorney William Tam explains it this way: "Water issues are a very deep foundation. Understanding water is a very long-term, complex thing. It comes once you're involved in a situation. It's very hard to describe abstractly. You don't tend to sense the importance of it, because in the water you pump, turn on a pipe, the faucet, there's water and you don't understand the context for water until you get into land use issues, you get into fisheries issues, you get into environmental issues, and you start to see that water is the link between all these things." In addition to taro, the farmers were growing a broad base of support for their water struggle. In the taro patches, sociopolitical alliances were being forged between environmentally or culturally minded educators, children who would grow up to be professionals and entrepreneurs, Hawaiian cultural practitioners in other fields of knowledge, and people who wanted to try something new and simply be a part of nature.

This informal network became more formalized in the mid-1990s. A Hawaiian family on the island of Moloka'i sought to reopen lo'i in Hālawa Valley, which once was renowned for its extensive cultivation of kalo, and called upon the Waiāhole taro farmers and allies for help. The farmers brought to Hālawa their troops: more than two hundred volunteers who worked tirelessly for three days. The Queen Lili'uokalani Children's Center, one of the four Hawaiian chiefs' endowed trusts, subsequently sponsored 'Onipa'a Nā Hui Kalo (The Taro Association Is Steadfast) because, as Gwen Kim explains, they "felt that one way to empower the Hawaiian community was to begin to do kalo restoration." Since this first collective restoration in Hālawa, the Hui has gone on to reopen different lo'i in different locales each year, with as many as five hundred people coming out to help. 'Onipa'a Nā Hui Kalo has established a set of Hawaiian protocols combined with state guidelines for restoring lo'i. When a traditional irrigation system—an 'auwai—is identified, along with identifiable taro patches watered by this ʻauwai, then it is rehabilitated. In this way, ʻOnipaʻa Nā Hui Kalo does not open new taro patches but rather reopens previously existing ones—which conceivably date back hundreds of years. In so doing, reopened loʻi and ʻauwai that are continually maintained are conceivably protected by state laws protecting Hawaiian cultural practices and resources.

The collective work of taro cultivation effectively built a community. It is a taro farming community not confined to one locale, but spanning multiple places and involving many overlapping multiethnic peoples who are linked together in common practice or common cause. These alliances proved invaluable for the Waiāhole taro farmers when they sought the return of long-diverted waters. Farmer John Reppun explains: "When we went to fight the water fight, we were amazed at the support that came forward, and then not amazed—because we've been taking kids up to our farm for twenty-five years and we were having adults coming up to us going, 'I came to your farm in the fourth grade' and they're at a [government] hearing . . . on Waiāhole water saying 'We need [the water] back in the stream.'" The Waiāhole taro farmers and allies instinctively understood that they needed to take advantage of this water in order to safeguard it against future takings while the Waiāhole case proceeded. As a deliberate strategy in their water struggle, and as part of the movement to restore loʻi throughout the islands, they reopened a community taro patch in Waiāhole Valley, called the Mauka Loʻi (mountainside taro patch). This community taro patch was the first of its kind in contemporary Hawaiʻi, and community here has multiple references: (1) a community taro patch for and within the Waiāhole community; (2) a community taro patch located within Waiāhole but for the broader taro farming community that spans the islands; and (3) a community taro patch in the Hawaiian ahupuaʻa system of shared subsistence and sustenance uses and collective resource management.

In the ensuing years, weekly workdays brought together diverse people from across the islands who would come to the Mauka Loʻi to practice Hawaiian culture in a traditional way. Those who contributed labor had rights to share the products of their labors in the form of harvested taro or produced poi. The Mauka Loʻi served as an alternative to American fast-food consumerist culture and as a source of personal and communal rejuvenation. Moreover, the Mauka Loʻi reflected an important shift that occurred among taro farmers: the contemporary kalo movement, which began in personal loʻi on lands that were either privately owned or leased, gave way to collective loʻi on lands which were now claimed as public—and Native Hawaiian—places. The Mauka Loʻi was quietly established on public land, that is, on state-owned open space. This was an act of civil disobedience inasmuch as it was unauthorized by the state—no permission was sought and no permission granted. While the Mauka Loʻi has since closed, its legacy lives on in the enduring success of the Waiāhole water struggle.

A broad range of issues concerning land use, governmental decision making, sustainable growth, ecosystem viability, and Native livelihoods are encapsulated in the Waiāhole water struggle. They have operated effectively and enduringly on both the politico-legal terrain and on the sociocultural level, because they have embodied the idea that, as Liko Hoe put it, "The legal stuff should be . . . a reflection of the nonlegal stuff." Perhaps even more important than their success in the Waiāhole Ditch Combined Contested Case, Waiāhole taro farmers have persistently demonstrated that the reestablishment of Hawaiian lifeways and livelihoods within renewed manifestations of the Native ahupua'a management system is not only possible, but also often preferred and increasingly practiced in Hawai'i's contemporary multiethnic environment.

Conclusion

As repeatedly shared with me by the diverse people of Waiāhole-Waikāne, here are some of the main lessons to be learned from their community struggles: the need to address problems collectively; the strong leadership of individuals who worked together; the decision-making process that prioritized talking things out followed by unity behind the decision; the action-oriented process that prioritizes doing more than talking; the importance of maintaining internal control of a struggle while utilizing outside resources and alliances; the ability to work across ethnic differences to avoid divisions and to focus on common causes; the capacity to articulate a struggle as part of a broader systemic problem in ways that draw support from the general populace; the need to use the law in ways that help create policy practices that reflect what is occurring on the ground; the importance of fostering place-based community reconnection; and the importance of multigenerational and extended family networks. Gwen Kim, an allied activist involved in both the antieviction and water struggles, adds this:

> The main lesson from Waiāhole-Waikāne is that the latent untapped power of the people is so great. It's unbelievable how much power there is if we could just unleash it, focus it. . . . The things that divide us now in the valley, or anywhere—we all have to look in terms of the larger picture. . . . I just believe with knowledge—it's so critical that we have knowledge—that with a lot of knowledge, combined with experience, I think we can win anything. We just have to have the strategy and the message and the love. If we lose the love, what is it all for? [*laughter*] . . . And hope.

Notes

All the community members and activists quoted in this chapter were interviewed by the author during the years 2003–2007.

1. Geschwender, "Social Context of Strategic Success"; Modavi, "Land, Environment and Power"; Scheuer, "Water and Power in Hawai'i"; Sproat and Moriwake, "Ke Kalo Pa'a O Waiāhole."

2. Geschwender, "Lessons from Waiahole-Waikane"; Nakata, "Struggles of the Waiahole-Waikane Community Association."

3. Sproat and Moriwake, "Ke Kalo Pa'a O Waiāhole."

4. Lasky, "Community Struggles, Struggling Communities."

5. Siddall, *Men of Hawai'i.*

6. McCandless acquired land by various, and often dubious, means that included outright purchase from the American government that took the land from the Hawaiian Kingdom, loan-shark mortgaging and foreclosures on private landowners, fathering children with Hawaiian landowners, discreet purchasing, swindling or theft of land as part of cooperative land associations (called Hui), and other questionable practices. C. (descendant of McCandless and Hawaiian landowner in Waiāhole), interviewed on August 8, 2005, in Kailua, Hawai'i. See also Stauffer, *Kahana.*

7. Danny Bishop retains a copy of this letter written by his wife's grandmother.

8. Wilcox, *Sugar Waters,* especially pp. 27–31 detailing testimony by the Kingdom's Water Commissioner Daniels (1866) and in the cases of *Beckley v. Ohule* (1873), *Cartwright v. Gulick* (1886), and *Horner v. Kumuliilii* (1895).

9. Handy, Handy, and Pukui, *Native Planters in Old Hawai'i*; MacKenzie, *Native Hawaiian Rights Handbook.*

10. 'Ohā is the sprout that shoots off from the taro root and is the basis for the word 'ohana (extended family).

11. Griffen and Pyle, *The Archaeology of Koolau-Poko, O'ahu.*

12. Devaney et al., *Kāne'ohe.*

13. Young, *The Chinese on Windward Oahu.*

14. Cooper and Daws, *Land and Power in Hawai'i.*

15. McMillen, "Social Organization in Waiahole-Waikane."

16. Geschwender, "Lessons from Waiahole-Waikane," 122.

17. Geschwender, "Lessons from Waiahole-Waikane," 123. In old usage, *Kuleana* meant "a portion or share of a thing or enterprise. It was chosen as the legal term applicable to the claims filed by tenants who sought permanent title to parcels of land then being allotted under the law of 1848. The word in old Hawaiian also meant a man's right, affairs, interests, being derived from the adjective *kulea* meaning competent or successful." Handy, Handy, and Pukui, *Native Planters in Old Hawai'i,* 54.

18. Nakata, "The Struggles of the Waiahole-Waikane Community Association."

19. These early struggles included preservation of surfing sites at Mā'ili Point, Kaimū, Queen's, and Baby Queen's; continued tenancy for residents of Old Vineyard and Old Young Street; and other small yet significant specific struggles.

20. Geschwender, "Lessons from Waiahole-Waikane," 125; Modavi, "Land, Environment, and Power."

21. Bowman, "The Valley That Was, and Is," emphasis added.

22. 1968, *Palama v. Sheehan* (50 Hawaii 298, 440 P.2d 95); 1968, *In re application of Ashford* (50 Hawaii 314, 440 P.2d 76); 1973, *Country of Hawaii v. Sotomura* (55 Hawaii 176, 517 P.2d); 1973, *McBryde Sugar Co. v. Robinson* (54 Hawaii 173, 504 P.2d 1330); 1977, *In re application of Sanboru* (57 Hawaii 585, 562 P.2d 771); 1977, *State of Hawaii v. Zimring* (58 Hawaii 106, 566 P.2d 725).

23. 1982, *Reppun v. Board of Water Supply* (65 Hawaii 531, 656 P.2d 57).

CHAPTER 2. "Our History, Our Way!"

ETHNIC STUDIES FOR HAWAIʻI'S PEOPLE

Davianna Pōmaikaʻi McGregor and Ibrahim Aoudé

No Marion Kelly

Hiki mai ka hōkū ʻai ʻāina
Hoʻolehua ke ʻau loa
Hiki mai ka wahine
Ke kama a Teanu Atu mai Tongareva mai
Ma o Waialua, ʻāina kū pālua i ka laʻi

Ua ʻau ʻia ʻoia i nā kai loa
I ka pae ʻāina Hawaiʻi
A i ka Pakipika mānoa

He hoaloha o nā mamo a nā kipi
Nā mamo i ka halo o kua
Eia ka wahine
He ʻaʻaliʻi ʻoia kū makani
ʻAʻohe makani nāna i kulaʻi

Eia ka wahine
Eia ka makuahine
Eia ke kumu aʻo
Eia ke kupuna aloha
E mau ana kona hana kūpono
o ka ʻāina
Aloha e, aloha e, aloha e

This chapter shares an overview of the evolution of the Ethnic Studies Department at the University of Hawaiʻi at Mānoa (UHM) as a center of knowledge about social justice and Hawaiʻi's multiethnic peoples. From its inception, the ethnic studies faculty and students focused on strengthening Hawaiʻi's communities, protecting island cultural

Marion Kelly speaks at an ethnic studies meeting at the Kaimukī Public Library in 1972.

and natural resources, supporting democratic processes and helping grassroots people cope with the pressures of a society in crisis. As the broader social movements developed in Hawai'i, ethnic studies faculty and students interacted and engaged with these movements at various levels. The establishment of the Ethnic Studies Department at UHM was itself a significant social movement of students, faculty, and community, and at the forefront was Marion Kelly (June 4, 1919–November 12, 2011), who is honored in the opening oli. As we begin this mo'olelo, telling the story of ethnic studies in Hawai'i, we want to acknowledge the compassionate leadership of Marion Kelly as indispensable in the establishment of the department. Marion Kelly was the preeminent authority on land tenure use and change in Hawai'i. Through her extensive ethnographic work at the Bishop Museum, she contributed significantly to the development of Hawaiian anthropology. She dedicated her research to perpetuating Kanaka 'Ōiwi culture and supporting the Kanaka 'Ōiwi national struggle for self-determination. Marion was clear that the Kanaka 'Ōiwi struggle for self-determination is at the heart of achieving social justice for the multiethnic communities of our Hawai'i nei.

In 2010, the Ethnic Studies Department celebrated forty years at UHM. At its inception, there was no guarantee that it would survive, much less flourish for four decades.

Mrs. Matayoshi, a resident of Waiāhole, in her sweet potato field, April 1973. She frequently sold her freshly harvested fruit out of a wheelbarrow alongside the Waiāhole Poi Factory on Kamehameha Highway and was called the "sweet lady of Waiāhole."

Roots

Ethnic studies was conceived at the end of the tumultuous 1960s, as an outgrowth of the civil rights, anti–Vietnam War, ethnic empowerment, and students' rights movements. Individuals influenced by all four movements converged into an alliance to support ethnic studies and defeat attempts to homogenize the history of Hawaii's immigrants into the Department of American Studies, whose textbooks focused on European migration. The formation of the Ethnic Studies Department occurred at a time when there was no redress for Japanese Americans illegally interned during World War II, the United States was using Kaho'olawe for military exercises, and Native Hawaiians were losing thousands of acres of land in adverse possession proceedings. While ethnic studies was conceived at UHM, its supporters extended beyond academia.

Massive evictions of poor ethnic, farming, and working-class communities across the state due to urbanization prompted the formation of minority rights organizations in the early 1970s. Groups such as Kōkua Hawai'i in Kalama Valley and Third Arm in Chinatown helped to organize ethnic communities against evictions at a time when there was little appreciation for preserving the history of Hawai'i's peoples. These com-

Terrilee Napua Keko'olani has been active in Hawaiian community, sovereignty, and demilitarization movements since the 1970s. Here, as an ethnic studies student in 1972, she speaks at a Save Our Surf–sponsored rally against a proposed resort development project at Wāwāmalu (Sandy Beach).

munities later played a key role in successfully supporting the continuation of ethnic studies by actively participating in an occupation of the UHM administration building in 1972 when the UH administration announced its plan to dismantle the program.

The demand to establish an Ethnic Studies Department at UHM was first raised in a 1968 Bachman Hall sit-in as part of a list of twenty demands by student activists protesting the Vietnam War, racism, and university governance issues.[1]

Throughout 1969, consultant English Bradshaw worked with students, faculty, and community supporters to develop a proposal for an ethnic studies program that would focus on Kānaka 'Ōiwi and the primary immigrant ethnic groups and their descendants in Hawai'i. Then in fall 1970, the Ethnic Studies Program was launched as a two-year experimental program, offering classes on the history of Hawai'i's ethnic groups.[2]

From the outset, the ethnic studies faculty actively engaged students in the community issues in which they themselves were involved. Prominent among these was the Kalama Valley struggle led by the Kōkua Kalama organization, which later transformed into Kōkua Hawai'i. Kalama Valley was a local political struggle that challenged U.S. control over Hawai'i in general and sparked organizing among other communities facing eviction as well as the Native Hawaiian community. Other community issues that the ethnic studies faculty and students helped support through 1972 included a broad range of organizations such as the Hawaiians, seeking reform of the Department of Hawaiian Home Lands; the Hālawa Housing eviction struggle (residents opposed to being evicted for the construction of the Aloha Stadium); the Legislative Coalition of Welfare Recipients; the Committee to Appoint a Hawaiian Trustee and its successor, the Congress of Hawaiian People; the Ota Camp eviction; and the People against Chinatown Eviction.

In spring 1972, then UHM president Harland Cleveland set up the Ad Hoc Committee on Ethnic Studies to make recommendations on the "continuation of the Program, its organization, curriculum, personnel and governance."[3] The political activism of the ethnic studies faculty and their students had drawn the attention of a critical and conservative university administration. Thus, it came as no surprise when the committee made a recommendation to terminate the program and disperse the courses and the faculty into existing departments—Japanese Americans, Chinese Americans, and Filipino Americans into American studies and Hawaiians into anthropology.

Immediately, faculty and students began to organize with the community to establish a permanent, unique, and distinct ethnic studies program. Over two hundred students marched on Bachman Hall and after seven hours of discussion got nowhere. This gave rise to a larger campus-wide movement, organized around the slogan "Our history, our way," which culminated in a three-night sit-in at Bachman Hall. At the end of the sit-in, the university administration agreed to establish the People's Committee on Ethnic Studies, comprising five students, five faculty, and five community representatives to review the program, recommend a core curriculum, and determine the future of the program. After members worked continuously throughout the summer, the report of the People's Committee on Ethnic Studies was finalized and accepted by the university administration. In fall 1972, the Ethnic Studies Program continued to offer its original courses and began to develop curriculum for an expanded set of upper-division courses.

This set a pattern that would be repeated throughout the next six years. The Ethnic Studies Program offered courses and developed curriculum as a provisional program and underwent academic reviews every two years. At the end of each review, the administration wanted to dismantle the program, but the faculty and students mobilized campus and community support for its continuation. Finally, the program gained permanent status with the appointment of a full-time director, Dr. Franklin Odo, in 1978.[4]

Pete Thompson, an early member of the UH Mānoa Ethnic Studies Program, bridged his studies with community organizing, including the Waiāhole-Waikāne Community Association. Here, he speaks at an ethnic studies meeting at the Kaimukī Public Library in 1972. Also pictured: Joy Ahn (far left) and Kalama Valley resident George Santos (far right).

Throughout the period that the program was provisional, the ethnic studies faculty, lab leaders, and students functioned as an organizational and ideological center for the broader political movement engaged in multiethnic local struggles of land and housing. Ethnic studies faculty, lab leaders, and students organized and participated in independent study groups in Marxism-Leninism and Mao Tse-Tung Thought. Inspired by this theory, they engaged in the social practice of developing strategy, tactics, and educational materials for local grassroots communities facing evictions.

It was an exhilarating era when youthful idealism achieved significant victories. Working with ethnic studies faculty and students, the communities of Waimānalo, Old Vineyard St., Young St., Ota Camp, and Mokauea Island all obtained long-term leases and funding for the construction of affordable housing through a combination of state and county funding. The residents of Niumalu-Nāwiliwili and Chinatown eventually negotiated their relocation into alternative housing and rental units. Heʻeia Kea residents successfully stopped construction of a windward electric generation plant and retained their rental units. In 1971, Save Our Surf organized one of the largest rallies ever held at the state capitol to protest the evictions from and the threats to Oʻahu's surfing sites. The Waiāhole-Waikāne struggle escalated into the largest antieviction struggle in the history of Hawaiʻi and resulted in long-term leases for the farmers and the residents. The end of the Vietnam War in 1975 seem to confirm the popular slogan of these serve-the-people initiatives, "The people united can never be defeated!"

In 1976, the ethnic studies faculty and lab leaders organized students around the call to stop the bombing of Kahoʻolawe—setting up informational tables, organizing rallies, selling T-shirts, getting petitions signed. The Kahoʻolawe movement signaled the beginning of the Kanaka ʻŌiwi renaissance and a focus on the quest for sovereignty and self-determination distinct from that of the multiethnic local grassroots movements. Organized around the slogan Aloha ʻĀina or Love Our Land, the Protect Kahoʻolawe ʻOhana evolved into an islands-wide grassroots movement that not only stopped the bombing of Kahoʻolawe but, more importantly, revived and restored Kanaka ʻŌiwi religious and cultural practices.[5]

Another development in 1976 was the shift of the organizational and ideological nexus with the broader political movement outside of the Ethnic Studies Program and into various Marxist-Leninist–Mao Tse-Tung Thought formations from the U.S. continent, which began to establish Hawaiʻi branches. These included the Revolutionary Communist Party, the Communist Workers Party, the Union of Democratic Filipinos, the Communist Labor Party, and the Line of March. This led to an exodus from the program of activists who saw their role as integrating into the working class and broader social and political organizations.

The activist faculty who remained within the program saw their role as training a new generation of critical thinkers and compassionate leaders grounded in their communities. They engaged in research on Hawaiʻi, national and international political and economic trends, and the intersection of these trends with the dynamics of race, class, and gender. Their research involved and benefited the community and resulted in an expanded upper-division curriculum and notable publications.[6]

Developing Institutional Presence

Throughout the 1980s, the part-time UHM ethnic studies faculty focused on developing the program and completing their own doctoral programs of study. By 1991, the program was able to double its number of faculty positions. That June, the program celebrated its twenty-first anniversary and the faculty initiated a series of steps in a focused campaign to develop a national and international academic reputation. The program hosted the Eighth Annual National Conference of the prestigious Association for Asian American Studies. The faculty developed a working relationship with the International Working Group for Indigenous Affairs with headquarters in Copenhagen, Denmark.

Professor Marion Kelly worked with Dr. Kekuni Akana Blaisdell to launch and sus-

Marion Kelly and her husband, John Kelly, at her eightieth birthday celebration in June 1999.

tain the Pro-Hawaiian Sovereignty Working Group as part of the Ka Pākaukau coalition of Kanaka ʻŌiwi organizations committed to sovereignty for Hawaiʻi. In 1993, the Ka Pākaukau organized Ka Hoʻokolokolonui Kānaka Maoli, the People's International Tribunal, and Professor Kelly helped to publish its lengthy findings. Faculty published a special issue of *Social Process in Hawaiʻi*, volume 35, *The Political Economy of Hawaiʻi*, which spotlighted the role of ethnic studies in creating and publishing analytical information about political and economic issues in Hawaiʻi. Professor Kelly continued to provide her expertise in land use and tenure in Hawaiʻi and Kanaka ʻŌiwi cultural customs, practices, and rights for Kanaka ʻŌiwi communities from Mokauea Island, Hālawa Valley, and Mākua on Oʻahu to Kaʻū on Hawaiʻi Island.

In 1991–1992, members of the ethnic studies faculty helped launch the Hui Naʻauao Sovereignty Education Project to prepare the Hawaiian community for the one hundred-year commemoration of the overthrow of the Hawaiian monarchy. In conjunction with this project, Professor McGregor helped develop a draft of the 1993 Apology Law, Public Law 103-150. McGregor helped work on legislation providing for the return of Kahoʻolawe to the people of Hawaiʻi, whereby the island was set aside as a trust for the sovereign Hawaiian nation and commercial activities were banned.

Finally, in 1995, the UH board of regents transformed the program into a department offering a bachelor of arts in ethnic studies. In summer 1995, the department hosted the Institute for Hawai'i History Teachers in conjunction with the Historic Hawai'i Foundation and funded by the National Endowment for the Humanities. The goal of the institute was to recognize the best secondary education teachers in Hawai'i history and provide them with the most exciting and important information and perspectives in the field. The institute inspired twenty-six teachers to return to their schools throughout the islands and transmit new knowledge and teaching methodologies to approximately three thousand students in the 1995–1996 academic year alone.

The 1993 Apology Law and activities commemorating the overthrow of the Hawaiian monarchy a hundred years earlier thrust the Hawaiian movement into the forefront of issues related to race, social justice, and peace in Hawai'i. The Hawaiians course together with courses on land tenure and use in Hawai'i were cornerstones of the department's curriculum. The courses, Hawai'i and the Pacific, Economic Change and Hawai'i's People, Social Movements in Hawai'i, and Change in the Pacific, designed by Marion Kelly, all foreground the experiences and culture of Kanaka 'Ōiwi.

Engaging students in service learning evolved from the community activism of the 1970s into a key component of the Program for Engaged Scholarship and Service Learning and a hallmark of the BA in ethnic studies. In particular, the Mālama i nā Ahupua'a program, originally called Adopt an Ahupua'a, involves students in cultural, historic, and environmental learning at various sites including Ala Wai Canal and Watershed, the One'ula Limu Project, Hālawa Valley Heiau, Loko I'a 'o He'eia, Kahana Valley, Kanaloa Kaho'olawe Island, Kaniakapūpū in Nu'uanu, Ka Papa Lo'i 'o Kānewai, Kawainui, Keāiwa Heiau, Mākua Valley, Mokauea, Pālehua, Pālolo Valley, Ulupō Heiau, Waihe'e Lo'i, Loko I'a Waikalua, and Wāwāmalu Beach Park/Ka Iwi Shoreline. Another service learning program that has gained national recognition is the Pālolo Pipeline Program, a long-term, broad community involvement program focused on improving life and education for housing residents who are low-income immigrant Pacific Islanders and Southeast Asians. The service learning program also involves ethnic studies students in the Kaka'ako Next Step Shelter for houseless families, primarily from Micronesia and other Pacific Islands and with low-income families at the Kūhiō Park Terrace.

In 1998, the Ethnic Studies Department hosted the Fifteenth Annual Conference of the Association for Asian American Studies, with a critical focus on the expansion of the American empire into the Pacific and Asia with the Spanish American War and the colonization of Hawai'i, Guam, Samoa, and the Philippines.

Our Future, Our Way

The Ethnic Studies Department entered the twenty-first century with the hiring of a second generation of faculty and the development of a strategic plan that focused on the development of a program of study for the master of arts degree. Reflecting the positioning of Hawai'i in the era of a global political economy, the MA program projected an interdisciplinary curriculum of advanced courses focused on racial and ethnic formations, indigenous peoples, migration, diaspora, and transnationalism. While having a particular emphasis on Hawai'i, the Pacific, and the continental United States, the courses would examine global trends and would focus on three major thematic areas: racial and ethnic formations; indigenous peoples; and migration, diaspora, globalization, and transnationalism. Unlike other comparable academic MA programs, students would be required to undertake service learning activities for at least one semester as part of their core course requirements.

A new generation of ethnic studies faculty are engaged with Hawai'i's community, including Professors Ty Tengan with the Hawaiian community, Monisha Das Gupta with Local 5 and Hawai'i's immigrant communities, Rod Labrador with the Filipino community, and Brian Chung with the Chinese community. Dr. Ulla Hasager coordinates the service learning and civic engagement program for the Ethnic Studies Department and the College of Social Sciences.

The saga of the UHM Ethnic Studies Department and Hawai'i's social movements will continue to unfold and develop. Despite global economic and political forces, Kanaka 'Ōiwi and the people of Hawai'i continue to organize as agents of change to shape our own destiny in our beloved islands—Ka Pae 'Āina Hawai'i. A department at the University of Hawai'i dedicated to research and teaching about Hawai'i's people and the intersections of ethnicity, race, class, and gender in Hawai'i, the Pacific, the continental United States and other areas of the world provides a historical perspective and a critical analysis to scope out future trends.

In a globalizing world, Hawai'i cannot afford for its new generations not to be fluent in this new language of diversity. As public intellectuals, ethnic studies faculty have offered their research for the benefit of the community in its struggle for justice and equality. It is in this way that the university could say that it actually is a public university, serving those sections of the community that have often been neglected in the rush to connect with money and power.

Given the precarious nature of the economic recovery and, more importantly, the global economy, the future will be fraught with considerable challenges that social movements will have to contend with and compel the public and private decision makers to find solutions in the interest of the overwhelming majority of the people, not only the powerful few. To be resolved, those challenges would require a polity informed about the dynamics of ethnicity, race, class, and gender as main dimensions of social motion. Here is where the value of ethnic studies is located, and it is here that ethnic studies will serve the cause of social justice and equality.

Notes

Epigraph: This chant was composed by Davianna Pōmaikaʻi McGregor in honor of Marion Kelly upon the occasion of Kelly's receipt of the Association for Asian American Studies Distinguished Lifetime Achievement Award, June 26, 1998. The English translation is as follows:

Of Marion Kelly

The star ruling land rises (navigator's star)
The current runs strong and swift
The woman arrives
Child of Teanu Atu from Tongareva
Through Waialua in the calm

She traveled the distant seas
In the Hawaiian Archipelago
And the wide Pacific

Friend of the descendants of rebels (of Kaʻū)
Descendants in the gills of kua (shark ʻaumakua of Kaʻū)
Here is the woman
She is an ʻaʻaliʻi standing in the wind
There is no wind which can blow her over

Here is the woman
Here is the mother
Here is the teacher
Here is the beloved kupuna
May her good and upright work for
the land continue always
Love, honor, respect

1. Students for a Democratic Society organized a sit-in to protest what they felt was a politically motivated denial of tenure to their faculty advisor, political science professor Oliver Lee.

2. While we could not locate the fall 1970 schedule, the fall 1971–spring 1972 academic year class schedule listed the following thirteen classes and eleven instructors: ES 101 Ethnic Groups in Hawaiʻi, Ian Lind; ES 121 Introduction to Hawaiian Studies, Marion Kelly; ES 200 Japanese Americans, Dennis Ogawa; ES 201 Chinese Americans, Nancy Young; ES 202 Filipino Americans, Rick Trimillos; ES 205 Black Americans, Katherine Brundage; ES 221 Hawaiian Americans, Larry Kamakawiwoole; ES 301 Ethnic Identity, Glenn Grant; ES 320 001 Dominant and Minority Culture, Thomas Gladwin; ES 320 002 Dominant and Minority Culture, James Anthony; ES 390 Study of Social Movements, Herbert Takahashi; ES 397 Field Experience, Larry Kamakawiwoole; ES 499 Directed Research, Dennis Ogawa.

3. The members of the committee were Professors Stephen Boggs, David Cromwell, James Linn, Seymour Lutzky, and Fritz Seifert.

4. The interim directors included: 1972, Larry Kamakawiwoole; 1972–1973, Nancy Young; 1973–1974, Jerrold Chung; 1974–1977, Davianna Pōmaikaʻi McGregor; 1977–1978, Miriam Sharma.

5. Aloha ʻĀina also means Patriotism, as in Hui Aloha ʻĀina or the Hawaiian Patriotic League orga-

nization that the Protect Kahoʻolawe ʻOhana claimed as a predecessor. At a deeper level, Aloha ʻĀina also means to love and honor the life forces of the land that Kanaka ʻŌiwi ancestors honored as deities.

6. Alegado, *Sinking Roots*; Aoudé, "Public Policy and Globalization in Hawaiʻi"; Aoudé, "Ethnic Studies Story"; Aoudé, "The Political Economy of Hawaiʻi"; Kelly, *Loko Iʻa o Heʻeia*; Kelly, *Historical Study of Kawainui Marsh Area*; Kelly, *Nā Māla o Kona*; Barrère, Kelly, and Nakamura, *Hilo Bay, a Chronological History*; Barrère and Kelly, *Background History of the Kona Area*; Kelly, *Majestic Kaʻu*; Kelly and Quintal, *Cultural History Report of Makua Military Reservation*; Kelly, "Changes in Land Tenure in Hawaii"; Kent, *America in 1900*; Kent, *Hawaiʻi*; McGregor and Revilla, *Our History, Our Way*; McGregor, *Nā Kuaʻāina*; Odo, *No Sword to Bury*; Odo and Sinoto, *Pictorial History of the Japanese in Hawaiʻi*; Fujikane and Okamura, *Asian Settler Colonialism*; Okamura, *Ethnicity and Inequality in Hawaiʻi*; Okamura, *The Japanese American Contemporary Experience in Hawaiʻi*; Okamura, *The Japanese American Historical Experience in Hawaiʻi*; Okamura, *Imagining the Filipino American Diaspora*; Okamura, *Filipino American History, Identity and Community in Hawaiʻi*; Tengan, *Native Men Remade.*

CHAPTER 3. E Ola Mau ka ʻŌlelo Hawaiʻi

THE HAWAIIAN LANGUAGE REVITALIZATION MOVEMENT

Katrina-Ann R. Kapāʻanaokalāokeola Nākoa Oliveira

I ka ʻōlelo nō ke ola; i ka ʻōlelo nō ka make. Our kūpuna (ancestors) remind us, "in language there is life; in language there is death." In a flourishing native society, commerce and governmental affairs are carried out in the ʻōlelo makuahine (mother tongue) of the land and numerous native speakers remain. The native language is alive and thriving; the ʻōlelo makuahine is a living language.

The identities of Indigenous peoples are inextricably linked to our languages. Embedded in our native languages are our worldviews and cultures. ʻŌlelo Hawaiʻi (Hawaiian language), for example, carries nuances and multiple layers of meaning that are uniquely Kanaka (Native Hawaiian) and that can only be fully understood and appreciated by speakers of ʻōlelo Hawaiʻi. As a Kanaka columnist writing in 1917 warns, "I ikeia no ke kanaka no kekahi lahui ma kana olelo. Ina e nalowale ana ka olelo makuahine o kekahi lahui, e nalo hia aku ana no ia lahui." Indeed, the language of a person reveals his nationality. Should the mother tongue of a nation be lost, so too will the people. Furthermore, the writer cautions, "I keia la, ua nalohia aku ko kakou kuokoa, a i ka pau ana o ka kakou olelo makuahine, o ka pau ana no ia o ka lahui Hawaii."[1] Inasmuch as the loss of sovereignty was a devastating blow to the Kingdom of Hawaiʻi, the writer laments that if the native tongue of Hawaiʻi goes extinct, so too will the Kanaka people.

The warning of this early twentieth-century columnist continues to resonate in the twenty-first century. ʻŌlelo Hawaiʻi educator Noʻeau Warner also expresses grief over the loss of the sovereignty of the Kingdom of Hawaiʻi, adding, "One by one, the markers of Hawaiian identity as a people have been stripped away, starting with the land, sovereignty, language, literacies (knowledge), histories, and connection to our ancestry."[2]

Mother tongues tend to thrive in sovereign native nations. With the suppression of sovereignty, the introduction of a new language of commerce and government, and the decline of a native population, many Indigenous languages become endangered. Some even succumb to language death. The death of a language signals the demise of a people, their culture, and their identity. As Kanaka scholar and activist Haunani-Kay Trask asserts, "A dead land is preceded by a dying people. As an example, indigenous languages replaced by universal (read colonial) languages result in the creation of 'dead languages.' But what is 'dead' or 'lost' is not the language but the people who once spoke it and transmitted their mother tongue to succeeding generations."[3]

The recently coined 'ōlelo Hawai'i word for colonization is kolonaio, meaning "crawling with worms."[4] One of the best ways to disempower a people is to burrow into their minds, infecting and incapacitating them at every level of consciousness, while simultaneously stripping them of their language—thereby erasing their historical memory and undermining their traditional knowledge systems. To add insult to injury, the colonizing power suppresses any meaningful use of the native language, yet perversely appropriates the native language and twists history for its benefit.

The state of Hawai'i has appropriated the motto of Kamehameha III, "ua mau ke ea o ka 'āina i ka pono," and has suppressed the fact that Kamehameha III made this statement on Lā Ho'iho'i Ea (Sovereignty Restoration Day) to commemorate the Kingdom's restored independence after a five-month occupation by the British. A more appropriate translation is "The sovereignty of the land is perpetuated in righteousness." As evidenced by the plight of our 'ōlelo makuahine, neither the sovereignty of the land nor the life of the land have been perpetuated in righteousness since the naio (worms) began to kolo (crawl).

Outside of individual families, a few rural communities, and Kanaka churches that maintained their ability to speak 'ōlelo Hawai'i, by the latter part of the twentieth century most Kanaka were no longer able to speak the 'ōlelo makuahine of our ancestors. Whereas other struggles discussed in this book started on the streets, the movement to revitalize 'ōlelo Hawai'i has clearly been waged in schools. Beginning at the University of Hawai'i, the movement grew through the education of thousands of second-language speakers of 'ōlelo Hawai'i, the creation of 'ōlelo Hawai'i researchers and curriculum developers, and the support of kula kaiapuni (public and private pre-K–12 Hawaiian language immersion schools). This chapter discusses the near death of 'ōlelo Hawai'i and some of the efforts to revive it.

A Brief History of 'Ōlelo Hawai'i

In spite of a 2,000-year history of speaking the mother tongue of our kūpuna and a 114-year history of publishing more than 125,000 newspaper pages in 'ōlelo Hawai'i, within a century of foreign occupation 'ōlelo Hawai'i became an endangered language. As Paul Nahoa Lucas points out, "Given Hawaiians' rapid and successful transformation from an entirely oral culture to a literate culture, Hawai'i had the opportunity to become a bilingual nation comparable to some European countries."[5] In addition to the decimation of the native population by disease and the loss of inalienable rights to the land that Kanaka enjoyed prior to the mid-1800s, the illegal overthrow of the Kingdom of Hawaiʻi in 1893 was one of the most devastating blows dealt to the Kanaka people. The loss of sovereignty was marked by a language shift from ʻōlelo Hawaiʻi to namu haole (English). Laws were created to limit the use of ʻōlelo Hawaiʻi in educational institutions. Act 57 of the 1896 Laws of the Republic of Hawaiʻi stated: "The English language shall be the medium and basis of instruction in all public and private schools, provided that where it is desired that another language shall be taught in addition to the English language, such instruction may be authorized by the Department, either by its rules, the curriculum of the school, or by direct order in any particular instance. Any schools that shall not conform to the provisions of this Section shall not be recognized by the Department." Act 57 effectively banned ʻōlelo Hawaiʻi-medium education. Lucas explains, "although schools had the option not to participate, nonparticipating schools would not continue to be recognized and thus would not receive government funding. As a direct result of the 1896 law, the number of Hawaiian-medium schools dropped drastically from a high of 150 in 1880 to zero in 1902. Conversely, the number of English-medium schools rose significantly from 60 in 1880 to 203 in 1902."[6] In 1900, four years after the enactment of Act 57, when Hawaiʻi became a territory of the United States, "all schools, government operations and official transactions were thereafter conducted in English, despite the fact that most people, including non-Natives, still spoke Hawaiian at the turn of the century."[7] Those caught speaking ʻōlelo Hawaiʻi in school, students and educators alike, were severely punished.[8]

THE EARLY DAYS OF ʻŌLELO HAWAIʻI AT THE UNIVERSITY OF HAWAIʻI

During those dark years of the Territorial period, there remained some efforts to keep ʻōlelo Hawaiʻi alive in institutional spaces. Created in 1907 as a land-grant college under the auspices of the Morrill Act, the University of Hawaiʻi at Mānoa was originally known as the College of Agriculture and Mechanic Arts of the Territory of Hawaiʻi. During the first fourteen years of the institution, ʻōlelo Hawaiʻi was not offered. According to Rubellite Johnson, "In early 1921, after the territorial legislature had expanded the College of Hawaii to become the University, the Board of Regents was asked in a legislative inquiry to declare its intentions with regards to Hawaiian. The board replied that ʻit has been a part of the plan of the University of Hawaii to give instruction in the Hawaiian language. . . . The University should become the center for the study of Hawaiian and a strong effort made to preserve the language in its purity.ʼ"[9] The first instructor of ʻōlelo Hawaiʻi at Mānoa was Frederick W. Beckley, the last ʻōlelo Hawaiʻi interpreter in the Supreme Court of the monarchy. Between 1922 and 1926, Beckley taught elementary to advanced ʻōlelo Hawaiʻi courses and a Polynesian comparative study course. His courses focused on pronunciation, conjugation, proverbs, religious history, literature, law, land tenure, song composition, syntax, and arts and crafts.

Beckley was succeeded by noted Kanaka patriot John Henry Wise, who left government service to join the professoriate. Professor Wise initially adopted the course descriptions of his predecessor. Shortly thereafter, he began incorporating the Hawaiian-English New Testament into his courses. In 1926, there was a breakthrough: ʻōlelo Hawaiʻi became a second language elective. Undergraduate students then had the option of choosing ʻōlelo Hawaiʻi to fulfill their elective requirements. This was a bold move, as very few schools offered ʻōlelo Hawaiʻi in their curriculum at the time. Even students at the Kamehameha Schools, an institution for Kanaka, did not begin offering ʻōlelo Hawaiʻi courses until the 1930s.[10]

Rubellite Johnson writes, "What Beckley and Wise accomplished between 1922 and 1934 (when Wise retired and was succeeded by the Reverend Henry Judd) was to lay the foundation for what eventually became the University's degree program in the Hawaiian language, a curriculum unique in the academic world."[11]

Following Beckley and Wise, a series of professors and instructors continued to push for modest expansion in the ʻōlelo Hawaiʻi curriculum. These included Henry Judd in the mid-1930s, Reverend Edward Kahale beginning in the mid-1940s, Samuel Elbert in the late 1940s, and Samuel A. Keala in the mid-1950s. From 1955 to 1968, under Elbert and Keala, the course offerings in ʻōlelo Hawaiʻi doubled. To accommodate the expanding curriculum and student demand, more instructors were hired. By the later 1960s, Alberta Pualani Anthony, Rubellite Johnson, Dorothy M. Kahananui, and Zaneta Richards all joined the ʻōlelo Hawaiʻi instructional faculty. This growth both contributed to and benefited from a larger cultural movement beyond the campus.

THE HAWAIIAN RENAISSANCE

During the Hawaiian Renaissance of the 1970s and onward, interest in ʻōlelo Hawaiʻi increased dramatically. Several hundred students enrolled in ʻōlelo Hawaiʻi at the university level. Many recognized that if the Kanaka people, our traditions, and our culture were to survive and thrive, we needed our language to live. A conscious resistance to cultural imperialism ensued; activists worked diligently to revive ʻōlelo Hawaiʻi as a living language. Central to the movement was the work of University of Hawaiʻi faculty who applied a multipronged approach to perpetuate and revitalize the language by preserving and recording the voices of native speakers, encouraging policymakers to repeal the law prohibiting the use of ʻōlelo Hawaiʻi as a medium of education, establishing preschool through twelfth grade kaiapuni schools, and pushing for ʻōlelo Hawaiʻi to be recognized as an official language of Hawaiʻi. Activists armed themselves with the traditional knowledge systems of our kūpuna to shield against the rapid fire aimed at annihilating the Kanaka people, our traditions, and our culture.

In 1972, *Ka Leo Hawaiʻi*, a Hawaiian-language weekly talk show hosted by instructor Larry Kimura, launched on KCCN 1420. Hui Aloha ʻĀina Tuahine, the ʻōlelo Hawaiʻi student organization of the University of Hawaiʻi at Mānoa, along with ʻōlelo Hawaiʻi faculty and staff, raced to preserve the voices of native speakers as a legacy for future generations of Kanaka. Native speakers throughout the islands were invited to speak about a variety of topics. Guests typically spoke about their experiences and memories of places in Hawai'i where they were born and raised. The original *Ka Leo Hawai'i* program ran until 1988, and during those seventeen years of programming, 674 shows were recorded. *Ka Leo Hawai'i* returned to the air in 1991 with Puakea Nogelmeier and Hau'oli Akaka serving as cohosts until 2000. Contemporary scholars continue to rely on this rich repository to glean insights about the worldviews of these 'ōlelo Hawai'i speakers and their oral traditions regarding Kanaka history, culture, traditions, and environment.

Along with the other 1970s movements related to land and culture, Kanaka organizers advocated for changes to the state's laws. In 1978, two important measures related to language and schooling were added to the state of Hawai'i's constitution. First, 'ōlelo Hawai'i was reestablished as an official language of Hawai'i. Second, an article that requires the state to "provide for a Hawaiian education program consisting of language, culture and history in the public schools" was included. In spite of the adoption of these measures, systemic oppression continued for 'ōlelo Hawai'i, as it was not granted full, equal status with English. 'Ōlelo Hawai'i was not required for "public acts and transactions," except if expressly required by law. Furthermore, the state failed to act on the mandate to initiate a publicly funded educational program in 'ōlelo Hawai'i. Disparity between 'ōlelo Hawai'i and English continued in governmental and educational systems. It was only through the persistent efforts of educators, students, and families that institutional spaces for 'ōlelo Hawai'i learning opened up.

The Birth of Kaiapuni Pre-K–12 Schools

In the early 1980s, less than fifty native speakers of 'ōlelo makuahine under the age of eighteen remained.[12] In 1983, 'ōlelo Hawai'i activists—many of whom began their careers as 'ōlelo Hawai'i faculty members at the University of Hawai'i—recognized the need to grow new generations of 'ōlelo Hawai'i–speaking children in order to ensure the survival of the language. Tired of waiting for state action, 'Īlei Beniamina, Hōkūlani Cleeland, Kauanoe Kamanā, Larry Kimura, No'eau Warner, Koki Williams, and William Wilson formed 'Aha Pūnana Leo Inc., a private, not-for-profit entity supporting kaiapuni education. In 1984, 'Aha Pūnana Leo opened the first kaiapuni preschool in Kekaha, Kaua'i. Pūnana Leo, or language nests, were modeled after Māori Kōhanga Reo in Aotearoa. Like birds feeding their young from mouth to mouth, teachers would feed the native language to youngsters so that they would be raised as native speakers.

The same educators helped fight for legislation that finally struck down the ninety-year-old law banning 'ōlelo Hawai'i as a medium of publicly funded education. After years of protest, in 1986 the state legislature affirmed that "special projects using the Hawaiian language" could be approved by the state's board of education.[13] This change was intended to support the unique needs of students from the Niʻihau community whose first language was ʻōlelo Hawaiʻi.[14] The fact that Pūnana Leo preschools began two years earlier is an example of civil disobedience. In fact, ʻōlelo Hawaiʻi instruction, in and of itself, is "both a cultural and political assertion; *cultural* because it seeks to preserve the core of a way of being and living that is uniquely Native, and *political* because this attempt at preservation takes place in a system where the dominant group has employed legal and social means to deny the use and inheritance of the Native language by Natives themselves."[15]

ʻŌlelo Hawaiʻi activism has paid off, especially in the area of ʻōlelo Hawaiʻi-medium education. In 1987, the board of education approved Ka Papahana Kaiapuni Hawaiʻi (Hawaiian Immersion Program), kindergarten to first grade, as a one-year pilot project. In 1992, permanent status was granted to Ka Papahana Kaiapuni Hawaiʻi as a K–12 public school program.[16] In 1999, the lead classes of Ānuenue in Pālolo, Oʻahu, and Nāwahīokalaniʻōpuʻu in Hilo, Hawaiʻi, graduated. As ʻōlelo Hawaiʻi educators William Wilson and Kauanoe Kamanā assert, "Having established Hawaiian-medium programs from pre-school through graduate school, Hawaiʻi has the most developed movement in indigenous language–medium education in the United States."[17]

Revitalization of ʻŌlelo Hawaiʻi at the University of Hawaiʻi

Faculty members at the University of Hawaiʻi continued to stand at the forefront of efforts to revitalize the language. ʻŌlelo Hawaiʻi educator and activist Laiana Wong echoes this sentiment by stating, "Although the Hawaiian movement involved participants from many segments of the wider community, its epicenter can be traced to the efforts of several Hawaiian language professors at the University of Hawaiʻi who provided the initial tremors that eventually rippled outward affecting the entire community."[18] The University of Hawaiʻi also served as a stage for highly contested Kanaka issues related to language, traditions, culture, and politics to be publicly debated and exposed.[19]

In 1979, a year after the Hawaiʻi state constitution was changed to declare an official language of Hawaiʻi, a provisional bachelor of arts degree in Hawaiian was approved at the University of Hawaiʻi at Mānoa. For the first time, students were able to earn a four-year degree in ʻōlelo Hawaiʻi. In 1986, eighteen Kanaka scholars representing all ten University of Hawaiʻi campuses met to provide guidance to the University of Hawaiʻi system on matters related to the study of Hawaiian language, culture, and history. This guiding document, "Kaʻū: University of Hawaiʻi Hawaiian Studies Task Force Report," was the impetus that catapulted Kanaka education forward at the University of Hawaiʻi. That document laid out a vision that set the stage for a generation of efforts: end-to-end integration of Kanaka and Hawaiian studies into the academy, with undergraduate and graduate curricula, a research center, services for Hawaiian students, tuition waivers, and a new Center for Hawaiian Studies. However, financial and administrative support for ʻōlelo Hawaiʻi was intermittent, and Kanaka programs were constantly vying with other programs for fiscal support.

Faculty, students, and community supporters went to great lengths to fight for space for ʻōlelo Hawaiʻi (Kekai Perry discusses one campaign in chapter 12, this volume). Perhaps no campus event better exemplifies this point than the Bachman Hall protest of 1995 when more than three hundred supporters stormed into the lobby of the university system's central administration offices, including the office of the president, to demonstrate against a proposal to reduce the Hawaiian language program's budget by 60 percent.[20] ʻŌlelo Hawaiʻi proponents warned that cuts to the program would not only impact 320 university students per semester but would also threaten to cause the extinction of the ʻōlelo makuahine of Hawaiʻi.

Laiana Wong implored, "If the English language department were shut down, the language would not die. Hawaiian isn't spoken anywhere else, it can't be learned in any other place." Noʻeau Warner contended, "Immersion will die without teachers," stressing that six of the seven kaiapuni teachers hired the year before were graduates of the University of Hawaiʻi at Mānoa's Hawaiian program. Proponents further reminded university officials that the University of Hawaiʻi at Mānoa sits on Hawaiian Trust Lands and that the university realized a 500 percent increase in Hawaiian enrollment between 1985 and 1995. ʻŌlelo Hawaiʻi protesters argued cuts to the program were a form of institutional racism.

After several hours of negotiation, acting president Joyce Tsunoda pledged, "You will get it. I don't know where we have the money now, but the first available dollar will go to Hawaiian language."[21]

In spite of the progress made in advancing ʻōlelo Hawaiʻi, the Hawaiian language program has yet to garner the complete and unconditional backing of the university. The level of support for the language is contingent upon the ever-changing administration. Within the past decade, several high-ranking administrators who have been staunch supporters of Kanaka serving programs at the University of Hawaiʻi at Mānoa have been either terminated or reassigned duties.

Conclusion

ʻŌlelo Hawaiʻi is a spring of life for the Kanaka people;[22] our identity, culture, and worldview pour forth from our native language. Centers for Hawaiian language within the university system, shaped by intense debate within the Kanaka community as a whole, are sources of these springs of life. To revitalize ʻōlelo Hawaiʻi as a living language, teachers, students, and families have established various niches for the language to thrive in schools and in the community at large: adult education classes, children's books, conversational groups, immersion camps, ʻōlelo Hawaiʻi clubs, language competitions, language showcases, mele (song) institutes, newsletters, newspaper columns, newspaper digitization and translation projects, radio programs, scholarly publications (e.g., theses, dissertations, journal articles, books written in ʻōlelo Hawaiʻi), sports teams, and theater productions have all contributed to breathing life back into a language that was once on the brink of extinction. Through school-based efforts, new generations of ʻōlelo Hawaiʻi speakers from preschool to graduate school are working to ensure that ʻōlelo Hawaiʻi is no longer in danger of becoming a dead language. If ʻōlelo Hawaiʻi is to thrive, we must employ sustained, systematic approaches that ensure our ʻōlelo Hawaiʻi is spoken intergenerationally in our homes, schools, workplaces, mass media, sites of worship, and in all aspects of our communities. We must resist the kolonaio by speaking our ʻōlelo makuahine. E Ola Mau ka ʻŌlelo Hawaiʻi!

Notes

1. "Olelo Hawaii."
2. Warner, "The Movement to Revitalize Hawaiian Language and Culture," 133.
3. Trask, *From a Native Daughter*, 81.
4. The term "kolonaio" was developed through discussion between Kaleikoa Kaʻeo and Hone Harawira, and later with feedback from Noʻeau Warner and Laiana Wong.
5. Lucas, "E Ola Mau Kākou i ka ʻŌlelo Makuahine," 2.
6. Lucas, "E Ola Mau Kākou i ka ʻŌlelo Makuahine," 9.
7. Trask, *From a Native Daughter*, 188.
8. Kawaiʻaeʻa, Housman, and Alencastre, "Pūʻā i Ka ʻŌlelo, Ola Ka ʻOhana"; Lucas, "E Ola Mau Kākou i ka ʻŌlelo Makuahine"; Warner, "*Kuleana*."
9. Johnson, "The Hawaiian Language and Hawaiian Studies," 138.
10. Pukui, Haertig, and Lee, *Nānā i Ke Kumu*, vol. 2, 62.
11. Johnson, "The Hawaiian Language and Hawaiian Studies," 138.
12. Kawaiʻaeʻa, Housman, and Alencastre, "Pūʻā i Ka ʻŌlelo, Ola Ka ʻOhana," 183.
13. Hawaiʻi Revised Statutes, section 298-2.
14. Lucas, "E Ola Mau Kākou i ka ʻŌlelo Makuahine," 24–25.
15. Trask, *From a Native Daughter*, 52–53.
16. Kawaiʻaeʻa, Housman, and Alencastre, "Pūʻā i Ka ʻŌlelo, Ola Ka ʻOhana," 228 and 230.
17. Wilson and Kamanā, "ʻMai Loko Mai o ka ʻIʻini," 147.
18. Wong, "He Hāwaʻe Kai Nui a Kau Ma Kula," 31.
19. NeSmith, "Tūtū's Hawaiian and the Emergence of a Neo-Hawaiian Language," 69.
20. Fernandes, "UH Tries to Cut 14 Classes."
21. "Protesters Besiege Bachman Hall."
22. Thiong'o, *Decolonising the Mind*, 3.

CHAPTER 4. Kaua'i

RESISTING PRESSURES TO CHANGE

Joan Conrow

Kaua'i, the northernmost of the main Hawaiian Islands, has always held itself apart from the rest of the archipelago. It is the only island that was never conquered by Kamehameha, and its earliest residents spoke Hawaiian in a distinctly different dialect. Even today there is a desire among its citizens to retain that separateness, that uniqueness, which for many translates as resisting the forces of development that continue to transform the rest of Hawai'i. Or as a popular phrase puts it: "Keep Kaua'i, Kaua'i."

In the nineteenth century, a wave of capital infusion from missionary descendants sought to transform Kaua'i, like the rest of the Hawaiian archipelago, into a sugar producer for export to the United States. Sugar production in Hawai'i, as in Latin America, Cuba, and elsewhere, is a labor-intensive process, and required the importation of immigrant workers to meet production quotas. On the sugar plantations of Kaua'i, as on the other islands, a new kind of local was created—Japanese, Chinese, Filipino, or Hawaiian laborers with a shared experience of plantation life. These communities grew and intermixed, but by the 1960s the shifting flow of global capital began moving sugar production (and later pineapple) to lower-wage nations. In the race to the bottom, Kaua'i plantations needed a new raison d'être. Into that void stepped the opportunities of the post-statehood capital boom: jet travel and mass tourism.

The first half of this chapter describes the efforts of Kaua'i locals to protect their communities from displacement by tourist development. The second section deals with the subsequent evolution of the Kaua'i grassroots movement and its efforts, in the wake of setbacks, to realize a vision for the island, resulting in a hard-won reputation for rebellion, activism, and what some would criticize as an almost rabidly antidevelopment sentiment. Still, there's a widespread sense, even among those who would not consider themselves activists, that the island's rural landscape and close-knit community are valuable and worth protecting.

Protecting a Lifestyle

The island's modern history of civil disobedience and social unrest harkens to the earliest efforts to unionize the workers who labored in the red clay fields of the island's

Keiki of a former plantation camp on the southeast side of Kaua'i Island, August 1973.

extensive sugar and pineapple plantations. As a result, Kaua'i holds the dubious distinction of being the site of the most violent episode in the Hawai'i labor movement—the infamous 1924 Hanapēpē Massacre. Seventeen striking sugar workers and three police officers were killed in the standoff. With its leaders dead, jailed, or deported, the Filipino labor movement was effectively derailed, and unionization wasn't achieved until 1946.

Spirited disputes over land development did not begin until the late 1960s on Kaua'i, when citizens of the predominantly rural island began mobilizing in opposition as plans for resorts slowly started to emerge. By 1969 a vibrant environmental and antieviction movement was focusing its attention on developments at Po'ipū, which is now a primary tourist destination on the island's south side. The activists were predominantly young and local, meaning born on Kaua'i. Many were the offspring of Japanese, Portuguese, and Filipino immigrants who had been brought in to work on the plantations, and others were Native Hawaiians. They shared a common interest: preserving the close-knit community, open spaces, and access to mountains and ocean that allowed them to fish, hunt, camp, and enjoy a country lifestyle rooted in Hawaiian traditions. The cry of the activist movement on Kaua'i was, and continues to be today, "we don't want to be like Maui or O'ahu"—two islands that are widely viewed as spoiled by excessive resort development and residential sprawl.

Arthur Chow and son, "Atta Boy" Chow, relax with their family dogs outside their Nāwiliwili home in August 1973.

Though earnest, the activists proved no match for the development forces that saw profit in the area's sunny coastline, and they were unable to halt resort construction. Their primary victory occurred when students of Kaua'i Community College gathered some five thousand signatures on a petition calling on Kaua'i County to expand a public beach park by condemning a lot that was leased to a corporation that wanted to expand the Waiohai Hotel. The county ultimately bought the lot.

Saving People's Homes

Another major skirmish arose three years later, near the island's main port of Nāwiliwili Harbor, which was also slated for tourist development. About twenty working-class families, many of them of mixed Hawaiian ancestry, received eviction notices from landowner Kanoa Estate Inc. Banding with another twenty nearby families who also feared eviction, they formed the Niumalu-Nāwiliwili Tenants Association (NNTA). Though the group included many Native Hawaiians, they organized primarily around social justice concerns, rejecting the premise that local people would be evicted so that visitors could take their place on the land instead. The NNTA was headed up by Stanford

A native of Niumalu, Stanford Achi got politically activated after receiving an eviction notice from the home he had lived in since birth. He became a key organizer in Kaua'i land struggles. A canoe paddler and coach, he is pictured here speaking with another paddler in 1971.

Achi, the fourth son of Kaua'i judge William Achi and an avid outrigger canoe paddler who coached the Kaua'i Canoe Club. Achi had grown up in Niumalu, and didn't want to see the area developed at the cost of people's longtime homes. In hopes of pressuring government officials to halt resort-oriented plans by Kanoa and other developers in the harbor area, the group staged a major political demonstration in December 1972, with a hundred sign-carrying citizens marching from the harbor to the county building in downtown Līhu'e, the county seat.

The group continued to gain strength, turning out in force to attend a 1973 public hearing on a plan recommending a resort in Niumalu. The crowd of about two hundred persons was the largest ever to that date to attend a hearing on a land use question on Kaua'i. The county ended up rejecting the recommendation, and the group's victory prompted NNTA to serve as an organizing model for other residents who were concerned about development in their communities.

Meanwhile, the group had been able to stave off the evictions, largely because the land use designation for most of Kanoa Estate's acreage in the harbor area did not allow development. But there was one fourteen-acre parcel that was zoned for multifamily housing, and in 1974 Kanoa sold it to an O'ahu-based development group, which drew

Stanford Achi, leader of the Niumalu-Nāwiliwili Tenants Association, speaks at a demonstration, Stop All Evictions Now, at the Hawai'i state capitol, February 14, 1976. The event brought together people from various eviction struggles across the islands.

up plans for a condominium project. When NNTA heard about the proposal, it sought unsuccessfully to have the land rezoned to prohibit a resort. Members then announced they would risk arrest in order to prevent eviction of the ten low- to moderate-income families that lived there.

By 1976, Kanoa had sold the parcel to Nāwiliwili Joint Venture, a partnership of Bishop Development Inc. (which has no affiliation with Bishop Estate) and Read Development Inc. In September 1976, Stanley Ota, half-owner of Bishop, was one of six men arrested on O'ahu in a heroin bust. At the time, federal Drug Enforcement Agency officials linked those arrested to an organized crime syndicate in Hawai'i. Several months later, Ota was found murdered. The events underscored a prevailing sentiment that development was bringing unsavory outsiders to the island, and that those who opposed it were putting themselves at risk.

Tensions and fears mounted further when, in April 1977, a fire of suspicious origin completely destroyed the home of Edward Panui Jr., an NNTA leader overseeing activities in Nāwiliwili. Some NNTA members suspected arson. About a week later, a union leader was gunned down outside his office in Honolulu, fueling fears among NNTA

Retired sugar plantation worker Eustaquio Ocso was a healer in his community and a tireless supporter of the Niumalu-Nāwiliwili Tenants Association. At public meetings with corporate developers, he would wave his machete, saying, "You come Kaua'i, I cut!" 1973.

Mr. Obra speaks at a Niumalu-Nāwiliwili community gathering with antieviction supporters from O'ahu in November 1975.

members that they might also be victims of violence. In light of the growing unease, and with just sixty hard-core members willing to be arrested, Achi decided to avoid a direct confrontation with police. He instead negotiated a settlement with Nāwiliwili Joint Venture that resulted in a church, as well as the two families that had remained on the land, being given free lots.

The Movement Picks Up Steam

Although the Niumalu-Nāwiliwili conflict ended in peaceful agreement, the group's actions served to inspire other environmentalists and community activists to get involved in fighting development proposals around the island. At this point, the movement's emphasis shifted back to its original focus: protecting the natural environment and rural lifestyle that so many residents cherished. Simultaneously, Hawaiians were becoming more active in practicing their culture, which stemmed from an understanding that the land was sacred. It was an easy mesh between the interests of Hawaiians, environmentalists, and community activists, especially because most of them shared the overriding bond of having been raised in the islands. As a result, when plans were introduced in 1977 to develop three 500-room resorts on the windswept beach of Nukoli'i, which was popular with fishers, surfers, and other recreational users, a sizable group of opponents—some of them spillovers from the Niumalu-Nāwiliwili standoff—quickly formed.

They were met with an equally sizable force of supporters, primarily members of the building industry, who welcomed the jobs. Indeed, their presence at a 1977 Kaua'i County Council session represented the first time that construction workers turned up at a land use meeting on the island. It represented a major turning point in Kaua'i land use struggles, and from that time on, developers frequently bused in workers who were on their side, if not their payroll, to show support for a proposed project when it went before regulatory agencies.

The protracted fight over the proposed rezoning of the sixty-acre Nukoli'i parcel for resort use turned bitter, with one Kaua'i County councilman claiming he had been threatened with death if he supported the zoning upgrade. Ultimately, the rezoning was approved, although by that time the resort had been scaled back to 350 rooms on twenty-five acres of land.

But the rezoning did not stop opponents, who formed a group called Committee to Save Nukoli'i and collected the signatures of registered voters on a petition drive for a ballot referendum to overturn the zoning—the first time such an approach had been taken on the island. The vote was scheduled for the November 1980 election. The group also filed three court actions in an attempt to slow the project and keep it from gaining vested rights, but all three interventions failed. Meanwhile, Hasegawa Komuten Inc., a condominium developer, had come to own the controlling interest in the property, bringing substantial resources to the struggle.

Shortly before the election, in the midst of heavy campaigning on both sides of the issue, the project's contractor reported that his baseyard, or equipment staging site, had been broken into. The fuel and hydraulic lines had been cut on three large pieces of heavy equipment; on other machines, sand was poured into fuel tanks, tires were punctured, and crank cases were damaged. The vandalism didn't slow construction on the condominiums around the resort, however, and on the afternoon before the election was to be held, the county issued the building permit for the hotel itself.

Voters rejected the rezoning by a margin of two to one. But Hasegawa continued construction, and the county refused to revoke the building permits on the grounds that the developer's rights had been vested. Opponents then turned to civil disobedience to protest what they considered illegal construction, and blocked an access road to the site. The action resulted in thirty-two people being arrested, including one woman charged with biting police officers. Death threats were reportedly made to both the mayor and various members of his administration, prompting county officials to impose tight security during the January inauguration ceremonies, which were protested by about 150 picketers. This was followed by a small bomb going off in the mayor's office—a second bomb would be detonated in the fall of 1982, when the mayor announced he would not seek reelection—and the discovery of an unexploded bomb at the Nukoliʻi construction site. Such actions, which the Committee to Save Nukoliʻi disavowed, were unheard of on sleepy Kauaʻi. Never before, or since, has a development project generated such intense animosity. Activists were desperate to stop what they saw as an opening of the floodgates for tourism and resort development, while project proponents were keen on economic development.

In February 1981, Kauaʻi Circuit Court judge Kei Hirano ruled that Hasegawa had, indeed, incurred sufficient expenses to vest its development rights, and construction continued as the Committee to Save Nukoliʻi filed an appeal. In October 1982, the Hawaiʻi Supreme Court shocked proponents and opponents alike by overturning Hirano's decision and ordering the county to revoke the condominium and hotel building permits so as to halt all construction on the project.

Serious Setbacks

Then governor George Ariyoshi and other leaders were chilled by the ruling, fearing it set a troubling precedent and sent a loud antibusiness message to investors and developers. As a result, Ariyoshi supported Hasegawa in its unsuccessful bid to have the U.S. Supreme Court review the state court's decision. Meanwhile, a group calling itself Kauaians for Nukoliʻi formed to collect signatures for a second referendum to reestablish resort zoning at the site. A second vote was held, in February 1984, and the zoning was reinstated by a vote of 58 to 42 percent. More money was spent on the campaign than had ever before been expended on a Kaua'i election, but other factors also came into play. Hurricane 'Iwa had struck the island two years earlier, causing widespread damage and contributing to unemployment, abysmal hotel occupancy rates, and an overall poor economy that likely caused voters to look more favorably upon a project that would generate jobs and revenues.

The Nukoli'i episode represented a major setback for Kaua'i's environmental community, which subsequently fragmented and weakened as activists primarily focused on development projects in their own backyards through the remainder of the 1980s. Meanwhile, the island had begun to see an influx of new residents from the U.S. mainland. Some of the local activists eyed the newcomers warily and were hesitant to build alliances, while others were drifting away from land use struggles and focusing instead on raising families.

Still, two large resort projects did generate widespread opposition. These included renovating and expanding the former Kaua'i Surf at Nāwiliwili into a luxurious Westin resort, and a proposal to build a hotel and golf course at Māhā'ulepū, a beloved southside beach where a resort had earlier been fought off. Both projects were approved, although community resistance did force Grove Farm to push its Māhā'ulepū hotel—now the Kaua'i Grand Hyatt—well back from the shoreline to preserve the beach.

In 1992, Kaua'i was struck by Hurricane 'Iniki, which heavily damaged the island's resorts, as well as many homes. Environmental activism fell by the wayside for the remainder of the decade as residents struggled to rebuild their houses and lives. The visitor industry had shriveled in the aftermath of the hurricane, and developers were not proposing new projects. Though the economy was weak, many residents were pleased that the hurricane had served to stymie what they feared would otherwise have been runaway growth. It was not uncommon in later years to hear Kaua'i residents call for a hurricane, or even a tsunami, when they felt development was getting out of hand.

Fighting Gentrification

By the turn of the new century, the visitor industry had picked up again, and activists were facing a new threat: gentrification of the island's extensive agricultural lands. The demise of the sugar plantations had left vast tracts of land vacant, and developers began pressing to convert some of the acreage to the newly lucrative market of vacation homes and gentleman's estates. Though this trend was occurring on all the islands, it came as a particular jolt to many Kaua'i residents, who feared it would undermine the island's treasured egalitarian social structure and simple, nonmaterialistic lifestyle. As one man described it in early 2000, "Nobody on Kaua'i cares if you don't have a nice car. In fact, they probably like you better if you don't."

Though land use activism on Kaua'i had previously been dominated by local residents of Asian ancestry, most of whom were the descendants of plantation workers, Hawaiians now moved to the forefront. They began speaking out as traditional trails to mountains and beaches were fenced off by new landowners and luxury home construction—much of it for the vacation rental market. They were also disturbed as gentrification began to encroach into traditionally Hawaiian communities that previously had not experienced direct impacts from tourism, such as Anahola and Hā'ena. Land prices began to escalate, and many Hawaiians and local families were forced to sell because they couldn't pay the property taxes. Alarmed by the rapid changes to the island's small, isolated, very rural communities, transplanted mainland haole and Native Hawaiians came together to advance a shared goal: halting the gentrification of agricultural lands and stopping the proliferation of luxury vacation rentals, especially along the coast.

As the economy picked up steam in the early to mid-2000s, even longtime residents who hadn't taken a stand on development issues began to express concern about skyrocketing real estate prices and rapid social changes that were destroying the tight-knit community. People fretted about how to "Keep Kaua'i Kaua'i," prompting widespread community support for a moratorium on development in Po'ipū, which was being engulfed by tourism, to the dismay of many longtime area residents. The council rejected the moratorium in 2006, clearing the way for a massive development project by Alexander and Baldwin—one of the Big Five companies that dominates politics and business in Hawai'i. Alexander and Baldwin is also one of the state's largest landowners, most of it agricultural land. At Po'ipū, the company secured state and county approval to significantly rezone its land for the massive Kukui'ula resort project. At build out, it will comprise some 1,500 mostly upscale homes, a hotel, golf course, and shopping center. Alexander and Baldwin also won approval to build another 1,700 units catering to the vacation home market.

Cultural Issues Move to the Forefront

Frustrated by the unwillingness of the county planning commission and county council to limit growth, activists began turning to the courts for relief. Though the tactic wasn't especially effective in slowing development, it further cemented environmental and cultural concerns and claims, at least legally. This marriage of common interests also strengthened the activist community, which had not regained its pre-'Iniki solidity. Environmentalists and Hawaiians joined together to file suit against two hotels approved for the Wailua area, raising cultural concerns about protecting ancient burials and fishing areas, and environmental worries about shoreline development and congested roads.

The citizen groups failed to prevail and were planning an appeal when attorneys for the developers moved to collect legal fees, threatening to go after the personal assets of Angie Puanani Rogers, who was the plaintiff in the suit with 1000 Friends of Kaua'i, a nonprofit organization. The coercive tactic worked, and the appeal was dropped, paving the way for the projects to proceed and exposing the legal vulnerability of Native Hawaiian individuals who pursued activism through the courts.

But that wasn't the only antidevelopment action that ended with a chill being cast over opposition to land use decisions on Kaua'i. Another highly volatile case involved Los Angeles developer Joseph Brescia, who encountered some thirty-one ancient Native Hawaiian burials when he began constructing a luxury home at Naue, on the island's North Shore. The discovery resulted in a public outcry, and citizens pressed the planning commission to revoke Brescia's building permits. The commission—chaired, ironically, by James Nishida Jr., a participant in the NNTA and Nukoli'i protests—refused to revoke the permits.

The Kaua'i-Ni'ihau Island Burial Council, an appointed panel that has jurisdiction over certain ancient burials, voted to preserve the remains, known as iwi kupuna (ancestral bones), in place, rather than dig them up and move them to another site. In taking that position, a majority of the council believed the house would be redesigned to avoid impacting the burials, or perhaps would not be built at all. Instead, archaeologists working for Brescia and the state's Historic Preservation Review Division decided to cap the burials in concrete so that foundation posts for the house could be erected above them.

The Native Hawaiian Legal Corporation stepped in on behalf of Jeffrey Chandler, who claimed a lineal connection to the iwi, and filed suit to halt the project, arguing in court that the state's Historic Preservation Review Division had handled the matter improperly. Kaua'i Circuit Court judge Kathleen Watanabe found the state had indeed erred, but she refused to issue an injunction to stop construction. Throughout the proceedings, numerous protests and vigils were held at the site, resulting in criminal trespassing charges being filed against a number of protesters. Brescia, meanwhile, had taken the unprecedented step of filing civil suits against some of his most vocal opponents, claiming slander of title and other harm. Brescia ultimately prevailed in court. Though he chose to collect only minimal damages, the stress and expense of fighting off his claims left the defendants, nearly all of them Native Hawaiian, wary of where land use activism might lead them.

New Enthusiasm

Kaua'i activists were more successful in halting the Hawai'i Superferry, in part because opposition to the high-speed ferry was widespread, crossing the lines of ethnicity and length of residence on the island that had previously divided activists with common interests. The protest began to swell when then governor Linda Lingle determined the ferry could begin operations without conducting an environmental impact study. Residents of Maui and Kaua'i were outraged, fearing their islands would be inundated with people and cars from O'ahu. The boat's maiden voyage to Kaua'i's Nāwiliwili Harbor was met with spontaneous mass protests that grew steadily each day, eventually totaling about eight hundred persons on the ferry's fourth visit to the island. The decisive moment came when surfers paddled out to block the boat, causing it to turn back to O'ahu. After that, Lingle imposed a security zone around the harbor, threatening citizens with federal charges if they protested the ferry. When she came to Kaua'i to announce the crackdown, she was met with a hostile crowd of more than a thousand persons, the island's largest protest gathering to that date.

The ferry never returned to Kaua'i, leaving residents feeling energized and empowered. The protests sparked a new enthusiasm for civil disobedience among some of those who had been active in land use issues in decades prior but had since dropped out. It also helped newer residents cement their ties to the island and increased awareness overall about the land use process and the power of community activism. While the issue ultimately was decided legally in a case brought by Maui residents, with the Hawai'i Supreme Court ruling an environmental impact statement was needed, Kaua'i's civil disobedience attracted international attention and was widely viewed as the final nail in the Superferry's coffin.

The highly publicized Superferry protests catapulted Kaua'i into the spotlight, with many O'ahu business leaders and residents characterizing the island as clannish, backward, even lawless, and freakishly antidevelopment. Many Kaua'i residents reveled in the characterization because it reinforced the perception that they had managed to remain separate and apart from the rest of Hawai'i, insistent on charting their own destiny, even in the face of intense financial and political pressure from outside.

Most recently, some Native Hawaiian activists have joined a movement against the biotech companies that are growing conventional and genetically engineered seed crops. Their concerns have focused on possible contamination of water and soil, as well as possible health risks to people living near the fields. They've also become increasingly involved in issues involving the development of new water sources and stream diversions, since water is a public trust resource in Hawai'i.

The land use struggles on Kaua'i, waged primarily over a desire to retain a lifestyle that is rooted in Hawaiian cultural traditions, have played an important role in Hawaiian movements for life, land, and sovereignty by demonstrating over and over that even a small group of people can make a difference if they are willing to stand up and be counted.

CHAPTER 5. Kū i ka Pono

THE MOVEMENT CONTINUES

Manu Kaʻiama

A Kīlauea eruption in 1790 took the lives of a number of Keōua's warriors, thus assisting Kamehameha to eventually win the battle to rule Hawaiʻi Island. Kīlauea again erupted 134 years later. This time her moʻolelo (story) lasted eighteen days, a stark reminder that she was still alive and well. On January 3, 1983, she began to erupt again and this flow has yet to cease. We, the citizens of the Nation of Hawaiʻi, treasure this ea, these vapors and fumes, this awesome activity as an essence of Pele's existence. She moves independently as the lava, teaching us how to rule.

This essay tells the story of a series of events that took place in the late 1990s and early 2000s, whose time in history is commonly characterized as the Kū i ka Pono movement. It included the political mobilization of major Hawaiian forces that had been lying dormant, such as the hula community, the Kamehameha Schools (KS), and a broad base of Kanaka Maoli.

ʻAʻole i pau.

The PASH Decision

Many ignorant people comment flippantly that Kanaka Maoli (people with native lineage in Hawaiʻi) have done nothing over time to show their displeasure at their current circumstances. In reality, this is more an indication of the lack of publicity given to our protests. The very real smoldering frustration bubbled over in January 1993 when Ka Lāhui Hawaiʻi organized a march to commemorate the overthrow of the Hawaiian government by U.S. Marines and white sugar plantation owners a hundred years earlier. This march was characterized as being "the single largest demonstration in the history of modern Hawaiʻi" with "over 15,000 people participating."[1]

In the wake of this grand display of Kanaka Maoli unity and mana (power) in 1993, in 1995 the Hawaiʻi State Supreme Court ruled in *Public Access Shoreline Hawaiʻi v. Hawaiʻi County Planning Commission*, commonly referred to as the PASH decision, that the state had a duty to protect all customary and traditional Native Hawaiian rights exercised for cultural, religious, and subsistence purposes.[2] The case stemmed from the concern that Kanaka Maoli gathering rights be protected on undeveloped land. It was considered a landmark decision because it plainly supported our right to gather, which originates from our land-based religion and the belief that land is not owned by anyone. The PASH decision thus intended to protect such practices within certain parameters under state law. In essence, though seen as a win, truly Kanaka Maoli rights are subject to the state's right to regulate them.[3] The term "state" is used to identify the settler government in power currently. As a result of this law, with every subsequent legislative session, Kanaka Maoli have had to be diligent in ensuring that these rights are not eroded through some sort of midnight special-interest legislation. At the same time, numerous landowners and developers were fearful that Hawaiian gathering rights would interfere with their ability to build on and profit from lands. Nervous settler capitalists moved expeditiously and cleverly to secure their own business interests by trying to change this law.

The 1997 session of the Hawai'i State Legislature hosted a number of bills designed to address the traditional and customary gathering rights of Kanaka Maoli. Though disguised as attempts to better define the PASH decision, they ultimately would have terminated our rights. The proposed bills were but one more example of how laws are used strategically to dismantle our native ways of life. If passed, a significant cultural practice would have been severely if not completely curtailed, and the law would have criminalized us for simply being Kanaka Maoli.

Upon learning about these bills, Vicky Holt Takamine, Kumu Hula (hula master) of Hālau Pua Ali'i 'Ilima, knew instantly that this would forever change the way hula dancers and other Kanaka gathered our necessary lā'au (resources of the land). As such, it would compromise our very identity as Kanaka Maoli. She rushed to inform as many Kumu Hula as possible to enlighten them to these new, proposed pieces of legislation. In three short days, through her leadership and with the help of other Kumu Hula, she successfully planned a twenty-four-hour protest at the state capitol building. She brought together twenty-eight pahu (drums) and approximately 250 people for what would be a culturally appropriate protest.[4]

Every hour on the hour chants were recited and hula was performed. At 6 p.m., we switched to every three hours throughout the night. At 6 a.m., we returned to the hourly presentation. The deep and rich sounds of the pahu filled the air of the capitol rotunda—sounds so ancient they gave us "chicken skin."[5] The drums were pounded purposefully, deliberately, sending a message to the upper levels of this modern tower of Babel, home to state lawmakers, echoing all the way up to the governor's office. The haunting, hallowed beat was a message from our ancestors, a message from Kanaka Maoli, a message that could not be ignored. We had had enough.

There were no warm smiles or lei. There was no aloha. Instead, an undercurrent of anger was prevalent. Finally, Senators Randy Iwase and Mālama Solomon came to the protest to address the crowd.[6] The senators' arrogant demeanor was not tolerated

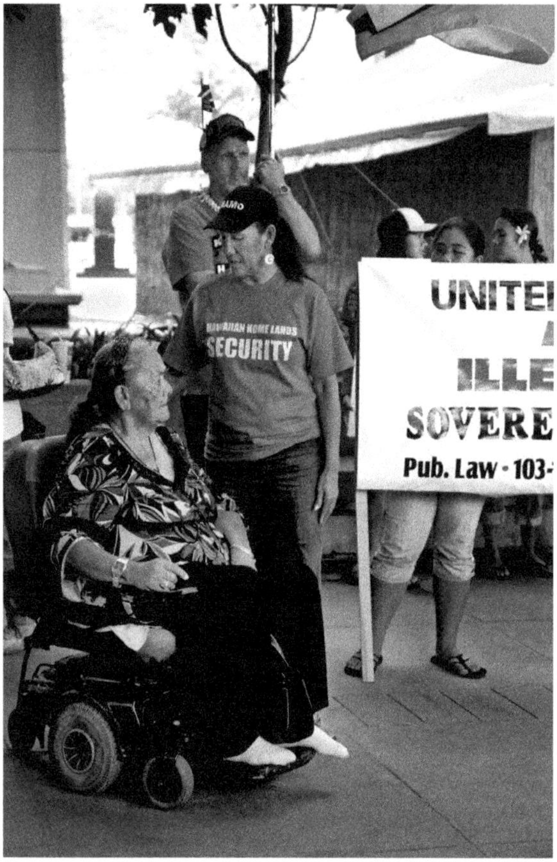

Kumu Vicky Holt Takamine (standing) and Adelaide "Frenchy" DeSoto (in wheelchair), her inspiration, at the state capitol during one of the many demonstrations demanding justice for Kanaka Maoli. Richard Kinney holds the Hawaiian flag in the background. 2008.

by those gathered. As Iwase attempted to admonish the crowd, we chanted: "Kill the bill!" After numerous taunts back and forth between the microphone and the crowd, Solomon dramatically ripped the bill in half.[7] The crowd erupted.

Interestingly enough, volcanic activity occurring at the Kīlauea Crater included significant movement in early 1997. Scientists recorded an eruption at Pu'u 'Ō'ō Kupaianaha on January 30, 1997.[8] And so the volcano continued to be restless and we were to follow.

'A'ole i pau.

The Birth of 'Īlio'ulaokalani

With this victory, Kanaka embraced once again the reality that there is power in organizing, that we do have a voice, and that we have every right to demand respect and protection of our cultural ways. Unfortunately we needed to testify in a more bombastic manner than most, just to be heard. Because of this prevailing oppressive illegal environment, exacerbated by the constant social and cultural attacks on our ways of life, Kumu Hula who participated in the vigil continued to meet and proceeded to divide up two responsibilities among themselves. The first responsibility was to care for our traditional practices through an organization called Lālākea (a white-tipped shark). The second group that formed took up the task of being politically alert, or maka'ala. It would be their duty to watch out for other laws intruding upon our way of life. Led by Vicky Holt Takamine, the 'Īlio'ulaokalani Coalition, "the red dog of the heavens," was born.

The vigil at the capitol reminded us of the unity and empowerment experienced in 1993 as Ka Lāhui Hawai'i marched to 'Iolani Palace. In many ways, 'Īlio'ulaokalani's later vigils were a continuation of that effort. Its first vigil at the capitol marked a point in history when culturally grounded organizing had an effect on anti–Kanaka Maoli legislation. In retrospect, Vicky Holt Takamine believes that this was where the Kū i ka Pono movement began, though that name had not yet been articulated. It is only fitting that this movement was born among a chorus of pahu and that ceremony inspired our ability to assume and fulfill our kuleana (responsibility). Which way will the lava flow next?

'A'ole i pau.

Anti-Hawaiian Movements and Legal Attacks

While the 'Īlio'ulaokalani Coalition was coalescing, an anti–Kanaka Maoli movement was gathering its own momentum. In 1996, a wealthy rancher and landowner of missionary descent, Harold Freddy Rice, filed suit against the state of Hawai'i claiming that he should have the right to vote in the election of Office of Hawaiian Affairs (OHA) trustees.[9] The *Rice v. Cayetano* case went all the way to the U.S. Supreme Court, after losing at both the state and appellate court levels, and in 2000, the Supreme Court ruling opened OHA elections to all registered voters in Hawai'i. Since at that time, approximately 80 percent of Hawai'i's population were settlers, the ruling effectively gutted the Native people's ability to determine who would lead an organization expressly created to benefit Kanaka Maoli.[10] Rice's win encouraged a plethora of lawsuits against Kanaka Maoli–serving institutions.

With a court decision claimed to be driven by the U.S. Constitution and for the protection of equal rights, the race was on to make illegal all services and programs attempting to assist Kanaka Maoli to reach parity with all other settlers in Hawai'i. The more renowned cases included attacks against the Queen Lili'uokalani Trust, OHA, the Department of Hawaiian Homelands (DHHL), and KS. Additionally and insidiously, the laws and legal ideology of the settlers were invoked to extinguish our independent National identity and birthrights.

Among the anti–Kanaka Maoli lawsuits were a few specifically targeting the admissions policy of KS, a private institution founded by the last will and testament of a Hawaiian female chief, Ke Ali'i Bernice Pauahi Pākī Bishop, for the betterment of our people. The institution had humble beginnings, being land rich and cash poor. It historically stressed industrial, vocational training and later shifted to become a college prep school for students of Kanaka Maoli ancestry. As KS's assets and holdings grew astronomically after the 1960s development boom, the quality of KS facilities and programs have come to rival those of other elite private schools in the islands while tuition, because of subsidy, remains only a fraction of its peer institutions. There exists no Kanaka Maoli blood quantum for a student to attend KS, only a stipulation in Pauahi's will that preference goes to students with Native Hawaiian ancestry. The result has been that KS is the "school for Hawaiians." With the majority of Kanaka Maoli at the bottom of every good statistic, such as good health, gainful employment, and home ownership, and at the top of every bad statistic, such as disease, poverty, suicide, and incarceration, KS has become a symbol of opportunity for hope and change through education for Kanaka Maoli. With the onset of affluence, suddenly settlers want their children to attend and further claim it to be their American right.

Under the pressure of numerous legal attacks, on July 11, 2002, then KS chief executive officer Hamilton McCubbin informed the public that a "non-Hawaiian" student had been offered admission to the KS Maui campus.[11] A meeting was called four days later at the KS Kapālama, O'ahu, campus to discuss this decision. The Ke'elikōlani Auditorium was filled to capacity with alumni, parents, and staff. The spirit there was dangerously anxious. One by one the Kamehameha trustees stood to explain to the angry crowd why a non–Kanaka Maoli had been admitted. Each and every time they attempted to state that this child was the most qualified out of all the remaining applicants, the crowd roared back at them. It was a defining moment for the illustrious trustees, historically revered and considered sacred by the very group that now demanded their resignations.

It is fair to say that 99 percent of everyone in that room did not care about the admission preference policy. Instead we were incensed that any Kanaka Maoli child would be denied before a settler child. There was no settler child more qualified than a Kanaka Maoli child. Education is the key to a better life for our people, especially opportunities offered at Kamehameha. A handout was distributed to all in attendance attempting to explain the reasoning behind the decision. In bold, so we wouldn't miss it, they highlighted the following from Codicil 1, Section 13 of Princess Bernice Pauahi Bishop's will: "I also give unto my said trustees full power to make all such rules and regulations as they may deem necessary for the government of said schools and to regulate the admission of pupils, and the same to alter, amend and publish upon a vote of a majority of said trustees."[12]

For some odd reason, they thought they would be able to garner support from the crowd for this decision. Instead, the hundreds in attendance that evening were livid. They jeered at Trustee Diane Plots when it appeared that she was falling asleep. They cat-called Trustee Constance Lau when she continually mispronounced Hawaiian words. Even the darling, Trustee Nainoa Thompson, could not seduce or silence the audience. Our anger erupted as the well-prepared speeches continued. All three KS campuses still collectively service approximately only 5 percent of all Kanaka Maoli K–12 children in Hawai'i.[13] How could a non–Kanaka Maoli be so self-serving as to take this spot away from a Kanaka Maoli? How could those settler parents encourage such behavior?[14] Being an alumna myself, I was amazed at the irreverence displayed by an audience so well disciplined in the missionary ways of politeness and obedience. We continued to push for real answers and the trustees were ill prepared. Alas, it was only at this moment that the trustees and administrators realized to whom KS really belonged.

As the evening wore on and the administration realized that they were not going to appease this crowd, they reminded us that the meeting would end promptly at 8:30 p.m. with no exception. Again, the audience hissed in disgust. At 8:30 on the dot, the reverend stood up and cut off an audience member by commanding in a bellowing voice, "Let us pray!" Like magic, his invocation of Akua (Gods) made everyone hush each other quiet. We might as well have been hushing each other out of existence. I looked around at everyone, whom only moments earlier I was so proud of, now being controlled, obedient, and silent. I turned to my daughter and said, "Let's go" in a semiloud voice. Those sitting near us turned toward me with wide eyes and mouths hanging open with their assumption that I lacked respect. I felt that this orchestrated call to God was completely wrong on so many levels, not to mention exploitive and disrespectful to Akua, that I refused to participate in it or to allow my daughter to do so. We stood and meandered through the dutifully praying audience and left. Strategically, the admission of a settler child may have been an opportunity for Kamehameha to prove to the litigious public that they did in fact bestow only a preference on Kanaka Maoli. But we in the audience needed and wanted leadership, not cowardly moves to appease the condescending settler. Those in power should have known about the growing frustration in our communities from cases occurring year after year, attempting to dismantle our programs and our way of life. How could a Kanaka Maoli institution do such a thing?

As Tūtū Pele flows through man-made cities, she does not ask permission to take what is rightfully hers. She commands you to recognize her mighty strength and bow down to her power. She does not pass by and apologize; she does what is naturally her right. Instead, you must apologize to her and thank her for borrowing her 'āina (land) for that fabulous period of time you were able to live there. Slowly, yet purposefully, she sets all on fire that happen to be in her way, including your home and belongings. She swallows up the road and smiles seductively, reminding you who is truly superior. We, Kanaka Maoli, must be more like Tūtū Pele.

'A'ole i pau.

"Kū i ka Pono!"

When the lava accumulating in Pu'u 'Ō'ō, Kīlauea, gets too heavy, the floor collapses. This historically caused a number of earthquakes throughout the Hawaiian archipelago. Hawai'i volcanoes are geologically identified as shield volcanoes. Shield volcanoes are not known for their explosive outbursts like composite volcanoes found elsewhere in the world. Yet do not take this for granted. Pele is not inviting. Pele's home is dangerous, sacred, and forbidding. We know not when she will present herself next and demonstrate her mighty power.

A year after the admission of the non–Kanaka Maoli student to KS Maui, the KS Kapālama campus conditionally accepted Brayden Mohica-Cummings to the seventh grade pending verification of his Kanaka Maoli ancestry. After numerous inquiries, the applicant's Caucasian mother attempted to explain that she had been hānai (foster or adopted) by her mother's husband, Melvin Cummings, who was Kanaka Maoli.[15] Mohica-Cummings's biological father was not Kanaka Maoli either. Kamehameha Schools rescinded the invitation for admission. The next day, three days before school was scheduled to start, the family filed suit in U.S. District Court claiming discrimination. On August 20, 2003, Judge David Ezra ordered that KS must temporarily allow Mohica-Cummings admission.[16]

A graduate of KS, my daughter, Mehana Ka'iama, was with friends when they heard the news of Ezra's ruling, and she insisted that they must "do something." She took the lead in organizing a protest the very next day. We stayed up until 2 a.m. making phone calls and signs for the protest that was to commence at 6:30 a.m. We hoped at least ten to fifteen people would show up at the bottom of Kapālama to protest the temporary admission of Brayden Mohica-Cummings on his first day of school. About fifty supporters came, most of whom had to rush off to their day jobs afterward. After a short blessing, the protest began. We took our signs to the road by the entrance of the school and began waving at cars heading to campus. The unfriendly Kamehameha guards instructed us not to come onto their property, so we were limited to standing between parked cars and on the street, but that didn't deter us. We were not going to leave.

Cars sped by too fast to read our signs, but as the hour wore on traffic got heavier. At first some thought we were celebrating the first day of school, but they soon realized we were protesting Judge Ezra's ruling about admitting a non–Kanaka Maoli. Most people smiled and waved. Others honked their horns in support, including bus drivers.

Although we did not inform anyone at Kamehameha that we had planned this protest, about half an hour into it the school's headmaster, Dr. Michael Chun, and his wife came by on their morning walk. We approached him, and when he recognized us he gave us a big smile and a hug. He mentioned to me that they did not condone any protest that was personally attacking the new student but would allow us to voice our distress at the judge's ruling. He then directed the guards to allow us to protest on the Kamehameha sidewalks, as it would be safer for all of us. It was also much easier for the drivers to see us and our signs. We ended half an hour later with a closing prayer, thankful for a safe and meaningful protest.[17]

A few days later, the Kamehameha trustees and administrators called a meeting with a small group of community representatives to discuss this latest development, including Professor Lilikalā Kame'eleihiwa of the Kamakakūokalani Center for Hawaiian Studies at the University of Hawai'i (UH); Vicky Holt Takamine from 'Īlio'ulaokalani Coalition; and myself, as executive director of the Native Hawaiian Leadership Project.[18] The trustees were looking for community suggestions regarding how to respond to the Mohica-Cummings admission situation. Those of us who had been invited were more interested in responding to all of the court cases that were attempting to systematically destroy Kanaka Maoli institutions and rights. We collectively agreed to protest in a dignified, peaceful manner, and we agreed that it needed to happen soon.

A follow-up meeting was held at the Center for Hawaiian Studies at UH, and representatives from large Hawaiian organizations such as the Queen Lili'uokalani Children's Center, OHA, DHHL, and the Hawaiian Civic Clubs were encouraged to attend. Those gathered decided to plan a march in less than two weeks, on Saturday, September 7, 2003. To draw the most attention, the march would have to occur in Waikīkī. Kamehameha Schools offered to take a few buses to select rural areas to transport people in.[19] The school also fronted the costs of T-shirts to symbolize unity in our protest.

A motto had to be chosen, and it needed to encapsulate the deep frustration we lived with day to day. It needed to inspire hundreds to come out on a Sunday. Our first and foremost consideration was that we could not assume that all people cared about Kamehameha's admission policy. Moreover, criticisms by Kanaka Maoli could be targeted at any one of the large institutions that were involved, including OHA and DHHL. How could we unite our people in spite of legitimate differences of opinions and politics? Finally, after a few suggestions, Vicky Holt Takamine sat up suddenly and with wide eyes offered the word "justice." Like a lit fire, she quickly went on to say that we could all agree that at the most basic level we, Kanaka Maoli, still need justice. We needed to stand for justice. Kū i ka Pono! The march became a response to all of the recent challenges to Hawaiian rights and institutions, but it was also about social justice and economic justice, as well.

Lilikalā Kame'eleihiwa insisted that the shirt be red, the color of our blood, and Shane Pale, a young Hawaiian activist and artist, was asked to design it. Red fit in perfectly with the season; fishermen were sighting the red 'āweoweo fish running. In Kanaka Maoli tradition, when this occurs, it is a portent that something significant is about to happen. The back of the shirt listed predominant issues concerning Kanaka Maoli at that time: Nā Iwi Kūpuna, Mauna Kea, Pōhakuloa, Ali'i (royalty) Trust Lands, and the Northwestern Hawaiian Islands.[20] It was challenging to have different factions working together, but everyone involved toiled diligently day and night to make sure the march would take place without a hitch. However, OHA was uncooperative and disinterested. Their leadership seemed cautious about being involved, and we suspected they were in bed with State Attorney General Mark Bennett.[21] Instead of being grateful that the march would actually end at Kapi'olani Park, bringing marchers directly to a Family Sunday event they had been planning, they participated only reluctantly.

Twenty-four hours before the march was to take place, the permits that OHA had been responsible for securing were not in hand. It appeared that the city and county had calculated that with no permits, there would be no march. Vicky instructed Wayne Kaho'onei Panoke, an 'Īlio member and the person in charge of this task, to let the city and county know that we would be marching with or without permits. Kaho'onei was no stranger to American politics. He was the first student member of the UH board of regents and the right-hand man for Vicky at 'Īlio. As luck would have it, a friend and a comrade from the Civil Defense Department heard about the difficulty of securing permits to protect especially our kūpuna (elderly) and keiki (children). We were informed not to worry. They would protect our group. They had the power to shut down the streets and get the police to escort us. We had no money to pay them for this service, but we had come to the point of no return. It didn't matter if permits or protection came through or not—the march would commence as we had planned. We decided that we would be happy if three hundred people showed up.

An estimated twelve thousand Kānaka Maoli and supporters took to the streets of Waikīkī for that first march in September 2003. Six truckloads of Kū i ka Pono T-shirts were sold out within an hour before the march commenced. People found ways to get there, even flying in from neighboring islands. Tourists watched in awe as the endless sea of marchers in red walked the three-lane boulevard, some carrying signs, many chanting. They looked curiously at us. In brief conversations and with flyers, we explained to inquisitive bystanders why we were marching. Many tourists reacted in disbelief, unable to comprehend the situation because they had never been taught the true history of America's continued illegal occupation of Hawai'i.

From the hotels above, the mass of people walking through the streets keenly resem-

Thousands of Hawai'i's people donned red Kū i ka Pono shirts and marched for justice down Kalākaua Avenue in Waikīkī. Photograph used with permission of the photographer, Michael J. Puleloa.

bled a never-ending school of 'āweoweo swimming. In addition, the red represented lava flowing from its source, like the blood flowing in our veins. It was magnificent. It was an honor to be a part of lines and lines of Kānaka and allies never seeming to end, just flowing down the street in protest. It was empowering. This movement had its gestation in 1893, its birth at the capitol in 1998, and now the Kū i ka Pono movement clearly made its debut in the crimson red streets of Waikīkī in 2003.

Unfortunately, so much time was put into planning the march that not much attention was given to how to end it appropriately. As we added thousands more Kānaka to their planned Family Sunday event than ever would have gathered, OHA received the largest benefit from this march. But as the crowds of people found their way into the park, adrenalin pumping, they naturally looked for the next step. Members of the planning committee instantly knew this and attempted to persuade OHA organizers to allow a number of activists to speak on their microphones. But OHA refused. Not realizing the ultimate importance of the moment, they continued to passively resist, reminding all of us that OHA is a part of the fake state institution. For the most part, marchers left feeling great about participating but a bit confused and disappointed about not obtaining additional information about things to come.

'A'ole i pau.

Ne'e Mua

In subsequent meetings, we agreed that we had to sponsor more activities and be proactive rather than reactive. We accepted that there would be times when our plans would be well supported and times when our support would wane. We were willing to do the work in either case. A second protest was planned for Sunday, November 16, 2003, the day before the federal courts were scheduled to decide on the *Doe v. Kamehameha Schools* case and on the *Arakaki v. Lingle* case.[22] The Mohica-Cummings case was to be determined in Ezra's court on November 18. Rather than walking through Waikīkī, this march went from the burial grounds of Mauna 'Ala to 'Iolani Palace.[23] There, at that symbol of Hawaiian sovereignty, an overnight vigil was held, with pule (prayer) every hour on the hour until the next morning. Those who were able slept at the Palace and just before daybreak, the campers walked down to the federal courthouse holding candles and torches in the dark, waiting for the court's decisions to be announced.

There was no room at Mauna 'Ala for all of the people, dressed in their Kū i ka Pono T-shirts, that showed up. Hālau offered ho'okupu (offerings) to this sacred place. Chanters performed oli. We then flowed onto Nu'uanu Avenue in a purposeful but dignified manner. Kumu Hula John Keola Lake led the procession, and I was humbled to be asked to walk with him at his side. His Hālau followed closely behind, dressed in traditional attire. The kia'i who guarded our safety consisted of the men of Hale Mua o Kūali'i. They spread themselves throughout the march.

Approximately 950 people walked the three miles in light rain showers to 'Iolani Palace, where there was music, speechifying, hula, and pule. Though the speeches were electric, there was something calming about the evening air. As the sun set, coolness filled the grounds. While some of the KS trustees spoke, it was painfully obvious that KS students were underrepresented at this event. We were proud, however, to see our charter school and Hawaiian language immersion students out in full force. As darkness fell we all retreated to our sleeping places to be awakened every hour by the deep sound of a conch shell being blown. Downtown Honolulu took on another face in the evening, uncharacteristically quiet and beautiful. We gathered carefully in a circle, recited our chants, and then returned to sleep once more. Finally, in early morning before sunrise, we gathered and began to light all of the candles and torches, ensuring that children were safe. About three hundred of us proceeded quietly down Punchbowl Street to the federal courthouse, accompanied by police, who reserved a lane on the roadway for us. We filled the courtyard fronting the federal building and made ourselves comfortable for the wait, watching the sunrise.

When the building opened, as many of us as were allowed entered the courtroom. After a number of procedural comments, Judge Alan Kay issued his decision: "The court finds that Kamehameha Schools has a legitimate justification for its admission policy and that it serves a legitimate remedial purpose by improving Native Hawaiians' socioeconomic and educational disadvantages, producing Native Hawaiian leadership for community involvement and revitalizing Native Hawaiian culture; thereby remedying current manifest imbalances resulting from the influx of Western civilization."[24] Upon hearing the news, the crowd outside roared in jubilation. We won! For now the admissions policy at Kamehameha was intact. Songs were sung and chants performed.

During the same time, in Judge Susan Oki Mollway's courtroom, oral arguments in the *Arakaki* case were made, but it was announced that a decision would not be made until days later. On November 21, Judge Mollway made a ruling that effectively removed the DHHL, Hawaiian Homes Commission, State Homesteaders' Association, and other intervening parties from the *Arakaki* suit. She followed up in January 2004 by deciding to dismiss the case against OHA, stating that these were political questions that should be decided by the U.S. Congress and not the courts.[25] In effect, the decision was favorable for Kanaka Maoli as it left Hawaiian institutions intact.

A much smaller number of us returned the next day to hear Judge Ezra's decision in the Mohica-Cummings case. Essentially, he decided not to decide, encouraging the two parties to come up with a solution between them. We left, wondering what would transpire.

Like a sharp blow to the na'au (gut), the news of an out-of-court settlement reached between KS and Mohica-Cummings came on November 28, 2003. Kamehameha announced that the settlement included Mohica-Cummings's continued attendance at KS and an undisclosed amount payable to his family.[26] In light of KS participation in the first Kū i ka Pono march, this came as a complete shock. Why would Kamehameha decide to do this? Though Kamehameha's public message showed great appreciation for our marches and efforts, it was very disconcerting, especially to those of us who had dedicated much time and energy to this cause.[27]

When Kīlauea is erupting at night it is a beautiful sight. Streams of lava shoot up into the black air to spatter on the darkened earth below. She builds up massive rivers that find their way down the mountain, through the villages, sometimes even venturing into the protesting sea. Accompanying this majestic display are the sulfur pits that dot the mountaintop. There is no escaping the rancid mist that percolates up through Papa's (earth mother) skin to fill the air with an acid stench and taste. It is a reminder to all of the diametric opposites that constitute life as we know it. With beauty there is wretchedness, and with goodness, evil.

'A'ole i pau.

The Consistent Flow

On September 6, 2004, Labor Day, about five of us on the planning committee showed up early on the streets of Waikīkī, feeling that old, familiar excitement about what was about to happen in a few hours. That same trepidation filled our na'au, as we wondered if anyone would show up, but it was tempered now by a bit of confidence from our previous experiences. We were here again, being proactive by marching for a number of old and new issues. The cold air lifted and the beating sun replaced it as morning took hold. I was busy coordinating trucks full of red T-shirts for sale as the street filled with people. The police had arrived and closed off the boulevard for us, and we prepared to march to Kapi'olani Park. This time, we had secured the use of the Waikīkī Shell at the end of the march for speeches and a small concert. It took close to three hours for fifteen thousand people dressed in our now familiar red Kū i ka Pono T-shirts to march through Waikīkī. Various Kanaka Maoli organizations set up information booths at the endpoint. Many of these booths represented opposing views in our community, but they coexisted nicely that day. We believe we would have had even more Kanaka, had we had one galvanizing issue to bring us together as we did the previous year.

In the year following the first, highly visible Kū i ka Pono marches, U.S. Senator Daniel Inouye decided to push for the U.S. Army to bring to the Islands 291 eight-wheeled, light armored Stryker vehicles. The vehicles weigh nineteen tons and were specifically designed as part of the army's mission to be able to deploy infantry quickly to any part of the world. They are especially effective in urban settings. The U.S. Congress authorized millions of dollars for the Hawai'i brigade before the environmental review process was even completed.[28] Was this a sign of America flexing its muscle with us Kānaka Maoli? The timing seemed so coincidental. Community testimony was largely against the Strykers being located here, but the decision had already been made. This issue was added to the Kū i ka Pono agenda, and another march was planned for September 2005 on the leeward side of O'ahu ending at Kūkaniloko.[29] This protest was less well attended, definitely because of its location and perhaps because of its direct criticism of the U.S. military. Certainly it was less noticed by the international community since we did not interrupt anyone's Waikīkī vacation.

Other actions have warranted gatherings of the red shirts in recent years. As of this writing, the most recent Kū i ka Pono march was held on January 17, 2009—the anniversary of the illegal overthrow of Queen Lili'uokalani—to protest Governor Linda Lingle and Lieutenant Governor James "Duke" Aiona's support for legislation that would allow the sale of Hawaiian Kingdom Crown and Government lands (commonly but incorrectly referred to as ceded lands) currently held in trust by the state of Hawaiʻi. During the march of 2003, Lingle stood in front of thousands of Hawaiians and proclaimed: "What's good for Hawaiians is good for Hawaiʻi!" Six years later, betraying our trust would be good for us? Their blatant hypocrisy was not forgotten.

ʻAʻole i pau.

Ua Mau Ke Ea

The Kū i ka Pono movement has continued on throughout the past decade as one of the longest-standing movements we have witnessed in contemporary times. Regardless of these years of organizing success for Kū i ka Pono, it is challenging to keep up the momentum. Movements require people, and people become exhausted. The same people do the lion's share of work willingly without hesitation, but without pay or recognition. It takes its toll. Our supporters also become disillusioned when they see that our gains are few and our battles constant. Insider fighting can become fierce. It is disheartening when the criticism comes from within our Kanaka Maoli communities. I have heard comments, for example, that anyone who wears that red shirt is a sheep. How insulting to those masses who came out! Others state casually that if we secured permits for these marches then we have basically gone institutional. How ridiculous is that?

Beside these occasional insults, we have had to deal with the continual co-opting of protest moments through all types of media. Video, pictures, and sound bites of our successful protests have been appropriated to initiatives that are completely unrelated to the original purposes that gave birth to Kū i ka Pono. For example, OHA, who was least supportive, has used a number of clips of our marchers in Washington, DC, trying to imply that thousands of Natives came out to march in favor of the Native Hawaiian Government Reorganization Act, popularly called the Akaka Bill. It is enough to say here that the lack of any congressional hearings or forums on the bill throughout the first twelve years of the century shows that the bill hardly represents the voice of the people. Discussion regarding our independence as an alternative has always been silenced.

On a positive note, other organizations have gone on to utilize the theme of Kū i ka Pono made popular by our numerous marches, thousands of T-shirts, bumper stickers, hats, and posters in forums that align nicely with our original cause. For example, the youth strand of the Rights of the Indigenous Symposium of 2011 named their strand Kū i ka Pono!

Our true enemies do not need rejuvenation. They are so numerous, located inside and outside of Hawaiʻi. They are inspired by greed and fueled by pompousness. We cannot wait for our Martin Luther King Jr. We have had many great Kanaka Maoli leaders, all unfortunately a bit ahead of their time. While education helps to peel away the layers of indoctrination from our people, these leaders have grown old waiting. Instead, our revolution has taken on a form similar to that of the lava flows of Kīlauea. Slow, steady, purposeful, and focused we move forward. We build one fishpond at a time. We are restoring more land to cultivate taro. We find the funding to support one more Hawaiian immersion school. We refurbish another heiau (Hawaiian temple). We celebrate Makahiki (Hawaiian New Year) in more traditional ways. We continue to demand respect and lawful protection of our cultural ways and customs.

Kīlauea continues to erupt. Each significant movement is called an episode. Her history is a series of episodes woven together to form new land masses. Similarly, our own episodes pull together our continued resistance against those who attempt to take what is rightfully ours. This is our ea, never ending.

'A'ole i pau.

Notes

1. Trask, "Settlers of Color and 'Immigrant' Hegemony," 46.

2. Sproat, "The Backlash against PASH."

3. Sproat, "The Backlash against PASH."

4. Vicky Holt Takamine, interview by the author, December 2010.

5. Kamahele, "'Īlio'ulaokalani," 90.

6. Senator Mālama Solomon came from a long line of Kumu Hula (Beamer family) and she represented District 1 (areas with numerous Kānaka Maoli) on the island of Hawai'i for close to twenty years. It is believed that she was not reelected in the subsequent 1998 election because of her support for this bill.

7. For a complete account of this historic event, see Kamahele, "'Īlio'ulaokalani."

8. Garcia, "Summary of Eruption Episodes."

9. OHA came into existence through a state constitutional convention in the late 1970s with the purpose of directing use and profit of Crown and government lands for Kanaka Maoli people. Originally, only Kanaka Maoli could vote for trustees that oversaw the office.

10. See U.S. Census 2000, "Resident Population," http://www.census.gov/population. Total population for Hawai'i is recorded at 1.2 million, and total Kanaka Maoli population is recorded at approximately 240,000, or 20 percent of the total population.

11. This announcement was made in an e-mail of July 11, 2002, that was sent to members of the Kamehameha 'ohana, including an advisory board to the school. The e-mail read, in part: "Kamehameha Schools' admissions policy gives preference to Hawaiians to the extent permitted by law and the rules governing tax-exempt organizations. . . . KS selects applicants who demonstrate potential for success in this rigorous educational program. When all accepted applicants of Hawaiian ancestry meeting this criteria have been exhausted, non-Hawaiian applicants may be considered for admittance on a space available basis. . . . This year . . . after admitting all of the Hawaiian applicants who met the criteria, there was space available and admission was offered to a non-Hawaiian applicant."

12. See Bernice Pauahi Bishop's will at http://www.ksbe.edu/pauahi/wil.php. The original document is located at the Hawaii State Archives.

13. "The KS Impact."

14. See "Kamehameha-Maui Grad Is First Non-Hawaiian." Written when Maui settler "Kalani" Rosell graduated from Kamehameha, the article sugarcoats Rosell's tenure at the Maui campus and the stereotypical "aloha spirit" of Kanaka Maoli is fronted in the piece, as if the truth is just too much for these settlers to admit and bear. The uninformed and purposeful ignorance of his parents regarding the initial enrollment of their son is displayed in comments like, "It didn't even occur to us that it would be a problem." One would have to assume that such people must have lived a very sheltered life in the islands not to have known better. The article goes on to highlight Mr. Rosell's intention to attend Yale. This hints that the young man would have been successful no matter what high school he attended, and therefore the decision to take that spot at the Maui campus was definitely a lost opportunity for a Kanaka Maoli.

15. "Hānai" is a Kanaka Maoli term commonly mistranslated as the English term "adopt." See the resolution put forward by the Association of Hawaiian Civic Clubs in 2003 regarding the accurate and traditional use of the term "hānai."

16. Waite, "Court Order Due Today in Kamehameha Suit."

17. Gordon, "Protest Held at Kamehameha Schools."

18. The Native Hawaiian Leadership Project was supported by U.S. Department of Education monies from 1998 to 2004. Over that period of time, over $10 million was used primarily to support students seeking higher education degrees at accredited colleges of their choice. Additional amounts were budgeted to support initiatives that increased the number of Kanaka Maoli teachers and professors, culturally appropriate pedagogy, and Kanaka Maoli research support. Thousands of Kānaka Maoli students and adults benefited from this program.

19. Since a number of Kanaka Maoli do not own cars, and the state was in the middle of a bus strike, this seemed an important course of action, and proved very useful and appreciated.

20. Nā Iwi Kūpuna is in reference to our ancestors' bones being dug up from their original resting places without regard and in many cases not following appropriate laws in place to protect them, in order to make room for new developments like hotels. Mauna Kea is our sacred mountain, which continues to be overdeveloped by the university astronomy community, who maintains a $1 per year lease to use the mountain. Pōhakuloa is over 108,863 acres located on Hawai'i Island, designated for American military practice. Ali'i Trusts include Kamehameha admissions cases but also forced lease-to-fee condemnation of Queen Lili'uokalani Children's Center land holdings. The Northwestern Hawaiian Islands were included as we were striving to protect the natural fisheries from depletion by commercial fishermen.

21. Mark Bennett was the attorney general of the state of Hawai'i, responsible for taking the ceded land case to the U.S. Supreme Court to get permission to sell Kanaka Maoli trust lands.

22. *Doe v. Kamehameha* was another case against Kamehameha's admission policy. *Arakaki v. Lingle* was another case challenging the constitutionality of OHA and the Hawaiian Homes Commission Act, claiming a violation of the Equal Protection Clause of the Fourteenth Amendment and a demand that both agencies should be dismantled. *Arakaki v. Lingle* later came to be known as the Arakaki 2 case since Earl Arakaki was part of another case in 2000, claiming that all citizens should have a right to serve as OHA trustees, not only Kanaka Maoli. They were successful in this action. The courts were full of cases against Kanaka Maoli.

23. Mauna 'Ala is the Royal Mausoleum of Hawai'i, located in Nu'uanu, O'ahu. It is the final resting place for many members of the Kamehameha and Kalākaua royal families. See National Park Service, National Register of Historic Places, for more information regarding Mauna 'Ala.

24. See Daysog and Barayuga, "Federal Judge Upholds Hawaiians-Only School."

25. See "Sovereign in Hawaii," http://www.sovereignstories.org.

26. This announcement was included in an e-mail of November 28, 2003, that was sent to a number of Kamehameha alumni and supporters.

27. It is interesting to note that even after all of this, Mohica-Cummings was expelled from KS during his high school years for zero-tolerance behavior. Though a complete discussion of the complexity of the legal case is not warranted in this chapter, it was believed by those advising KS leaders that the initial settlement with Mohica-Cummings's family would improve their chances of winning the *Doe* case, which went up to the Ninth Circuit Court of Appeals. In May 2006 the full board of the Ninth Circuit Court of Appeals found in favor of Kamehameha in the *Doe* case in a vote of eight to seven. The community was elated, as a favorable ruling was unexpected. Kamehameha was immediately informed that an appeal to the U.S. Supreme Court would occur. Their team of legal experts began to strategize and once again decided to settle out of court. Once the plaintiff's attorneys realized that Kamehameha would never take their chances with the predominantly conservative highest court in the United States, they began to solicit for more clients, knowing this could be a profitable way to line their pockets. As Kamehameha continues to settle rather than fight, it is much harder to garner support and loyalty to their causes. It is unfortunate that they envision this as their only option.

28. See "Stryker Brigade in Hawai'i," http://www.dmzhawaii.org, for an in-depth look at the ramifications of Stryker vehicles residing in the Hawaiian Islands.

29. Sacred area near Wahiawā on O'ahu, known for its large birthing stones used by ali'i.

Portrait. Sam Kaha'i Ka'ai

Ty P. Kāwika Tengan

Every story is a ceremony for Sam Kaha'i Ka'ai. With half-remembered prayers and bright shining eyes, he has shaped countless histories, images, and men in the likeness of their ancestors. It is impossible to adequately represent his life or works in a book (which I have tried) or a gallery (which others have tried).[1] Thus, it is fitting that this piece, based on recorded conversations between 1999 and 2011, is a portrait, or a ki'i. Like most things Hawaiian, ki'i is a multivalent term filled with kaona (deeper meaning). On one level, it refers to an "image, statue, picture, . . . likeness," or something "carved"; as a verb, it means to "fetch, get, procure, send for, go after, summon, attack," or "seek for sexual ends"; in hula, it names a step or gesture; and in the cosmogonic prayer of the Kumulipo, it represents the first man (who in turn represents the gods).[2] A kālai ki'i (carver of images) and haku mo'olelo (composer of histories and stories), Sam has summoned Kanaka Maoli to "be real" in the quest for ea (sovereignty and self-determination) by petitioning the heavens for life on earth.

Remembering

Born in Hāna on April 17, 1938, to Edward and Caterina Marciel, Sam was given in hānai (Hawaiian customary adoption) to Edward's childless sister Christina and her husband Samuel Kaha'i Ka'ai Sr. of Moloka'i. Sam spent his early years on the Marciel homestead in the rural sweet potato growing and fishing village of Kaupō on the southeastern side of Maui. There he learned carving from his uncles as he first watched them work, then fetched and carried materials, then learned to sharpen and tie the adze, and finally began to carve wooden boards and boxes. He later lived on O'ahu where he went to McKinley High School, served briefly in the Army Reserves, attended the Honolulu Academy of the Arts, and worked as a carver at the International Marketplace in Waikīkī.

Sam moved back to Maui in 1960 to open a shop on Front Street (Lāhainā) called Ka Honu (The Turtle), which sold carvings he made and crafts he imported from thirty-eight different Pacific islands. At twenty-three he married a schoolteacher from Michigan, and they had three daughters. At this time he also began to visit his great-uncle Līhau Ka'ula Ka'aihue in Kaupō to talk about "Hawaiian subjects," which "were not popular at the time."[3] He had a growing sense of unease and dissatisfaction with the state of Hawaiian affairs, a feeling that was only compounded when he went through a divorce in 1985.

After much soul searching, Sam came to the realization that Hawaiian "material culture was missing." In his view, things considered Hawaiian were either adaptations of foreign objects (e.g., the ʻukulele, which was the Portuguese braguinha) or Hawaiian-looking items produced elsewhere (e.g., kukui [candlenut] lei made in the Philippines and lauhala [pandanus leaf] mats made in Sāmoa and Tonga). He summarized Hawaiians' collective alienation from their material culture in his maxim, "When you eat poi from plastic bags, you burp foreign sounds." He argued, "Hawaiian things will be in Hawaiian hands when Hawaiians pick it up, and you can't pick it up in the store, you gotta make it."

All of this became clear to him in 1988 when he went to Aotearoa / New Zealand on a Fulbright scholarship to study carving with Māori artisans. He explained, "To a Māori . . . accident of birth did not make you who you were. . . . So they would say, 'A ʻoe Māori? Are you real? Do you go in the street with your father's good name?' And . . . that hit as a kind of a clear answer to the things that you kinda not put your finger on at home." Sam lamented the fact that instead of doing the things that make us Maoli, Hawaiians look to written accounts by foreign observers like Captain James Cook.

In contrast, he spoke of what and how he learned "in the doing" when he was growing up in Kaupō:

> My tūtū [Līhau] used to say "Kālai kālai, nānā ka maka, hana e ka lima [carve, carve, the eyes watch, the hand works]. Your hand coordination, your eye coordination was you, but the sharpening of the adze before you started was the foundation, and the binding, the making of the handle. . . . And then you have to allow for this little extra. It's for the blisters, cause as you concentrate on your carving and you shaping the wood, the adze on the other hand is shaping the hand, shaping the tolerance, shaping the judgment, shaping the ʻuhane [spirit]." . . . So by doing all of dese tings increases our familiarity, and then you can feel the same pain of the people before you and have some kinship that is not measured by this time and that time, but time in work.

Sam's own familiarity with the material culture led him to carve the stern images for the Hawaiian voyaging canoe Hōkūleʻa's maiden voyage in 1976 and to conduct ceremonies for her departure from Hawaiʻi and arrival in Tahiti. On one stern was a female image: "Kiha, ka moʻo o malu ʻulu o Lele, represents all the kūpuna. She is the heavenly watcher, a caring spirit, a clear voice of guidance."[4]

On the other side was a male holding a mother of pearl disc above his head, Kāne o Hōkūleʻa o ka lani. Sam explained that he was

Sam Ka'ai with the ki'i: Kiha, ka mo'o o malu 'ulu o Lele, 2000. Photograph © Franco Salmoiraghi.

> an effigy of our time, reaching for the hōkū, the stars. . . . Some people were crying in their heart that they were born too late, see. The trouble is . . . when they pray, they wen look down, they nevah look up. Cause if you get up before dawn, the heavens have not changed. . . . Their relationship to each other is there, so if you lost your way . . . on the land because the streets are changed and the bulldozah making new alanui [road], well, 'a'a ke alanui o ka lani [brave the path of the heavens], the heavenly roads are still there. Look up, see your star, *remember* where your kūpuna said the island was. . . . So, choose the right star, set the course, give your life to eternity, ma mua [in front or the historical past], go forward.

As has been noted elsewhere, the voyages of the Hōkūle'a were instrumental in stimulating cultural revitalization in Hawai'i and the revival of ocean voyaging throughout Polynesia.[5] For Sam personally, Hōkūle'a "taught many lessons" that "allowed probing. . . . Everybody looking at Oriental and Occidental ideas; Hawaiians only had to look south to other islands." Over the years Sam visited such places as Tahiti, Sāmoa, Rapa Nui, Rarotonga, Fiji, and Aotearoa / New Zealand, all islands "on the chain of vertebrae that make up the lei of ancestors and connections."

Rededicating

With a renewed Oceanic intercourse came a new set of challenges. Sam remembered meeting a Māori leader named John Rangihau (from the Tūhoe tribe) who asked him, "What do your Hawaiian men do on their maraes [meeting places]? What do Hawaiian women do? . . . I see you grow a lot of . . . weeds."

The occasion to respond to these questions came in 1989. That year Sam became the chair of a committee to organize the bicentennial commemoration of Pu'ukoholā Heiau, the temple of state at Kawaihae associated with the unification of the Hawaiian Islands. On this site in 1791, Kamehameha sacrificed his primary rival and cousin Keōua in fulfillment of a prophecy that foretold the end of war when one was laid upon its altar. When the ruler of Kaua'i peacefully ceded control of his island to Kamehameha in 1810, the entire archipelago came under his rule, and the Hawaiian Kingdom was established.

The 1991 commemoration was to be called Ho'oku'ikahi, which meant To Reconcile and To Unify as One. Sam worked with a committee that included respected leaders such as John Keola Lake, Fred Kalani Meinecke, Parley Kanaka'ole, Hale Kealoha Makua, and the Kahaiali'i 'Ohana (Manu, Thelma, and Ulu), as well as staff of the National Park Service (that managed Pu'ukoholā as a National Historic Site) and members of the Hawaiian Civic Clubs, to ensure that the event was not a pageant, but a happening. Ho'oku'ikahi represented a unification of Hawaiians today and an integration of their modern selves with their ancient ones. Re-membering the mo'olelo of Pu'ukoholā would involve the reunification of elements of Hawaiian culture and society that had been dis-membered. This involved healing the divisions and animosities between the descendants of Kamehameha and those of Keōua; unifying Kanaka Maoli searching for cultural identity, spiritual guidance, and political sovereignty; and reconnecting with other Polynesian and Indigenous peoples whose histories we shared. There at the temple of state, where Hawaiians had successfully petitioned the heavens once before, new prayers would be lifted as modern Kānaka dedicated themselves to being Maoli—real.

Ho'oku'ikahi was also meant to answer the question, "Where are the men?" This question came not only from Māori quarters, but also from within the Hawaiian community. The high visibility of Hawaiian women taking up leadership roles in the cultural and political arenas contrasted with the perceived absence of their men. To correct this, Sam sought to connect men with the values and practices of koa—a culturally and spiritually grounded bravery, courage, and warriorhood that had been lost. He decided to gather a group of forty men to stand at the heiau as Nā Koa, The Courageous Ones / Warriors. He explained that Nā Koa was "not about being *warlike*," but "being courageous enough to look at your *spirit*. . . . It's about spending yourself, and in the *spending* you know more about yourself, things you already *are*."[6]

Sam gave a speaking tour throughout the islands and called all Hawaiians (espe-

Sam Ka'ai at Ka Lae, Hawai'i Island, with Hōkūle'a in background, prior to arrival at Kawaihae for Ho'oku'ikahi 1991. Photograph © Franco Salmoiraghi.

cially the men) to gather at Pu'ukoholā at Kawaihae in 1991 to remember who they were as a people. On one occasion, he said, "History is either a *living* thing, or it's already been blown away. How important is this metaphor? In the *canoe*, the navigator holds a story, a song, that's *all* he has. And exactly three hundred yards behind the canoe, his road is being erased. He pushes into the unknown and has only a *small* glimpse of the past; except that he remembers the song, and sings it again. So *you* will *live* if you remember the song."[7]

After two long years of manufacturing the various weapons and ceremonial implements and garb that would be used, as well as learning the chants, prayers, and ceremonies that would be conducted, the day of Ho'oku'ikahi finally came. The Hōkūle'a sailed into the harbor to open up the day's events, which included a reconciliation between descendants of Kamehameha and Keōua; a ceremony honoring Hawaiian dignitaries and those who came from across Polynesia (including Tahiti, Sāmoa, the Marquesas, Rapa Nui / Easter Island, and Aotearoa / New Zealand); a presentation of offerings to the heiau and to the deity of Kūnuiākea; and a display of weaponry usage and martial formations by Nā Koa.

When all was said and done, Pu'ukoholā succeeded in ways that were unexpected.

"You know outta all da things we planned, about forty percent collapsed. But, for the sixty that was, there were two thousand percent blessing."[8] The hōʻailona (spiritual signs) appeared as sharks and turtles circled in the water and cameras that tried to record the phenomenon inexplicably opened up and lost their film. "Had *wonderful* stuff like that, had happened. You know what I mean? You plan things, and there are *other* things that happen, eh. *Those* people have mana [spiritual power] also. And they are called, and the other side of the veil *pours* over."

Returning

Puʻukoholā became a gathering place for both men and women to practice and live their culture. For men, it held a particular appeal as it revitalized cultural and spiritual traditions that were both authentic (i.e., not performed for tourists or as a pageant) and masculine (i.e., aggressive, strong, and disciplined). Nā Koa embodied this gendered reclamation of cultural identity, and they inspired an important segment of the Hawaiian male population who had previously been uninvolved in the cultural politics of sovereignty and revitalization. Both men and women returned to Puʻukoholā each year thereafter to renew and rededicate themselves.

The groups of Nā Papa Kanaka o Puʻukoholā (the organizational body of the Puʻukoholā ceremonies), Nā Koa (the warriors or courageous ones), and Nā Waʻa Lālani Kahuna (ritual specialists) that were "born" at Puʻukoholā added a greater level of spirituality to the political rallies and protest marches such as the 1993 ʻOnipaʻa commemoration of the illegal overthrow of the Hawaiian Kingdom and the 1998 Hawaiʻi Loa Kū Like Kākou centennial of the so-called annexation. Sam served ʻawa ceremoniously at the ʻIolani Palace grounds, and he heralded the coming of the masses when he blew his pū (conch shell trumpet) during the marches. In each of these events, Nā Koa was a visible force whose presence signaled the new strength, aggression, and resolve with which cultural nationalists had engaged in their struggles for self-determination and sovereignty.

The assembly of Nā Koa at Puʻukoholā in 1991 signaled the beginning of what today might be called a warrior movement that came out of two related though separate developments: Puʻukoholā on the one hand, and on the other the revival of the Hawaiian fighting art lua in 1993. Though separate, these two strands of cultural revitalization frequently overlapped so that many of the members of Nā Koa were also involved in the lua schools.

On Maui, Sam Kaʻai mentored a number of young men who wanted to take up the kuleana (responsibilities and rights) of their forefathers. Kyle Nākānelua, a firefighter, taro farmer, and lua practitioner, became the poʻo (leader) of a group of Nā Koa from Maui that would return annually to Puʻukoholā. Eventually the group grew and reorganized as a Hale Mua, a cultural organization that took as its model the men's eating

Sam Kaʻai at Puʻukoholā with Nā Koa, 1991. Photograph © Franco Salmoiraghi.

house and domestic temple of precolonial Hawaiʻi. Sam recalled that when Nākānelua and others conferred with him, he told them, "Be Maoli. . . . The Hawaiians had a house, the hale mua. Basically the word means 'to go forward.' You suffah da pain, and now we mad. . . . Let's pound each addah until we meld togethah like poi. . . . That means, whatever you are, you must transform by being meld into one. And what it's done fo'? To go *forward.*" The basic aim of the Hale Mua was to establish a foundation for Hawaiian men by creating a safe space for learning and practicing culture, engaging in the ritual process of self-transformation, and establishing networks of support and community. The general premise of the group was that colonization and modernity had led to a loss of Hawaiian life and culture, especially for the men. By reestablishing a Hale Mua, men would gain a deeper understanding of their history and acquire the skills, knowledge, and courage to be more effective as members and leaders in their families and communities.

When asked how he would describe the "average Hawaiian man today," Sam once replied:

> I don't know what an "average man" is. You know we have a syndrome called the "galvanizing ʻalamihi [black crab]." Everybody say when a Hawaiian try to climb

> up, another one pulls him down, all in the same galvanized [steel] bucket. The trouble is that the bucket is galvanized. If it was a basket they crawl in and out. If a clay pot, they can crawl in and out; it's the fact that it's a galvanized bucket. So I don't think it's the fault of the crabs as it is the fault of the environment. And so there's some galvanizing stuff in Hawaiians, but Hawaiian men are trying to raise their families, some cope well, some don't.
>
> "Average Hawaiian man." There are men coping at every level. . . . I think the only thing "average" about Hawai'i is the galvanized bucket. Rules and restraints of society on man and how we handle it. Some handle wit aloha, some handle wit anger. Hopefully wit thoughtfulness and discipline, is what the Hale Mua is for.

Over the years, the Hale Mua of Maui, under the leadership of Kyle Nākānelua and Sam Ka'ai, proceeded to redefine the average by introducing a new generation of Hawaiian men and boys to the ways of their kūpuna. In 2004, Hale Mua visited their "younger brothers" (the Māori) in Aotearoa / New Zealand to deliver the long-awaited response to the questions posed decades earlier—Hawaiian men are here.[9] An affiliated Hale Mua o Kūali'i became active on the island of O'ahu, participating in the Kū i ka Pono marches for social justice from 2003 to 2009 and conducting the Makahiki Nui ceremonies and competitions at Kualoa between 2006 and 2011. Kamana'opono Crabbe, one of the po'o (heads) of the Hale Mua o Kūali'i, worked with 'Umi Kai and Billy Richards (both lua teachers) to organize three 'Aha Kāne Native Hawaiian Men's Health Conferences (2006, 2010, 2012) that drew over five hundred men from across the islands each time. For Sam, all of this has been an affirmation that "things like men did in the past are now being translated in a new song."

Reflecting

The year 2010 marked the bicentennial of the Hawaiian Kingdom's establishment under Kamehameha. As he did at the 1991 rededication at Pu'ukoholā, the god of state Kūnuiākea presided. This time, it was at a historic gathering at the Bishop Museum in Honolulu where the last three remaining temple ki'i carved in his image were brought together for the first time in nearly two hundred years. Members of the Hale Mua from Maui and O'ahu went with the museum's staff to fetch the two images residing outside of Hawai'i in Massachusetts and London; theirs was a journey filled with hō'ailona. At the exhibit's opening, Sam Ka'ai spoke to a large audience and clarified some widely held misconceptions of Kū, who is commonly known only as the god of war. As he had been doing prior to (and ever since) the first Pu'ukoholā ceremonies, Sam explained that there are seventy-two names of Kū that correspond to his multiple attitudes and activities, of which war is only one. Kū more broadly is the deity of industry, governance, and men's activities. The eight-hundred-pound wooden statues are icons of a nation's values, and their faces are "the reflection of a time before us." Like the stars in the heavens and the place names on the land, the carved features of the ki'i are the signs that remind us whose grandchildren we really are and what sacrifices we need to make.

Sitting in his living room in September 2011, Sam reflected on developments in the Hawaiian community over the last fifty years: "[Hawaiian] things were unfashionable, and [then] they became [fashionable]. There was a hunger, and as things were answered, more things were asked for. So kahiko mā [the company of old] stepped forward." And as the ancestors came into our world, we too stepped into theirs. Sam noted that when men put on the malo (loincloth), there was a special kind of transformation: "In reality by getting undressed you disappear into your father's shadow. I've seen people that said their son and nephews are in that group and these people run past them and they don't even see their own family. Their family always turns into five generations back and the night marchers." One of his last comments was specifically referring to the Hale Mua, but could equally apply to all who have striven to remember, rededicate, return, and reflect in the manner of the kūpuna: "You folks are the image of your ancestor; you are the only people in Hawai'i . . . who go off into the world half naked, and are filled with mana, and no one doubts your presence."

Notes

1. Kua'āina Associates, "The Lifework and Collective Song of Sam Kaha'i Ka'ai"; Tengan, *Native Men Remade.*
2. Liliuokalani, *The Kumulipo;* Pukui and Elbert, *Hawaiian Dictionary,* 148.
3. Interview with author, Pukalani, Maui, July 23, 2002.
4. Kua'āina Associates, "The Lifework and Collective Song of Sam Kaha'i Ka'ai," 5.
5. Finney, *Sailing in the Wake of the Ancestors.*
6. Meyer, *Ho'oku'ikahi.*
7. Nā Maka o ka 'Āina, *A Presentation by Sam Ka'ai.*
8. Interview with author, Makawao, Maui, September 30, 2011.
9. Tengan, *Native Men Remade,* 202–215.

PART II *Land*

Ululani Bierne harvesting kalo in a Kahana, Oʻahu loʻi, August 29, 1982.

Puhipau, also known as Abraham Ahmad, made regular deliveries of ice to Sand Island residents and lived there himself from 1970 to 1980. Politicized by the state's arrests and subsequent destruction of 135 homes, Puhipau joined forces with Joan Lander to become one of the most prolific and widely known documentary film teams in Hawai'i—Nā Maka o ka 'Āina, the eyes of the land. November 10, 1979.

(Self-)Portrait. Puhipau

THE ICE MAN LOOKS BACK AT THE SAND ISLAND EVICTION

Puhipau

My name is Abraham Ahmad or Abe Ahmad or Puhipau. These three names have been part of my identification for the past seventy-five years. I started out as Abraham, a name inherited from my Palestinian father, who married my mother, Caroline Aku, a widow of Keālia, Kona, with seven sons from her first husband, John Henriques.

I was born in 1937, second oldest of four children of this Palestinian-Hawaiian union: a "hapa-stinian." Walter Keli'iokekai Paulo, half brother to my half brothers, played a critical role in my life, almost like a second father.

The name I took for myself in 1982 is Puhipau, a name found on my family's genealogy chart from the 1700s. According to the Pukui dictionary, puhi pau means blown away, completely burned.[1] Puhi pau 'ia nā mea huna, all the secrets were revealed. The name of Susanna Puhipau can be found on the first page of the 1897 Kū'ē petitions, protesting the annexation of Hawai'i to the United States.

Just about all my brothers were men of the sea: fishermen, sailors, a ship captain, merchant seamen. That's the direction I wound up taking after high school and one year of a football scholarship at the University of Oregon. I was an ordinary seaman, ten years on the ocean, shipping out from California to Vietnam (delivering Coca Cola and beer to the troops) and to South America where conveyor belts brought raw ore from the mountains straight into the freighter holds.

In many of the Latin American ports where we docked I saw a lot of guns. Local resources were being ripped off and governments had to use martial law to protect the thieves. The local people in these countries didn't see me as American. They saw me as a Hawaiian. Being Hawaiian was my passport into their homes and communities.

In 1970, I returned home to Hawai'i from California with my three sons and my first wife, Vivian Aulani Fish, my classmate from the Kamehameha class of 1955. I was now able to spend time with my extended family. There was always a party going on at someone's house, especially when my brother Frankie used to get off the ship. He would go to each of our siblings' homes and spend some time until he overextended his stay. So my brother Julian came up with an idea. We often went fishing down at Sand Island and he had seen a shack over there. "Hey, that's a good place for brother Frank. That way he'll be out of everybody's hair." So they built a shack for him. Now instead of

A diver shows off he'e (octopus) caught in the waters just off Sand Island in January 1980, when the area was one of the few fishing villages on O'ahu. The iconic silhouette of Lae'ahi—Diamond Head—and the hotels of Waikīkī are seen in the distance.

Frankie coming to our houses, the whole family would go down to Frankie's place on Sand Island for family gatherings.

That little shack we started out with became a place to sleep, keep dry, cook up some food. Instead of going to the bars, everyone would pick up a couple six packs after work and head down to Sand Island. Go fishing, drink, sing, play 'ukulele, sleep. That was our humble beginning on Sand Island.

Sand Island had started out as just a small spit of sand in Honolulu Harbor. By the 1970s it had been slowly built up from scraps of the torn-down sections of Honolulu. It was a no-man's-land when we were first there. As it became more and more expensive to live in modern-day Hawai'i, people began to come down, at first just to sleep in their cars, then to put up a lean-to, eventually to build a shack where they could welcome friends to come over, drop some nets, pick up some fish, limu, lobsters, crab. Watch the sunset. Nobody bother.

For me personally, it meant rediscovering a relationship with the ocean that my ancestors had. Sand Island was part of the great Mokauea fisheries, a series of fishponds and lagoons that made up the most productive fishery on the west side of O'ahu,

After the state of Hawai'i ordered the removal of all Sand Island residents, this Samoan father and daughter ponder their future. Taken shortly before the January 1980 evictions.

Kāne'ohe Bay being the major fishery on the east side. The abundant gifts of the ocean were brought in by the boatloads and shared with family and the growing Sand Island community.

Those were the best of times. We thought it would go on forever.

The reality, of course, was that we were living in the midst of a garbage dump. The beautiful sights, sounds, and smells of shoreline living were matched by the grind of dump trucks bringing more trash, the odor from the sewage treatment plant, and the deafening noise of planes taking off and landing at Honolulu International Airport just across the lagoon from Sand Island.

We had watched the reef runway being built right on top our fishing grounds. Dillingham's huge dredge chewed up the reef and spit it back out—living crabs, fish, lobster, coral, limu, and all—onto the rest of the reef.

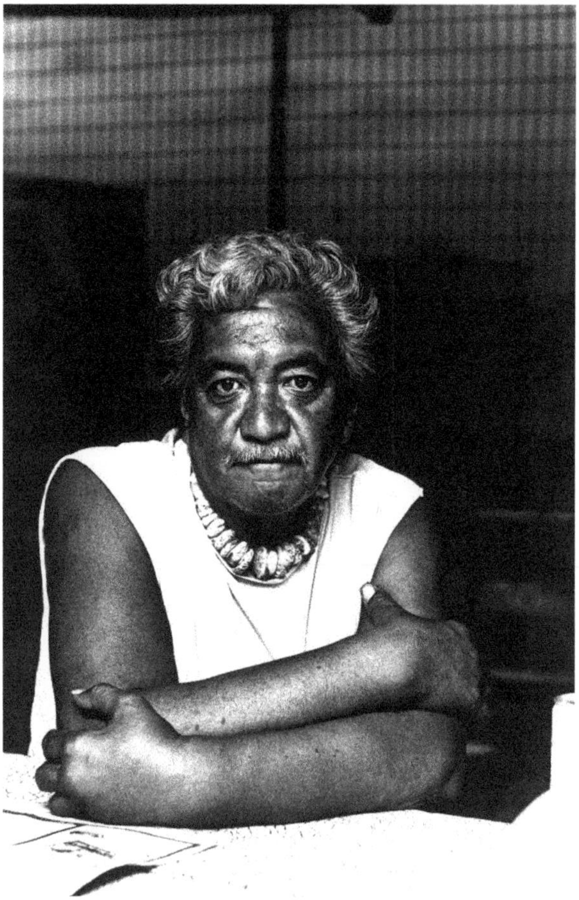

George Cash lived with his ʻohana in the Sand Island brush for over ten years. Each time Ed Greevy visited Sand Island to take photos, George introduced Ed's four-year-old son to kids in the community and ensured they had toys to play with. This photo was taken shortly before the 1980 eviction. On January 23, 1980, the state arrested residents and bulldozed 135 homes. George burned his own home to preempt the state's destroying it.

At Sand Island we were making do among the dredged landfill, the leftovers, the trash, the wastes of the city. Honolulu Harbor and Keʻehi lagoon are filled with the waste pollution of Honolulu and Kalihi Valley. The rain brings everything down. This is where we went to gather food and live. Amazing, but we had a good time and enjoyed it. When we turned our backs on Honolulu and looked straight out to sea, we could enjoy the same sunsets our kūpuna (elders or ancestors) saw. We could enjoy those moments of quiet in between the takeoffs and landings.

We tried to make the place as nice and as clean as we could. Instead of living in shacks, we eventually built houses. But when we started living like humans instead of junkyard dogs, the state of Hawaiʻi started noticing. They didn't like to see people taking back the land, even if it was only a garbage dump.

In October 1979, the state Department of Land and Natural Resources (DLNR) issued eviction notices. There was panic. For the first time the people of Sand Island felt under threat. Would we have to find other places besides Sand Island to keep our fishing gear and put up our hālau and hale (houses), find other ways to keep ourselves alive?

Over the years, Sand Island had evolved into a magnet, attracting people from youngsters to kūpuna, providing a place to go when they had problems, when they needed to connect with the land and sea. Sand Island allowed them to take a shot at it, to experience that same relationship that has been under threat since the arrival of greedy peoples. That's why we went to Sand Island, primarily to find ourselves. We didn't realize what it was going to take to hold on to this connection with our culture.

At first we were willing to work with the system, to gain permission to continue staying on the island. We met with state officials and presented a plan for a cultural live-in park that would allow residents to live there, practice traditional ways, and be an educational resource for the people of Honolulu. But DLNR authorities had made up their minds.

We began to hold meetings and discuss our options. The Sand Island community by that time had grown to 134 dwellings with approximately four hundred residents. I had a way to gauge the population because for several years I delivered ice on Sand Island. Since everyone knew me, the ice man, I was designated spokesperson and represented the community to the TV and newspaper reporters who started coming down to Sand Island.

Among those who came with a camera were Victoria Keith and Jerry Rochford of Windward Video. They introduced themselves and asked if they could document the eviction issue. I agreed to help by serving as a liaison with members of the community. Over the next few months, Vicki and Jerry were able to capture the unique Sand Island lifestyle along with stories of homelessness and dispossession.

As the eviction date drew closer, the majority of the people chose to remove themselves and their belongings. For me, my two brothers and several others, the decision was made to stand up to the fake state of Hawaiʻi. We would stay until they forced us out.

On eviction day in January 1980, the state came down with enforcement agents, dogs, guns, and bulldozers. The Coast Guard patrolled the area offshore. Helicopters flew overhead. A police riot squad was stationed at a nearby park near the entrance to the harbor. Nineteen people were arrested when they refused to move. Some set their houses on fire. The rest of the residences were bulldozed.

My brother Tony, who was in the merchant marines, had built his house out over the water on fifty-gallon drums filled with concrete. My brothers Bobby Henriques and Walter Paulo and I were arrested and taken out of that house in handcuffs. Deputies put a chain around the house (after prying my niece from her grip on the house post), pulled

Sand Island resident and fisherman Walter Keli'iokekai Paulo critiques the state as cameras film his arrest. His brother, Puhipau, is led handcuffed by a plainclothed Honolulu Police Department officer in the background. January 23, 1980.

it ashore with a bulldozer, and smashed it to bits. Tony's ship was just then coming into port and he listened to radio reports of the evictions. Those of us arrested were taken to a temporary holding area on the island, then to the police station where we were booked. The charge: obstructing government operations.

By the end of the day, the whole west end of Sand Island was smoking rubble.

Windward Video's documentary of that eviction, *The Sand Island Story*, ended up being broadcast throughout the United States on PBS.[2] When it was later screened at the United Nations, it had such an impact on the U.S. ambassador that he called the Hawai'i authorities to confirm that the eviction had actually taken place and wasn't just a dramatization.

Those of us who got arrested were now headed to court. Most had differing positions, but my brothers Bobby Henriques and Walter Paulo and I retained Hayden Burgess (Pōkā Laenui) as our attorney, who advised taking the position of "no jurisdiction." The United States had no jurisdiction over us because we're not Yankees.

My attitude toward the American justice system had been molded during a time when being a Hawaiian was not the "in" thing. Having been born just before World War II, I was taught to be American. When I went to school, I went to an English-standard

Honolulu police officers stand guard as the Sand Island community is bulldozed on January 23, 1980. Handmade signs reflect Hawaiian nationalist consciousness.

school that prepared me to enter Kamehameha Schools, where I was programmed to become a full-on American. I cried when I sang "God Bless America."

It took a while to decide on taking a "no jurisdiction" stand. It was after I read Queen Liliʻuokalani's book, *Hawaii's Story by Hawaii's Queen*, that I learned the true history of the so-called overthrow of 1893.[3] When I then learned that Sand Island actually belonged to the Hawaiian Kingdom government, I began to understand the extent of my brainwashing.

We looked forward to our day in court where we could assert this new understanding, where we could stand up and proclaim that American law does not apply in Hawaiʻi. The irony of trying to prove in a court that they don't have jurisdiction was later described by Hayden (Pōkā) as "a thief in judgment of itself."

However, even our day in court was denied.

Between our arraignment and the actual court hearing a year later, the legislature changed the law. Instead of a misdemeanor, "obstructing government operations" was now a petty misdemeanor, which did not allow us a jury trial. The judge told us he had to follow the law. If we wanted to make political and social change, we needed to go to the legislature and make new law.

In 1975, state of Hawai'i transportation director E. Alvey Wright ordered the destruction of homes on Mokauea, a small islet near Sand Island where families still practice subsistence fishing for survival. When Wright admitted to retaining a private contractor to set the homes on fire, public opinion turned in favor of the Mokauea families. Here Billy Molale drives his boat as John Kelly, Lorna Omori, Antonio Andres, and Ed Greevy document the state destruction. Not long after the burnings, the state backed off the evictions and signed a long-term lease with fourteen 'ohana who have ancestral ties to the 'āina.

So we went to the legislature, trying to advocate for recognition of our right to be on Sand Island. The first year they tell you, you have to do this, do that. So you do this, you do that. Then they say maybe next year we "get chance." The next year you go back, do this and do that. They tell you, you "get good chance," but come back next year. I'm looking at the whole scenario of going through the system, one year in court, two years in the legislature, and realized this was going be a stroke job: all stroke and no 'gasms.

The final insult occurred about a year after the evictions when the DLNR held public meetings seeking input on how to develop self-sufficient communities.

So I started to look in another direction. A teacher had once told me if you want to make changes, you have to build a base. And the base he was talking about was a base of consciousness. And I'm thinking, wow, consciousness. That's pretty deep for somebody on Sand Island like myself. No more higher education. No more all the certificates that you need to build a base.

Then I realized that all you need are tools to create the change, to build the consciousness of people who have been brainwashed like myself. What I felt was needed was a knowledge of our history and that knowledge needed to be gathered from wherever and whoever we could find. The however I could handle: it turned out to be video.

Sand Island was a calling. Everybody who has come and gone to that island went there for a reason. It calls you. You get your calling. And my calling was to educate the masses, to puhi pau, blow away the dust and reveal the secrets. But first I had to gather the information and package it in such a way that it could be spread out to our children, the folks in Hawai'i and the world.

And that's what happened. With Joan Lander I began to produce documentaries on Hawaiian history, culture, environment, language, music—and independence and sovereignty.

As part of the video production team Nā Maka o ka 'Āina, we documented other evictions and land rights issues over the years: Mākua, Waimānalo, Ka'ū, Kaho'olawe, Kohanaiki, Kapalua, Wao Kele o Puna, Waiāhole, Ka Lae, Mauna Kea.[4] Our work is to keep these stories alive for future generations. Although many teachers have used our videos in the classroom, there is still a long way to go to incorporate this Hawaiian history into the public education curriculum.

What Sand Island did was to enlighten me about who I am, who we are, where I come from, where I'm at, and where I'm going. That vision is the kingdom, the Hawaiian Kingdom in place among the family of nations, where it was, where it is, and where it will be.

Amen.

Puhipau
Ka'ū, Hawai'i
February 2012

Notes

I would like to acknowledge the assistance of my partner, Joan Lander, in the preparation of this chapter. As the video production team Nā Maka o ka ʻĀina, Joan and I documented other evictions and land rights issues over the years.

1. Pukui and Elbert, *Hawaiian Dictionary*.

2. Keith and Rochford, *The Sand Island Story*. Available through Victoria Keith Productions at http://www.victoriakeith.com.

3. Liliʻuokalani, *Hawaii's Story by Hawaii's Queen*.

4. For the catalog of Nā Maka o ka ʻĀina's documentary films, see http://www.hawaiianvoice.com. A number of documentaries and trailers can also be viewed online at http://www.youtube.com/HawaiianVoice.

CHAPTER 6. Hawaiian Souls

THE MOVEMENT TO STOP THE U.S. MILITARY BOMBING OF KAHOʻOLAWE

Jonathan Kamakawiwoʻole Osorio

On March 8, 1977, two young men from Molokaʻi were reported missing in the waters between the islands of Maui and Kahoʻolawe. The disappearances of George Helm and Kimo Mitchell, two very active members of the Protect Kahoʻolawe Association, signaled the end of a series of confrontations between the association and the U.S. Navy and the initiation of Protect Kahoʻolawe ʻOhana (PKO, or ʻOhana) as a recognized negotiator over the future of that island.

While the movement to stop decades of bombing of the island owes much of its momentum to the antiwar and civil rights issues of the 1960s and 1970s, the movement was, and continues to be, as much a cultural expression as it is political. What makes the PKO story especially important political history has been its persistent abnegation of violence, its continuous challenge of the Navy's use of the island, its emergence as a partner in any decision made—federal or local—regarding the island, and finally, its existence as a distinct, significant entity within a growing Hawaiian nationalism. The PKO is unique because of its longevity; unlike numerous political organizations in Hawaiʻi that have opposed institutional powers, the PKO has thrived for over three and a half decades.[1]

The ʻOhana helped shift Hawaiian movements from a reparations to a sovereignty framework. This transformation of Hawaiian activism from isolated voices pleading for special considerations to well-organized groups linking their concerns and contentions with other Indigenous movements both inside and outside the United States is a direct and indirect result of a decade of leadership that received much of its training and focus on the parched surface of Kahoʻolawe.

When I interviewed Davianna McGregor of the PKO in 1989, she reported that somewhere between three thousand and four thousand people had been transported by the ʻOhana to the island since the initiation of the 1980 consent decree between the Navy and the PKO. A PKO visit was called an "access," a word that claimed a right to visit and care for the island and contested the Navy's description of their efforts as trespass. In January 1988, we celebrated the closing of Makahiki, the traditional period devoted to the annual visit of Lono, a male akua (deity) representing agriculture and bounty. Several Hawaiians on that access to the island spoke about the importance of the religious ceremonies to the island and to themselves. Adrian "Age" Makanani from Kauaʻi had this to say: "Some of you folks are here to look around. I'm not. I'm here to worship my gods. This ceremony is very serious to me . . . and if you're not serious, then I have no time for you. . . . This ʻāina depends on our aloha. This is why we come, this is why we bring the Makahiki here, to bring our ʻāina back to health."[2]

The sense of mission has always been strong among the ʻOhana. The strain of mobilizing each access consumes a member's time and finances. But in addition to time spent on the island, the ʻOhana undertook continual negotiations with the Navy and continues to assert a responsibility for the island even since the Navy's departure, with the current administrating authority, the Kahoʻolawe Island Reserve Commission (KIRC). As a partner in the 1980 consent decree, the ʻOhana took responsibility for monitoring the Navy's revegetation program and, in fact, initiated several of its own.[3] As a result of its lobbying efforts, the Hawaiʻi legislature granted funds for a water study in 1988. While consultants for that study, as well as the revegetation, came from outside the ʻOhana, it was invariably the ʻOhana and not the Navy that assisted with the work.

Since March 1981, the entire island of Kahoʻolawe has been recognized as an archaeological district after it was placed on the U.S. National Register of Historic Places. One of the ways in which the ʻOhana continued to challenge the Navy's activities was in its capacity as stewards of the archaeological sites that were not only threatened but occasionally struck by shells and bombs.[4] When this occurred it was the ʻOhana that challenged the Navy both in and out of court to improve their procedures. Working with the Haida nation, the PKO also petitioned the Canadian government to refrain from shelling the island during the biannual RIMPAC exercises conducted under the auspices of the U.S. Department of Defense.[5]

I have tried to briefly outline the scope and nature of the PKO's activities in the 1980s and responsibilities with regard to Kahoʻolawe in order to impress the reader with its unique capacities. For a grassroots organization, the PKO wielded tremendous influence in its dealings with the U.S. Navy. As a partner in the consent decree the ʻOhana used its right to access not only to publicize what they perceived as gross misuse by the U.S. federal government, but as a resource to revitalize traditional practices and cultural beliefs.[6] The organization has persisted since the U.S. government relinquished the island to the KIRC. Despite the fact that PKO members have been KIRC commissioners, the two organizations have had a complex and, at times, strained relationship.[7]

Before bringing about a complete halt to the bombardment of the island and removing Kahoʻolawe from the military's jurisdiction, the PKO was successful in severely limiting the Navy's options and managed to insinuate itself into the negotiations between the state and the federal government on all matters concerning the island. The history of the PKO's emergence as an important agent on behalf of Hawaiians and Hawaiian culture is historically significant for several reasons. Having its roots in the protest decade of the 1970s, the 'Ohana's endurance should be of some interest to the student of contemporary American history. Second, the PKO represented a significant confrontation of Western liberal ideologies by Indigenous peoples claiming the primacy of their traditions. This confrontation fueled a decades-long sovereignty movement and a cultural resurgence that has quite clearly changed the political culture of Hawai'i. Finally, the story of the disappearance of one of its most important leaders has profound meaning for many people, whether they are 'Ohana sympathizers or not. George Helm left behind important symbols as a legacy for the movement he helped found. These symbols, aloha 'āina and ho'oulu lāhui (increase the nation), have been crucial for the continuity of the PKO and have helped shape the focus and development of Hawaiian sovereignty movements since the 1980s.

I first trace the emergence of the PKO from a milieu of political and cultural ferment that marked the 1970s in Hawai'i. I then examine the concept of aloha 'āina and its development as the primary symbol of cultural identity among those who participated in political activism. One of the points I hope to make clear is that this concept, although not universally enunciated as aloha 'āina, is an integral part of Hawaiian consciousness and unifies a number of seemingly disunified Hawaiian organizations.

Ho'omaka (Beginnings)

The controversy over Kaho'olawe has no definite beginning. My grandmother, a pure Native Hawaiian who considered herself a patriotic and God-fearing American, told me that the Navy's bombardment of the island was pohō (wasteful) when I was still in elementary school back in the early 1960s. It would be difficult to ascertain precisely what the Hawaiian attitudes toward the Navy's use of the island were before 1969. With the exception of a few letters to the editors of the Honolulu dailies, not much public attention was paid to Kaho'olawe until increased military use of the island during the Vietnam War began to alarm citizens and officials on the neighboring island of Maui.

Maui's mayor in the late 1960s was Elmer Cravalho, one of the first officials to publicly pursue the end of naval jurisdiction over the island. His antagonism to the Navy, exacerbated by the discovery of an unexploded five-hundred-pound bomb on his property in September 1969, was primarily based on economic concerns. "On a visit to Maui, [Rear Admiral] Bakutis was confronted by Elmer Cravalho who brought up the possibility of discontinuing the Naval bombardments altogether. Cravalho was holding considerable acreage under lease on lands adjacent to the target island and, not too surprisingly, his half of the conversation centered on the subject of distant financial opportunities."[8] Cravalho's public opposition to the military use of Kaho'olawe was ultimately ineffectual, even when he was joined by U.S. senator Daniel Inouye.

The Navy employed several tactics to reduce public pressure to relinquish the island. One was an appeal to American patriotism, arguing that Kaho'olawe's use was essential to national security. Another argument was that the island was unrecoverable due to the sheer amount of unexploded ordnance scattered over it. Neither argument convinced state officials. Inouye and others challenged both arguments, citing the provisions of the 1953 executive order giving the Navy possession. The order stipulated the Navy's responsibility for controlling erosion and assumed eventual return of the island. Inouye accused the Navy of a "deliberate lack of candor" with its insistence that only 70 percent of Kaho'olawe could be made safe for habitation and industry.[9] "It would appear that the Navy continues to insist that no rehabilitation is possible and further—or perhaps therefore—there is no need to determine the cost of feasibility because the Navy has no intent to ever return Kaho'olawe to the State of Hawaii even if the Navy's need should diminish."[10]

The Navy responded to the senator's criticism by maintaining that the Kaho'olawe exercises were crucial, tying them to the military presence in the Hawaiian Islands. Even if Inouye found the Navy's threat to transfer large numbers of personnel to Guam and Micronesia amusing, organizations like the Chamber of Commerce did not. Indeed, the Navy's contention that the loss of Kaho'olawe could mean a transfer of men and material elsewhere set off alarms in the working community as well as the business community. "This argument found widespread adherents in civilian employees (as well as their friends and relatives) of the military. It affected them at a basic level; the threat of unemployment for the sake of an uninhabited island which many viewed in the popular stereotype of the 'barren rock' was hardly conceivable, much less supportable."[11]

The origins of the Kaho'olawe protest are firmly rooted in ordinary economics and politics. For Cravalho and the Maui County Council, the bombardment of Kaho'olawe in 1969 threatened the planned resort and residential development of Kīhei. For Senator Inouye, it was, perhaps, a political opportunity enabling him to maintain solidarity with the local Democrats—of whom Cravalho was among the most powerful—and take a shot at the military, which had become an increasingly popular target for Democratic politicians as the war escalated under the Republican administration.[12]

For a variety of reasons, the campaign for the return of Kaho'olawe in 1969 was not successful. The United States was at war. This made the Navy quite adamant and its case for needing the island more convincing than it would be a decade later. Furthermore, the issue appeared to be severely localized. Outside of a few Maui residents and a former resident of Kaho'olawe, there was little public pressure on state officials to seek the return of the island.[13] Kaho'olawe did not become an issue for the peace movement in

Hawai'i. It is possible that Kaho'olawe was beneath public notice and that peace activists, if they considered the island at all, may have seen it as a barren and deserted place that could not possibly arouse public sympathy. It is also true that the peace movement in Hawai'i was relatively minor compared to the social movements, particularly those dealing with land and land use, that erupted in the islands throughout the 1970s.[14]

Davianna McGregor and Haunani-Kay Trask attribute the flourishing of protests over land use to the increasing urbanization of rural areas that had provided opportunities for many Hawaiians to maintain a semblance of traditional life. "High cost housing, condominium developments, resort complexes and golf courses replaced many farmers and families in the rural areas. For these families, rents had been cheaper than in town and their incomes had been supplemented by fishing and raising livestock. Displaced, they were now faced with drastic changes in their lifestyle and possible dependence on welfare."[15] As Trask also noted, protests over land were also a result of a new consciousness among Hawaiians that they had been subjugated by Western institutions. "One result of this consciousness was a growing activism in rural Hawaiian communities to preserve the remnants of their life-ways against encroaching urbanization and military use."[16]

These movements, such as that in Kalama Valley, provided some critical precedents for the Kaho'olawe struggle. One was the example of radical Hawaiian leadership. Another was a renewal of a traditional perception of the land. A third was a strategy of opposition that was to become a key element in the Hawaiian (re)occupation of Kaho'olawe. Trask notes that "KKC (Kokua Kalama Committee) members devoted themselves to serious study hoping to uncover the 'real history of Hawai'i.' As Kalani 'Ohelo put it, 'the history about the overthrow, the old haole oligarchy, the Republican Party, the plantations, the origins of the Democratic Party, the 442nd. . . . ' Reading and research led them to an understanding that 'these corporations—Kaiser-Aetna, the Bishop Estate—were going to make profits at the expense of people being in dire poverty.'"[17] As these young, modern, political activists reached into their own history for substantive support of their claims, some of them discovered an even deeper, more fundamental basis for their struggle against profiteering landlords in the ancient traditions of Hawaiian land tenure. This tradition, based on communal use and access to land for agriculture, fishing, and gathering, was given a political dimension. Larry Kamakawiwo'ole, for instance, criticized the fact that Kalama Valley resistors had been arrested and convicted for trespassing. "In our heart and soul today, Hawaiian people know that what happened in Kalama Valley was not morally wrong . . . not our law. . . . It was forced on us by the white man. . . . Trespassing was foreign to Polynesia. . . . The land was a vital part of our life. To divorce someone from their land was inhuman."[18]

The perception that our historic rights to the land had been violated by American institutions began to filter throughout the Hawaiian community. In 1972, a new organization called ALOHA (Aboriginal Landowners of Hawaiian Ancestry) was organized out of Moloka'i by Louisa Rice. Motivated by Queen Lili'uokalani's account of the illegal overthrow of the Hawaiian Kingdom government, ALOHA proposed massive reparations to the Hawaiian people.[19]

The sense that a tremendous injustice had been done to earlier Hawaiians by missionaries, planters, and the U.S. government was somewhat overshadowed during the mid-1970s by the realization that every Hawaiian community on O'ahu was in danger of dispersal before the onslaught of suburbia. This consciousness emerged in Hawaiian musicians mourning the loss of the countryside in popular recordings like "Waimanalo Blues" and "Me Kealoha Ku'u Home o Kahalu'u" and a flurry of organizing and protest.[20] From 1972 to 1975 Hawaiians organized to protect rural agricultural lands that had been rezoned to residential and light industrial. While Hui Mālama 'Āina o Ko'olau was losing its battle to protect Kahalu'u's forests and streams, the Waiāhole-Waikāne Association was able to forestall the McCandless Estate's attempt to turn those valleys into another Kalama.

The McCandless heirs would have suceeded in Waiāhole-Waikāne, as the Bishop Estate had in Kalama, were it not for an increasingly adept Hawaiian leadership. While the residents fought development in part for their own economic survival, they imparted to the public the emotional attachment that they had to their homes. Ultimately, those same activists who had organized the Kalama protests were able to build public opinion favorable to the tenant farmers, forcing the governor to intervene on their behalf.[21] Their intent and ideology was Marxist in part—especially with regard to their perceptions of class conflicts—but they also drew on what they understood to be traditional values.

Not long after the last resident had been evicted from Kalama Valley, Kōkua Hawai'i advertised their agenda for land management in a Honolulu newspaper. They said, among other things: "We must take care of our air, land and water. If we kill water, nature will kill us. . . . We must use our land to house and feed our people and learn to rely on ourselves to do it—not on the mainland. . . . We must get our land back from the few big landholders that have almost all of it. It was stolen from us in the first place."[22] Within this manifesto are three key ideals that would help shape the Kaho'olawe movement: self-sufficiency and autonomy, sovereignty over the land, and the need to care for the land as a vital resource. These were the ideals that would be included five years later in George Helm's articulations of ho'oulu lāhui and aloha 'āina.

Aloha 'Āina

On January 4, 1976, nine people landed on Kaho'olawe, slipping past a net of naval helicopters that attempted to prevent anyone from reaching the island. These nine were part of a demonstration organized by ALOHA to publicize Hawaiians' demands for reparations for the illegal seizure of Hawaiian lands after the 1893 overthrow. The demonstration began with a small flotilla of fishing boats and pleasure cruisers, most of which turned back at the Navy's first warning.

It was a strange confluence of events that brought the future originators of the PKO to Kaho'olawe for the first time. The proposed occupation of Kaho'olawe had not been organized for the sake of stopping the bombing. Indeed, from the very beginning, Kaho'olawe was meaningful as a symbol for Hawaiians' aspirations as well as their resentments.

Three of the nine who landed were Moloka'i activists working to preserve Hawaiians' right of access along the trails that criss-crossed their home island. In 1975, Walter Ritte, Emmett Aluli, and Adolph and George Helm formed Hui Alaloa to protest the closing of those trails by Moloka'i Ranch, which intended to develop a resort on the west end of the island. Hui Alaloa was trying to legitimize the right of Hawaiians to pursue traditional gathering and fishing activities in an area that had the potential of becoming an important tourist destination. Their success in opening up the trails to Kawākiu Beach led them to undertake other access attempts in different parts of Moloka'i. Although they failed to gain access to an abandoned military gunnery range at 'Īlio Point, their activities generated a tremendous amount of publicity. "So, Walter was contacted by Charles Maxwell. . . . Big publicity, we were just high profile at the time. . . . Here Moloka'i is doing access. . . . And the rationale for going to Kaho'olawe [for Hui Alaloa] was we had to organize Maui, because the decisions were made on Maui for Moloka'i. We thought that getting involved with Kaho'olawe would further the credibility of Moloka'i people in their access claims."[23]

For the Moloka'i contingent, Kaho'olawe access meant the opportunity to further publicize their efforts on their own island and gain some political recognition, or even a measure of influence nearer the county seat. But for the people who were organizing the access—the Maui chapter of ALOHA led by Charlie Maxwell—the occupation was planned to dramatize Hawaiians' frustrations at not being taken seriously in their quest for reparations.

> What [Charlie] explained was that the reparations bill was not being taken seriously because people don't believe that Hawaiians had problems. They think Hawaiians are all happy playing 'ukulele sitting on the beach, dancing hula and catering to the tourists. And so he explained to me that what we need to do was have a "Wounded Knee" like the Indians did to draw attention to the seriousness of the claims that Hawaiians were pressing through to Congress. That would mean occupying some federal lands in the islands. At some point . . . they decided that Kaho'olawe would be the appropriate place to stage the occupation.[24]

Since it was ALOHA's intention to publicize the event, it is not surprising that the operation was leaked to the press the day before. While guaranteeing press coverage, however, it also guaranteed a reaction by the U.S. military. Shortly after the flotilla left Mā'alaea, they were confronted by Navy helicopters ordering the group to turn back and warning that boats that did not comply could be confiscated. Most of the flotilla was made up of fishermen who depended on their boats for a living. Maxwell, his point made, directed the group to turn back.

The single boat that made it to Kaho'olawe was owned by David Padgett, the son of a prominent Honolulu attorney. He was persuaded to carry the nine people to shore by Maui reporter Jeanette Foster. Their landing accomplished, Padgett, carrying only George Helm, returned to Maui.[25] Ritte and Aluli—the remaining members of Hui Alaloa—quickly separated themselves from the rest of the group and wandered off into the bush. The two made no effort to rejoin the others when the Navy came to remove the group. Aluli attributes this to what he perceived as unfitting levity among the other participants. "We didn't agree with what was happening on the beach. It wasn't just a party. There was a little more seriousness . . . and I just wanted to get away and look at where we were," he remembered.

The two men were experienced hikers who had grown up in rural areas of Hawai'i, and their motivations and perceptions had been shaped by a period of activism on Moloka'i that sharpened their appreciation for the land. Ritte was a hunter, accustomed to spending lengthy periods of time in the wild. What they saw over the next two days as they hiked across the island committed them to Kaho'olawe. "Pain. We really felt pain. We really felt that the island was bleeding into the ocean. And sure enough, you'd look around, it was a windy day and you would have like, the whole layer that we could see was just filled with dirt and blowing to the ocean. And the bays were just all red."[26]

Despite the destruction wreaked by the bombardment and the uncontrolled population of goats, the two men developed a new appreciation for the island. Part of it was the sense that despite the abuse, Kaho'olawe provided a clear and direct record of Hawaiians' ancient past. Aluli commented on the heiau (temples) and shrines that had been bombed and insisted, "If our grandparents had seen that, they would have cried."[27]

The experience also affected Ritte on a deeply personal level. In a press interview following their removal from the island, Ritte, in tears, demonstrated his attachment to it. "It never really hit me until we were ready to leave. . . . As the helicopter went up . . . straight up . . . I was looking at this one rock. I was just glued to that one rock. And as we got higher, the rock became the whole island. . . . It was like a communication and all I knew was that it said, it was going to die. That if we allowed what was happening, it was going to die."[28]

The differences between the two men, which would become more pronounced as time went on, was reflected by their differing styles and even by their perceptions of

Walter Ritte discusses the PKO's efforts to stop the bombing on Kaho'olawe, in an interview with *SunBums* magazine on May 3, 1977. The Hui Alaloa, which preceded and supported the PKO, was a Moloka'i-based group that aimed to protect Hawaiian access to traditional trails to important sites for subsistence, ceremony, and travel.

their experience on the island. For Aluli, educated and urbane, the outrage was generalized, and the abuse included Hawaiians, their history, and their culture as well as the island itself. For Ritte, the connection was direct. He and the island committed to one another through the power of their communion. The differences between them did not so much create problems for the movement as it created a tremendous dependence on George Helm, who came to be the link between the more visionary Aluli and the more spiritual and contentious Ritte.[29]

George met the two men when they returned to Maui in Jeanette Foster's Mā'alaea home. Greeting them as heroes, George encouraged them to stay and plan their next move, particularly their strategy with the press. Aluli was still trying to come to grips with what he had done. As an intern at Queen's Hospital in Honolulu, he was worried over possible repercussions of his action and insisted that some definition be given to what they had accomplished. "I told him that we needed a motto or we needed something to tell people what we did and why we did it. The only research I had done on Kaho'olawe was a song that they were learning that my Aunt Irmgard had written the melody for. . . . The repeat stanza was 'Ke aloha kūpa'a o ka 'āina.' And that's what I had tried to convince George we should be saying. He said, 'Too long, too long, should be just cut down to aloha 'āina.'"

Aloha 'Āina became the official motto of the 'Ohana, appropriate not only for the meaning of the words, to cherish and care for the land, but for the historical symbolism of the name. *Ke Aloha 'Āina* had been the name of Joseph Nāwahī's turn-of-the-century newspaper distinguished by its whole-hearted support of Hawaiians and their culture and its biting criticism of the haole elite.[30] Aloha 'Āina as an idea would quickly distinguish the 'Ohana from Hawaiian movements like ALOHA and later organizations like the Office of Hawaiian Affairs that pressed for monetary reparations from the government rather than contesting the issues of land use and land management. "We [were] beefing with Charlie Maxwell, with Gail Prejean guys . . . 'cause they were using us . . . for their own motives. [We thought] they're not really sincere 'cause they had kind of busted it to the press. . . . So in a sense then, we excluded them from the whole Kaho'olawe movement."[31]

Three more occupations of Kaho'olawe would take place over the next year, and these men discussed Aloha 'Āina with anyone who would listen. They spoke at high schools and clubs, to civic groups and even to veterans, spreading an idea that was easily grasped by Hawaiians and often misunderstood by those who were not. While they were occasionally misunderstood by Hawaiians as well, they were consistently successful among the young people and the elders.

The integration of the kūpuna (grandparents) into the movement began earlier, when Hui Alaloa members turned to elders for explanations about the heiau and other historic sites they had discovered on the Moloka'i trails. Moloka'i kūpuna in particular began to have a tremendous influence on the movement as Helm repeatedly turned to them not only for descriptions of older cultural practices and their meanings but also as legitimate authorities on the traditional practice of Aloha 'Āina.

On January 12, 1976, Emmett Aluli, Loretta Ritte, Scarlet Ritte, and Walter Ritte made a second landing to make clear to the federal government that the island would continue to be occupied until the bombing ceased.[32] Aluli left after one night on the island, exchanging passage on a press helicopter for his description of their experience. Walter, Loretta, and Scarlett remained until the seventeenth, after which they signaled searching aircraft and were taken from the island. Walter was arrested, taken to Honolulu, and charged by order of the federal court not to set foot on Kaho'olawe again.

Ritte's arrest encouraged both support and opposition within the Hawaiian community. To a certain extent, however, the Moloka'i hui was never imprinted with the

Aunty Emma DeFries arrives on Kahoʻolawe for a blessing at Kealaikahiki in August 1980. Dropped by boat, she swam over one hundred yards to shore and was greeted by, among others, her student Kawaikapu Hewett and surfer Rell Sunn.

radical image that Oʻahu activists had had to contend with. Molokaʻi people recognized them as their own, if they were at times seen as errant and impatient youth. The integration of the kūpuna into the movement, therefore, was natural and unforced. As the younger activists regarded the kūpuna's contributions as essential, so did the kūpuna see themselves as wise and patient counselors.

The kūpuna involvement became critical in the decision to hold religious services on Kahoʻolawe to cleanse and replenish the island. The third access, conducted with the Navy's permission, was framed as a religious ceremony. Aluli remembers, "We used to say, 'If you could bring the kūpuna together, you could bring Hawaiʻi together.' Then we started to say, 'If you could get the kahuna together. . . .'"[33] The decision to conduct a blessing of Kahoʻolawe on the island created some disagreement between ʻOhana members. Some kūpuna were more traditional Christians than others. Some, like Emma DeFries and Sam Lono, were not Christian at all. Ultimately, the Christian members

George Helm and Wayne Reis warm up for a performance on February 3, 1973, under the supervision of their teacher, Kahauanu Lake. The show, Hawai'i Stars Present Hawai'i's Youth, was held at McKinley High School auditorium a few years before Helm's involvement in the Protect Kaho'olawe movement.

quite gracefully attended the ceremony, held on February 13 at Hakioawa, that was obviously designed to please Hawaiian gods.

The bringing of the kāhuna into the 'Ohana signaled a deeper commitment to Hawaiian values and traditions. The kūpunas' importance to the movement had never been questioned. The retrieval of Kaho'olawe was seen by the activists as a retrieval of their culture, which in turn meant the renewal of traditional relationships with the elders. But it also revealed the necessity of turning to ancient religious practices in order to explain the proper care of the sacred artifacts on Kaho'olawe. The kāhuna, in turn, insisted that the entire island was a sacred entity.

The February 13 ceremony aimed to restore mana to the island. Mana, like aloha, is a concept that Hawaiians find difficult to explain to foreigners. While it refers to personal power, mana also implies personal purity and rectitude. Mana is understood as a power that an individual inherently possesses and can only be manifested through correct and responsible actions. The kāhuna recognized that the island—a living and breathing entity—had been defiled through misuse and neglect, and they sought to restore Kaho'olawe's mana by calling the ancient gods back to the island.

The ho'oponopono—literally, making things right—symbolized the determination of Hawaiians to practice Aloha 'Āina on the island that symbolized their neglected heritage. Mana was to be restored not only to the island but to the people who would care for it. From this time on, the 'Ohana became even more active and visible in public. George Helm, whose dedication to Kaho'olawe seemed limitless, was their chief spokesman.[34]

New members very quickly became spokespersons and organizers as the 'Ohana organized around a loose network of activists on each island. One O'ahu member, Charles Warrington, remembers that period as being extremely hectic, proceeding from organizational meetings to public discussions, trying to educate Hawaiians about the issue. In particular, he remembers Helm's effect on people: "Once when we were trying to address one of the civic clubs here, you know, the Hawaiian Civic Club . . . well, they didn't want to let George speak . . . the directors anyway. So George went into the hallway with his guitar and started singing. Pretty soon everyone was crowding around him listening to him sing, and then he stopped singing and started talking."[35]

Helm's voracious appetite for information that could assist him in the cause sent him in a number of different directions. During the later months of 1976 he consulted with numerous prominent Hawaiians seeking the advice and counsel of anyone who could offer him a different understanding of Hawaiian culture, trying to accommodate his own vision of the future with the expectations of other Hawaiians. He met with musicians like Richard Kauhi, businessmen like Larry Mehau, educators, administrators, politicians, and, of course, kūpuna.

Perhaps, as Emma DeFries insisted, he listened to too many voices.[36] Certainly, he gave himself unequivocally to meeting the demands of a movement that was growing in size and momentum. It would have been a monumental task simply to deal with the sheer variety of personalities and conflicting ideologies that were pulled into the 'Ohana. Marxists from the university and activists from the newly formed Richardson Law School brought urban perspectives and tactics. There were even some who advocated direct and violent action against the military.[37]

But the leadership remained firmly in the hands of the Moloka'i community, which managed to direct the 'Ohana toward continued, nonviolent, and highly publicized confrontations with the Navy and public officials. While they exhorted the community to understand the principles of Aloha 'Āina, they challenged elected officials to meet with them and to take their share of responsibility.

The movement, therefore, was not mainstream politics. It was far too confrontational for that. Neither, however, was it an extremist movement. Radicals had little leverage precisely because the ideology of the movement, Aloha 'Āina, was so rooted in traditional kinds of behavior. But especially for those furthest from rural culture,

Aloha ʻĀina was even more revolutionary than the dialectic. It challenged not only one's notions of economics and history but one's sense of place in the universe as well. It questioned Western assumptions of individuality and placed the community of humans on an equal plane with the rest of nature. Finally, it gave credence to spiritual values that Hawaiians, conditioned by a century of Christianity and rationalism, had come to doubt.

No one has written a more eloquent testimony to the concept of Aloha ʻĀina than the late Samuel Crowningburg Amalu. No great friend of controversial movements, Amalu was, nevertheless, quite comfortable with controversial ideas. Significantly, he wrote about Hawaiians' love for the land just a few days after Helm and Aluli met at Māʻalaea and gave their beliefs a name.

> And if we as a people have looked upon earth as holy through all our history, can it be any wonder that we are outraged when we find aliens and strangers who come upon our lands, our earth, only to defile her? . . . And we care because it is our soil. It belonged to us Hawaiians long before the Americans ever got their hands upon it. And we love that soil—It is part of the living flesh of Papa who was our ancient mother. O yes, our mother and our bride. In most things we can become Americans—but not when our land is tortured and destroyed.[38]

The fact that Aloha ʻĀina was understood and articulated by different classes of individuals within the Hawaiian community is evidence of either a cultural link or an overwhelmingly compelling idea. Perhaps it was both.

Hoʻomana (Empower)

There is actually no way to measure the growth of the ʻOhana in the years between 1976 and 1978.[39] For that matter, one can only estimate the size of the ʻOhana today. There never was any formal membership. One is simply recognized as a member through participation. The federation style of the ʻOhana created individual island groups, known as lāhui, in which individuals, often activists in other causes, participated. Some individuals, like Charles Warrington, were very visible for a period of time, taking very active roles in more than one ʻOhana action. Others became involved for specific actions and then were not heard from for several years.[40]

One sign of the movement's success was the increasing approval by state officials of the Navy's return of the island. Mayor Cravalho had actually attended the hoʻoponopono in 1976 and two neighbor island legislators, Gerald Machida and Richard Kawakami, had toured much of the island by helicopter and promised to introduce resolutions for the island's return.[41] At the national level, the ʻOhana was hopeful that Senator Inouye would take the active role he had once taken in 1969.

That hope was shattered early in 1977 when the 'Ohana learned that the senator planned to submit a Castle and Cooke proposal to U.S. president Jimmy Carter that the federal government purchase a portion of the company's land on Lāna'i with the $77 million it would take to clear Kaho'olawe of unexploded ordnance.[42] Although there was some disagreement, the 'Ohana decided to reoccupy the island, this time for a much longer period.

On January 30, 1977, five men landed on Kaho'olawe: Charles Warrington, Francis Kauhane, George Helm, Richard Sawyer, and Walter Ritte. Of the five, only Ritte and Sawyer were prepared to stay. The others hiked over the island by night for two days before signaling the military search parties. At the time, Aluli stated that they were occupying the island because "people [were] starting to play politics . . . and losing sight of the Hawaiian issues involved on Kaho'olawe."[43]

The strategy was twofold. First, the 'Ohana wanted to clarify their objective to end the bombing. Each of the five "invaders" left behind statements of their reasons for going to the island, which made the front page of the *Honolulu Star-Bulletin*.[44] Both Helm and Ritte reaffirmed their sense of commitment to the land and the idea of Aloha 'Āina.

Their second strategy was to leave two on the island so that the Navy could not resume bombing. Ritte and Sawyer carried enough provisions for a two-week stay, assuming that Helm and Aluli would secure some kind of federal action before their food and water ran out. But the 'Ohana's telegrams and letters to Washington officials went unanswered, and the Navy stunned the group by resuming bombing on February 10.[45] The 'Ohana's response to this development verged on desperation. *Hawaii Observer* journalist Pam Smith called their reactions "hasty . . . and ill-timed."[46]

On February 12, Helm did something that had never been done before, addressing the State House of Representatives with the assistance of Jann Yuen and Henry Peters. Some were moved to tears as Helm spoke: "God can hear us. . . . Why can't the politicians? . . . If you don't understand what Aloha 'Āina means, go do your homework."[47]

In response, the House passed a resolution calling for a halt to the bombing. With resolution and petitions, Helm and Kauhane flew to Washington to seek the aid of the congressional delegation. Unfortunately, three of the four, including Inouye, were in Hawai'i being briefed by the Navy. The two men found Washington officials largely ignorant of the entire issue and "unwilling to move without pressure from Inouye." Frustrated, and angrily denouncing the uncaring official stance, Helm announced that "there were Hawaiians willing to stand on the bombing targets and let the bombs come . . . and there was no reason to stop them."[48]

The 'Ohana scheduled an invasion of more than one hundred people for February 20, 1977. But word leaked to the Coast Guard, and Helm was forced to call off the action. Instead the 'Ohana landed ten men and women on Kaho'olawe. The operation was something of a debacle. None of the ten were able to make contact with Ritte and Sawyer. Two actually swam back to Maui and the rest were picked up by U.S. Marines search parties, arrested, and charged with trespassing.[49]

On Kahoʻolawe, Ritte and Sawyer had exhausted their provisions and had turned to gathering coconuts and fishing.[50] The necessity of remaining in hiding limited their ability to gather food, and on February 27, faint with hunger, Ritte expressed in his journal his anger at the military, the politicians, all of the forces that sanctioned the bombing. "I can't believe they let the military bomb while we are still on the island. . . . It seems to me today that we have exhausted all of our cards in playing this hand within the system. . . . I wish I was militant like the Marines, Army and Navy, but I cannot act as the Haole and condone destruction and violence as he does."[51]

By February 28, Ritte and Sawyer had decided to give themselves up. For two days they attempted to signal passing military aircraft, but no one saw them. On Molokaʻi, the ʻOhana despaired that nothing would be done and worried for the safety of the two men. George decided to go himself to find them and bring them off, not knowing at that point that the Navy had already located the men and taken them off the island.

The tragedy that followed has been mythologized partly because the events were so inexplicable, partly because of Helm's incredible stature. On March 5, 1977, Helm, accompanied by Billy Mitchell of Honolulu and activist Kimo Mitchell (no relation to Billy) from Keʻanae, Maui, landed on Kahoʻolawe. The plan was to find Ritte and Sawyer, return to Kūheia together, and wait for the boat, owned by Sluggo Hahn of Maui, to pick them up.

The last person to see George and Kimo alive was Billy Mitchell. He was extremely reluctant to publicly discuss the event when it occurred, saying only that he "would like to keep their memories good" and that George was wrecked by spirits.[52] The boat that was supposed to rendezvous with them never made it. It actually sank at its dock. Mysteriously, the bilge plugs in the hull had been pulled. This is one unsolved mystery in the disappearance of George and Kimo. The other was what exactly took place between the three men on Kahoʻolawe on March 5.

Billy Mitchell, in one of his few statements to the press, said that when the boat failed to return and having failed to locate Ritte and Sawyer, the three men decided to paddle back to Maui on two surfboards that had been part of an emergency cache from an earlier trip. George was, according to Mitchell, wrecked both physically and emotionally and in poor shape when he entered the water. For this reason it was decided that Kimo would paddle one board with George and Billy would take the other. The water was rough that day, and George struck his head against some rocks. At some point they were separated and Billy went back to Kahoʻolawe to seek help at the military installation.[53]

The PKO was devastated by the loss. Family members Harry Mitchell and Adolph Helm and other PKO members joined in the search, assisted by the Navy, but no trace of the men was ever found. The mystery of their disappearance spawned an unbelievable

Uncle Harry Mitchell alongside Mo'olele a double-hulled canoe from Maui when it came to visit Kaho'olawe, October 1980.

profusion of rumors, with which the 'Ohana was forced to deal even as they grieved. Even within the membership, however, there was considerable dissent over the reliability of Billy Mitchell and his account. Still, they carried on. On March 19, 1977, a blessing for the young men was held on all of the islands. The ceremony on O'ahu was distinctly Hawaiian, conducted by mourners, many of them in traditional dress, directed by a descendent of Ka'ahumanu's high priest, Hewahewa. Emma DeFries, who had been very close to George and who had warned him not to go to Kaho'olawe at the end conducted the ceremony at Sandy Beach. "We must not be angry at nature. Nature does not punish us. We punish ourselves when we are out of tune with the elements."[54]

As fascinating a story as this had been for the press, the PKO was not through making headlines. As soon as the rumors began to die down, the 'Ohana began to gear up for the trespass trials. The Navy had charged seven people, and they were tried in two separate cases in June 1977. Two of the defendants, Joyce Kainoa and Samuel Kealoha, sparked press interest a month before their trial. Arraigned in Circuit Court on May 11, Kainoa refused to accept bail. She insisted that would recognize the validity of a judicial system which she would not accept.[55]

At the U.S. federal court in May 1977, Kānaka stood in support of the PKO members Joyce Kainoa and Sam Kealoha, on trial for landing on Kaho'olawe. According to Davianna McGregor, the masks mark affiliation with the god Kū.

Even more striking was Kealoha's flight to the sacred pu'uhonua (place of refuge) at Hōnaunau on the island of Hawai'i. Traditionally, kapu breakers and defeated chiefs would be spared if they were able to reach the pu'uhonua. Kealoha's claim that the government had no respect for Hawaiian culture was amply demonstrated when federal marshals turned up at Hōnaunau to bring him before the court.

Kainoa and Kealoha were tried in Circuit Court by Judge Samuel King—a Hawaiian himself—in the third week of May. The proceedings were rich in symbolism as the gallery, made up of PKO members and sympathizers dressed in malo (loincloth), kīkepa (cloth wrapped around the body), headdresses, and gourd helmets, singing "Hawai'i Pono'ī" as the Navy witnesses sat quietly in dress whites. Both defendants were without counsel and constructed their defense as a rejection of a judicial system that did not recognize their right to act as their own culture demanded.

The five defendants in the second trial, conducted June 21–23, were all found guilty by visiting judge Gordon Thompson. In rendering his verdict, Thompson said, "What the court did today is not what the court wants to do."[56] The judge had, in fact, been quite sympathetic to the defense, allowing them to present testimony on the religious significance of Kaho'olawe, even after Judge King had ruled on a defense motion, saying that the religious issue was not pertinent to the trespassing charge.

The defense called two religious experts and an anthropologist who testified that "a deep spiritual relationship to the land lay at the roots of Hawaiian culture."[57] The prosecution responded with a witness of their own, David Kenn, a consultant for the Kamehameha Schools and writer of numerous articles about Hawai'i's archaeology. He contended that there was "no such thing as Hawaiian religion today," identified Aloha 'Āina as a turn-of-the-century political concept, and stated that Kaho'olawe had no significance to anyone but fishermen.[58] However, under cross-examination, Kenn admitted that he knew "very little about ancient Hawaiian religion."

For the defense, the point of the trial was to show that the activists had gone to Kaho'olawe for cultural rather than political reasons. Judge King's ruling had effectively cut the legs from under that argument. It was symbolic of the struggle that the 'Ohana had confronted throughout its existence. Government officials, even those who were Hawaiian, refused to acknowledge the cultural expression of the movement, insisting that that expression had to be subordinated to American legal traditions.

Ho'oulu Lāhui

Ho'oulu Lāhui, to increase the nation, was the last concept that George Helm was working with before he disappeared in March 1977. Appropriately enough, these words also came from a song, this one by Alvin Issacs. George learned the song and was sharing its message with the others. When the first statewide meeting of the 'Ohana took place in 1977, it was called Ho'olulu Lāhui, the Gathering of the Nation.

Ultimately, the movement has had a tremendous social impact and even, although far more disputably, a political impact as well. It certainly influenced the 1978 Constitutional Convention, where John Waihe'e, one of the PKO's attorneys in the June trial, helped introduce and pass the so-called Hawaiian Affairs package. Included in that group of proposals were reforms of the Hawaiian Homes Commission; recognition of Native Hawaiians' rights to land and natural resources for subsistence, cultural, and religious purposes; a mandate that the state promote Hawaiian studies within the public schools; and eventually the creation of the Office of Hawaiian Affairs.[59]

But it is actually in the areas of education, environmental awareness, and even economic development that the notions of Ho'oulu Lāhui and Aloha 'Āina have had the most significant impact. The heightened awareness of Hawaiian values regarding land has resulted in continued challenges to capital developments over Hawaiian sacred sites and in resurgent Native agriculture and aquaculture on every island.

Today the terms ahupua'a (traditional Hawaiian land division) and mālama 'āina (caring for the land) are widely used by teachers and school administrators, planners

A PKO member begins thatching a hale hālāwai (meeting house) in Hakioawa, Kaho'olawe, August 18, 1983.

and policymakers, providing a vocabulary for a host of strategic plans and mission statements for institutions ranging from nonprofits to banks and multinational companies. Hawaiian studies curricula at the University of Hawai'i has been greatly shaped by the awareness of our people's essential connection to the 'āina. A growing number of young Native men and women have forged careers in managing lands for the state and for the Kamehameha Schools, fortified by a vision of restoring ancient best practices to land management in Hawai'i. While the adoption (and co-opting) of these terms may not have created a viable new political party, or resulted in the return of an independent Hawaiian government, Native Hawaiians' continued presence and our cultural values continue to infuse the political discourse and climate in Hawai'i.

As the Hawaiian sovereignty movement grew from the 1980s onward, it drew leadership and inspiration from the 'Ohana. At a 1988 Sovereignty Conference held at the state capitol, six organizations, including the PKO, submitted position papers on sovereignty and four of them specifically called for the implementation of Aloha 'Āina.

The PKO has made significant contributions to Hawaiian leadership. ʻOhana members gathered to help create Mālama i nā Kūpuna o Hawaiʻi Nei, the organization that works to protect the sanctity of ancient burial grounds. Leaders of the PKO like Davianna McGregor, Emmett Aluli, and Palikapu Dedman were key figures in the struggle to stop geothermal development in Wao Kele O Puna (see chapter 8). Many of Ka Lāhui Hawaiʻi's officers were also members of the PKO. Some of those who have been involved with that organization have maintained a confrontational stance toward the political system in Hawaiʻi and are usually involved with social programs and cultural activities that promote Hawaiians. Some have penetrated the political system and have become elected officials.[60]

The ʻOhana continues to speak for the responsibility that we Kanaka have for the ʻāina. Even though the U.S. military stopped using Kahoʻolawe for target practice in 1990, the PKO still has a remarkable vitality and relevance. The PKO might argue that its most important contribution has been to the island of Kahoʻolawe. After more than thirty-five years of protest, confrontation, organization, and sacrifice, the island has begun to heal. Many thousands of people, Kānaka and non-Kanaka, have made the journey to Kanaloa (Kahoʻolawe), some with the KIRC, others with the PKO.

Interestingly, these two organizations maintain a kind of studied distance. In fact their bases of operations are literally on opposite sides of the island. Whatever political or other differences may separate the two agencies, however, one gets similar stories from those Kānaka who go to the island to work, study, or practice our culture and religion. They are affected in deeply meaningful ways, observing in the punishment and neglect dealt to the island a corollary to their own lives. The island's survival is an inspiration to hoʻomau—to endure, to continue.

In the end, this is one aspect of ea; sovereignty, life, spirit, and breath emanate from Kanaloa and touch us. The island lives because of us, and we live because the island lives. It is truly a remarkable thing that we came so close to permanently forgetting this relationship. And we owe so much to the elders who refused to forget, and to the young men and women who risked and sacrificed their lives to teach us.

Notes

1. In the 1960s a number of organizations, led by a new generation of college-educated Hawaiians, began lobbying for reparations based on the illegal nature of the Hawaiian annexation by the United States. These groups were cataloged in a pamphlet published by the Ethnic Studies Program at the University of Hawaiʻi at Mānoa.

2. Osorio, "Unpublished Journal of Huakaʻi to Kahoʻolawe."

3. U.S. District Court, Hawaiʻi, Consent Decree Civil No. 76-8380, *Aluli v. Brown*, 1980. Under the consent decree and order, the Navy agreed to survey and protect historic and cultural sites on the island, clear surface ordnance from ten thousand acres, continue soil conservation and revegetation

programs, eradicate the goats from the island, limit ordnance impact training to the central third of the island, and allow monthly PKO access to the island.

4. Commander Third Fleet, "Second Endorsement on Capt. J.D. Grice USN, Investigative Report of 5 Nov 87," unpublished correspondence to the judge advocate general via CINCPACFLT, February 17, 1988. In this two-page report, the fleet commander attributes the off-target delivery of the cluster bombs to errors in planning and execution and concluded that while no damage was sustained by any of the archaeological sites, it "was fortuitous and not the result of sound strike planning."

5. Several nations have regularly participated in RIMPAC training on Kahoʻolawe, including Great Britain, Australia, Japan, and Canada. Since 1984 only Canada and the United States continued to use live ordnance during the RIMPAC exercises.

6. At Hakioawa, the ʻOhana has directed the rebuilding of several small heiau, the erection of a permanent Hale Mua (men's meeting house), and the construction of a Pā Hula (hula area) using, in traditional fashion, resources provided by the island. ʻOhana members and other volunteers have contributed their labor and knowledge of traditional technologies to build a Hawaiian settlement in the valley.

7. At this writing, current members of KIRC include highly admired Kānaka like Nāmaka Whitehead and William Ailā, as well as long-time Molokaʻi activist and Office of Hawaiian Affairs trustee Collette Machado and Hōkūleʻa captain Kaʻiulani Murphy. The PKO does not have the resources of KIRC and while they share some of the same visions for the future of the island such as revegetating and restoring water resources, there are differences over methods and ultimately over who speaks for the island.

8. MacDonald, "Fixed in Time," 78.

9. MacDonald, "Fixed in Time," 79. MacDonald cites "Dan Raps Navy on Kahoʻolawe," A4.

10. MacDonald, "Fixed in Time," 83.

11. Tuggle, "The Protect Kahoʻolawe ʻOhana," 98.

12. This may appear to be an overly cynical evaluation of the senator's motives. Yet how else can one explain his public determination to secure Kahoʻolawe for the state during the Nixon administration and his almost total abstention from the issue when it was raised during the Carter presidency?

13. MacDonald, "Fixed in Time," 80.

14. Protests of the war were minor only in a relative sense. In 1968 and 1969 there were several dramatic and well-publicized incidents including the burning of the ROTC building on the Mānoa campus, the occupation of the university's Bachman Hall, and a number of public draft card burnings.

15. McGregor-Alegado, "Hawaiians," 35.

16. Trask, *From a Native Daughter*, 119.

17. Trask, "The Birth of the Modern Hawaiian Movement," 139.

18. "ʻWhite' Laws Unacceptable the Court Told," C2.

19. Liliʻuokalani, *Hawaii's Story by Hawaii's Queen*.

20. Martin, "Waimanalo Blues"; Santos, "Me ke Aloha Ku'u Home o Kahaluʻu."

21. Pete Thompson, Kehau Lee, Kalani ʻOhelo, and Terry Kekoʻolani were all heavily and visibly involved in the support group. I know because I was also there.

22. *Honolulu Advertiser*, June 13, 1971, cited in Trask, "The Birth of the Modern Hawaiian Movement," 149.

23. Emmett Aluli, interview by the author, Puʻuohoku, Molokaʻi, November 15, 1989.

24. Davianna McGregor, interview by the author, Puʻuohoku, Molokaʻi, November 15, 1989.

25. Aluli, interview. Many of the details of this particular landing were supplied by Emmett Aluli. His perceptions as one of the principal members of the PKO are key to an evaluation of the group's

intentions and motivations. Since Walter Ritte was not interviewed for this chapter, it is important that the reader approach Aluli's observations with the usual caution.

26. Aluli, interview.

27. "2 Claim Isle Desecrated," A1.

28. *Mo'olelo o ka 'Āina*. Although produced in 1984, this section of the program consisted of the 1976 television broadcast.

29. In his interview, Aluli mentions a conflict that arose within the 'Ohana before the access in February 1977 that resulted in Helm's and Mitchell's disappearance. Contending that several 'Ohana members, including Helm, voiced their objections to Ritte's occupation, Aluli states that several Moloka'i people felt that Ritte was "going for himself." Aluli had already initiated a civil suit against the Navy (*Aluli v. Brown*) and, according to him, the general consensus was that this access would be "burdensome." None of this was revealed to the press at the time nor even to other, non-Moloka'i members of the 'Ohana. Charles Warrington of Honolulu made the trip in complete ignorance of the dissent. George Helm also went on that access.

30. Silva, *Aloha Betrayed*.

31. Aluli, interview.

32. "Hawaiian Activist Invades Kaho'olawe Again," A1.

33. Aluli, interview.

34. It is difficult to avoid turning a discussion of George Helm into a hagiography. His disappearance translates, for many, into a martyrdom. Every person I have interviewed and spoken to over the years insists that George was indeed a special individual. As someone who knew him, I can only say that I believe he was fundamentally changed by his connection with Kaho'olawe.

35. Charles Warrington, interview by the author, at Warrington's home in Pana'ewa, Hawai'i, November 23, 1989.

36. Smith, "The Ohana," 23.

37. Warrington, interview.

38. Amalu, "Sing a Song of Love for Hawaii Soil," A12.

39. The consent decree allowed access for up to seventy-five members of the PKO in certain months, while limiting it to forty-five in others.

40. Warrington, interview.

41. "Legislators Impressed by Their Trip to Island," C2.

42. Castle and Cooke was one of the Big Five powerful corporations that controlled the cultivation, shipping, and marketing of sugar in Hawai'i. According to Davianna McGregor, Ritte was working on some kind of arrangement with Inouye. If so, his disappointment with Inouye after the senator's talks with Castle and Cooke may have triggered his determination to return to Kaho'olawe against the wishes of some members of the Moloka'i group.

43. McGregor, interview.

44. "Why Hawaiians Value Kaho'olawe," A1.

45. Smith, "The Ohana," 21.

46. Smith, "The Ohana," 19–20.

47. Smith, "The Ohana," 19–20.

48. Smith, "The Ohana," 22.

49. Whether it was intended or not, this action resulted in a great deal of publicity for the 'Ohana during their court trials later that year.

50. Ritte and Sawyer, "Na Mana'o Aloha o Kaho'olawe," 41–42. Ritte writes that, while the Navy claimed that they believed no one was on the island, they continued to search.

51. Ritte and Sawyer, "Na Manaʻo Aloha o Kahoʻolawe," 41–42.

52. Smith, "The Ohana," 22.

53. Smith, "The Ohana, 23. There are several conflicting accounts of Billy Mitchell's actions at this point. He has made almost no public statements about what took place, since his sole interview with reporters and the PKO following the tragedy. There are also a number of people, including this author, who believed his account to be largely fabricated.

54. Smith, "Kahoʻolawe," 11.

55. "Activist's Choice: Jail, Not Bail," A3.

56. "Six in Kahoolawe Trial Found Guilty of Trespass," A3.

57. Smith, "Kahoʻolawe," 14. The expert witnesses for the defense were Emma DeFries, Edward Kanahele, and anthropologist Stephen Boggs.

58. Smith, "Kahoʻolawe."

59. McGregor-Alegado, "Hawaiians," 50.

60. Haunani-Kay Trask was the president of the Oʻahu Lāhui in the early 1980s. Charles Warrington worked with foster children in Hilo. Both Office of Hawaiian Affairs trustee Peter Apo and former governor Waiheʻe have identified themselves, in the past, as ʻOhana.

CHAPTER 7. Pu'uhonua

SANCTUARY AND STRUGGLE AT MĀKUA

Kalamaoka'āina Niheu

When the sun rose over Mākua on the morning of June 18, 1996, it illuminated a scene at odds with the typical quiet of this isolated valley far along the western shore of O'ahu. Against a backdrop of green stretching from the ocean to the base of sharply carved mountains, a trail of lights like a string of pearls wound sinuously along the road, flashing in the morning gloom. Helicopters and boats were ready, positioned strategically around the beach. Hundreds of men with holstered guns waited in canopied trucks at the nearby Army training reservation, waiting for the signal to move.

The state of Hawai'i's Department of Land and Natural Resources (DLNR) and then governor Benjamin Cayetano had issued the order to forcibly remove a community of approximately three hundred people, predominantly Kānaka Maoli, from the valley and to destroy their homes. The stated reason was to clear the area for a public park.

Eighty sheriffs, also predominantly Kānaka Maoli, strengthened by their overwhelming backup, descended on this community with semiautomatic guns drawn and handcuffs ready to arrest and destroy a community. Sixteen people were arrested. Dozens of supporters were cleared from the area and the entire coast closed off as bulldozers razed their homes to the ground.

The story of Mākua was at the center of public attention in 1996, but the history of the conflict goes much further back and continues to this day. As this chapter shows, it is part of the ongoing dispossession of the Indigenous peoples of Ka Pae 'Āina—the archipelago of Hawai'i—and the progressive encroachment of military interests through land seizure for the purpose of American security.

History of Mākua

Mākua is an ahupua'a, or traditional island division extending from mountain to sea, located on the northwestern coast of O'ahu, Hawai'i. What is usually referred to as Mākua Valley actually consists of three different ahupua'a: Mākua, Ko'iahi, and Kahanahaiki. The ahupua'a are ringed by mountains on the eastern side with the valleys stretching out to the sea. The wide, white sand beach of Ōhikilolo forms a bay of deep waters. On the west end of the beach at Kalaeopa'akai Point, depressions in the

The author, as a child, is carried by her mother, with father and siblings walking out of Mākua on July 11, 1977. During one wave of efforts to stop live fire training in Mākua, the Protect Kaho'olawe 'Ohana had entered the valley without permission from the U.S. military. They wanted to publicize and show the connections between the bombing at Kaho'olawe and Mākua. The PKO spent the day surveying damage to the valley.

ocean-side rocks can still be seen where rock was carved to cultivate and harvest salt, or pa'akai. The isolated valley was known as a training ground for warriors in the ancient Kanaka Maoli martial art of Lua.[1] Two large heiau, or temples, built of stone and a fishing shrine stand testament to the community that lived there.[2]

In 1848, King Kamehameha III, Kauikeaouli, under the advice of several of his former missionary advisors, began the transition to a system of private property land tenure.[3] Anyone of Kanaka Maoli ancestry who could provide evidence of continued cultivation and ancestral presence on areas of land could file with the government to claim land awards, called kuleana. In the Mākua area, the Māhele Act resulted in the allocation of only twenty-four kuleana awards to twenty-one petitioners for a total of approximately two hundred acres. Kelly estimated that in 1836 approximately 114 people lived in Mākua-Kahanahaiki. Consistent with the trend throughout the islands, less than 5 percent of the area's 4,190 acres were awarded in title to a fraction of the residents.

Over the next forty years, sugar industry businessmen (many of them missionary

A site for live fire testing, Mākua Valley has been contaminated by ordnance such as that pictured here, as well as a toxic cocktail of chemical pollutants. In this photo, taken in 1977, Protect Kaho'olawe 'Ohana members attempt surface cleaning in the background.

descended) worked to gain control over the majority of land leased by the Hawaiian Kingdom government. Many more thousands of acres were purchased outright. The conversion of land to haole, or foreign, control was aided by the physical presence of U.S. and English military might. The majority of Mākua land belonged to the Crown as public lands, and during the late 1800s and early 1900s ranchers leased Mākua from the Hawaiian Kingdom for pig, cattle, and horse ranching.

The armed coup against Queen Lili'uokalani and the Hawaiian Kingdom in 1893 resulted in a seizure of the national lands. The majority of lands in Mākua, once belonging to the Crown, became what is now called ceded land, even though it was not ceded by the Hawaiian people or their lawful government. After the beginning of the U.S. occupation of Hawai'i, without a government to protect the rights of the Native population, the remaining kuleana owners were besieged. Ranching became dominant in Mākua. Maria Kamaka lived in the valley as a young girl on her family's kuleana, which was surrounded by the ranch. The cattle would routinely overrun their garden. Even trained dogs were unable to control the decimation of the food they relied upon for daily sustenance. Eventually fighting off the cattle proved to be too much of a hardship and her family had to relocate to the beach. Kelly noted that this was a common tactic used at the time by ranchers throughout the islands to drive kuleana owners off their land.[4]

In the aftermath of Pearl Harbor, the U.S. Army declared martial law in Hawai'i in 1941. Mākua Ranch and any remaining kuleana lands were seized for military training. All of the remaining residents of the three ahupua'a—Mākua, Kahanahaiki, and Ko'iahi—were ordered from the land, and the Mākua Military Reservation was created. Mākua Church, the home of a former rancher, and any infrastructure in the area were used for target practice by the Army and subsequently destroyed.

After 1941, another four waves of land clearances were orchestrated at Mākua: in 1964, 1977, 1983, and 1996. The majority of the evictions were carried out with the stated intention of improving access, establishing a state park, and removing squatters. The issue of public access has been repeatedly used as a wedge to isolate and vilify the people of Mākua, limit support by the general public, delegitimize any claim to the land by the residents, and obscure the primary motivation of keeping the land clear for military exercises.

In 1964 the Mirisch Motion Picture Company leased Mākua Beach from the Army to film the motion picture *Hawaii*. Mākua Village did not fit in with the picturesque backdrop needed for the movie. The state Department of Land and Natural Resources labeled the residents "squatters." The Honolulu chief of police ordered that the homes be destroyed and everyone who lived there removed. The primary justification for this action was that residents were purportedly restricting public access to the beach. Although many who lived there had ancestral ties to the land, few in Hawai'i had the legal and organizational knowledge to protest their removal. Once filming for the movie was completed, Mākua Beach again fell out of the government spotlight. People began to congregate and a community arose again.

Plans for a state park were first documented in 1969. The Division of State Parks, Outdoor Recreation and Historic Sites proposed a plan to create a Mākua-Ka'ena Point State Park, covering several thousand acres from Kea'au Beach Park (south of Mākua) to Ka'ena Point. The state government allocated $1,808,000 to start acquiring the land on an incremental basis, in the hopes that the park could begin development in 1973.

In 1977, 1983, and 1996, the state of Hawai'i again used the rationale of public access and plans for a park to remove the community and destroy their homes. Each time, plans for the park were widely touted, including the installation of picnic tables and shower facilities.[5] At least $2.308 million dollars have been appropriated to develop a park at Mākua; $1,808,000 in 1969 and $500,000 in June 1996. To date the only structures erected are two large, yellow steel gates that block residents from moving back in.

Sanctuary

> We're not homeless, we're Hawaiians. Before the word "homeless" they called us squatters. But let's go even further back. Before that it was a Hawaiian lifestyle. Were we homeless then? Or did we say, "Welcome to our land"? It is our culture we're talking about that's getting destroyed. Everyone says: respect everyone else's culture. But when it comes to the Hawaiian, we're odd, we're different. So Mākua brings us and reminds us you're not odd. You're Hawaiian. You're not unorthodox; this is your culture.
>
> —HENRY DAVID ROSA, IN *MĀKUA: TO HEAL A NATION*
> (VIDEO RECORDING, NĀ MAKA O KA 'ĀINA)

In traditional times there were many pu'uhonua, commonly known as "places of refuge," where those who violated the strict kapu, or laws, could flee and find sanctuary, even from penalties requiring death. There were several pu'uhonua throughout the Hawaiian Islands prior to the Māhele, including but not limited to Pu'umau in Maui, Waipukua on Hawai'i, and Kalua'aha in Moloka'i. In modern times, places like Mākua, Waiāhole, and Waikāne are critical examples of cultural, political, and economic power based upon land that provided a means for the 'ohana—functioning, extended family—to remain intact. Unlike the state-run Department of Hawaiian Homelands, which focuses on a nuclear, Western-style family model, organic communities maintain and build upon the 'ohana unit.

Residents began to return to Mākua shortly after the 1983 sweep. The villagers declared Mākua a modern pu'uhonua in a society that criminalizes poverty. Their goal was to create a model where some would stay but that would be open to anyone who needed sanctuary. By February 1996, the community had grown to a population of 282 people. Kanaka Maoli represent approximately 20 percent of the total population in Hawai'i. In contrast, Mākua Village was overwhelmingly Indigenous, as they were 83 percent of the community.[6] The remainder was a local mix: thirteen residents were Pacific Islander, eleven Caucasian, nine Filipino, three Puerto Rican, and one Japanese.

Driving down Farrington Highway along the Wai'anae Coast, the green valleys of Mākua are clearly visible on the ma uka, or mountain side, of the road. A high brush of wild grasses and kiawe almost completely obscures the view of the ocean from the road. Most of the residents built their homes along the short dirt road that runs parallel on the ma kai, or ocean side, of the highway, carving out a home among the thorny trees.

I was introduced to the community by Leandra Wai, one of the residents and a member of the Mākua Council, at the Pai 'Ohana occupation in Kohonaiki.[7] Leandra had lived in several different places on O'ahu before she moved to Mākua. Her financial

Leandra Wai, a Mākua Council member, at one of the council meetings in 1996. Even after the bulldozing of her home, she continued to mālama iā Mākua, including caring for sacred sites and monitoring the U.S. Army's usage of the valley.

situation had become increasingly difficult, and eventually she could not afford the rent for a house. Houseless, her faith in mainstream society and her relationship to it had changed. She needed a sanctuary to recover from the wounds received in a struggle to survive. She arrived in Mākua with her husband, two daughters, and almost no possessions. "It was a garbage dump," as she remembered the place when she first arrived. "I was really torn between running away and staying, but I had no place to go. So I built, and as I started to build I started to realize that everyone here had a reason for coming here. Life had shattered in one way or another."[8]

Leandra's home was probably the most beautiful in the community. Her entry was a small part in the grasses along the dirt road that opened onto a short, graceful stairway made of sand and plywood flanked by lovely stone patterns that opened onto a broad platform fashioned from wooden pallets and covered by carpets. All of the materials were scavenged from elsewhere: other people's trash, painstakingly restored to functional use. Near the entrance she gathered bits of grass, branches, and flammable rubbish that she lit at night to chase away mosquitoes.

Henry David Rosa was a Vietnam veteran. David, as he was better known, met, fell in love with, and married his wife, Noe, in 1971. They had several sons and managed to make a decent living. When he fell ill in 1991 from a disease that doctors were unable to diagnose, Noe believed that he was dying. Unable to work and with medical bills piling up, they moved to Mākua Beach. As he began to look around at the people who lived there, he realized they had a common bond. "These people here today can all state the same story. A huge machine, a vast modern machine was moving in on them and no one was there to reach them."

David's home was at the junction of the dirt and main roads. He lived there with Noe and their sons. Their living area also served as a meeting place for the entire community. There were usually at least a dozen residents there at any time, often coming to cook together over the grill, strategize, or simply talk. Their home was a cluster of three hale (homes, one-room structures). The tents had been salvaged from materials discarded by the military. David often referred to his home as the Forty-Dollar Wonder because it cost slightly more than that to build. He claimed that the tents could last about five to ten years and withstand up to eighty- to one-hundred-mile-an-hour winds. "I got the majority of my materials from other men's trashes," he told Nā Maka o ka 'Āina. "My motto is that you can live poor but you don't have to live poorly."[9]

Data confirm the economic and housing crisis. In 1990 the cost of a median single-family home on O'ahu was $363,000, a 41 percent increase from 1989. In the same time period, condominium prices increased 54 percent to $200,000 and the average cost of a one-family rental unit was $1,450 per month. Simultaneously, the number of those living in poverty, as defined by having a total family income below $15,000 per year, increased to 11 percent of the population, primarily Filipino and Kanaka Maoli.[10] On the Wai'anae Coast, which was approximately 60 percent Native Hawaiian in 1996, the percentage of those living in poverty conditions was approximately 17 percent.[11]

Wai'anae Coast human service providers identified the villagers at Mākua as the direct inheritors of the legacy of lost land. "The current Beach residents are refugees from high rents, housing projects, and an educational system that doesn't educate.... Unless the root causes are addressed this cycle of homeless people seeking refuge at Mākua Beach, confrontation with the State, forced eviction, then gradually families drift back seeking refuge at Mākua Beach and the cycle repeats itself decade after decade."[12]

Once people arrived at Mākua, protecting themselves from the elements became a major concern. The sun on the west side of the island is particularly brutal as the coast lies in the rain shadow of the Wai'anae Mountain Range, resulting in extremely arid summer conditions with limited trees to provide protection from the hot sun. During

Barbara Avelino, a Mākua Beach resident and Mākua Council member in the 1990s, also lived at Mākua as a child. She and her family were forcibly removed during her childhood, and then again in 1996, a few months after this photo was taken. Mākua Village was destroyed and homes bulldozed to the ground.

the winter months, the heat of the sun is less severe. The clouds bring rain every day and the surf rises up to the road, sometimes sweeping through people's homes.

Hurricane 'Iniki swept through the islands in 1992, destroying several homes and buildings throughout Hawai'i. Along the Wai'anae Coast huge waves crashed on the beaches and over Farrington Highway. Telephone lines were downed by waves and boulders. Some of the boulders, the size of cars, swept into the streets and smashed into buildings. Most of the hale at Mākua Village were destroyed, but unbelievably some of the structures were sturdy enough to survive the storm. Most of the villagers evacuated the area, retreating to the emergency shelters, and returned the next day to salvage what they could.

Barbara Avelino and her husband lived right next to Leandra's 'ohana, separated by the high brush. Barbara was a slender woman with straight, brown, shoulder-length hair. She walked with a slightly sassy strut and spoke in a low raspy voice. Barbara was raised at Mākua. She was a survivor of the 1983 land clearance and believed that her family might have ties to Mākua even further back. As an adult, she returned and worked doing auto body repair. Her hale was an open, uncovered living area with chairs and a small table facing the ocean next to a small enclosure built of plywood where she and her husband slept.

Food and water were a challenge at Mākua Village. The residents used barrels to haul water from Kea'au Beach Park, which had shower facilities, approximately a mile down the road. Those who owned cars would pool money for gas to get water or buy food from the local grocery store. As the residents became more established, many began to grow their own food. The most successful was a Samoan family headed by a matriarch named Sia. Her family grew sweet potato, pumpkin, green onion, watermelon, squash, and tapioca. Sia, also a member of the Mākua Council, was one of the few non–Kanaka Maoli living at Mākua. Fishing was another source of available food. Kaimana, another resident, spoke of the variety of fish he caught with his blue nets lined with dark orange floaters. Akule, moi, papio, and ulua provided the majority of the protein in his diet. He also gathered different types of edible seaweed such as limu pepe'e, limu 'ele'ele, and limu kohu.

A pu'uhonua, or sanctuary, is what the residents called Mākua. With the tightening of state control of the homeless and the simultaneous increase in the price of housing, the residents felt strongly that Mākua was the last safe place. "It's peaceful here and we just want to stay," said Noreen, another Mākua resident. When she heard of the planned eviction, she was alarmed. "Now we have nowhere to go. It's either left in the ocean or right in the hills, and this is the end of the road."[13]

More than shelter, Mākua was where the residents could heal what was often called the wounds of society. At one time the Mākua Council accurately compared their situation to post-traumatic stress disorder. "Symptoms listed are as follows, feeling isolated, loss of identity, violent reactions and tendencies, suicidal tendencies, hearing voices, tendency to drug abuse to cope, nightmares, manic depression, unable to focus, cannot hold a job, and often homeless and derelict situations."[14] The council believed cultural traditions were critical to healing the trauma.

"I had no idea that this land, this water . . . something about the soil, the sand here, the salt air. Makes the fruit sweeter, beans sweeter," said Leandra. "And we're healing our past of torment and destruction."

Most of the community admitted to being survivors of various forms of abuse, domestic, physical, mental, or substance related. The effectiveness of culturally based interventions in the healing of Kanaka Maoli has been well established.[15]

One of the remarkable aspects of Mākua Village was that families were rebuilt. Poverty makes it difficult for families to stay together. The constant mobility required by those who shuffle from park to car to park again leads to instability of interpersonal kin networks. Large families often have to split up to find space for themselves wherever they can.

"For me, Mākua is everything," stated Noelani Rosa. "This is where my family all got back together again. I buried a son here." All of the members of the Mākua Council had or were able to rebuild their kin networks and play critical leadership roles in the organization of the village.[16] By 1996 the council had organized systems that included the sharing of food, water, transportation of the children to school, and a neighborhood watch.

Residents and Mākua Council members stand defiant on the beach where their homes were located. In the background, Cory Cidade's home is visible. At far left, with two fists raised, stands Sparky Rodrigues, who was arrested protesting the destruction of his and others' homes in 1996. He and Leandra Wai helped to form Mālama Mākua, which envisions the return of Mākua to the Hawaiian people.

Representatives, previously inexperienced in community organizing, researched the legal rights of land ownership in the area, coordinated public relations with the media, and went out to various organizations to increase awareness and garner support. A significant proportion of the research in this chapter was conducted, collected, and organized by the Mākua Council in 1996, in particular Sparky Rodrigues.

Prior to the 1848 Māhele, the 'ohana as an extended family was the fundamental basis of Kanaka Maoli economic and interpersonal relationships. Therefore, the destruction of 'ohana has been devastating. Land alienation separates people from their foundation—water, food, and natural resources. In addition, clearing people from the land also separates them from the social processes that organize harvesting, sharing, processing, exchange, transfer, and storage, and the passing on of this knowledge of those processes. Cultural extinction is often considered an event fixed at a point in time. The events that have occurred at Mākua reveal that dispossession is an ongoing process, a process that continues to this day.

On Military and State Parks

The most recent Mākua land clearances were primarily justified on the basis that the residents of Mākua Village were illegally occupying the beach and obstructing public access to the beach. In 1996, state officials, such as the chairman of the Board of Land and Natural Resources, claimed there were complaints about the residents restricting public access to the beach, public health risks, and growing rubbish that prompted a site inspection. But these public statements hid the underlying military needs for the area.

Following World War II, the Wai'anae community became increasingly opposed to the continuing occupation of Mākua by the Army. Many of the former Mākua Valley residents saw the use of the valley as destructive and wasteful. "They don't need that place for bombing," said one. "During the wartime they had to use it, but when it is peacetime again, they should change it back to the people." Another former resident criticized the argument that too many bombs had been dropped on Mākua for it to be safe for human habitation: "Give 'em back. You see all the bombing, all that crap, they had more damn bombs fall on Germany and everything; they clean 'em up; they all back living there again. What the hell!"[17]

The U.S. Army was not interested in returning the land. Mākua Valley is an ideal training site for military maneuvers and live fire munitions training. The 1964 Mākua Military Reservation lease reveals the strength of the Army's negotiating power. On an island known for the high cost of real estate, the lease fee for 1,500 acres was set at a pittance of $1 from 1964 to 2029. The lease also states that any disputes that should arise between the state of Hawai'i and the Army would be settled by the U.S. Army Division Engineer assigned to Hawai'i. If the state disagreed with the decision, the appeal would be sent to the Secretary of the Army.[18] Identifying the valley as the ideal training area for soldiers to practice invading an island nation, the Army continued to consolidate control over the valley and by 1996 Mākua Military Reservation comprised 4,190 acres.[19]

In the 1970s, all military reservations in the United States were required by U.S. federal mandate to report on the cultural and environmental effects of their activities. The U.S. Army contracted the Bernice Pauahi Bishop Museum on O'ahu to conduct the necessary research. In April 1977 the *Cultural History Report of Mākua Military Reservation and Vicinity: Mākua Valley, O'ahu, Hawaii* was completed and submitted to the Army.[20] The report details the history of human occupation in the valley by Kānaka Maoli, ranchers, and the U.S. Army and their impact on the natural resources of the area. The research was the result of archival and archaeological study and interviews with twenty-two informants. The final recommendation was that any activity that could cause further damage to the area—including gunnery practice and the use of fire to dispose of munitions—be discontinued and a committee composed of representatives from the federal and state governments, scientists, and Wai'anae community members be convened to investigate the future use of the area.

Marion Kelly, respected anthropologist and primary researcher of the report, revealed that a representative of the Army attempted to modify it before accepting it. He insisted that she remove her recommendations. When Kelly refused, the Army simply

Gwen Epuni Kim holds a piece of unexploded ordinance at Mākua Valley on July 11, 1977. A proud Korean, Gwen has been a tireless ally for Kanaka Maoli, playing key but often behind-the-scenes roles in water, land, welfare rights, taro restoration, and demilitarization movements.

rejected this thoroughly researched report by an established scholar. In spite of this, the manuscript has survived in the community via photocopies passed from hand to hand.

Hawaiian opposition to the U.S. military usage of Mākua dates back to at least the mid-1970s. Organizers buoyed by successes like the Waiāhole-Waikāne antieviction struggle took what they had learned and moved to support other struggles. Walter Ritte, Richard Sawyer, and other prominent members of the Protect Kaho'olawe 'Ohana were occupying Kaho'olawe despite ongoing live bombing. Shortly after George Helm died in an attempt to stop the bombing of Kaho'olawe, the O'ahu chapter of the PKO announced an open house at Mākua in an effort to connect the different sites of U.S. military live munitions training. The main organizers of the event were Terri Keko'olani, Gwendolyn Kim, Kīhei Soli Niheu, Sam Kealoha, and the Papakōlea brothers. Due to the momentum of the movement at that time, no military or police presence ever arrived to stop the access even though a Mākua Military Reservation guard shack was burned to the ground.[21]

In 1992, opposition to the military's presence again became an issue when the Army applied to the Environmental Protection Agency (EPA) for a permit to operate a hazardous waste treatment facility at Mākua.[22] The Washington, DC–based Military Toxic Projects brought local attention to Mākua again when the EPA proposed a rule in 1995 to allow the Department of Defense to independently regulate its management of military munitions waste.[23]

Within an unfriendly atmosphere, the U.S. Army continued to conduct training exercises at Mākua. The Army wanted free use of the beach for military training exercises without the impediment of the residents of Mākua Village. After more than a decade of relative peace for Mākua Village, Major General Robert L. Ord, commanding general of the U.S. Army, Hawai'i, wrote a letter in 1992 urging William Paty, chairman of the Board of Land and Natural Resources, to remove the community from the beach: "Our Mākua Range Safety Officer has advised that each day more people are taking up residence at Mākua Beach. . . . We request that you expedite your coordination with the state Department of Human Services to determine the 'homeless' status of these people and initiate appropriate measures to relocate them from Mākua Beach."[24]

The relocation was a delicate matter. The Wai'anae Coast community's opposition to the use of Mākua for live-fire munitions training was still high and any direct action by the Army against the community would raise that ember to a flame. It was critical to deflect attention away from the military intent and begin setting public opinion against Mākua Village.

In 1995 representatives from the DLNR began informing the media that they were receiving complaints about restriction of the park's public access, public health risks, and growing rubbish attributed to the residents at Mākua Beach: "We are extremely concerned about the situation at Mākua," stated DLNR chairman Michael Wilson, "especially with the welfare of the occupants, the conditions of this once-beautiful beach, and the general public who may wish to utilize the area."[25]

Hawaii Community Action Program (HCAP), a Wai'anae community organization, contradicted this statement and reported that the significant trash noted on the beaches of Mākua had been left by businesses and individuals from outside the village.[26] The Mākua Council issued a press release in response: "We're tired of being treated and talked about like trash. We've been cleaning and picking up trash at Mākua for years. Not only our own trash but the trash left by others."[27]

Although DLNR's accusation was reported on all the major local news stations and two newspapers, Mākua villagers' response and the report from HCAP were never published. Mainstream Hawai'i believed the media reports, and anger and resentment toward the Mākua residents began to rise. Demonstrations by Mākua residents and their support were met with angry calls to "get a job!"

Early in the morning on March 1, 1996, Mākua residents woke to find their village occupied. A DLNR state parks administrator, Ralston Nagata, and more than forty police officers, with identification badges reversed so that they could remain anonymous, descended upon the community. Additional armed men were seen on a nearby hillside, raising fears of a SWAT team. Although the residents had lived for months with the rumors of eviction, it was the first time since 1983 that a large armed force had entered their community. When David Rosa approached Nagata, he was immediately surrounded by armed police officers and given a flier with a list of human service resources for employment, housing, and health services. No explanation was provided at the time. None of the information provided was new. An identical flier had already been provided months before. Although DLNR later announced that the purpose of the visit was to provide resources and conduct a site inspection, the message was both clear and frightening: utilize the listed resources or deal with armed force.

On March 8, 1996, the Board of Land and Natural Resources leased 11.1 acres at Mākua Beach from the U.S. Army for the purposes of a state park for a mere five years. Although the stated purposes were to "optimize the management of Mākua Beach by the State Parks Divisions," the details of the lease reveal that the true intent was to increase military access to the area while simultaneously deflecting responsibility for the eviction. According to the contract:

> [The state] will obtain written permission from the commander, US Army Garrison, Hawai'i, prior to any construction. . . . No overnight camping shall be authorized on the premises except by US Military Personnel. . . . The government shall retain the right to conduct military activities . . . and restrict public use. . . . The use and the occupancy shall be under the general supervision of the Commander US Army Garrison, Dir. of Public Works . . . and subject to such rules and regulations as may be prescribed from time to time by said officer. . . . The Secretary reserves the right to use the premises from time to time for such purposes deemed necessary in the interest of national defense.[28]

The license also stated that the state must vacate the area and remove any property that had been erected at Mākua upon the termination of the lease. Structures not removed would become the property of the U.S. Army. No monetary compensation was to be provided to the Army. In a bureaucracy often satirized for its lack of speed, the license was presented, heard, and approved in a single meeting. It is clear that retaining the use of Mākua for military exercises was a top priority. Second, the stated desire to increase public access and develop the area for a state park was a fallacy. Third, the U.S. Army and the state of Hawai'i worked together efficiently to achieve the first priority while simultaneously obscuring their primary objective from the public.

Four days after the license was granted, representatives from the DLNR returned to Mākua Village and delivered a notice to vacate the area by April 15 or face a $500 fine. Any property found would be either confiscated or destroyed.[29] The notices were delivered early in the morning, and the roar of the bulldozers driving past their homes awoke residents with the fear that they were to be bulldozed while they slept. As the representatives spread throughout the village, some of the residents wept but most received the papers with stoic faces, standing protectively in front of their homes and families. A DLNR spokeswoman, Aulani Wilhelm, told reporters that the eviction notices were a result of the March 1 inspection where the state found evidence of health risks and excessive trash in the area. The justification for the presence of the bulldozers was to clear public access ways to the beach even though they were never used.[30]

Supporters crafted Senate Concurrent Resolution (SCR) 48, "Requesting the Department of Land and Natural Resources and the Hawai'i Housing Authority to study the homeless problems at Mākua Beach, Wai'anae." It was heard at the legislature on March 19, 1996. The Mākua Council arranged for transportation for two dozen residents, joined by more than 150 supporters. In spite of two hours of testimony in support of the resolution, the Senate Housing Committee deferred action until Governor Ben Cayetano was consulted. Governor Cayetano denied Mākua residents access to the meeting and refused to suspend the evictions after a five-minute meeting with HCAP representative Danette Rayford. The next day, the governor issued a press release extending the evictions to June 15 to allow the children who lived at Mākua to finish school.[31]

The March 8 license between the Army and DLNR and its terms were not made public until June 13, 1996, less than a week before the planned eviction and only after the efforts of community activists. The Wai'anae Neighborhood Board convened a public meeting to address community concerns over the agreed licenses. The DLNR director, Michael Wilson, and representatives from the Army appeared to discuss the terms of the lease. Colonel Randy Tucker admitted at that meeting the Army's plans to conduct operations with rubber boats and dry fire training activities on the beach.[32]

Frustrated that the mainstream media would not report their side of the story, the Mākua Council sought alternative means of getting their story out. Nā Maka o ka 'Āina, a Hawai'i-based documentary company that has covered the Hawaiian movement for thirty years, began filming what would eventually become the documentary *Mākua: To Heal a Nation*. The council began to strategize, issuing press statements and collaborating with other, small independent media outlets, community newsletters, and 'Olelo, the public access channel, to combat the negative press. Unfortunately, the information could reach only a limited audience and the village was combating the fear and disdain of poverty and the overwhelmingly negative spin provided by mainstream media. "Squatters" were the perfect villains for the average struggling Hawai'i resident.

On May 6, 1996, more than thirty different service providers, special interest groups, and church representatives arrived at Mākua. Later, Cory Cidade, a Mākua resident, said the day succeeded in doing what the two visits by DLNR failed to do: dishearten the residents. For those whose primary goal was to find a way to leave Mākua, the options were extremely limited and temporary. For the residents who wanted to create a pu'uhonua, no legal representation was offered. They were faced with the realization that the chances of the state allowing them to stay were incredibly slim.[33]

In the weeks that followed, many of the residents began to believe that they were fighting a losing battle. If forcibly removed, their precious but meager belongings would be either confiscated or destroyed. People began moving out of the village, some into transitional housing and others onto a different beach. Although those who left promised to continue supporting the struggle, the cohesiveness of the group had been lost, and they were no longer operating with the full effectiveness of their community. A large gathering of support from the general public would have brought hope to the community, but the press had been successful at vilifying and isolating the residents.

By the beginning of June, less than a third of the community remained at Mākua. When the sun rose on the morning of June 18, 1996, most of those remaining at Mākua, both villagers and supporters, were already awake. As police cars were spied across the bay, winding along the road, someone called out the warning: "They're coming!" Those who remained gathered in their homes where they would make a stand. Hundreds of police descended upon the village, identification concealed, weapons holstered. Sixteen residents refused to leave. Among those arrested were Sparky Rodrigues, Barbara Avelino, Cory Cidade, Linda (last name unknown), Skippy Ioane, William Gosline, Bernard Keli'ikoa, Kaliko Kanaele, Steven Tayama, Richard Pomaika'iokalani Kinney, Kaleo Patterson, and myself.

Observing the police, I was filled with a choking sadness. All of the officers were brown-skinned Polynesians, primarily Kānaka Maoli. My mother, seeing me dragged out to the road, told me not to weep. She said that what we did was a good thing, something to be proud of. Sparky Rodrigues, who had extensive connections within law enforcement, reported that the Sheriff's Department and DLNR recruited personnel from all the major islands, including prison guards, the fire department, SWAT, and the Sheriff's Department. "What happens if no one shows up?" Sparky asked of Cappy Caminos, head of the Sheriff's Department, and Gary Moniz, head of enforcement for DLNR. Their response was that any who refused to go would lose their jobs.[34]

When I joined the rest in the paddy wagon, my heart became piha (full). Each person put into the paddy wagon was greeted as a hero by the others. Irritated, one of the policewomen yelled at us to shut up. My sadness turned to anger. "Remember the Overthrow?" I called out to her. "The U.S. might have invaded our country but there were also Hawaiians standing on the steps of 'Iolani Palace with open arms. When your children look back at your picture, where will you be in history?" She tightened my cuffs in retaliation until I could no longer feel my fingers. I knew where we would stand in the history of our people.

The charges were ultimately dismissed, the occupation was over, and the village was razed to the ground. Despite the evictions, Mālama Mākua, a group composed of several members of the Mākua Council, continues to fight the military's abuse of Mākua and advocate for its return to nā Kanaka Maoli. In March 1997, almost a year after the forced evictions of the people of Mākua, the U.S. Marine Corps announced their intention to practice amphibious landings at Mākua Beach. The exercise was to include small amphibious craft and 2,000 troops.[35] Mālama Mākua successfully halted those exercises and a second attempt that same year. Among those leading that charge were two former Mākua Council members, Sparky Rodrigues and Leandra Wai, along with physician and activist Dr. Fred Dodge.

Conclusion

The lessons from the history of Mākua are manifold. Destroying the 'ohana as a fundamental basis of Kanaka Maoli culture has caused immeasurable damage. Land clearances separate people from land, water, food, and natural resources. More subtly, land alienation separates people from the social processes that organize the harvesting, sharing, processing, exchange, transfer, storage, and the passing on of this knowledge of said processes. Healing and repairing the trauma requires systems that involve rebuilding and repairing that foundation. A solid base is the key to a successful movement. The current system does not allow us to define the process of our own healing.

Direct, frontline action is a trial by fire. Many of our greatest community leaders started out faced with an injustice, and they made a decision to kū'ē—to resist. In that fight to correct that injustice these leaders were educated in history, community organizing, and the application of revolutionary theory. There is no faster or deeper way of understanding what is at risk and what can be gained than fighting for a home.

We must not rely upon others to distribute the truth. The means to collect and distribute information is a critical component of educating our community and protecting our resources. Relying upon mainstream media to do so will leave our people vulnerable and subject to division and misinformation. We need to cultivate and further support independent, Kanaka Maoli–created media, such as Nā Maka o ka 'Āina and the *Hawai'i Independent*.[36]

Houselessness in Ka Pae 'Āina has its fundamental roots in the dispossession of Kanaka Maoli as a people. Poverty is a slippery slope, and most of us are one paycheck away from being without a home. Human service providers should be aware of this even when service is provided with the best of intentions. In the Mākua case, well-meaning people were, perhaps unwittingly, positioned in a role that was ultimately meant to divide and dishearten the community. Understanding the greater context can help us to avoid such pitfalls.

Finally, the threat of violence against us is often being wielded by our own people.

Kānaka Maoli are being sent to arrest and contain other Kānaka Maoli. I challenge with aloha for all of our people to stand down at times like these. Ask why you are being selected from among your colleagues of other ethnic backgrounds to participate in particular events such as evictions of other Hawaiians. Understand that we fight for the future of all our children, including yours.

Notes

1. Sterling and Summers, *Sites of O'ahu.*
2. Kelly and Quintal, *Cultural History Report of Mākua Military Reservation and Vicinity.*
3. Kame'eleihiwa, *Native Land and Foreign Desires.*
4. Kelly and Quintal, *Cultural History Report of Mākua Military Reservation and Vicinity.*
5. "Homeless Beach Person Criticizes State Tactics," *Honolulu Star-Bulletin,* March 8, 1996.
6. Suka, "Mākua."
7. In the mid-1990s, the Pai 'ohana were threatened with eviction from their ancestral lands and fishing grounds by the U.S. National Park Service. As was the case in Mākua, the settler state wanted to clear out the Indigenous people in order to "protect" the area as a park.
8. Nā Maka o ka 'Āina, *Mākua.*
9. Nā Maka o ka 'Āina, *Mākua.*
10. Minerbi, "Sustainability versus Growth in Hawai'i," 71–73.
11. "Hawaiian Socio-demographic Community Health Indicators," prepared for the Queen Lili'uokalani Children's Center, Honolulu, Hawai'i, 1993, A4.8, B4.2.
12. Suka, "Makua 'Ohana Project," Executive Summary.
13. Paoa Productions, *Wahine Mākua Speak.*
14. Makua Council Minutes, unpublished, on file with Kalama Nīheu, 1996.
15. Shintani et al., "Waianae Diet Program"; Blaisdell, "The Meaning of Health"; Mokuau, "Culturally Based Interventions for Substance Use and Child Abuse among Native Hawaiians."
16. Carol Stack has written of the importance and effectiveness of kin networks, especially in situations of limited resources. See Stack, *All Our Kin.*
17. Kelly and Quintal, *Cultural History Report of Mākua Military Reservation and Vicinity.*
18. General Lease No. S-3848, Hawai'i State Department of Land and Natural Resources, August 20, 1964.
19. "Makua Valley Ideal Training Area for Soldiers to Fine-Tune Skills," A4.
20. Marion Kelly, interview by author, Honolulu, Hawai'i, January 28, 1997.
21. Kīhei Soli Niheu, interview by author, Waimea, Hawai'i, February 15, 2012; Gwendolyn Kim, interview by author, Ka'a'awa, Hawai'i, February 16, 2012.
22. "Army's Application for EPA Permit Is Long, but Not Informative."
23. "Environmentalists Enraged by These Military Practices."
24. "First the Cattle, Then the Bombs Oust Hawaiians from Mākua Valley."
25. "Homeless Beach Person Criticizes State Tactics."
26. Suka, "Makua 'Ohana Project."
27. Makua Council, "Mahalo for All Your Kokua," unpublished press release, March 22, 1996.
28. Department of the Army License for State Park Purposes, Contract No. DACA84-3-96, Hawai'i, March 8, 1996.

29. DLNR Notice to Vacate Mākua and Kahanaiki, state of Hawaiʻi, March 12, 1996.
30. Rosa, "Letter to the Editor."
31. "Cayetano Meets with Squatters' Sympathizer."
32. "Agreement Prohibits Camping at Mākua."
33. Edmond Suka, *Makua Service Providers Day Evaluation*, unpublished report to Hawaiʻi Community Action Program, May 1996.
34. Sparky Rodrigues and Leandra Wai, interview by author, Waiʻanae, Hawaiʻi, June 17, 2012.
35. "Marines Cancel Mākua Exercise."
36. For information on Nā Maka o ka ʻĀina and their catalog of documentary and educational videos, see http://www.hawaiianvoice.com/. The *Hawaii Independent*, an online news source, can be found at http://hawaiiindependent.net/.

CHAPTER 8. Wao Kele O Puna and the Pele Defense Fund

Davianna Pōmaika'i McGregor and Noa Emmett Aluli

Ha Pele Ha

You come to us as the *kai ea pele*
Your families creating, decorating
Give life to our land
Pele ha, pele ha

You *pele* with *kū, kāne, kanaloa and lono*
Alive, the living god
Akua to our people
Pele ha, pele ha

You have given us these lives *pele*
Our dreams, the images of your beauty
Wili the sennit closer to you
Pele ha, pele ha

You pele are the *oli*, the *hula*
Your sisters honoring you
Connect us, *pili* us tighter
Pele ha, pele ha

Pele you give *mana* to our existence
Your forests' scent we can not do without
Care for our seas, shelter us
Pele ha, pele ha

—PALIKAPUOKAMOHOALII DEDMAN
AND NOA EMMETT ALULI, EXCERPT
FROM "PELE HA," IN *MĀLAMA HAWAIIAN LAND AND WATER*, 1985

The proposed development of geothermal energy in the Wao Kele O Puna volcanic rainforest in the 1980s on Hawai'i Island threatened to destroy this forest, obstruct access to its natural resources utilized by Kanaka 'Ōiwi cultural practitioners, and desecrate the Goddess Pelehonuamea. The Hawai'i Geothermal Project (HGP) would have transformed the pristine Wao Kele O Puna into an industrial wasteland of approximately 155 production wells on thirty-nine separate well sites with thirty-seven injection wells and twenty-one power plants on 22,000 acres in Puna, Hawai'i. It would also have served as a gateway to the industrialization of Hawai'i Island and development on O'ahu. The plan was to generate 500 megawatts of electricity to power a spaceport in Ka'ū, the expanding population of O'ahu, and the processing of manganese nodules mined from the ocean floor off Hawai'i Island. To reach O'ahu, high-voltage overhead transmission lines were to run from Puna through the saddle between Mauna Kea and Mauna Loa to Mahukona and connect with undersea cables. The submarine cables would transmit the electricity under the 'Alenuihāhā Channel to southeast Maui between Apole Point and Huakini Bay. From there, the electricity was to have been transmitted twenty miles by overland transmission lines to connect to undersea cables off 'Āhihi Bay; laid under the 'Au'au, 'Alalākeiki, Pailolo, Kalohi, and Kealaikahiki Channels; pass near Moloka'i; go under the Kaiwi Channel; and surface at Waimānalo, O'ahu. Promoters of the HGP included U.S. Senator Daniel K. Inouye, Governor John Waihe'e, Hawai'i State Senator Richard Matsuura, Hawaii County Mayor Dante Carpenter, the influential Campbell Estate, the Hawaiian Electric Company, the International Longshoremen and Warehousemen's Union, Wyoming-based True/Mid-Pacific Geothermal Venture, Italy-based Pirelli International, and Israeli-based Ormat.

The Pele Defense Fund (PDF) was formed in 1985 by religious practitioners and lineal descendants of Pelehonuamea to protect her life force and realm, as well as the rights of Kanaka 'Ōiwi in the Wao Kele O Puna. The poem above succinctly conveys the heartfelt beliefs about Pele, the goddess of the volcano. Given the powerful and affluent forces aligned in favor of geothermal energy, the PDF forged a broad alliance with Puna and Maui residents, Native Hawaiian organizations such as the Protect Kaho'olawe 'Ohana and Ka 'Ohana o Ka Lae, and national and international environmental organizations, including the Rainforest Action Network, Earth First, Sierra Club, Friends of the Earth, and Greenpeace International.

This chapter discusses the nature of this struggle and some of the actions undertaken by the Pele practitioners from 1983 through 1994, and highlights the major accomplishments. It illustrates how the development of alternative energy can potentially alter Native Hawaiian cultural beliefs and practices, because Native Hawaiians honor the elemental energy forces of nature as spiritual deities. Although the development of geothermal energy for transmission to O'ahu via an undersea cable was discredited and abandoned by 1994, a similar proposal reemerged in 2010. Hopefully this chapter can help to inform the reader about the dangers of developing geothermal energy and reinforce those who continue to believe in and honor Pele to persist in resisting these twenty-first-century proposals.

Pelehonuamea and the Fire Clan

Pelehonuamea is widely acknowledged as the principal Hawaiian deity to be continuously and publicly honored and worshipped despite the 'Ai Noa or abolition of the Kapu in 1819.[1] Kanaka 'Ōiwi have worshipped her throughout the nineteenth and twentieth centuries and into the twenty-first century. Her periodic dramatic, magnificent, and spectacular eruptions reinforced the faith of her followers, who persist in honoring her life force through offerings, chants, and hula.

The core practitioners of the Pelehonuamea religion are those who trace their genealogy to the deity and her family. Primarily, these are families who trace their lineage to the districts of Ka'ū and Puna on Hawai'i Island. Their ancestors came to Hawai'i and established themselves in these districts and very quickly affiliated themselves with Pelehonuamea as their deity because she was very visible for them and readily available. They established their genealogy with her and became part of her worship.

According to ethnographer Martha Beckwith, many heiau dedicated to the goddess Pelehonuamea were erected by traditional practitioners beside lava streams and at the edge of the crater.[2] The bodies of the dead were offered to the goddess in the belief that their spirits would live again with Pelehonuamea in a beautiful home beneath the burning pit, which is the goddess's material body. From there, they would go out as her messengers in bodies of flame to avenge any infringement of her kapu (sacred law) and to work her will in the land. Only those connected with the Pelehonuamea family have a right to such a burial.

Beckwith reported that, according to her sources, the worship of Pelehonuamea was not taught in the schools of the priesthood. Pelehonuamea's descendants alone worshipped her. Only actual relatives invoked her and became her keepers. Pelehonuamea names are given to children born into her family.

Pele Hula Tradition

One line of Pelehonuamea families is connected to the deity through the hula tradition. In the hula tradition, the saga of Pelehonuamea and Hi'iakaikapoliopele has varying levels of meaning. It conveys not only the history of the family, their accomplishments, their natures, and their powers but also the history of the origin and growth of hula.[3] In performing the hula, the dancer repeats the story and keeps the memory and knowledge of the deity, the family, and the hula alive.

One form of worship of Pelehonuamea is the composing of chants in honor of her eruptive phases. Chants that specifically focus on volcanic eruptions and provide a description of volcanic eruptive phases are called Hulihia chants. "Hulihia" means overturned, overthrown, and upheaval. These chants begin with this word. Whenever Pelehonuamea has erupted, chants have been written for her, describing the beauty of her manifestations and reaffirming her existence.[4]

Until the geothermal controversy, the performance of Pelehonuamea hula and chants were the only public way of honoring the deity. Most families and practitioners conducted their ceremonies in private.

Pele Dwells in Kīlauea

The principal place to honor Pelehonuamea is at her home at Kīlauea, but it is also a common practice to offer ho'okupu to Pelehonuamea when and where she is actively erupting. Park rangers at the Volcanoes National Park report observing numerous offerings being made or left at Halema'uma'u Crater, the central crater of Kīlauea volcano reputed in legend to be the home of Pelehonuamea. They have also observed people placing offerings on top of moving tongues of lava in lower Puna, or leaving them where they could watch a moving tongue of lava consume them and know that Pelehonuamea had accepted the gift.[5]

Every family has their own special area at Kīlauea to make their ho'okupu. Palikapuokamohoali'i Dedman, a Pelehonuamea descendant from Ka'ū and founder of the PDF, explained how as a young child his family would leave Ka'ū at night in the family's Model T and go up to the volcano to pay respect to Pelehonuamea. His grandmother would spend a few hours chanting softly, moving her lips and hands with no sound coming out. Her offering was herself and her family's continued connection to the deity. Throughout the years he observed that other families had their own special place that they went to praise and honor Pelehonuamea.[6]

Society-Wide Recognition of Pele

In addition to those who can trace their genealogy to Pelehonuamea or are trained in her hula, most people in Hawai'i, Hawaiian and non-Hawaiian alike, widely acknowledge and respect her as the premier Hawaiian deity of the volcano. People not of the Pelehonuamea clan also make offerings to the deity and perform her chants and dances.

When Pelehonuamea erupts, thousands of people are attracted and journey to the site. Pelehonuamea practitioners who visit usually take offerings. Harry Kim, administrator of the Hawai'i Civil Defense Agency from 1977 to 1993, testified in court proceedings on February 19, 1991, that in his years of working with the volcano in the Puna district he had observed that the chief deity acknowledged and honored by Hawaiians is Pelehonuamea. Families and individuals regularly requested permission to go beyond barricades to where the volcano was flowing to make offerings of lei, flowers, and gifts.

Anthropologist H. Arlo Nimmo in his article "Pele, Ancient Goddess of Contemporary Hawaii" recorded 108 newspaper and magazine articles that attribute the volcanic activity on Hawai'i to Pelehonuamea. In the conclusion to his article, Nimmo noted:

> Pele is a significant ingredient in the culture of the contemporary Hawaiian Islands. Belief in the volcano goddess is widely held by a broad stratum of society—doctors, professors, scientists, writers, housewives, engineers, hotel managers, and countless others. Children in Hawaii are weaned on Pele stories and throughout their lives they hear of encounters with the goddess, see evidence of her wrath on the Big Island, and observe her periodic portrayal in island arts. . . . It is important to emphasize that the traditional belief in Pele as goddess of the volcanoes and special deity to Hawaiians in the volcano area is unbroken from the past.[7]

In addition, grandparents and parents perpetuate the belief in Pele through stories that have been passed down through oral tradition.

The volcano as well as the volcanic matter in the area is widely respected as belonging to Pelehonuamea. According to park rangers, Hawai'i Volcanoes National Park receives a dozen to two dozen packages and letters a day addressed to Madame Pele. The packages usually contain pieces of rock or sand that were taken from the volcano during a visit. Having experienced mishaps or misfortunes, which they attributed to having removed the volcanic material, the individuals mail the material to the park rangers to return to the volcano.

Sacred Realm of Pele

At the time of the geothermal controversy, Pualani Kanaka'ole Kanahele, one of four daughters of Aunty Edith Kanaka'ole, was the Kumu Hula or hula master for Hālau O Kekuhi, together with her sister Nālani Kanaka'ole. Hālau O Kekuhi is widely recognized as the premier hālau or school of hula dedicated to the perpetuation of the Pele chants and hula. Kanahele documented the Pele beliefs, customs, and practices as part of the Native Hawaiian Ethnographic Study for the Hawai'i Geothermal Project Environmental Impact Study. In 1992, she published the study for the State Foundation on Culture and the Arts as *Ka Honua Ola: 'Eli'eli Kau Mai / The Living Earth: Descend, Deepen the Revelation.*[8]

According to Kanahele, the lava form and the energy that comes out of the earth are godlike. Pelehonuamea is the energy that produces the elements, which come out of the volcano, and she is the raw energy that produces those elements. Pelehonuamea takes the form of rocks, flowing lava, magma bursting through the earth giving new life, earthquakes, projectiles, fire, steam, and fireballs. According to the Pele traditions, Pelehonuamea had lived among people, and she was deified upon her passing by her living family of relatives.

As an opponent of geothermal energy development, Kanahele argues that traditional chants establish the tenet that whatever area of land is hot or still has steam coming out of it is sacred to the deity and should not be disturbed by human activities. According to Kanahele, the chant "Hulihia Ke Au, Ka Papa Honua O Kona Moku" recounts this principle, called the "law of the burning back." However, it is not only her back that is sacred; the entire section of the land that is hot is recognized as sacred. Kanahele also explained that the chant "E komo maloko o Halema'uma'u" more clearly defines this when the chanter, speaking in the first-person persona of the deity, declares that whatever is hot is sacred to her. In the chant, the first-person voice representing the deity invites the listener to go into Halema'uma'u and see her display and her movements. The listener is invited to view her inner parts and how she dances and moves. However, the listener is admonished not to take what belongs to the deity, and that whatever is hot belongs to the deity. In other words, if the earth is hot it still belongs to the goddess and if it belongs to her it is sacred. If the earth steams or if any other sign of heat still exists on the land or the water surrounding the land because of volcanic activities, then the effect of the law still exists. The heat of the earth is the realm of Pelehonuamea, which is sacred to her. It is not meant for human use and development.[9]

Geothermal Desecration and the Defense of Pelehonuamea

The Hawai'i Geothermal Project planned to extract the steam of the volcano from wells 7,000 to 8,000 feet deep to run turbines and generate electricity. This desecration of the realm of Pelehonuamea compelled Pele practitioners to take action and publicly proclaim their beliefs, customs, and practices in a prolonged political struggle to stop the project.

The primary concern of the practitioners was that the extraction of geothermal steam is tantamount to draining the goddess of her life force. They compared the steam within the volcano to the bloodstream of Pelehonuamea. Long-term extraction of the steam would deplete the goddess of her energy, such that she would no longer manifest to her followers and their future generations as steam flowing out of the volcano or as erupting molten lava. Pelehonuamea practitioners were also concerned that the goddess would move on from Hawai'i Island and that the culture as we know it would die.

The desecration of the goddess would also have a psychological impact upon those who believe and honor her. Injury to the goddess would also be an injury to the spirituality and dignity of Kanaka 'Ōiwi. The diminishing of her manifestations, her moving beyond Hawai'i Island, would exacerbate this cultural impact. Essentially, the development of geothermal energy is another form of cultural trauma that Kanaka 'Ōiwi have experienced throughout the centuries since Western contact in 1778 and will further contribute to the disparities of future generations.

In January 1983, Pelehonuamea began to erupt in Kahauale'a, right at the center of the Campbell Estate lands where the geothermal wells were to be drilled. Throughout 1983 and 1984, she built up Pu'u 'Ō'ō and eventually covered 15,000 acres of surrounding forest. The areas slated for geothermal wells were buried under fifteen feet of newly erupted lava. The eruption continued through the beginning of the twenty-first century, flowing out of subterranean tubes from the Kupaianaha lava lake. Kahauale'a was protected from geothermal development, but the geothermal developers and Campbell Estate began to work with the state of Hawai'i on an exchange of their lands at Kahauale'a for the state-owned Wao Kele O Puna Natural Area Reserve of the Puna Forest Reserve.

Pelehonuamea practitioners interpreted the continuing eruption as a hō'ailona or a supernatural sign of defiance by the deity against geothermal energy. Her active manifestation inspires them to be resolute and determined in their efforts to protect the deity and to shut down the development of geothermal energy.

By 1985, the practitioners realized that their individual efforts on behalf of Kanaka 'Ōiwi religious rights had made little headway and that they would need to build support from around and outside Hawai'i for what they knew would be a costly and lengthy struggle. In April 1985, Palikapuokamohoali'i Dedman, a Pelehonuamea descendant from Ka'ū and member of the Protect Kaho'olawe 'Ohana; Dr. Noa Emmett Aluli, a Native Hawaiian physician on Moloka'i and founder of the Protect Kaho'olawe 'Ohana; and Lehua Lopez, a Kanaka 'Ōiwi environmental activist, formed the PDF to stop the Hawai'i Geothermal Project.[10]

Dedman and Aluli met on the island of Kaho'olawe in 1981 and worked together to stop the bombing and all military use of the island. Along with other men of the Protect Kaho'olawe 'Ohana, they took on the responsibility of mo'olono (stewards of Lono). Their kuleana (responsibility) was to reestablish on Kaho'olawe the Makahiki harvest ceremonies honoring Lono, the god of agriculture. Aunty Edith Kanaka'ole and her daughter, Nālani Kanaka'ole, provided them with the chants, rituals, and protocols to conduct the ceremony.

Palikapuokamohoali'i is named after the cliff in Halema'uma'u that is sacred to Kamohoali'i, the shark god who is a brother of Pele. According to Dedman, when the experimental geothermal well was dug in Kapoho in 1976 and the experimental power plant came online in 1981, he and other practitioners felt that Pele would take care of it. However, as the drilling continued and the plans for generating electricity expanded into the rainforests of Kahauale'a, he and the other practitioners who eventually formed the PDF believed that they had to do something within their capacity to try to stop geothermal energy development.

Dedman explained that he had been conditioned by the Western practice that one could simply go to church on Sunday and ask the god to clean up damage done during the week. However, one night it came to him that he, as a Pele practitioner, bearing a Pele name, and tracing his genealogy to the deity, had to do something. He explained, "It comes upon you at night and grabs you by your neck and sits on your chest and tells you that, 'You go out, and you do it as a Hawaiian because you are intelligent, you got the ability, and this is Hawai'i.' You don't pass the buck or lay your rubbish down to your gods to clean it up. You clean it up yourself. You made it, you clean it."[11]

Noa Emmett Aluli credits Aunty Edith Kanaka'ole as someone who helped to solidify his belief in Pele. In her lifetime, Aunty Edith was a distinguished Hawaiian scholar and master of the chants and dance sacred to the volcano goddess. Aunty Edith founded Hālau O Kekuhi. She took Aluli to Halema'uma'u Crater and appealed to Pele to guide and protect the young men in their movement to protect Kaho'olawe. In an interview with Dr. Aluli in 1994, he spoke of this moment:

> I was arrested on Kaho'olawe. I had gone to UH-Hilo to give a talk to a whole auditorium of students about Kaho'olawe. Aunty Edith whisked me away and we drove to Halema'uma'u Crater. She gave me a haku lei. At the crater we offered the lei. It hung in the mist for several minutes before falling down. As it slowly fell into the crater I knew that Aunty Edith had opened the way. I knew that I could call upon Pele and think of Pele to help with Kaho'olawe. Pele was the last living god. The Pele religion has the responsibility to care for the land. Not just Pele's land. Not just Ka'ū. She protects the more frail areas. When people need her they can call upon her to help protect what is sacred on the other islands.[12]

Dedman and Aluli met Lehua Lopez, who lived in the volcano community of Glenwood, when she gave testimony against geothermal energy development at public hearings. As a member of the Sierra Club and the Volcano Community Association, Lopez was concerned about the impacts of geothermal energy development on the health and well-being of the residents who lived near Kahauale'a and upon the volcanic rainforest. As a Kanaka 'Ōiwi who honored Pelehonuamea, she saw the importance of forming the PDF to organize broad-based opposition within and beyond the Kanaka 'Ōiwi community.[13]

Pele Perspectives and Concerns

When they formed the PDF, Dedman, Aluli, and Lopez issued a statement of their beliefs, which essentially stated that from a religious standpoint, geothermal energy development is totally unacceptable to those who descend from Pele and who continue to honor, respect, and worship her. They believe that geothermal energy will have a fatal and irreversible impact on the deity. Moreover, Pele is singularly important to the survival of Hawaiian culture as a whole, because she is the only Hawaiian deity to be continuously honored and worshipped by Hawaiians despite two hundred years of contact with the West.

National Ad Campaign and Alliance with Environmental Groups

One of the unique and successful tactics utilized by the PDF was a national ad campaign designed in coordination with the San Francisco–based Public Media Center. In February 1988, they ran a full-page ad in the Sunday editions of the *New York Times, Los Angeles Times, Washington Post, San Francisco Examiner, Hilo Tribune, West Hawaii Today, Maui News, Garden Island,* and the *Honolulu Star-Bulletin* and *Advertiser.*[14]

The ad summarized the impact of geothermal energy development in twelve points. It also featured sidebars on the desecration of Pele from the Hawaiian religious viewpoint, a list of endangered species in the Wao Kele O Puna, and a cartoon image of an industrialized Hawai'i Island. Readers were asked to mail protest coupons to Hawai'i Governor Waihe'e, U.S. Senator Daniel Inouye, and Hawai'i County Mayor Dante Carpenter. It drew national attention to the geothermal project in Hawai'i as "Ugly, Toxic, Costly and Sacrilegious." Donations raised from the ad coupons covered the $35,000 cost of the ad. More importantly, it was a major breakthrough for the PDF in gaining the attention and support of national environmental groups.

A critical element in the struggle to stop geothermal development was the successful alliance of the PDF with national and international environmental groups concerned with saving rainforests throughout the world from destruction. These groups included the Rainforest Action Network, Greenpeace International, Friends of the Earth, Sierra Club, and the Sierra Club Legal Defense Fund, now called Earthjustice. The PDF was also able to raise major funding to sustain a long-term struggle from the San Francisco–based Tides Foundation, the Alexander Gerbode Foundation, and private contributors. This alliance educated national and international environmental groups about the valuable natural resources in the Wao Kele O Puna and the potential destruction of this largest expanse of tropical rainforest in the United States by geothermal energy development. Wao Kele O Puna became the focal point of an international movement to save rainforests throughout the world.

John Echohawk, executive director of Native American Rights Fund, later observed, "The struggle for this rainforest dramatically brings together Native cultural rights and environmental issues; the need to protect sacred, unspoiled areas for Native peoples gives Wao Kele O Puna national importance."[15]

Lawsuits

Throughout the struggle against geothermal energy, ten civil suits were filed and two hundred persons were arrested in political acts of peaceful civil disobedience. The team of attorneys included Hawai'i attorneys from the Native Hawaiian Legal Corporation, Yuklin Aluli, lawyers from the Native American Rights Fund, and New Mexico Native rights attorney Tom Luebben. The net effect of the lawsuits was to stop the large-scale development of geothermal energy; reaffirm and expand Native Hawaiian rights of access for religious, cultural, and subsistence purposes; and educate the general public about the threat of geothermal energy to Hawaiian culture, public health, the environment, and rate payers. The prominent lawsuits are discussed below.

RELIGIOUS RIGHTS SUIT

The legislature passed Act 296 in 1983 providing for the Board of Land and Natural Resources (BLNR) to designate geothermal resource subzones (GRS). The PDF opposed the GRS designation of Kahauale'a and the Middle East Rift Zone (MERZ). In a series of hearings and contested case hearings, the PDF argued that the designation of geothermal resource zones violated their religious beliefs, customs, and practices. Despite opposition, the BLNR designated 8,477 acres of the MERZ as a GRS. In 1987, the PDF appealed the ruling of the BLNR through the lawsuit *Dedman v. Board of Land and Natural Resources*.[16] The PDF claimed that the development of geothermal energy in the KMERZ would violate the right of Pelehonuamea practitioners to freely exercise their religion. The suit also claimed that the board failed to adequately consider the religious claims of Pelehonuamea practitioners in weighing criteria for establishing a GRS. The Hawai'i Supreme Court held that geothermal development of an area considered sacred by Native Hawaiian worshippers of the volcano fire goddess, Pele, was not an unconstitutional infringement of the right to free exercise of religion as guaranteed by the first amendment to the U.S. Constitution and article 1, section 4 of the Hawai'i Constitution. The PDF appealed this decision to the U.S. Supreme Court, but the court denied certiorari review of the case and the Hawai'i Supreme Court ruling prevailed. Despite the loss, this was the first civil suit to advocate for the free exercise of the religious beliefs, customs, and practices sacred to Pelehonuamea.

WAO KELE O PUNA LAND EXCHANGE SUIT

In October 1985, the BLNR approved the exchange of 25,641 acres of Campbell Estate's lands at Kahauale'a for 27,644 acres of the Puna Forest Reserve, including the Wao Kele O Puna Natural Area Reserve. This land exchange became the focal point of a lawsuit and local and national protests, as discussed below.

Campbell Estate had originally proposed to develop geothermal energy on their Kahauale'a lands located on the northern boundary of Hawai'i Volcanoes National Park. Pele's spectacular and protracted eruption on these lands began in January 1983 and continues through 2013. While this foiled plans to develop geothermal energy at Kahauale'a, it did not deter Campbell Estate. They successfully negotiated an exchange of their 25,807 acres of lava-charred lands for 27,785 acres of the pristine Wao Kele O Puna rainforest.

The lawsuit was first filed in the U.S. District Court for the District of Hawai'i as *Ulaleo v. Paty*.[17] Mr. Kaolelo Ulaleo was a Pele practitioner who lived in Ke Ahi a Laka and gathered traditional lā'au or medicinal plants in the Wao Kele O Puna. The federal court dismissed all of the claims. Ulaleo and the PDF appealed the dismissal. While the case was pending appeal, Ulaleo passed away. The PDF pursued the appeal on its own and also filed a new case, *Pele Defense Fund v. William Paty, et al.* in the Third Circuit Court in Hilo. The federal case was dismissed on appeal, but the case in the state court was pursued.

The PDF's attorneys argued that the land exchange constituted a breach of the trust created under section 5(f) of the Hawaii Admission Act and article 12, section 4 of the Hawai'i Constitution. The PDF also alleged that the exchange violated the constitutional right to due process. In addition, the PDF stated that the relinquishment of state lands on which Native Hawaiians customarily and traditionally exercised subsistence, cultural, and religious practices violated the rights guaranteed under the Hawai'i Constitution, article 12, section 7. The suit sought a declaration that the exchange was a breach of trust and a violation of law and asked for the return of the exchanged lands to the ceded public lands trust via a constructive trust or another land exchange. The Hawai'i Supreme Court upheld the circuit court ruling with regard to the land exchange and due process of law and dismissed the case against the BLNR. However, the claim alleging the violation of article 12, section 7 by Campbell Estate for the denial of access to the undeveloped areas of the Wao Kele O Puna was remanded to the Third Circuit Court for a trial.[18]

The Hawai'i Supreme Court ruling set a precedent with regard to Native Hawaiian rights by ruling, "If, as argued by PDF, the customary and traditional rights associated with tenancy in an ahupua'a extended beyond the boundaries of the ahupua'a, then article XII, § 7 protects those rights as well. The drafters of the constitutional amendment emphasized that all such rights were reaffirmed and that they did not intend for the provision to be narrowly construed. We therefore hold that native Hawaiian rights protected by article XII, § 7 may extend beyond the ahupua'a in which a native Hawaiian resides where such rights have been customarily and traditionally exercised in this manner." Previous to this ruling, customary and traditional rights associated with tenancy in an ahupua'a were limited to the ahupua'a in which the practitioner resided.

For the remand trial, the case was renamed *Pele Defense Fund v. the Estate of James Campbell*. The trial was held in August 1994, but the final Findings of Fact, Conclusions of Law, and Order was filed in August 2002. The order set an important precedent by acknowledging the following persons as having a right to enter the Wao Kele O Puna for customarily and traditionally exercised subsistence and cultural practices:

(a) Hawaiian subsistence or cultural practitioners who are descendants of the inhabitants of the Hawaiian Islands prior to 1778;
(b) Person or persons accompanying Hawaiian subsistence or cultural practitioners described in (a); or
(c) Persons related by blood, marriage or adoption to Hawaiian subsistence or cultural practitioners described in (a).[19]

While this suit originated with the PDF and cultural practitioners in the Puna district, it resulted in important precedents for all Kanaka 'Ōiwi.

HEALTH SUIT

In March 1986, the Hawaii Electric Light Company announced that it had signed an agreement with Puna Geothermal Venture to develop 25 megawatts in Kapoho by 1993, with 12.5 megawatts projected to go online by December 1989. The PDF allied with Kapoho residents to raise concerns about the pollution of the air in their neighborhood from emissions of hydrogen sulfide, lead, arsenic, mercury, and radon from the geothermal plant. In January 1990, PDF and five named individuals filed a suit, *Aluli v. Lewin*, against the Department of Health for permitting True Geothermal and Ormat/Puna Geothermal to drill twelve geothermal wells before ambient air quality standards for hydrogen sulfide (H2S) gas were adopted. The suit sought cessation of construction and of operations of geothermal wells in the Kīlauea Middle East Rift Zone. While the circuit court ruled against the PDF, the Hawai'i State Supreme Court reversed the ruling and required the Department of Health to adopt rules to uphold ambient air quality standards before issuing permits for geothermal drilling. In part, the ruling stated: "The director [of health] may require private persons or agencies or governmental agencies engaged or desiring to engage in operations which result or may result in air pollution to secure a permit prior to installation or operation or continued operation. The director shall refuse to issue the permit unless it appears that the operations would be in compliance with the rules of the department and the state ambient air quality standards."[20] Important precedents were set in the *Aluli v. Lewin* lawsuit. The Hawaiʻi State Department of Health was instructed to promulgate rules to establish and monitor standards for the emission of hydrogen sulfide into the air. It was also required to stop any action based on an authorization to construct permit that was issued prior to the promulgation of the rules and standards.

ENVIRONMENTAL IMPACT STATEMENT SUIT

In 1990, the Sierra Club Legal Defense Fund filed a civil suit on behalf of the Blue Ocean Preservation Society, Sierra Club, and Greenpeace Foundation against the U.S. Department of Energy. The lawsuit asked the court to issue an order to compel the preparation of a federal Environmental Impact Statement (EIS) for the Hawaiʻi Geothermal Energy Project and to enjoin any further federal involvement in the project until the EIS was completed. In an unexpected victory, the court ruled that the U.S. congressional appropriation and expenditure of $5 million for the development of geothermal energy in Hawaiʻi constituted a major federal action. In June 1991, the court ruled that the government was "enjoined from any further participation in the Project other than the preparation of the EIS itself, until such EIS is complete."[21]

Significantly, in recognition of the impacts of geothermal energy development on Native Hawaiians, a cultural impact study was required to be conducted as part of the federal EIS. This was the first cultural impact study ever conducted in Hawaiʻi. The authors of the Native Hawaiian Ethnographic Study for the Hawaiʻi Geothermal Project Environmental Impact Study—Jon Matsuoka, Davianna Pōmaika'i McGregor, Luciano Minerbi, Marion Kelly, and Pualani Kanaka'ole Kanahele—set a high standard for the conduct of cultural impact studies, which are now regularly conducted as part of EIS in Hawaiʻi.

WAO KELE O PUNA V. JOHN D. WAIHEE III

Following the above victory, the Sierra Club Legal Defense Fund filed a state EIS lawsuit on behalf of the Wao Kele O Puna, a Native Hawaiian rainforest, the PDF, and eleven national and local environmental and community groups. This case resulted in a settlement agreement in February 1995 that ended the participation in and any future pursuit of the Hawaiʻi Geothermal Project by the state of Hawaiʻi for the duration of the administration of Governor Benjamin Cayetano. In part, the settlement stated: "By their signing of this Agreement, State of Hawaiʻi Defendants, including Governor Benjamin J. Cayetano, hereby declare and commit, publicly and officially, that: (1) the Large-Scale Geothermal/Cable Project is terminated; and (2) in the future, they will not support, proceed with, participate in, or directly facilitate any geothermal project that is intended to explore the feasibility of or which will actually result in or contribute to the export of geothermal energy from the Island of Hawai'i." This settlement agreement terminated the large-scale geothermal energy development and cable project through the end of the Cayetano administration. It was not until 2010 that the state of Hawai'i again began to consider geothermal energy development and an undersea cable project.

Significantly, section 11 of the settlement agreement commits the state of Hawai'i to conduct an EIS in compliance with Hawai'i Revised Statutes (HRS) Chapter 343 before any large-scale geothermal or cable project can be initiated. It states: "State of Hawai'i Defendants agree that they will not undertake, initiate or instigate any acts or actions in furtherance of a Large-Scale Geothermal/Cable Project unless and until an environmental impact statement has been prepared in compliance with H.R.S. Chapter 343." This section applies beyond the Cayetano administration and requires compliance by the state of Hawai'i in any future pursuit of geothermal energy for export to neighbor islands or of an undersea energy cable.

Ceremonies and Peaceful Protest

In June 1989, despite all of the legal challenges of the PDF, the Wyoming-based True/Mid-Pacific Geothermal Venture had all of its permits. They started to bulldoze a road into the Wao Kele O Puna to establish a drilling site for geothermal resource exploration. True/Mid-Pacific Geothermal Venture was owned by a Wyoming family who made their fortune by wildcat drilling into the earth for oil.

This signaled the beginning of a phase of direct cultural actions on the part of the PDF and its supporters. The PDF insisted on taking a Kanaka 'Ōiwi cultural approach to the direct actions that we organized, standing on our rights of access to the Wao Kele O Puna for cultural, religious, and subsistence purposes. Environmental allies respected this approach and also organized their own independent actions of protest.

In 1989, the PDF worked with the Nā Maka O Ka 'Āina film crew to produce a documentary called *Pele's Appeal*. The video graphically documented the religious beliefs of the Pele practitioners, the customary and traditional activities in the Wao Kele O Puna, and the impacts of geothermal energy development on Puna residents. It was also an appeal for help from viewers to support the customary religious and gathering rights of Kanaka 'Ōiwi. The response was demonstrated in the large turnouts of practitioners and supporters to participate in religious ceremonies and processions in the Wao Kele O Puna.

On October 14, 1989, approximately 350 Pele practitioners and supporters entered the Wao Kele O Puna in a religious procession and built an ahu or rock altar on the site where the geothermal drilling would start. They made offerings and chanted traditional oli (chants) to heal the scar made by the bulldozers that had cleared a three-mile gravel

"Stop Corporate Crime." On October 14, 1989, approximately 350 Pele practitioners and supporters entered the Wao Kele O Puna in a religious procession led by Kumu Hula Dr. Pualani Kanakaʻole Kanahele, accompanied by kūpuna (elders) and members of her Hālau O Kekuhi. They built a religious altar on the site where the geothermal well would be drilled. Photograph © Franco Salmoiraghi.

road in the forest. The drilling rig went into the forest on October 28, 1989, and on the following day Pele practitioners again conducted a religious ceremony at the drilling site. The drilling at the site began in November 1989.

On March 25, 1990, 1,500 Pele practitioners and supporters attempted to enter the forest to conduct a religious ceremony at the drilling site. Referring to this ceremony, Randy Hayes of the Rainforest Action Network stated, "WKOP was the site of the largest single act of peaceful disobedience for a rainforest in the United States."[22] The Campbell Estate and True Geothermal Energy Co. called in the police. The PDF assured the landowner, representatives of the developer, and the police that the intent was to carry out a peaceful religious ceremony of healing. Nevertheless, the PDF was informed that the gate into the forest would be locked and that anyone who walked beyond that point would be arrested. A total of 141 practitioners and their supporters were arrested and charged with trespassing. A large contingent of attorneys from Hawaiʻi and Oʻahu were organized into a pro bono defense team by attorney Hayden Aluli. In the trials of the Pele practitioners, the testimonies they offered described how they felt an obligation

"Reclaim the Rainforest." Fifteen hundred Pele practitioners and supporters attempted to enter the Wao Kele O Puna on March 25, 1990, to conduct a religious ceremony of healing at the drilling site. Some 141 practitioners and supporters, including elders and young adults, were arrested and charged with trespassing. Photograph © Franco Salmoiraghi.

to go into the forest to conduct ceremonies to heal the forest and the wound made by the geothermal drilling into the deity Pele. The trials also provided additional insights into the Pele beliefs, customs, and practices related to the volcanic rainforest and to the Puna district.[23]

Punahele Lerma, a chanter and dancer of Hālau O Kekuhi, had conducted the healing ceremonies in Wao Kele O Puna in October 1989 and in March 1990. In his trial for trespass he described his sense of responsibility and obligation to protect the forest. The first chant, "Na 'Aumākua," was intended to link up each individual native person to the ancestral spirits of the area. The second offering was the reaffirmation of the migration chant of the Pele line starting from Tahiti to the northern islands of Hawai'i and to Puna. The protocol he performed was to begin the process of restoring a relationship of lōkahi or unity and harmony between the people and the forest and the deities of the forest.

Dr. Pualani Kanaka'ole Kanahele, Kumu Hula for Hālau O Kekuhi, provided expert witness testimony in the trial involving Mr. Lerma, one of the leading members of her hālau. She explained that if there was an act of disrespect to the deity, the burden of responsibility did not fall upon those who were unaware, but upon the tradition bearers, those who have the responsibility to maintain respect and reverence to that akua. She also explained that when there is desecration of the land, a lot of ceremonies are necessary to heal the land and restore the balance. There must be a lot of giving back, of caring and showing sincerity and connecting to the spirits of the ancestors. Those who were raised in traditions related to Pele and the forests of Pele, such as members of the PDF, feel a responsibility to try to protect the deity and her family and their manifestations.

Victory

In March 1994, True/Mid-Pacific Geothermal withdrew from the HGP following the ruling in favor of access rights. The company did not want to contend with providing access to Native Hawaiian practitioners and protecting the historic cultural sites in the forest, such as lava tubes with historic burials. Moreover, after miles of drilling for geothermal steam in five different directions, the resource still eluded them.

In response to their withdrawal, Dedman stated: "When True geothermal opened a wound in the volcanic rainforest to drill into Pele, we conducted rituals to heal that wound. Hundreds of people supported us, even risking arrest for trespass. Today, we see that our diligence and persistence made an impact. We, in the Pele Defense Fund, would like to thank everyone on the island of Hawai'i, the other neighbor islands, nationally, and internationally who supported us in carrying out our spiritual responsibility to protect Pele. Pele still dances on the Kilauea East Rift and we have a lifelong commitment to protect her."[24] If the PDF had not stood up and challenged the proposed HGP, the last large expanse of lowland tropical rainforest in Hawai'i would have been destroyed, forever. In turn, the traditional lifestyle of the Puna Hawaiians who hunt pigs and gather native plants for traditional medicine and hula would also have been negatively affected.

Soon after the withdrawal of True/Mid-Pacific, the Wao Kele O Puna lawsuit, as discussed above, resulted in a settlement terminating the participation in and promotion of the large-scale geothermal energy and cable project of the state of Hawai'i, through 2010.

Purchase of Wao Kele O Puna by the Office of Hawaiian Affairs

Despite the failure of the geothermal project in 1994, Campbell Estate held on to the Wao Kele O Puna lands. With the passing of the last heir, Campbell Estate underwent a process of dissolution, which then led to a decision in 2001 to sell the rainforest lands.

At that point, both U.S. senators Daniel Inouye and Daniel Akaka got involved and pressured the U.S. Forest Service to commit $3.35 million from its Legacy Program to purchase Wao Kele O Puna. In 2007 the Trust for Public Land, under their Tribal and Native Lands Program, raised the remainder of the $3.65 million asking price and signed the sacred forest over to the Office of Hawaiian Affairs (OHA), which funds the management of Wao Kele O Puna in partnership with the Hawai'i State Department of Land and Natural Resources.[25]

On August 27, 2007, OHA held a dedication ceremony. Haunani Apoliona, then chair of OHA's board of trustees, stated, "I congratulate the trustees of our OHA board for joining with our partners to seize this moment by demonstrating leadership that reminds our Native and our non-Native community that despite disagreements of the past, reconciliation and healing can occur one opportunity at a time." U.S. Senator Daniel K. Inouye apologized for his earlier support of drilling for geothermal energy in the forest. The Edith Kanaka'ole Foundation conducted ceremonies of healing and thanksgiving. Palikapu Dedman, president of the PDF, stated, "We took a stand for this land two decades ago in the courts and have never given up the fight to find a permanent way to protect this forest." He thanked all of the supporters of Pele and the rainforest.[26] Officially, OHA now holds title to Wao Kele O Puna for eventual transfer to a sovereign Native Hawaiian governing entity.

Ha'ina 'ia mai

New proposals for geothermal development began to be considered in 2010, as the price of oil made the risks and challenges of this unreliable, nonrenewable, volatile, and expensive source of energy profitable. In the words of the PDF, the geothermal resource is still "ugly, toxic, costly, and sacrilegious."

The chant "E komo maloko o Halema'uma'u," which declares that whatever is hot is sacred to Pele, is still applicable. The heat of the earth, the steam, and associated natural elements belong to the goddess Pele. It is sacred. This realm of Pele that is sacred to her is not for human exploration and development—and it is not for sale.

Ha'ina 'ia mai ana ka puana no Pelehonuamea a me Wao Kele O Puna. Tell the story of Pelehonuamea and the Wao Kele O Puna. It will continue to unfold for new generations. It is part of the legacy and the destiny as well as the kuleana responsibility of Nā Kanaka 'Ōiwi as long as Pele continues to dance at Kīlauea.

Pelehonuamea continues her 1983 eruption into the early twenty-first century. The defeat of geothermal energy and her continuing eruption continues to reinforce the living presence of Pelehonuamea. Indeed, Pelehonuamea dances at Kīlauea and rules in Hawai'i while her descendants and her followers continue to carry out a lifelong commitment to protect and honor her.

Notes

1. Upon the death of King Kamehameha I in 1819, those chiefs who were closely allied to him feared a rebellion from rival traditional chiefs. As a means of undermining their rivals, the Council of Chiefs, under the leadership of Mō'ī Kamehameha II, Kuhina Nui Ka'ahumanu, and High Chief Kalanimoku, instituted the 'Ai Noa or abolition of the chiefly religion under which rivals could claim rank, prestige, and position. Nevertheless, families continued to honor their ancestral deities; kahuna la'au lapa'au or herbal healers continued their healing practices using native Hawaiian plants and spiritual healing arts; burial caves and lava tubes continued to be cared for; hula and chants continued to be taught, in distinctly private ways. Among the deities who continued to be actively honored, worshipped, thought of, and respected, even to the present, was Pele and her family of deities. McGregor, *Nā Kua'āina.*

2. Beckwith, *Hawaiian Mythology*, 192.

3. Kanahele, *Ka Honua Ola*; Hālau O Kekuhi, *Holo Mai Pele* (film); Ho'omanawanui, "Pele's Appeal."

4. Kanahele, *Ka Honua Ola: 'Eli'eli Kau Mai.*

5. Russ Apple, former ranger at the Hawai'i Volcanoes National Park in the 1950s, and historian specializing on Hawai'i Island and Kīlauea in particular.

6. Matsuoka, McGregor, and Minerbi, "Native Hawaiian Ethnographic Study."

7. Nimmo, "Pele, Ancient Goddess of Contemporary Hawai'i."

8. Kanahele, *Ka Honua Ola:'Eli'eli Kau Mai.*

9. Matsuoka, McGregor, and Minerbi, "Native Hawaiian Ethnographic Study."

10. Dedman was president, Aluli was vice president, and Lopez was secretary-treasurer.

11. Matsuoka, McGregor, and Minerbi, "Native Hawaiian Ethnographic Study," 207.

12. Noa Emmett Aluli, interview by Davianna McGregor, March 21, 1994, for the geothermal cultural impact study.

13. Lopez was only involved initially. The volunteer staff included Hawaiian Homeland farmer and vocational rehab counselor Paul Takahiro; Ka'ū resident, secretary Margaret McGuire; and Dedman's cousin, bookkeeper Mark Luning.

14. E.g., *Honolulu Advertiser*, February 1, 1988, A5.

15. See Trust for Public Land, "Agreement Would Protect 25K Acres of HI Forest," September 13, 2005, http://www.tpl.org/news/press-releases/agreement-would-protect-25k-acres.html.

16. *Dedman v. Board of Land and Natural Resources*, 69 Haw. 740 P.2d 28 (1987).

17. *Ulaleo v. Paty*, 902 F .2d 1395, 1397 (9th Cir. 1990).

18. 73 Haw. 578, 837 P.2d 1247 (1992).

19. *Pele Defense Fund v. the Estate of James Campbell*, Civil No. 89-089 (Hilo) (Declaratory Judgment/Injunction) Findings of Fact and Conclusions of Law; Order.

20. *Aluli v. Lewin*, Civ. No. 89-358, 828 P.2d 802 (1992) No. 14815.

21. *Blue Ocean Preservation Society, et al. v. James D. Watkins, et al.*, Civ. No. 90-00407 DAE, 767 F.Supp.1518.

22. See Trust for Public Land, "Agreement Would Protect 25K Acres of HI Forest."

23. *State of Hawaii v. Davianna McGregor et al.*, Rep. No. D-27647.

24. Pele Defense Fund Press Statement, March 7, 1994.

25. For background and an analysis of the Crown lands, see Van Dyke, *Who Owns the Crown Lands of Hawai'i?*

26. See Trust for Public Land, "Agreement Would Protect 25K Acres of HI Forest."

CHAPTER 9. A Question of Wai

SEEKING JUSTICE THROUGH LAW FOR HAWAIʻI'S STREAMS AND COMMUNITIES

D. Kapuaʻala Sproat

When people visualize Maoli struggles for self-determination, they generally picture clashes over sacred spaces and land in particular. Yet other natural and cultural treasures besides land are often overlooked, except by those who have made the effort to protect and restore these resources their life's mission. One example is the pitched battle over Hawaiʻi's fresh water resources that continues on most of the inhabited Hawaiian Islands. In recent decades, this question of *wai*[1]—whether our fresh water is a public resource or private commodity—has been litigated on the islands of Oʻahu, Molokaʻi, and Maui. But this issue has far-reaching implications for Indigenous and other communities both within and beyond Hawaiʻi's shores. This question of wai raises other important issues as well: Why do government agencies allow private interests to subvert legal and cultural mandates, including protections for Kanaka Maoli resources and practices? Why has the kuleana (responsibility) of righting this wrong been consistently left to community groups, especially Maoli? And what does this reveal about the effectiveness of rights-based frameworks for underrepresented groups and Kanaka Maoli in particular?

Since time immemorial, fresh water has been the lifeblood of Hawaiʻi's Indigenous people, culture, and resources. Yet both the physical resource and the law of water in Hawaiʻi were appropriated by plantation barons for their private commercial profit despite significant harms to Kanaka Maoli and our environment. For generations now, Maoli communities have been working to regain control over our natural and cultural heritage, including fresh water, to rejuvenate both the resources themselves and the thriving culture and ways of life that depend on them. With the closure of all but one sugar plantation in Hawaiʻi, even greater impetus and opportunity are arising to return management of these resources to their rightful stewards. This chapter explores the quest to restore Hawaiʻi's streams and communities in the larger context of the Maoli renaissance and the pursuit of self-determination and cultural sovereignty.[2] In particular, it highlights both the promise and pitfalls of the legal process and other efforts to seek justice through law.

Water pours into a flooded lo'i in preparation for planting kalo, Waikāne, O'ahu, 1974.

From Wai to Kānāwai: The Flow of Water and the Law in Hawai'i

To understand Maoli struggles to reclaim water resources, and diverted streams in particular, one must internalize fresh water's foundational role as a physical and spiritual life force in Hawai'i nei.[3] "Kāko'o Ko'olau," a mele about the Ko'olau (Windward) side of O'ahu, describes how fresh water—whether in the form of rain, streams, or springs—permeates all aspects of life in our islands, including our natural resources and the cultural practices that they enable.

Kāko'o Ko'olau
A he lau ka makani
Kumu pali a'ea'e
I ka 'ohu a ka ua

ʻĀkoakoa mai
Lāhui paka ua
Mololani, ʻĀpuakea,
Kanikoʻokoʻo
Moʻomoʻo waʻawaʻa
Kahawai i ke kua
Huaʻina wai puna
Hoʻomoko i ka loʻi
Hoʻi mai Hāloa
Kuaʻana, Kualoa
Ola i ka wai ola
Ola ē kuaʻāina

Finding support in Koʻolau
With its abundance of cool, moist wind
The cliffs strive upward
Collecting and covered by the rain
Gathering together
Uniting the individual rain drops
From Mololani, to ʻĀpuakea,
to Kanikoʻokoʻo
The mountains are shaped by the water
Stream that comes from the source
Bubbling forth from the spring
Irrigating the loʻi
Hāloa returns
Elder sibling, long connection
Life through the life-giving water
Life for the people of the land[4]

As "Kākoʻo Koʻolau" illustrates, Kanaka Maoli have long understood the interconnection between Hawaiʻi's water resources and her people. Since the beginning of time in these islands, Kanaka Maoli recognized that lush forests and healthy watersheds gathered abundant rains to feed streams and seep deep into the earth to recharge drinking water supplies. We knew that fresh water flowing down streams and bubbling up as springs, especially in coastal areas, was vital to feed an estuary system where stream and marine life could thrive. Without this continuous connection between ma uka and ma kai (mountains and ocean), this cycle of life would cease. We understood that caring for our elder sibling Hāloa by cultivating kalo (taro) required an abundant supply of fresh water to flow through irrigated terraces and back into streams, and that this was necessary to sustain the larger community. "Ola i ka wai ola, ola ē kuaʻāina" (Life through the living waters, life to the people of the land). These fundamental truths were cultivated through generations of living symbiotically with our natural and cultural resources. Today, "Kākoʻo Koʻolau" epitomizes both the ongoing significance of wai to Kanaka Maoli and more recent efforts to infuse current management practices with ancestral knowledge.

As island people who rely on fresh water to survive, Kanaka Maoli developed an intimate and complex relationship with our resources. In addition to providing a foundation for Indigenous society, fresh water was also deified as a kinolau or physical embodiment of Kāne, one of the four principal akua (ancestors or gods) of the Maoli pantheon. As Handy, Handy, and Pukui explain, "Kāne—the word means 'male' and 'husband'—was the embodiment of male procreative energy in fresh water, flowing on or under the earth in springs, in streams and rivers, and falling as rain (and also as sunshine), which gives life to plants. . . . Regardless of all such distinctions, life-giving waters were sacred."[5] Given the physical and spiritual nature of our relationship to fresh water, Kanaka Maoli held these resources in trust for present and future generations.

Laws and customs preceding Western contact and continuing through Hawaiʻi's independent kingdom reflected these important principles, recognizing that water could not be owned in any sense, but instead must be proactively managed as a resource for generations to come.[6] For instance, the Kingdom of Hawaiʻi's first Western-style constitution in 1840 included strong public trust provisions, declaring that the land, along with its resources, "was not [the king's] private property. It belonged to the chiefs and the people in common, of whom [the king] was the head, and had the management of the landed property."[7] These values were strictly enforced by lunawai (water stewards) who managed the flow of water within and between ahupuaʻa to ensure, for example, that if water was taken from a stream for kalo cultivation, it was returned to the same stream so that downstream users had enough water to satisfy agricultural or other needs. These management practices respected the environment while also taking into account the competing needs of the larger community.

The institution of private property via the Māhele, subsequent consolidation of land ownership by foreign (largely American) interests, and growing recognition that Hawaiʻi's climate and year-round growing season made plantation agriculture, and especially sugar cane, a lucrative business, drove the foreign takeover of Maoli land. Water resources seemed destined to follow this history of dispossession.

To establish and expand plantations, massive irrigation systems were constructed to transport and use water in ways that nature never intended. Instead of utilizing water within ahupuaʻa and allowing geology and hydrology to maintain systems critical to ecological and cultural health, plantations radically redirected natural systems.[8] To satisfy their thirsty crops, sugar planters constructed ditches that diverted streams from wet, Windward (or Koʻolau), predominantly Maoli communities, to the drier Central and Leeward plains where sugar was cultivated. In addition, wells siphoned groundwater. This was often done with no consideration of or consultation with affected communities. Water was simply taken and streams and springs dried up. The impacted communities—both natural and human—were left to live, or die, with the consequences. This rapid change altered the natural environment while also inflicting significant physical and cultural harm on Kanaka Maoli, many of which remain unaddressed to this day. Within a short period, plantations and their irrigation systems took root on each of the major Hawaiian islands, fundamentally changing how and where water was used.

Sugar's rise to dominance rewrote the social contract. Plantations used public trust resources for private gain and, in turn, took over small towns, entire communities, and even whole islands. Plantations became the economy. This dominance pervaded the government as well. Management practices and even court decisions during the Hawaiian Kingdom and Territorial periods reflect increasingly Western notions of private property. Instead of continuing to respect water as a physical embodiment of Akua Kāne, and a fundamental requirement for a balanced and healthy environment, plantation interests commodified, diverted, and sold water with no regard for impacts on natural or cultural resources or Maoli or other affected communities.

Soon, conflicts over water ensued—first, between plantation interests and Kanaka Maoli, and later, between competing sugar plantations. A Commission of Private Ways and Water Rights was created in 1860 to address growing controversies over water.[9] Initially, a board of three commissioners (two Maoli and one foreigner) was appointed from each election district within the kingdom to resolve water disputes. Although both the boards and courts were directed "to declare and to protect these rights as they existed, under the ancient Hawaiian customs and regulations," the ability to respond to individual cases and reapportion water was constrained as decisions and practices reflected increasingly Western notions of ownership as opposed to management.[10] Amendments over the years substituted a single commissioner for the boards and changed the appeals process; after the overthrow, the boards' duties were transferred to circuit court judges in 1907 to maintain the new status quo. The Big Five sugar oligarchy's rise to power extended beyond water and resulted in almost complete control of the government.

After 1959, Hawaiʻi began to select its own judges as opposed to having them appointed in Washington, DC, which was the practice during the Territorial period. These locally appointed judges more fully understood Hawaiʻi's legal and cultural foundations, including Maoli custom and tradition.[11]

The case of *McBryde Sugar Company v. Robinson* (1973) brought the tensions over water as public resource or private property to a head.[12] Two sugar companies were embroiled in litigation over their respective rights to take water from the Hanapēpē River on Kaua'i. The Hawai'i Supreme Court, led by the late, great Chief Justice William S. Richardson (who was a Kanaka Maoli), took up the question of wai in *McBryde* and addressed the larger issue of water management in Hawai'i. The court clarified that although the parties in that case may have had rights to use water, they had no ownership interest in the water itself.[13] Those rights were never included when fee simple title was instituted in Hawai'i via the Māhele.[14] Instead, the court ruled that the sovereign—at that time, the court recognized the state of Hawai'i—holds all water in trust for the benefit of the larger community.[15] The sugar companies disagreed and filed multiple appeals with different courts. Ultimately, those appeals were resolved in favor of the state, upholding the determination that water resources are "reserved for the people of Hawai'i for their common good."[16]

Other cases followed, including *Robinson v. Ariyoshi* and *Reppun v. Board of Water Supply* (both decided in 1982), which respectively considered the public nature of Hawai'i's water resources and the rights of downstream kalo growers to maintain Maoli agricultural practices.[17] Despite the Hawai'i Supreme Court's consistent rulings upholding the public trust over Hawai'i's water resources, opposition by entrenched powers persisted. The black letter of the law carried moral and legal authority, which collided with the political power wielded by plantation and other aligned interests. Thus, more needed to be done to bring legal protections to life on the ground in the community.

Around the time that the *McBryde* litigation was unfolding, sugar plantations began to lose their economic dominance to tourism and the military. Concerned communities took this opportunity to reexamine the legal regime and to manage more proactively Hawai'i's water resources for the benefit of the larger community, rather than for the profit of a handful of private interests. The 1978 Hawai'i State Constitutional Convention (ConCon) proved critical in this regard. Thanks to the efforts of young Maoli and environmentally conscious representatives and staff, the 1978 ConCon crafted amendments that were later ratified by Hawai'i's voters to enshrine resource protection and Maoli rights as state constitutional mandates.

Article 11, section 1, of Hawai'i's constitution now declares, "For the benefit of present and future generations, the State and its political subdivisions shall conserve and protect Hawai'i's natural beauty and all natural resources, including land, water, air, minerals and energy sources, and shall promote the development and utilization of these resources in a manner consistent with their conservation and in furtherance of the self-sufficiency of the State." Article 11, section 7, affirms that "the State has an obligation to protect, control and regulate the use of Hawai'i's water resources for the benefit of its people."

Independent safeguards were also put in place for traditional and customary Maoli rights and practices. Article 12, section 7, "reaffirms and shall protect all rights, customarily and traditionally exercised for subsistence, cultural and religious purposes and possessed by ahupua'a tenants who are descendants of native Hawaiians who inhabited the Hawaiian Islands prior to 1778."

In 1987, the legislature fulfilled another provision of article 11, section 7, by enacting Hawai'i's Water Code, Hawai'i Revised Statutes chapter 174C. This established a new regime for water resource management that sought to balance resource protection with reasonable and beneficial use. The nearly ten-year travail to enact the code attests to the political wrangling that took place and the tension between Maoli, environmental, plantation, and other interests. With additional legal tools finally in place, the burden again fell on activists and kalo-roots groups to seek justice through law.

Ke Kalo Pa'a o Waiāhole

Community members and Maoli advocates in particular wasted no time utilizing these new tools in an attempt to redress the more than century-long theft of Hawai'i's life-giving waters. Although many different communities took action, the first major case seeking stream restoration under the new legal regime arose in Waiāhole, O'ahu.

Traditional mo'olelo (stories or history) about this area reference Ke Kalo Pa'a o Waiāhole, the hard taro of this region, which also metaphorically speaks to the character of the people from this district who are steadfast in the face of adversity.[18] Indeed, the spirit of Ke Kalo Pa'a o Waiāhole had persevered because for almost one hundred years the majority of the fresh water from Waiāhole and its neighboring communities of Waikāne, Hakipu'u, and Kahana had been drained to subsidize O'ahu Sugar's operations on the island's Central plain.

In 1916, a twenty-five-mile ditch system was completed that diverted water directly from area streams as well as from groundwater sources stored deep within the Ko'olau Mountains. The Waiāhole Ditch took almost 30 million gallons per day (mgd) from Windward streams and communities, through a three-mile tunnel in the Ko'olau Mountains, to O'ahu's Central plain. As Charlie Reppun, one of the key community organizers, recounted, "when the ditch was being constructed, community members raised concerns about whether there would be enough water left to support Windward people and agriculture. One concerned citizen wrote a letter to the governor in 1912, who responded that there was plenty of water with excess 'running to waste into the ocean' and there 'was no cause for worry.' Unfortunately, this couldn't have been further from the truth."[19] Ko'olau streams practically disappeared, with Waiāhole plummeting from 20 to 3 mgd and Waikāne dwindling from 7 to 1 mgd. Without sufficient ma uka to ma kai flow, kalo withered and native stream animals perished. The ditch system also took the major source of fresh water for the Kāne'ohe bay estuary and fishery, with similarly tragic results. Although a handful of families persevered, many Kānaka Maoli were forced to move from their traditional homelands. These degraded conditions persisted for nearly a century.

With the 1987 Water Code finally in place, community members petitioned the Commission on Water Resource Management to more actively manage Windward O'ahu's fresh water to rectify long-standing inequities, including the diversion of streams by the Waiāhole Ditch.[20] In 1993, O'ahu Sugar announced that it would be closing, sparking what became the epic battle over water in Hawai'i's recent history. A coalition of Kānaka Maoli, small family farmers, and environmentalists (Waiāhole-Waikāne Community Association, Hakipu'u 'Ohana, and Ka Lāhui Hawai'i—collectively the Windward Parties) in partnership with the public interest environmental litigation firm Earthjustice (formerly the Sierra Club Legal Defense Fund) petitioned to restore all of the diverted water to their streams and communities of origin.[21]

Over twenty other parties also coveted this water. Although several (such as Hawai'i's Thousand Friends and the Office of Hawaiian Affairs, OHA) supported stream restoration, the vast majority advocated draining Ko'olau streams in favor of agribusiness and urban development in Leeward O'ahu. These included some of the wealthiest and most powerful interests in Hawai'i at the time.[22] Even the agencies charged with safeguarding the public trust and Hawai'i's natural resources—such as the Department of Land and Natural Resources—followed suit, joining in the Leeward parties' request to maximize stream diversions. Yet Ke Kalo Pa'a o Waiāhole were undaunted, building capacity and other support throughout Hawai'i nei by holding concerts and using print media and public access television to share their story. Uncle Charlie explained, "Those who weren't crafting the legal strategy helped to raise the significant funds needed to litigate the case. Different events, including concerts, served a practical purpose of raising money as well as a therapeutic purpose of bringing our coalition and supporters together and keeping us united with a common vision. This was part and parcel of a broad campaign to educate the general public."[23]

In the midst of an extended contested case (or administrative trial), the Windward Parties exposed the ditch operator's dumping of water into dry Leeward gulches to avoid returning stream flows. A December 1994 mediated agreement between the parties limited the amount taken by the ditch system to 8 mgd, and immediately returned the balance to Ko'olau streams and communities pending the Water Commission's final decision in the case—this marked the first such restoration of water by plantation interests in Hawai'i's history. Kalā Hoe, a member of Hakipu'u 'Ohana, one of the community groups leading this struggle, noted, "This vindicated us because even those that were supposed to be working on our behalf—including government officials, business leaders, and Maoli kūpuna—used fear to try to keep us down and claimed that stream restoration was not just wrong, but impossible. This was also an opportunity to prove that we were not just capable, but could excel at managing our own resources, as our ancestors had for generations before us."[24]

After ten months of hearings, myriad witnesses, and many hundreds of exhibits from roughly twenty-five parties, in December 1997 the Water Commission issued a decision that divided the water between Koʻolau streams and Leeward users. Although similar to the 1994 mediated agreement, the commission's decision amending the interim instream flow standards provided greater assurance that the restored water would remain in Windward streams and communities for the long term.[25] Notably, it also awarded the Leeward Parties just about all the water they had sought. Although some flow was restored to Koʻolau streams, the process was riddled with political gamesmanship. For example, the Water Commission's attorney was fired after economic and government interests criticized the initial decision for returning too much water and the commission was left to finalize its order without legal counsel.[26] No one was completely satisfied with the commission's final decision, and three separate appeals were filed over the course of more than a decade.[27] Although more stream flow was returned, the Hawaiʻi Supreme Court played a crucial role in rising above the political wrangling that tainted the commission's decisions.

The Supreme Court's August 2000 *Waiāhole* decision built upon the foundation that Chief Justice Richardson initially elucidated in *McBryde* and that the constitution and Water Code later reaffirmed and clarified.[28] From a legal perspective, *Waiāhole* was hailed nationally for its public trust pronouncements. The court "adopt[ed] the public trust doctrine as a fundamental principle of constitutional law in Hawaiʻi" and recognized the Water Commission's responsibility to protect and restore these important resources.[29] "Under the public trust, the state has both the authority and duty to preserve the rights of present and future generations in the waters of the state."[30] To fulfill this kuleana, the court identified a handful of "public trust purposes" including environmental protection, Maoli rights and practices, appurtenant rights, and domestic water uses, all of which have presumptive priority over private commercial diversions.[31] After all, "any balancing between public and private purposes [must] begin with a presumption in favor of public use, access, and enjoyment."[32]

Many celebrated the 2000 Hawaiʻi Supreme Court decision as a major victory for Kanaka Maoli. In addition to affirming native rights, on remand the commission restored more water to Koʻolau streams and communities, enabling the rejuvenation of cultural practices—such as kalo cultivation—that had been precluded by the lack of fresh water. Through its decision, the Supreme Court began to redress some of the cultural harms imposed almost a century before and once again provided access to the natural resources necessary to improve social welfare conditions and more fully exercise cultural sovereignty. Legally, this decision created significant opportunities for Maoli and other underrepresented communities throughout Hawaiʻi nei to seek justice through law. Despite having been out-resourced financially and politically, the Windward Parties more than made up the difference in hard work, media savvy, and naʻau pono—that deep sense of justice that you can feel in your gut and that permeates and defines your whole being.

As Kalā explained, "the leaders of this struggle were visionaries. Our coalition understood the cultural, scientific, legal, and economic bases for restoring stream flow. But more importantly, we knew that to persevere over the long term, we had to build a movement by tapping into the thirst for pono. We worked to educate our lāhui so that folks realized that this was about more than restoring any one stream. This was about Hawaiʻi's future and whether Maoli communities would have the resources to continue to live in these islands and perpetuate our culture ā mau loa."[33]

The Hawaiʻi Supreme Court's 2000 decision in *Waiāhole* is over one hundred pages long and extraordinarily complex—impossible to summarize here. Suffice it to say, however, the decision affirmed the public nature of Hawaiʻi's water resources, clarified the burden of proof for those seeking stream restoration and diversions (including that diverters and the commission must demonstrate actual water uses and the absence of alternative sources or more efficient use), and recognized the value of free-flowing streams and Indigenous culture. Decades after the effort began, these rulings ultimately restored about 12 mgd to Koʻolau streams and permitted slightly less water (about 11.8 mgd) to Leeward users; they also vindicated the Windward Parties' legal, cultural, and moral case. Moreover, these decisions laid the groundwork for future efforts to more proactively manage water resources and restore diverted streams, hopefully making it easier for others to reclaim their resources and cultural heritage. The case went back and forth between the Water Commission and the appeals courts. Roughly twenty years after it began, more water has been returned to Koʻolau communities, but related issues are still being litigated. Interestingly enough, many of the Leeward interests who insisted on receiving Waiāhole water to stay in agriculture, such as Del Monte, Dole/Castle and Cooke, and Campbell Estate, have since closed Hawaiʻi operations or sold off land for urban development.

In many ways, communities throughout Hawaiʻi nei view Ke Kalo Paʻa o Waiāhole as a beacon of hope. This coalition strategically crafted and then tested the promise and possibility of justice through law, establishing that a group of culturally grounded farmers and practitioners could not just stand up against, but actually prevail in the face of overwhelming odds and adversity. This offers hope for the future, precisely as "Kākoʻo Koʻolau," which was composed after the return of water to Koʻolau streams, envisioned. "*Waiāhole* was like one of the first drops of rain; a sign of things to come. Hopefully, communities committed to these issues will continue to come together and unite so that many more of our streams will flow again from ma uka to ma kai."[34] Others have been inspired and empowered by this living legacy and have taken up the cause in their own communities.

Kaulana Nā Wai ʻEhā

Kaulana Nā Wai ʻEhā, famous are the four great waters—Waiheʻe, Waiehu, ʻĪao, and Waikapū streams—in the heart of central Maui. Traditional songs and stories about this area have lauded its abundant fresh water resources and the natural and cultural treasures that they enabled. Historically, Nā Wai ʻEhā boasted the largest contiguous area of wetland kalo cultivation in all of Hawaiʻi nei, with loʻi kalo stretching from Waikapū to Waiheʻe.[35] It also played a prominent role in the development of Maoli history in general as the site where Haumea planted the foundation of Maoli society in the waters of the Waiheʻe River.[36] A proliferation of heiau (places of worship), sizeable populations, and residences of aliʻi (leaders) also identified Nā Wai ʻEhā as a region of considerable political power and religious significance, much of which flowed from its wealth of fresh water.[37]

But like Waiāhole and too many other communities throughout Hawaiʻi nei, Nā Wai ʻEhā's once abundant water resources have been misappropriated by commercial interests. In 1862, a predecessor of what is now Wailuku Water Company LLC (WWC) began taking water from area streams to grow sugar cane.[38] By 1866, Maui residents including S. D. Hakuole began to document in Hawaiian-language newspapers the devastating impact of these diversions on their lives, land, and culture:

> AUWE! PAU WAILUKU I KA MAHIKO.—Ua hiki mai ma ko makou nei keena hana, he palapala na S. D. Hakuole, o Kula, Maui, e hai mai ana i ka pau loa o ka aina o Wailuku i ka mahiia i ke ko. A ke hai hou mai nei no ke hoomaloo ia nei na loi kanu kalo e na Haole, i wahi e kanu ai i ke ko. A ke makau nei oia, e pau ana ka ai ana o na kanaka oia wahi i ka ai ana i ka poi, a e ai wale aku ana no paha i ka balena oolea hoeha niho, a he paa palaoa mama e maona ole i na kanaka Hawaii. Oiai ua maa na kanaka i ka ai i ka poi.
>
> DESPAIR! WAILUKU IS BEING DESTROYED BY THE SUGAR PLANTATION.—A letter by S. D. Hakuole, of Kula, Maui arrived at our office, he was declaring that the land of Wailuku is being lost due to the cultivation of sugarcane. Furthermore, he states the current condition of once cultivated taro patches being dried up by the foreigners, where they are now planting sugarcane. Also, he fears that Hawaiians of that place will no longer be able to eat poi and that there will only be hard crackers which hurt the teeth when eaten, a cracker to snack on but it does not satisfy the hunger of the Hawaiian people. Although, let it be known that the Hawaiian people were accustomed to eating poi.[39]

Despite these and other concerns, ditch systems and diversions were built and expanded until they completely drained Nā Wai 'Ehā streams of their physical resources and spiritual mana (power). Plantation interests took 60–70 mgd each day for roughly 150 years, with heartbreaking costs. For example, in 2010, the Water Commission acknowledged that "cultural experts and community witnesses provided uncontroverted testimony regarding limitations on Native Hawaiians' ability to exercise traditional and customary rights and practices in the greater Nā Wai 'Ehā area due to the lack of freshwater flowing in Nā Wai 'Ehā's streams and into the nearshore marine waters."[40] Rose Marie Ho'oululāhui Lindsey Duey, a kupa'āina (native to a particular place) from 'Īao Valley and the heart and soul of that community's effort to restore stream flow, articulated the issue best: "For me, this struggle goes to the very essence of what it means to be Kanaka Maoli. When they take our fresh water, they are taking away a life force that feeds our culture and who we are as a people. This is genocide, plain and simple."[41]

Although streams continue to be diverted as they were during the height of sugar production, only one plantation—Hawaiian Commercial and Sugar Company Inc. (HC&S)—still cultivates cane, though on only a fraction of the original acreage. Also, WWC, which had previously used the majority of the diverted water for sugar, sold off its farmlands but kept its water diversion and delivery system and reorganized into a company selling stream water to private developers and the county of Maui. For many in these communities, the diversions were *hewa* (wrong) 150 years ago and have only gotten more offensive.

In 2004, Hui o Nā Wai 'Ehā and Maui Tomorrow Foundation Inc. (collectively the Community Groups), in partnership with Earthjustice, took on this question of wai and filed a petition with Hawai'i's Water Commission to restore continuous ma uka to ma kai flow to Nā Wai 'Ehā's streams and communities.[42] Like the Windward Parties in *Waiāhole*, despite having the apparent letter of the law on their side, Nā Wai 'Ehā's Community Groups faced an uphill battle against HC&S and its parent company, Alexander and Baldwin. In addition to being the last sugar plantation in Hawai'i, HC&S also happened to be the largest employer in Maui County and quickly and repeatedly demonstrated that it would miss no opportunity to exploit that leverage. Other parties to the suit included OHA, who strongly supported stream restoration for cultural and environmental purposes and was a significant player in the case; Maui County, who used some diverted flows from 'Īao Stream for municipal water supplies and also pumped groundwater from wells that are recharged by the streams; and WWC, which was selling diverted flows to developers and other customers, including a local golf course.

Initial efforts by the Water Commission to investigate the issues and determine what HC&S and WWC (collectively, the companies) were doing with all of the excess water they were taking proved futile;[43] the companies were in no rush to provide data or otherwise cooperate. After all, the status quo allowed them to continue to hoard the

"Ho'ākoakoa!" Nā Wai 'Ehā's water warriors gather in solidarity on the diversion grate of 'Īao Stream (traditionally Wailuku River), still fighting for water to flow with justice from ma uka to ma kai. 2011.

water they had been appropriating for over a century. After failed mediation and years of delay, the Community Groups pressed for a contested case hearing, which proved to be the only way to extract necessary information from the companies.

After eleven months of hearings, water commissioner and hearings officer Lawrence Miike had accepted testimony from seventy-seven witnesses and received over six hundred exhibits into evidence. After carefully considering all of that information, he relied on the Hawai'i Supreme Court's *Waiāhole* decisions and issued an April 2009 draft order that would have restored 34.5 mgd, or about half of the water diverted from Nā Wai 'Ehā's streams and communities each day. Miike determined that it was necessary to return water to each of the four streams, with a minimum flow ma kai of the major diversions of 14 mgd in Waihe'e, 2.2 mgd in North Waiehu, 1.3 mgd in South Waiehu, 13 mgd in 'Īao, and a provisional release of 4 mgd in Waikapū.[44]

Once the hearings officer issued his draft decision, HC&S circumvented the substantive issues by playing its economic card, repeatedly threatening to shut down the

"No be lōlō, restore stream flow!" The dry ʻĪao streambed, 2011.

plantation—and lay off roughly eight hundred employees—if it did not receive the bulk of the water it was taking. Union-led workers from HC&S joined the fray, claiming, "Our jobs are at stake, our very livelihood and the ability to support our families."[45] Executives of HC&S were just as shameless. During the final oral argument in the case, HC&S avoided addressing the actual case through its attorney and instead had its newly appointed manager, who was also Alexander and Baldwin's chief financial officer, essentially present the commission with an ultimatum: "We do not believe that there was any intent to shutdown HC&S through the proposed [stream restoration]. Nonetheless, that will be the end result if you adopt the recommended decision."[46]

The full commission responded with a dramatic about-face, returning even less water to Nā Wai ʻEhā than HC&S had advocated. In its June 2010 Final Decision and Order, a majority of the Water Commission bowed to political pressure and gave back a mere 12.5 mgd to Waiheʻe and Waiehu, only two of Nā Wai ʻEhā's four streams. This left ʻĪao and Waikapū completely diverted. "If you look at our stream, it's nothing but skeletal remains. They could have just as well reached into my chest and pulled my heart out," Aunty Rose explained.[47]

Miike—the only commissioner to have participated in all of the hearings and reviewed all of the evidence—sharply dissented, charging that "by its decision, the majority has failed in its duties under the Constitution and the State Water Code as trustee of the state's public water resources."[48] Miike also recognized the commission's duty to Kanaka Maoli, including the fact that "restoration of Nā Wai ʻEhā waters is of importance for traditional and customary purposes" and that "in addition to its duty to resolve uncertainty in favor of resource protection, the Commission has a duty to take feasible actions to reasonably protect native Hawaiian rights."[49] Although 12.5 mgd was ultimately restored to Nā Wai ʻEhā, the Community Groups felt strongly that the majority's rationale was grounded in politics—not justice or law. Hōkūao Pellegrino, a kalo farmer from Waikapū and one of the founding members of Hui o Nā Wai ʻEhā, recounted, "This should have been a no-brainer. We had the better legal case, but at the end of the day, it didn't matter. The full commission went with what it knew best: politics, power, big money, and the 'old boy' mentality. Their final decision was based on nothing that was legally relevant or what justice required."[50]

The Community Groups and OHA appealed, and in August 2012 the Hawaiʻi Supreme Court reversed the Water Commission's June 2010 decision: "Where the Commission's decision making does not display 'a level of openness, diligence, and foresight commensurate with the high priority these [public trust] rights command under the laws of our state,' the decision cannot stand."[51] The court first ruled that it had jurisdiction, or the ability to review the case. In doing so it rejected the commission's and diverters' attempts to bar the courtroom doors. The decision acknowledged that "the ramifications of an erroneous [instream flow decision] could offend the public trust, and [are] simply too important to deprive the parties of due process and judicial review."[52]

The court then invalidated the commission's decision in several respects. First, the court "concluded that the Commission did not discharge its duty with regard to the feasibility of protecting native Hawaiian rights" by failing to consider impacts on Kanaka Maoli traditional and customary practices, including kalo cultivation and gathering stream animals and other resources for cultural, spiritual, and religious purposes.[53] Second, the court reversed the commission's refusal to restore any water to ʻĪao and Waikapū streams.[54] Third, the court ruled that the commission erred when it arbitrarily reduced the amount of water that HC&S must use from Well 7, a brackish water well that was the primary source for its Nā Wai ʻEhā fields.[55] Based on these and other reasons, the Hawaiʻi Supreme Court sent the case back to the Water Commission for proper consideration of its legal duties to the public trust and to Kanaka Maoli.[56]

Isaac Moriwake, Earthjustice's lead attorney for the Community Groups, opined: "The Supreme Court's decision again brings home the need to move beyond the nineteenth-century mind-set of rivers and streams as plantation plumbing and to respect the twenty-first-century kuleana of the public trust. In the darkest hours of its troubled history, the commission allied with the plantation diverters in trying to block the public's and Native Hawaiians' access to justice. We're relieved that the court upheld the rule of law so that justice—and Nā Wai ʻEhā—can flow for present and future generations."[57]

The Community Groups in *Nā Wai ʻEhā* strategically modeled their case after *Waiāhole*, and the proceedings before the commission were eerily similar in disappointing ways. For example, political influences continued to be brazen. Like *Waiāhole*, a draft decision was issued in *Nā Wai ʻEhā* but later changed in response to political pressure. Similar to *Waiāhole*, some water was returned to the streams, but the final decision was appealed to the Hawaiʻi Supreme Court. Like *Waiāhole*, the Community

"Ho'i ka wai!" Water finally returns to the Waihe'e River and community after years of hard work. Hui o Nā Wai 'Ehā and Maui Tomorrow supporters, 2011.

Groups ultimately prevailed before the high court. Only time will tell whether the Water Commission will respect the court's decision or continue with politics as usual. As Hōkūao reflected, "Ultimately, this is about doing the right thing. It is as simple and as complex as that."[58]

The Community Groups' experience in *Nā Wai 'Ehā* exposed the lingering impacts of colonialism and plantation influences in particular. Even after years and generations of hard work to craft a seemingly sympathetic legal regime, and over a decade of litigation in *Waiāhole* to clarify any misperceptions, the Community Groups watched political forces subvert the legal process before the commission to maintain control of public resources for their private profit. This calls into question the effectiveness of rights-based frameworks for underrepresented groups and Kanaka Maoli in particular. As Aunty Rose shared, "We are beyond frustrated and it doesn't help to be taunted by other Hawaiians who say that we lose more by having faith in the law. By using the law, we got water returned to our streams and we will continue working at it until others get theirs. But I can see why people take matters into their own hands when they are driven to the extreme. I am hoping and praying for a positive outcome before the Water Commission in the next round of hearings because I know what will happen if things aren't rectified."[59]

As *Waiāhole* and other struggles have demonstrated, the legal process holds tremendous promise to provide justice through law and can help to level the playing field when politics are in play, as in the Supreme Court's decisions in *Waiāhole* and *Nā Wai ʻEhā*. But this path is protracted and expensive, and the results are by no means guaranteed. Maoli advocates and activists cannot blindly rely on the legal process to mete out justice. As Isaac explained, "Communities must appreciate the strategies and costs of engaging in a Western legal framework, where political powers including those from Hawaiʻi's colonial legacy have not hesitated to put a thumb on the scale of justice when necessary to maintain private control of public resources and deny public trust beneficiaries relief."[60] If *Waiāhole* and *Nā Wai ʻEhā* are any indicators, most agency decision makers have been content to go along, and the kuleana of righting this wrong has been left to affected community groups to seek redress via court appeals.

Larger Lessons Revealed by the Question of Wai

In both *Waiāhole* and *Nā Wai ʻEhā*, the question of wai uncovered a generational struggle to return the natural and cultural resources necessary for our Indigenous culture and people to thrive. At the same time, it imparted larger lessons for Kanaka Maoli and other communities seeking to understand the strategies and politics of movements for life, land, and sovereignty.

In both *Waiāhole* and *Nā Wai ʻEhā*, Kānaka Maoli and our allies elected to strategically engage the state of Hawaiʻi's legal system and political arena as an expression of ea. Many view ea as independence or life. It surely means both. But ea also means to rise, to go up against, or to raise up, as a person who was bowed down.[61] On both Maui and Oʻahu, Maoli communities used the legal system to rise up and challenge the plantation legacy of fresh water as the private property of sugar barons and their friends.

This was a difficult decision and not without cost. Many Maoli reject colonial vestiges and exhibit patriotism by refusing to acknowledge that the United States or state of Hawaiʻi have any legal or other authority in our islands. In *Waiāhole* and *Nā Wai ʻEhā*, Kānaka Maoli and our allies took a different tack, first working to craft the legal regime for water resource management in Hawaiʻi, then strategically deploying that system to reclaim fresh water resources that had been appropriated for over a century. While some community organizers welcomed the Water Code and Commission itself as avenues for justice through law, others remained skeptical.

Although ultimately successful, these hard-fought struggles came with a hefty price tag. Despite the legal precedent Chief Justice Richardson established in *McBryde* and other decisions, and even the new regime of Hawai'i's constitution and Water Code, the *Waiāhole* and *Nā Wai 'Ehā* communities bore the burden of giving meaning to laws and facts in a way that would be respected and would eventually prevail within a Western legal system.

In addition to shouldering financial and political costs, *Waiāhole* and *Nā Wai 'Ehā* community leaders also faced criticism within their own communities—as skeptics questioned their patriotism for seeking stream restoration through a state system. Although victories before Hawai'i's high court and the restoration of stream flow in both *Waiāhole* and *Nā Wai 'Ehā* muted most detractors, more work remains both within and beyond our Maoli community if we hope to finally resolve this question of wai.

Despite the challenges posed by the politics of water in Hawai'i, at bottom, this story is about courage, hard work, and the power of community. Specifically, how a handful of committed and strategic organizers and their attorneys were able to build a movement to seek justice through law for Hawai'i's streams and communities by engaging the legal system as an expression of ea.

Ultimately, the answer to the fundamental question of wai is ea. Thus far, one response has been communities rising up to reclaim cultural resources and sovereignty through the existing legal framework they helped to engineer. We look forward to the day that the question of wai will be resolved by the agencies and courts of our own lāhui. Until then, the best answer is for communities to continue to ea, whatever form that takes:

E iho ana o luna
E pi'i ana o lalo
E hui ana nā moku
E kū ana ka paia

The high which is above shall be brought down
That which is below shall be lifted up
The islands shall be united
The walls shall stand upright.[62]

Notes

1. In this context, "wai" refers to fresh water. See Pukui and Elbert, *Hawaiian Dictionary*, 377.

2. Cultural sovereignty describes Indigenous people's efforts to "exercise their own norms and values in structuring their collective futures." Rebecca Tsosie, "Engaging the Spirit of Racial Healing within Critical Race Theory," 21, 45.

3. Some text from this section previously appeared in Sproat, "Water."

4. Kelikokauaikekai Hoe, "Kāko'o Ko'olau," unpublished mele, or song, on file with the author, 2001.

5. Handy, Handy, and Pukui, *Native Planters in Old Hawai'i*, 64 (kahakō added).

6. *McBryde Sugar Co. v. Robinson*, 54 Haw. 174, 185–87, 504 P.2d 1330, 1338–39 (1973) (*McBryde*).

7. Nā Kumukānāwai O Ka Makahiki 1839 A Me Ka 1840 (the 1839 and 1840 constitutions).

8. An ahupua'a is a traditional Maoli land division that can roughly approximate a watershed, but is part of a larger resource management system that is both defined and inspired by Hawai'i's Indigenous culture. Beamer, "Living Ahupua'a."

9. Perry, "Hawaiian Water Rights," 96–99.

10. Perry, "Hawaiian Water Rights," 97–98.

11. Richardson, *Ka Lama Kū O Ka No'eau*, vi–vii; Hawaii Revised Statute section 1-1 (2009).

12. *McBryde*, 54 Haw. at 185–87, 504 P.2d at 1338–39.

13. *McBryde*, at 186–87, 504 P.2d at 1338–39.

14. *McBryde*, at 186–87, 504 P.2d at 1338–39.

15. *McBryde*, at 186, 504 P.2d at 1338.

16. *McBryde*, at 186, 504 P.2d at 1338.

17. *Robinson v. Ariyoshi*, 65 Haw. 641, 658 P.2d 287 (1982); *Reppun v. Bd. of Water Supply*, 65 Haw. 531, 656 P.2d 57 (1982).

18. Sterling and Summers, *Sites of O'ahu*, 189.

19. Charles Reppun, personal communication with the author, February 23, 2012.

20. The 1992 designation of Windward O'ahu as a groundwater management area imposed additional restrictions on water use in the area.

21. Other law firms also assisted the Windward Coalition including Paul, Johnson, Park and Niles and the Native Hawaiian Legal Corporation.

22. These interests included OHA, Kamehameha Schools (then called Bishop Estate), James Campbell Estate, Robinson Estate, Amfac and its subsidiary the Waiāhole Irrigation Company, City and County of Honolulu Board of Water Supply, Hawai'i Department of Agriculture, Hawai'i Department of Hawaiian Home Lands, the Hawai'i Department of Land and Natural Resources, and the U.S. Navy. *In re Waiāhole Combined Contested Case*, 94 Haw. 97, 110–11, 9 P.3d 409, 422–23 (2000) (*Waiāhole*).

23. Reppun, personal communication, February 23, 2012.

24. Kahikūkalā Hoe, Hakipu'u 'Ohana, personal communication with the author, February 15, 2012.

25. An interim instream flow standard (IIFS) is the amount of water required to be in a stream, or a particular reach of a stream, to protect beneficial instream uses such as fish and wildlife habitats and traditional and customary Maoli rights and practices. See Hawai'i Revised Statute section 174C-3 (2009). Because an IIFS is only temporary, it may be amended. Currently, the only IIFSs based on some scientific information have been established as a result of litigation (as in *Waiāhole*); the Water Commission has not yet adopted any permanent instream flow standards.

26. For more information regarding the political gamesmanship in the *Waiāhole* case, see Sproat and Moriwake, "Ke Kalo Pa'a o Waiāhole," 247, 277–279.

27. For more information on the Hawai'i Supreme Court decisions, review them directly. *Waiāhole*, 94 Haw. 97, 9 P.3d 409; *In re Waiāhole Combined Contested Case*, 105 Haw. 1, 93 P.3d 643 (2004).

28. *Waiāhole*, 94 Haw. 97, 9 P.3d 409.

29. *Waiāhole*, at 132, 9 P.3d at 444.

30. *Waiāhole*, at 141, 9 P.3d at 453.

31. *Waiāhole*, at 136–37, n.34, 9 P.3d at 448–449, n.34. The Hawai'i Supreme Court later ruled that

reservations of water for the Department of Hawaiian Home Lands are also public trust purposes. See *In re Wai'ola O Moloka'i, Inc.*, 103 Hawai'i 401, 431, 83 P.3d 664, 694 (2004).

32. *Waiāhole*, 94 Haw. at 142, 9 P.3d at 454.

33. Kahikūkalā Hoe, personal communication, February 15, 2012.

34. Kahikūkalā Hoe, personal communication, February 15, 2012.

35. See Handy, Handy, and Pukui, *Native Planters in Old Hawai'i*, 496–497.

36. Tengan, *Report on the Archival, Historical and Archaeological Resources of Nā Wai 'Ehā*, 1–7.

37. Tengan, *Report on the Archival, Historical and Archaeological Resources of Nā Wai 'Ehā*, 7–13.

38. Commission on Water Resource Management, "Findings of Fact, Conclusions of Law, and Decision and Order."

39. Tengan, *Report on the Archival, Historical and Archaeological Resources of Nā Wai 'Ehā*, 16 (translation of the January 13, 1866, article by Hōkūao Pellegrino).

40. Commission on Water Resource Management, "Findings of Fact," 10.

41. Rose Marie Ho'oululāhui Lindsey Duey, Hui o Nā Wai 'Ehā, interview by the author, February 19, 2012.

42. For more information on this issue, see Earthjustice, "Restore Stream Flow"; Earthjustice, *Kaulana Nā Wai 'Ehā*.

43. Despite the Water Commission's problems, it at least provided an avenue for Kanaka Maoli to seek justice through law.

44. "Hearings Officer's Proposed Findings of Fact, Conclusions of Law, and Decision and Order," Contested Case Hearing, No. CCH-MA06-01, April 9, 2009, 187–89, http://www.state.hi.us/dlnr/cwrm/; Earthjustice, "Restore Stream Flow."

45. Hamilton, "Na Wai Eha."

46. "Transcript of Closing Argument," Contested Case Hearing, No. CCH-MA06-01, October 15, 2009. In *Nā Wai 'Ehā* and other contested cases before the Water Commission, the practice has been to issue a proposed decision, allow the parties to file written exceptions to that decision, hold oral argument on the parties' exceptions to the proposed decision, then issue a final decision and order. See, e.g., Commission on Water Resource Management, "Findings of Fact," 7–8.

47. Duey, interview, February 19, 2012.

48. "Dissenting Opinion of the Hearings Officer/Commissioner Lawrence H. Miike," Contested Case Hearing, No. CCH-MA06-01, June 10, 2010, http://www.state.hi.us/dlnr/cwrm/.

49. "Dissenting Opinion of the Hearings Officer."

50. Hōkūao Pellegrino, Hui o Nā Wai 'Ehā, personal communication with the author, February 22, 2012.

51. *In re 'Īao Ground Water Management Area High-Level Source Water Use Permit Applications*, 128 Hawai'i 228, 262, 287 P.3d 129, 163 (2012) ("*Nā Wai 'Ehā*"). Justice Acoba filed a concurring opinion that separately addressed jurisdiction and the Water Commission's failure to comply with the mandates of *Waiāhole I*.

52. *Nā Wai 'Ehā*, at 244, 287 P.4d at 145.

53. *Nā Wai 'Ehā*, at 249, 287 P.2d at 150.

54. *Nā Wai 'Ehā*, at 249–251, 287 P.2d at 150–152.

55. *Nā Wai 'Ehā*, at 258–261, 287 P.2d at 159–162.

56. The Hawai'i Supreme Court's decision in *Nā Wai 'Ehā* also addressed other issues that are not included here; for more information, review the decision itself: 128 Hawai'i 228, 287 P.3d 129 (2012).

57. Isaac H. Moriwake, Earthjustice, personal communication with the author, November 18, 2012.

58. Hōkūao Pellegrino, personal communication, November 20, 2012.

59. Duey, personal communication, November 20, 2012.

60. Moriwake, personal communication, November 18, 2012.

61. See Pukui and Elbert, *Hawaiian Dictionary*, 36; Andrews, *A Dictionary of the Hawaiian Language*, 51.

62. Malo, *Hawaiian Antiquities*, 154 (oli adapted by the Kanaka'ole 'Ohana; kahakō and 'okina added).

CHAPTER 10. Aia i Hea ka Wai a Kāne? (Where Indeed Is the Water of Kāne?)

EXAMINING THE EAST MAUI WATER BATTLE

Pauahi Ho'okano

> Water is fundamental for life and health. The human right to water is indispensable for leading a healthy life in human dignity. It is a pre-requisite to the realization of all other human rights.
>
> —UNITED NATIONS COMMITTEE ON ECONOMIC, CULTURAL AND SOCIAL RIGHTS, *ENVIRONMENT NEWS SERVICE*, NOVEMBER 27, 2002

In the Ko'olau district of East Maui, the lush vegetation and windward showers are a backdrop to one of the largest water cases in Hawai'i's history. Fifty-seven bridges cross what were once perennial streams on the way to Hāna. These streams and rivers are now mostly dry, leaving farmers, residents, and tourists alike wondering, "What happened to the water?"

Water is power, and the power structure reflects who has access to the water. Those who have control of and a say in the management and usage of water, which is critical to the development of Maui's future, are by definition power brokers. Hence, although the taro farmer's preferential rights to the water are a part of the constitution of the state of Hawai'i, those rights have meant little under the so-called democratic system. It is only through the taro farmers' unrelenting, unrepentant, and decades-long struggle, and continued commitment to insist on and demand enforcement of these laws, in the face of overwhelming odds, that these laws have the potential to bear fruit or, more specifically, taro.

In the uplands of Maui's Ko'olau mountain range, faced with a history of theft and oppression, the actions of a group of brave taro farmers struck a powerful blow against the private water corporation, East Maui Irrigation (EMI), openly challenging their authority over the water in a way that was never done before. Their story, along with the history behind it, is the focus of this chapter.

Traditional Hawaiian Water Usage and Practices

Traditionally, water was considered sacred, and its use was regimented and regulated by the konohiki, or chief, of an ahupua'a, a pie-shaped wedge of land that ran from

Lynn Scott and Pauahi Ho'okano at Honopou, Maui, March 26, 2011.

the mountains down to the ocean. Although the konohiki was a manager of the commodity, that by no means translated into ownership of it. They were caretakers of the property of the gods or, more specifically in the case of water, of Kāne, the god of fresh water. Water, wai in Hawaiian, was so important culturally that the word for wealth is waiwai, a duplication of the word for water. In traditional Hawaiian society, water was taken from streams and put into 'auwai, irrigation ditches, that fed taro patches. The water then went from patch to patch, and upon exiting the final taro patch in the system, the water was returned to the stream so that stream flow was uninterrupted and allowed to flow into the ocean. At any point where the water was taken to go into the 'auwai, one could not completely dewater the river, as Hawaiians depended and used the flora and fauna that resided in the rivers themselves for food and medicines. In addition to this, it was the konohiki's responsibility to organize the maka'āinana (commoner, a person who does not have the genealogy or rank of an ali'i, royalty) in order to clear and maintain the 'auwai system to keep the water flowing freely. If a farmer or maka'āinana does not participate in the maintenance of the water system, the konohiki had the authority to cut off the water supply.

East Maui Irrigation: A Little Bit of History

In 1876, Samuel Thomas Alexander and Henry Perrine Baldwin entered into an agreement with the Hawaiian Kingdom to lease lands on the east side of Maui and to build a system of irrigation ditches and tunnels to transport water to Maui's central plain to irrigate sugarcane fields. The areas that Alexander and Baldwin leased were broken into four areas in East Maui: Nāhiku, Wailuanui-Ke'anae, Honomanu, and Huelo-Honopou. The original lease agreement was signed by Alexander, Baldwin (founders of what is known today as Alexander and Baldwin, Inc. [A&B], a company with much influence and power in Hawai'i), and Kalākaua, the sovereign of Hawai'i. Thus began the diversion of water from East Maui to its central plain, part of the beginning of a shift across the Hawaiian archipelago to privatization of water as a source of profit. An elaborate system of ditches was built as a result of the unrestricted access of A&B's subsidiary, EMI, to Crown lands for over one hundred years.

Today, EMI is one of the largest privately owned water corporations in the United States. The system of ditches and tunnels diverts an average of 160 million gallons of water per day, with a maximum capacity of approximately 450 million gallons of water per day. To put this into perspective, 160 million gallons per day is the average domestic use of water on the island of O'ahu, the most densely populated island in the chain with almost one million residents (about 80 percent of the state population).

The Maka'āinana Fighting for Their Water: It's Not New

Historically, the residents of East Maui protested this diversion with foresight of the potential of things to come. In 1881, a group of community members from the Ke'anae and Wailuanui area sent a formal letter of protest regarding the diversion of water to the commissioners of Crown Lands, the Hon. H. A. P. Carter and the Hon. J. S. Walker:

> Nonoi aku nei makou i ko olua oluolu. Aole e lilo kekahi pono wai o na aina lei alii, oia mai Honomanu, Keanae, Wailua i ka ona Miliona (Claus Spreckels) . . . No ka mea, ina e lilo kekahi pono wai o na aina lei alii i hoike ia maluna, alaila, e pilikia ana na makaainana o ke *'lii* e noho ana ma ua mau aina ala . . . Oiai ua ike ia na hana a ka ona miliona i ka wai o na aina i hala, a no keia pilikia i ike ia oia ka makou e noi aku nei ua oki loa ke kii ana mai i ka wai o na aina i hoikeia maluna.
>
> We request your kindness. Do not allow any water rights of the *Crown Lands* of Honomanu, Ke'anae, and Wailua to be lost to the millionaire Claus Spreckels . . . because, if any of the water rights on the *Crown Lands* that were mentioned above were lost, then, the subjects of the king living on said lands will be in [great] trouble. We already know what the millionaire has done with the water

> on other lands, and as a result of this previous trouble, which is well known, this is the reason why we are sending our plea to immediately stop taking water of the lands that were named above. (Translation by the author, emphasis original)[1]

The "ona Miliona" mentioned in the letter, Claus Spreckels, was born in Germany and came to Hawai'i from California to take advantage of the newest version of the Reciprocity Treaty of 1876, which allowed sugar to be imported to America duty free and guaranteed American markets for sugar from Hawai'i. He was the original owner of Hawaiian Commercial and Sugar Company (HC&S). He eventually returned to San Francisco, and sold HC&S to A&B.

The pleas did not stop there. In February 1902, "the majority of Nahiku homesteaders petitioned the Territorial governor to stop a proposed auction of a water lease governing the government water . . . which they believed would detrimentally affect the homestead program intitiated by the [illegal] Republic of Hawai'i."[2] As a result, the lease that was given to H. P. Baldwin included a condition not to interfere "with the vested interests in water of land-owners in Ke'anae or Wailuanui or of other third parties," meaning that only surplus water was to be taken from the streams, as in storm events, and normal stream flow would be uninterrupted.

In 1985, the Ke'anae-Wailuanui Community Association submitted comments regarding proposed interim instream flow standards. An interim instream flow standard was being decided upon at that time by the Commission on Water Resource Management (CWRM), which falls under the Board of Land and Natural Resources (BLNR). According to the Community Association's submitted comments, "Nothing in the Water Code requires the grandfathering in of all these diversions. The licenses to take the water from East Maui are currently being renewed from month to month, so that at the present no claim can be made that there is a vested interest in the taking of all this water. You (the Commission on Water Resource Management) are mandated by the new code to 'protect, enhance, and reestablish, where practicable, beneficial instream uses of water.'"

The foresight of the kūpuna over one hundred years ago was justified. Over time, the surplus water that EMI took became the water that was left for the farmers below the diversion, meaning that when a severe storm hits East Maui and overflows the ditch system in the uplands, this is the water that touches the streams and rivers. When there is no storm, the streams and rivers are a trickle at best, leaving taro farmers to rely on any existing springs that support water uses downstream of EMI's diversions. In 1987, the Ke'anae-Wailuanui Community Association said, "Right now, the flow immediately below the ditch on all streams is zero almost all the time. . . . Beneficial in-stream uses will be completely sacrificed. The assurances in the [Water] Code of the continuation of our Hawaiian gathering rights are meaningless if there is nothing in the streams to gather." One year later, in 1988, Uncle Harry Kunihi Mitchell intimated that "if the commission supported grandfathering all existing diversions, native Hawaiians will be forced to go to court to assert their aboriginal water rights."[3]

In order for taro in wetland lo'i to thrive, it needs cool, flowing water. Otherwise, pythium rot, also known as pocket rot, sets in, stunting or destroying the crop. Traditionally, Wailuanui and Ke'anae were major producers of taro. Up until the 1980s, the crop was exported out of the region to poi millers on Maui and O'ahu. Now, water in Wailuanui Valley is so scarce that it can barely sustain the farmers in the area. In 2006, and for the first time in the history of Wailuanui Valley, a part of the 'auwai, the system of ditches that irrigate the taro patches, went dry. These 'auwai are fed by the waterfall of Waikani, so named for the thundering sound that could be heard from the volume of water as it went over the waterfall. However, because of EMI's diversions on Wailuanui Stream, not enough water filled the pond below Waikani to allow for intake into the 'auwai that services the eastern portion of Wailuanui Valley.

One farmer in particular, Norman "Bush" Martin Jr., was unable to pull taro from his patch to send to Aloha Poi for over two months. Bush was raised in Wailuanui Valley, and he learned taro farming from his grandfather, Sammy Akina. His patches became dry and cracked, resulting in a potential loss of his crop, the income from which supplements what he makes at his day job. Taro is propagated by vegetative means, meaning that cuttings from one crop, when harvested, become the seed for the next planting. Therefore, when one crop is lost, future crops are lost as well, which was a pressing issue for Bush, as well as other taro farmers who were affected by the total lack of water coming from Waikani.

The long-term leases held by A&B began to expire. The Ke'anae license expired in 1972, the Nāhiku lease in 1977, Huelo in 1982, and Honomanu in 1986. At that time, A&B, through its subsidiary EMI, applied for another long-term, thirty-year lease. It was at this time that the original group of four taro farmers and residents of the region contested their lease, including Meiling Akuna, Harry Kunihi Mitchell, Marvin Hanchett-Ching, and Elaine Needham. The first challenge to the lease was in 1987 with Native Hawaiian Legal Corporation (NHLC) as their counsel. "We spent two years trying to determine whether or not Hawaiians had a right to challenge Alexander and Baldwin's application for a permit," stated Alan Murakami, a lawyer from NHLC, working on the case. After winning that right in court, the state and EMI attempted to negotiate a thirty-year lease to satisfy the concerns of these farmers. Ultimately, the state abandoned that effort, resorting instead to routinely annually renewing month-to-month revocable permits for the same lease areas. At the time, the state and EMI blamed farmers for failing to clean their 'auwai as the cause of the lack of water in Wailuanui Valley.

Over time, Uncle Harry Kunihi Mitchell, a key individual farmer who was working on the case, passed away. The communities of the Wailuanui-Ke'anae region banded

The Wendt ʻohana farm in Wailuanui, 2011. Ed Wendt cuts taro by the bucket. Ryan Wendt works in the taro patch. Lance Wendt at far left, and Māhealani Wendt at far right.

together again to create a 501(c)3 nonprofit organization called Nā Moku Aupuni o Koʻolau Hui, with Ed Wendt as the founding president. Edward Wendt comes from Wailuanui, where his family, like most of the Hawaiian families in the region, practiced taro farming since time immemorial. When he founded Nā Moku Aupuni o Koʻolau Hui, it was with the intention to protect and preserve the traditional taro farming lifestyle and practices, through water restoration, along with educating future generations of people who come from that region through scholarships.

This organization joined with Honopou kūpuna Beatrice Kekahuna and Marjorie Wallett to formally challenge the BLNR's practice of alternately issuing annual permits to A&B and EMI. In this process, they demanded a contested case hearing before the board, which operates like a court trial where the farmers can demand answers to pertinent questions from the BLNR and EMI, and make legal arguments in support of their constitutional rights to water.

Not only did Nā Moku file a petition challenging the BLNR lease of the water in Wailuanui Valley to EMI, it also petitioned the state agency in charge of managing and regulating water uses to restore and increase stream flow in twenty-seven major streams and rivers in East Maui, so taro farming, gathering, and fishing could once again flourish as it had for generations of Hawaiians. This petition went before the CWRM. The CWRM is mandated by Hawaiʻi state law to act upon a petition within six months to one year from the original filing. By 2008, seven years later, no action had been taken by the commission.

In 2007, partial relief was granted by the BLNR. It ordered the release of 6 million gallons per day average into Waiokamilo Stream, along with similar releases for another seven of the twenty-seven streams under petition. In order to enforce its order, the BLNR directed its Department of Land and Natural Resources (DLNR) staff to appoint a stream monitor. The original stream monitor was a DLNR land agent for the island of Maui, Daniel Ornellas. His duties were to monitor compliance by EMI and to make recommendations to address the needs of taro farmers, if their needs were not met. Barely

Steven Ho'okano (left) in Wailuanui, 2011.

a month after Ornellas began, the DLNR replaced him, over Nā Moku's objection, with another DLNR staff member who is based on O'ahu, Morris Atta, who Nā Moku feared would not be accessible to East Maui farmers. The justification for this action was the heavy workload of Maui's land agent.

The farmers of East Maui grew more and more frustrated as the delay of the site inspection wore on. Every year in April, Hāna hosts the Taro Fest. As it happened, 'Onipa'a Nā Hui Kalo, a Hawai'i-wide consortium of taro farmers under the auspices of Queen Lili'uokalani Children's Center, was having its quarterly meeting on Maui in order to be able to attend Taro Fest. To call attention to the delay, Steven Ho'okano organized the farmers and had a sign-waving campaign at Honomanu to bring awareness to the public about the contested case hearing that was happening on Maui. The general public would see, on their way to the Taro Fest no less, the actions that the state of Hawai'i was taking to delay and deny justice for the taro farmers of the area. This was one of several campaigns that Steven Ho'okano organized to get the word out regarding the water case, and to bring to light the plight of the taro farmers in East Maui at the hands of EMI.

After a year's delay, the O'ahu-based Atta had been largely inaccessible and conducted no site visits to determine the taro farmers' needs in Honopou and Wailuanui valleys, leading to intense frustration at the lack of any diligence toward implementing the 2007 BLNR order. Finally responding to farmers' complaints, on July 9, Morris Atta, Daniel Ornellas, Alan Murakami from the NHLC, and a group of approximately fifteen taro farmers from Wailuanui Valley participated in a site inspection of EMI's ditch system in the ma uka (upland) portions of Wailuanui Valley. East Maui Irrigation officials chose not to participate. A week earlier, Atta had witnessed the cracked taro lo'i of Wailuanui taro farmers due to the lack of water from Wailuanui Stream. When I spoke with Atta that day, as we were looking at the dry taro patches, he said, "I can't know for sure that the diversions are causing this situation," to which I replied, "By the same token, you cannot say that it is NOT the diversions that are causing this."

As the inspection began, the simmering frustration of the taro farmers affected by the lack of water in their 'auwai boiled over when Atta refused to take prompt action to ensure the restoration of flow to Wailuanui Stream. Although Atta had over a year to become familiar with the hydrology and the rivers of East Maui, particularly the streams in question, East and West Wailuanui streams, he claimed ignorance. In addition, Atta did not bring the correct maps to the site inspection, saying that he did not want to open any diversions until he was sure that the stream and the diversion were indeed the correct ones that if released would flow into Waikani waterfall and Wailua River. He refused to acknowledge the expertise and geographical knowledge of the taro farmers about their own water source.

The stream monitor insisted that he did not have the authority to release the water into the stream from the diversion, in spite of the fact that within the court order itself, the duties of the water monitor were "to insure compliance with its Order, to resolve if possible all complaints regarding stream flows by any of the parties to this proceeding, to be available in the field upon written notice to all affected parties, to make recommendations to the Board for disputes which cannot be resolved by the Monitor, to verify if the Board's understanding of the facts in this case are correct, to periodically record the temperature of the streams in question; and to make recommendation for further decreases of diversions should it appear such action is necessary to control pythium rot."[4] In an unplanned action, fueled by frustration with the appointed stream monitor and impatience with the state, the farmer directly affected by the diversion of Waikani waterfall in Wailuanui Stream, Bush Martin, decided to exercise his inherent right to the water by lifting the gates diverting water into EMI's Ko'olau ditch, realizing that he had no other option to protect his taro crop and to follow his ancient traditions. Bush took this action independent from Nā Moku 'Aupuni o Ko'olau Hui. He was a Kanaka farmer asserting his rights as a traditional user of the water that was being diverted. He was not acting as a member of the nonprofit organization which as a group is being represented by NHLC.

Immediately upon the release of water by the affected taro farmers, Morris Atta terminated the official site inspection. Both NHLC and the official representative of Nā Moku 'Aupuni o Ko'olau Hui, Ed Wendt, departed at the same time as the state official in order to preserve their formal case in court and in the BLNR. In the early hours of the next morning, the water released from the diversion, far upland of Waikani waterfall, reached the ditches and lo'i in the eastern portion of Wailuanui Valley.

Relief finally arrived to the dry, cracked, and parched lo'i. Bush's courageous action was historic not only because of the assertion of his rights as a Native Hawaiian taro farmer, but because a release of water from stream diversions had never happened while active sugar production was occurring on any island in the Hawaiian archipelago. East Maui Irrigation closed the sluice gate in the late afternoon on July 10.

Initially, Kimo Day and Steven Ho'okano, taro farmers again acting as individuals, without the support of Nā Moku, went ma uka to ensure that EMI kept the gate open so water would keep flowing. Kimo Day is a Vietnam veteran: "I went and fought for my country. Now I come home and now I gotta fight for my water."[5] Kimo is a strong, independent, and very intense man. He has no fear and will do whatever it takes to fight for his rights. This is what led him to walk ma uka every day for weeks at a time until eventually the workers from EMI stopped closing the gate, which further solidified the taro farmers' claim to the water. Steven Ho'okano, who accompanied Kimo Day, stated, "There comes a time to fight and now is that time."[6] He is a younger taro farmer who has followed in the footsteps of his father and his grandparents before that, stretching back through the corridor of time. It was the actions of these individual farmers that pushed the case further and faster than any court proceedings. They were willing, because of their passion for, and relationship to, taro and traditional wetland farming methods, to put their freedom and indeed their lives on the line, not just for what they believed in but for what was pono. Within the Hawai'i state constitution, the ultimate right to water is conferred upon Native Hawaiian practitioners, including taro farmers.

While these actions were occurring, Atta and other DLNR officials refused to engage Nā Moku in dialogue about how to deal with the situation of individual farmers asserting their rights, despite repeated requests by Nā Moku to meet and confer about it. To add insult to injury, the water monitor, Morris Atta, filed a faulty report misrepresenting the events that took place on the mountain during the site inspection. He was ordered to file a report by the BLNR by August 22, 2008, in order for the BLNR to review it thoroughly by the time of the motion to enforce hearing on October 1, 2008. Atta did not file his report until the day of the hearing. The report was supposed to include (as stated in the court order):

1. The monitor's efforts in fulfilling the interim order to date
2. What have been the results of its efforts
3. What monitoring programs are currently in place
4. What difficulties the monitor has faced in implementing the board's order

5. The cost to date of implementing the board's order
6. What future plans it has to continue to fulfill the interim order

Not only did Atta fail to address most of these issues in his late report, he stated, "As the discussion continued several Nā Moku members or their invitees began holding up their machetes and making confrontational statements such as 'Who going stop us if we open the diversion? You?' (While indicating the Water Monitor) . . . As the sound of the water rushing in the stream increased, the members and invitees of Nā Moku began to display increasingly hostile behavior and making loud statements that all of the stream diversions should be forcibly opened."[7] This statement is completely and totally false. I was present at the site inspection, and no one had machetes. What many people held in their hands, including my husband Steven, were video cameras. There is quite a bit of footage regarding what happened at the diversion that day, and it is plain to see that there were no machetes, that the taro farmers were not threatening Morris Atta in any way, and the only shouting was from my husband, who simply said, "How easy!" How easy indeed after waiting, in this case, over fifteen months for some sort of relief from the chronic drought caused by EMI's diversions, and, in the bigger picture, after waiting over one hundred years for relief from the oppression and genocidal practices of EMI, which, by taking all of the water, made it extremely difficult to farm and at times prevented a group of Native Hawaiians from practicing taro farming in the traditional way handed down to them by their kūpuna. No arrests were made in the matter, as no crime or terroristic threats occurred.

The footage taken by my husband, Steven Hoʻokano, has been aired many times on the public access station on Maui, called Akakū. Because of his media savvy, including the footage, the sign-waving campaign in Honomanu, and several public service announcements on Akakū, the stories of the farmers were becoming a part of the public consciousness. People were not looking only at the EMI, HC&S, and A&B side of the story.

The Water Commission

The commissioners on the CWRM are appointed by the governor, the president of the Senate, and the speaker of the House. Additionally, the chair of the BLNR is the chair of the CWRM, as determined by state law. The director of health is also a voting member. Seven members in total make up the commission. Throughout the period when the water diversions were being contested, the commissioners included Meredith Ching, who was also vice president of government and community relations for A&B. Other very influential people have a stake in A&B. Michael Chun, former headmaster of the Kamehameha Schools Kapālama Campus, is also on the board of directors for A&B.

Few realize that the law also prescribes that one member of the CWRM "shall have substantial experience or expertise in traditional Hawaiian water resource management techniques and in traditional Hawaiian riparian usage." For the past four years, Lawrence Miike has served as that designated member. His only familiarity with this requirement has been as a member of the CWRM for eight years as the Department of Health director under the Cayetano administration and as an author of a book on water rights. Many would argue that the governor has failed to comply with this mandate, but the Democratic Senate, which has the power to reject appointments, has not challenged the governor on this appointment, or other appointments like it, resulting in a commission weighted heavily in favor of corporate, commercial interests and continuing the disfavored practice of large-scale water diversions.

The taro farmers in this region have endured and continue to endure great hardships, because of the continued legal and political maneuvering of A&B to ensure "business as usual." The obstructions created by A&B in addition to the unresponsiveness, lack of legal enforcement, and lethargy of state agencies have only added to the frustration of taro farmers. It has taken more than ten years, in this latest version of the East Maui water struggle, to obtain agency action via formal petitions required for restoration of twenty-seven streams. When the agency has been forced to take action by the courts, those actions have been generally unsatisfactory, as they have resulted in only partial restoration to the streams, leaving the taro farmers with a continued lack of adequate water.

In December 2009, the CWRM voted against its own staff's recommendations for partial restoration of the remaining nineteen streams still under petition. These recommendations incorporated the results of lengthy scientific studies by the DLNR's Division of Aquatic Resources, studies that were originally requested by the commission itself. The commission further denied the farmers any right to contest its decision. As a result, more legal challenges are underway and will more than likely be as difficult and lengthy as earlier court challenges.

Because of these lengthy and protracted court battles, it is important for Kanaka Maoli farmers to remember to assert their rights in the real world. Not only does this punctuate the legal battles taking place in the courts, but actively asserting your rights sheds light on the injustice that is happening to the Kanaka Maoli. In the end, our rights are undeniable, and the actions taken by the brave taro farmers in the face of the Goliath corporation EMI, as well as the state of Hawai'i, serve as a reminder that we have rights to our 'āina, our resources.

Unfortunately, as of this writing, the East Maui taro farmers have been unable to get timely help from the state to follow the simple law that gives them the right to water, as stated in article 12, section 7, of the Hawai'i state constitution: "The State reaffirms and shall protect all rights, customarily and traditionally exercised for subsistence, cultural and religious purposes and possessed by ahupua'a tenants who are descendants of native Hawaiians who inhabited the Hawaiian Islands prior to 1778, subject to the right of the State to regulate such rights." Perhaps it is the state that needs to be regulated.

Notes

1. Letter from Ke'anae and Wailuanui residents to the commissioners of the Crown Lands, 1881, Hawaii State Archives.

2. This quote was taken from comments provided by the Ke'anae-Wailuanui Community Association to the State Commission of Water Resource Management.

3. Kubota, "Panel Hears Pleas to Both Increase, Reduce Water Flow."

4. Board of Land and Natural Resources, State of Hawai'i, Court order regarding the Contested Case Hearing for East Maui diversions: "In the matter of a contested case regarding water licenses at Honomanu, Keanae, Nahiku, and Huelo, Maui," DLNR, file MA-01-05.

5. Olaf Beretta and Steven Ho'okano, "EMI OUT," video-recording shown on AKAKU public access television station.

6. "EMI OUT."

7. Morris Atta, "Status Report of Water Monitor in the Matter of the Contested Case Hearing Regarding Water Licenses at Honomanu, Keanae Nahiku and Huelo, Maui," DLNR, file MA-01-05, filed October 1, 2008.

“Kahi i hoʻomaka ai ʻo Wailuku.” Here at the poʻowai, the headwaters of Wailuku that comprise a significant portion of Hawaiʻi Island’s freshwater, reside the akua of the Mauna. They continue to breathe life, despite the irreverent imposition upon their realm. Photograph used with permission of the photographer, Kalei Nuʻuhiwa.

Portrait. Mauna a Wākea

HĀNAU KA MAUNA, THE PIKO OF OUR EA

Leon No'eau Peralto

O hanau ka Mauna a Wakea,
O puu a'e ka mauna a Wakea.
O Wakea ke kane, o Papa, o Walinuu ka wahine.
Hanau Hoohoku, he wahine,
Hanau Haloa he 'lii,
Hanau ka Mauna, he keiki mauna na Wakea.

Born is the Mauna a Wākea,
The mountain of Wākea buds forth.
Wākea is the male, Papa Walinu'u is the female.
Born is Ho'ohōkū, a female,
Born is Hāloa, a chief,
Born is the Mauna, a mountain-child of Wākea.
—"HE KANAENAE NO KA HANAU ANA O KAUIKEAOULI,"
KA NA'I AUPUNI, FEBRUARY 10, 1906

It has been said that we are all branches of the genealogical trees established long ago by our kūpuna who birthed us into existence. I ulu nō ka lālā i ke kumu.[1] Nourished and sustained by the many piko (umbilical cord, center) that connect us to those kūpuna who came before, we, indeed, are the living embodiments of the sacrifices of their labor, and it is largely for this reason that I venture to articulate these thoughts in writing. The short mo'olelo I weave in these pages is that of a most-revered kupuna, akua, and 'āina on the island of Hawai'i. Known poetically by many names, Maunakea stands proudly as the highest peak, and piko, in all of Oceania. This mauna, home to a multitude of akua, or elemental forms, has long inspired the thoughts and aspirations of those who have been fortunate enough to experience its awesome grandeur.

As a way of beginning to familiarize the reader with Maunakea, this portrait opens with an excerpt from "He Kanaenae no ka hanau ana o Kauikeaouli," a birth chant composed for Kauikeaouli (Kamehameha III), who was born in 1813 at Keauhou, Kona, Hawai'i.[2] Infused with multiple layers of kaona, or veiled meaning, this portion of the kānaenae presents the genealogy of Maunakea and Hāloa in juxtaposition, showing

"Crossroads of Change." I ulu nō ka lālā i ke kumu. A koa tree stands resiliently upon Pu'u Huluhulu, a kīpuka and pu'uhonua in the saddle between Maunakea and Maunaloa. It survives and thrives at the crossroads, the convergence of old and new, foreign and familiar, reminding us of the trail our kūpuna traversed to bring us to this point, and the misty trail to the piko that lies before us. Photograph used with permission of the photographer, Kalei Nu'uhiwa.

the direct familial relationship between Kanaka 'Ōiwi and ka mauna a Wākea, the mountain-child of Wākea. Born of the union between Papahānaumoku and Wākea, Mauna a Wākea is an elder sibling of Hāloa, the ali'i. As such, both the Mauna and Kanaka are instilled, at birth, with particular kuleana to each other.[3] This relationship is reciprocal, and its sanctity requires continual maintenance in order to remain pono, or balanced.

According to the traditions that have been passed on to us today, our kūpuna, and especially our ali'i, intimately understood the importance of maintaining pono in their relationship with Mauna a Wākea. The kānaenae composed for Kauikeaouli is an exemplary representation of this understanding. Like the islands of Ko Hawai'i Pae 'Āina, Mauna a Wākea was born of the union of Papahānaumoku and Wākea. This union, as articulated by 'Ōiwi scholar Dr. Kekuewa Kikiloi, resulted not only in the birthing of 'āina, but also in the "birthing of a unified Hawaiian consciousness—a common ancestral lineage that forges links between the genealogies of both land and people."[4] In recounting this lineage following Kauikeaouli's troubled birth, the genealogical links between the chiefly child, the Mauna, Papa, and Wākea were essentially reaffirmed.[5] This not only established his kuleana to rule as an ali'i, but, as a stillborn revived after birth, it perhaps also invoked, or foretold, a rebirth of the 'āina, and a rebirth of 'Ōiwi consciousness during this ali'i's lifetime. Mauna a Wākea, as the highest peak, can thus be viewed, symbolically, as the highest potential of human consciousness. "Mauna," in this context, is interpreted as "prominent for excellence."[6] For the newborn Kauikeaouli, establishing a direct genealogical connection to this mauna of consciousness would have been extremely important, as an indication of chiefly mana and leadership potential. He—as we will see—would arguably become one of Hawai'i's most influential leaders of the nineteenth century.

In the second line of this kānaenae, the term 'ōpu'u is utilized by the composer to perhaps depict the birthing and growth processes of the Mauna. However, while 'ōpu'u, as noted in the translation, can be interpreted as "to bud forth," it could also be interpreted as a metaphor, likening the Mauna to the whale-tooth pendant, or lei 'ōpu'u, which was an important symbol of mana and ea for high-ranking ali'i of particular lineages.[7] During the time of Kauikeaouli's grandfather, Kahekili'ahumanu, a famed ali'i of Maui, it was foretold by Ka'ōpulupulu, the well-respected kahuna of the O'ahu Mō'ī, Kahahana, that relinquishing control of the sacred 'āina at Kualoa, Ko'olaupoko, O'ahu, and its palaoa pae would inherently lead to a loss of ea for the Mō'ī.[8] Kahahana, disregarding the warning of his kahuna, relinquished this 'āina and its palaoa pae to Kahekili, who gained control of the island soon after, and had the foolish Mō'ī of O'ahu killed.[9] Considering this mo'olelo, and the linkage drawn between the Mauna and the 'ōpu'u in this kānaenae, perhaps Mauna a Wākea stood, similarly, as an important symbol of mana and ea for Mō'ī of Hawai'i Island, like Kauikeaouli and his great-grandfather, Kalani'ōpu'u, who was named for the chiefly adornment.[10]

As mentioned earlier, Mauna a Wākea is, among other things, 'āina, which can be interpreted as "land," or "that which feeds."[11] These definitions surely hold true to this day for Mauna a Wākea, which continues to feed us both physically and spiritually. During the reign of Kauikeaouli (1824–1854), however, 'āina was imbued with yet another definition established within the context of the young Mō'ī's rebirthing of the archipelago. This era was marked by vast political and social transformation throughout Hawai'i, with the establishment of a constitutional system of governance, and the Māhele of 1848, which codified a new system of allodial title to, and private ownership of, 'āina.[12]

The highest, most sacred regions of Mauna a Wākea are situated within the ahupua'a of Ka'ohe, Hāmākua, and Humu'ula, Hilo. In the Māhele event of 1848, Victoria Kamāmalu relinquished to Kauikeaouli both of these ahupua'a, which were among the many 'āina she had likely inherited from the female high chief, Ka'ahumanu, through her mother, Kīna'u.[13] Kauikeaouli, in turn, relinquished Ka'ohe to the Aupuni and retained Humu'ula as one of his personal lands.[14] Both of these ahupua'a eventually became part of the Crown and Hawaiian Government Lands, which were seized by the United States in 1898.[15] This seizure came five years after the overthrow of Lili'uokalani, and three years after the Land Act of 1895, passed by the Republic of Hawai'i, which essentially renamed and reclassified these 'āina as Public Lands.[16] In 1959, the United States transferred control of these 'āina to the state of Hawai'i, establishing the Public Land Trust.[17] Since this seizure occurred and American occupation began in these islands, control of the allodial title to these 'āina mauna has framed the ongoing struggle by Kanaka 'Ōiwi, and many others, to mālama this keiki mauna na Wākea, in the face of increasing pressure to impose further desecration upon its summit.[18] Thus, as our struggle to recover the 'ōpu'u, Mauna a Wākea, parallels our enduring struggle to reestablish our ea as a lāhui in these islands, perhaps we can find relevance once again in the prophetic words that Ka'ōpulupulu uttered long ago.

Hanau ka Mauna, He makahiapo kapu na Wakea.
Oia ho'i, o ka Mauna, Hanau ka Mauna,
O ka mauna auanei ko lalo nei la.
Owai la hoi auanei ko luna la?
Owai la? O ka La, A—ia!, Aia hoi ha.

Born is the Mauna, a sacred firstborn of Wakea.
So it is, the Mauna, born is the Mauna.
The mountain shall be below here.
Who shall be above?
Who? The Sun, there! That is who.[19]

In the last five lines of the kānaenae above, we are reminded of the inherent sanctity that the Mauna was imbued with at birth, as the sacred firstborn of Wākea. Here, the Mauna is situated within the cosmos in a position subordinate only to the sun, the very source of energy that sustains all life on earth. As Hawai'i's most prominent peak, Mauna a Wākea is the piko that connects us to the heavens—it is the first to be touched by the rising sun's morning rays and the first to receive the highest clouds' life-giving waters. Upon its summit reside the akua water forms of Kāneikawaiola, Poliahu, Lilinoe, and Waiau, among others, who collectively form a predominant source of the island's fresh water aquifer. This important source of wai is perhaps alluded to in the name of the ahupua'a Ka'ohe, defined as "the bamboo," another kin olau, or physical manifestation, of Kāne, which was utilized for holding and transporting ceremonial waters.[20] As such, maintaining a pono relationship with the Mauna, and the akua of the Mauna, ensured continued waiwai for the 'āina as a whole.

In 1882, 'Emalani Kaleleonālani Naea Rooke, continuing in the traditions of her chiefly Hawai'i island lineage, embarked on a strenuous huaka'i for this very purpose.[21]

"He kapa hau ko Poliahu. He kapa lau ko Poliahu." Poliahu, akua of the snows, blankets the Mauna's summit regions with her sacred kapa hau, a protective, life-giving snow mantle. With the desecration that continues to tear away at her kapa hau, however, Poliahu has become increasingly engulfed by the looming shadow of the *kapa lau*, an alarming reminder that she is in dire need of our aloha. Photograph used with permission of the photographer, Kalei Nuʻuhiwa.

Ascending the steep Mauna trail to the piko o Wākea, Kaleleonālani is said to have immersed herself completely in Waiau's sacred waters at the "hena o nā kuahiwi," perhaps conducting a hiʻuwai, or bathing ceremony.[22] In honor of the Mōʻīwahine, a series of mele were composed to commemorate and chronicle this huakaʻi. One such mele piʻi kuahiwi, "A Maunakea ʻo Kalani," begins with four lines as follows:

A Maunakea o Kalani
Ike maka ia Waiau
Kela wai kamahao
I ka piko o ke kuahiwi

The Queen was at Maunakea
To see Waiau
That remarkable body of water
At the piko of the mountain[23]

Like the piko on our own bodies, Mauna a Wākea represents our physical and spiritual connections to past, present, and future generations. Waiau, in particular, where some ʻohana deposit the piko of newborn keiki, embodies this procreative continuum, as the convergence of akua, ʻāina, and kanaka. "When Emma immersed herself in Waiau," argues ʻŌiwi scholars and Kumu Hula, Kīhei and Māpuana de Silva, "she entered the piko wai kamahaʻo of her ancestor-gods, the wondrous liquid point of union from which all kanaka descend. She was reconnected; she was nourished; she was reborn."[24] Hānau ka mauna. The Mauna, thus, gave birth to her.

In essence, Kaleleonālani's huakaʻi of returning to the piko, Mauna a Wākea, was one of personal and conscious transformation, renewal, and rebirth in which the hiʻuwai served a very specific purpose. "Hiʻuwai," according to respected Kumu Hula and ʻŌiwi scholar Dr. Pualani Kanakaʻole Kanahele, "is the idea of returning back to the womb to again be innocent, without distractions. Therefore, the return to the fluid of the earth is the solvent to dissipate all negativity and distractions . . . before approaching any kuleana of great importance."[25] This return to the womb came at a critical time for Kaleleonālani, not long after the death of her kāne, Mōʻī Alexander Liholiho (Kamehameha IV), and her son, Albert Edward Kauikeaouli, during which her mana and kuleana to the ea of the Aupuni were being maligned by supporters of David Laʻamea Kalākaua.[26] Kalākaua had been elected as Mōʻī over Kaleleonālani six years earlier, and had recently embarked on his own huakaʻi around the world.[27] Many Kānaka, however, remained loyal to the Mōʻīwahine, despite Kalākaua's victory. As a staunch opponent to increasing American and missionary political influence in the islands, according to ʻŌiwi scholar Dr. Jonathan Osorio, Kaleleonālani was viewed by her supporters as "the more reliable champion of the kingdom's independence."[28] Considering the vastly different destinations of each aliʻi's huakaʻi, it is quite clear that each envisioned a fairly different route for the lāhui's uncertain path ahead. As de Silva and de Silva simply put it, "Kalākaua went around the world; Emma countered by going to the piko of the Hawaiian world."[29]

Huli hoi mai o Kalani
I ke ala kapekepeke
A he ala nihinihi ia
A hiki a i ke Mole
Ui ae nei o Kalani
E uleu mai oukou
He ihona loa ana ia
A hiki i Wahinekea
Emalani no he inoa
Ke ʻLii ae kuahiwi.

The Queen turned back
To the unsteady trail
It was a precarious trail
All the way to Kemole
And the Queen offered encouragement
"Be lively, all of you
It will be a very long descent
To reach Wahinekea"
For ʻEmalani, indeed, is this name chant
The aliʻi who entered the mountains.[30]

As portrayed in this and other mele piʻi Maunakea like it, the huakaʻi of the "aliʻi ʻaʻe kuahiwi" to the piko and back to the mole along the "ala kāpekepeke" was fraught with challenge, both physical and spiritual.[31] A verse from the mele "Hau kahiaka nui ʻo Kalani" further describes moments during this huakaʻi as being "huikau i ke anu," confused in the cold.[32] This is a huakaʻi to which we, as ʻŌiwi today, can collectively relate. Our journey as a people to mālama our kuleana to Mauna a Wākea over the past two centuries has been one of great adversity, struggle, and, at times, uncertainty. Since the state of Hawaiʻi gained control of the ʻāina of Mauna a Wākea, over a dozen astronomical observatories have been constructed upon its piko, despite the steadfast opposition of many ʻŌiwi and others alike. To this day, our journey along this path continues, as yet another observatory, the Thirty-Meter Telescope (TMT), has been proposed for construction within the next decade.[33] Projected to stand eighteen stories high, TMT would become the tallest building on Hawaiʻi Island, imposing itself on over eight acres of undisturbed ʻāina, and creating yet another permanent scar upon the mountain's sacred summit.[34]

The generations before us who engaged tirelessly in this struggle have essentially led us to the edge of Waiau's sacred waters. As we gaze at our own reflection on her placid surface, just as Kaleleonālani did over a century ago, we are confronted with a timeless reminder of where we came from, who we are, and who our grandchildren will grow to become. Just as Kaleleonālani found herself huikau (confused) at times along the steep path back to the piko, we too, as a lāhui, may become huikau at times today. Collectively, however, we cannot forget our kuleana to the many ancestors that surround us. We cannot forget our genealogies to place. We cannot forget our genealogies to the "makahiapo kapu," the sacred firstborn. Sacred places, like Mauna a Wākea, remind us of these genealogical relationships, and the kuleana that these relationships entail. Standing Rock Sioux scholar Vine Deloria Jr. explains further: "Sacred places are the foundation of all other beliefs and practices because they represent the presence of the sacred in our lives. They properly inform us that we are not larger than nature and that

"E Kānehoalani ē. E Kāneahoalani ē. Aloha kāua . . ." The rising and setting of the sun, and its cyclical journey along the ala loa, establishes the framework for our conception of time as a continuum. Change upon the ʻāina occurs in cycles—births and deaths—"but the sanctity left behind," states Kalei Nuʻuhiwa, "is embedded in the land's memory; waiting for the right one to come along and acknowledge its existence." Photograph used with permission of the photographer, Kalei Nuʻuhiwa.

we have responsibilities to the rest of the natural world that transcend our own personal desires and wishes. This lesson must be learned by each generation; unfortunately the technology of industrial society always leads us in the other direction. Yet it is certain that as we permanently foul our planetary nest, we shall have to learn a most bitter lesson."[35]

During the time of Kaiakahinaliʻi—a great deluge that engulfed the ʻāina—it is said that only the peaks of Mauna a Wākea, Maunaloa, and Haleakalā remained above the water.[36] The last lines of Wā ʻUmikumāmākahi (Era Eleven) in the epic cosmogonic moʻokūʻauhau, Kumulipo, chronicle such a cataclysmic event during which a great many were devoured by the sea, seemingly having left behind only those who had found refuge at the piko of Hawaiʻi's highest mountains.[37] In the Wā that follows this great deluge, the next eleven generations of male descendants of the survivors of this lineage are remembered as having carried the name ʻŌpuʻu, followed by five generations that carried the name Mauna.[38] Amid the destruction and turmoil brought by Kaiakahinaliʻi, the Mauna remained, unyielding, as the piko, the kumu, the firmly rooted ancestral source of life, from which the exalted branches of our resilient lāhui—like the stillborn Kauikeaouli, and the steadfast Kaleleonālani—were reborn, and budded forth once again. ʻŌpuʻu aʻe ka mauna. ʻŌpuʻu aʻe ka lāhui. The mountain, thus, budded forth, as did the nation.

I return now to the metaphor of the tree to bring this moʻolelo to a conclusion, for the time being. The foundation and source of life for every tree is the ʻāina. If we continue to poison the ʻāina in which our genealogical trees are deeply rooted, our children and grandchildren will surely be confronted with the harsh realities of the "most bitter lesson" that Deloria alludes to. We are the Mauna, and our treatment of it reflects a deeply ingrained notion of the ways in which we now view and treat ourselves and each other. In neglecting our kuleana to mālama this ʻāina, we ultimately neglect our kuleana to the future generations of our lāhui. Our time of reconnection and renewal is upon us. Let us return to our place of origin, the piko, the womb, and allow the Mauna to transform and rebirth us, as we bud forth from the sturdy trunk established by the many generations that came long before us. As this new generation of Kanaka ʻŌiwi emerges, we must recognize that it is our kuleana to continue to mālama our ʻohana that surrounds us, from the depths of Kanaloa's ocean, to the expanses of Wākea's sky, and to the sacred Mauna that connects us all. Kaleleonālani's voice beckons us. E ʻuleu mai ʻoukou (Be lively, all of you). He ihona loa ana ia (It will be a very long descent). I ola ke kulāiwi. I ola nā ʻŌiwi. A i mau nō hoʻi ke ea o ka ʻāina.

> The truth is, there is man and there is environment. One does not supersede the other. The breath in man is the breath of Papa. Man is merely the caretaker of the land that maintains his life and nourishes his soul. Therefore, ʻāina is sacred. The church of life is not in a building, it is the open sky, the surrounding ocean, the beautiful soil. My duty is to protect Mother Earth, who gives me life. And to give thanks with humility as well as forgiveness for the arrogance and insensitivity of man. (George Helm, "Reasons for the Fourth Occupation of Kahoʻolawe," January 30, 1977)

Notes

He Leo Mahalo: This moʻolelo, like all of our moʻolelo, is reflective of a collective consciousness, and the culmination of the feelings, thoughts, emotions, and experiences of a great many, among which I am but one. He leo mahalo kēia no nā akua, nā ʻaumākua, a me nā kūpuna. Eia nō kuʻu aloha no ka Mauna a Wākea, ʻo ia nō, ʻo kuʻu one hānau a ʻo kuʻu kulāiwi hoʻi nō ia. Mahalo nui to my kūpuna, my ʻohana of the Ua Kanilehua and the Ala ʻŪlili, to all our poʻe Aloha ʻĀina, past and present, who continue to mālama our Mauna, and to the kumu from which I have budded forth. Mahalo nui to all my kumu, mentors, and dear friends who have shared your ʻike, your time, and your aloha with me in shaping this moʻolelo as well as its author. Mahalo nui to the editors of this book for your leadership and guidance in this project and for allowing me the opportunity to share this moʻolelo as part of this amazing work. Finally, I'd like to extend a special mahalo to Dr. Kekuewa Kikiloi for your critical feedback and contributions to this moʻolelo; Aunty Pualani Kanakaʻole Kanahele and the Papakū Makawalu research team for opening my mind to the potentiality of our akua ingrained in our ancestral DNA; and especially to Kalei Nuʻuhiwa for contributing your ʻike and mana to this piece through your powerful photos, which tell epic moʻolelo all of their own. And to all those whose names are not mentioned here, but whose roles in shaping this moʻolelo, this moʻokūʻauhau, have not been forgotten, mahalo nui iā ʻoukou pākahi a pau.

Epigraph: The text of mele included in this essay is transcribed here as it appears in its original published form, without contemporary diacritical markings. This is to maintain the integrity of the multiple layered meanings that may have been intended by the original author. Translation by author, based on translation by Mary Kawena Pukui in Pukui and Korn, *The Echo of Our Song*, 23.

1. "The branches grow because of the trunk." Pukui, *ʻOlelo Noʻeau.*

2. Poepoe, "Ka Moolelo Hawaii Kahiko"; Kameʻeleihiwa, *Native Land and Foreign Desires*, 31.

3. Kuleana, as defined in Pukui and Elbert, *Hawaiian Dictionary*, can be interpreted as "right, privilege, concern, responsibility." Along this train of thought, it could be conceived that any right or privilege we have is gained through the fulfillment of our responsibilities to that which concerns us. We Kanaka, as the younger siblings of Mauna a Wākea, or all ʻāina for that matter, must first fulfill our kuleana to mālama our elder relations, in order to be afforded the kuleana of partaking in the physical and spiritual sustenance they provide for us.

4. Kikiloi, "Rebirth of an Archipelago," 76.

5. According to Pukui and Korn, Kauikeaouli was stillborn, and "'prayed in to life' by a high priest Ka-malo-ʻihi (also called Ka-pihe)." Pukui and Korn, *The Echo of Our Song*, 13.

6. Andrews, *A Dictionary of the Hawaiian Language.*

7. Kanahele et al., "Kūkulu Ke Ea a Kanaloa," 79.

8. Fornander, *Fornander's Ancient History of the Hawaiian People*, 217–218. Palaoa pae is beached whale ivory. Pukui, *ʻOlelo Noʻeau*, cites the ʻōlelo noʻeau, "O luna, o lalo; o uka, o kai; o ka palaoa pae, no ke aliʻi ia." According to her interpretation, "The chief owned everything in the land he ruled. Ivory obtained from the teeth of whales that washed ashore [palaoa pae] was very valuable" (273).

9. Fornander, *Fornander's Ancient History of the Hawaiian People*, 217–225.

10. Fornander, *Fornander's Ancient History of the Hawaiian People*, 204.

11. Handy, Handy, and Pukui, *Native Planters in Old Hawaiʻi*, 45.

12. Beamer and Duarte, "I Palapala No Ia Aina"; Kameʻeleihiwa, *Native Lands and Foreign Desires.*

13. Kameʻeleihiwa, *Native Lands and Foreign Desires*, 124; Kamehameha III, "Buke Kakau Paa No Ka Mahele Aina," 5.

14. Kamehameha III, "Buke Kakau Paa No Ka Mahele Aina," 186, 91.

15. Sai, *Ua Mau Ke Ea*, 94–95.

16. Iaukea, *The Queen and I*, 47–48.

17. Van Dyke, *Who Owns the Crown Lands of Hawaiʻi?*, 381.

18. In 1964, a single telescope was constructed on Maunakea's summit, which had been deemed to provide astronomers with "the best astronomical observing conditions in the world" (Parker, *Stairway to the Stars*, 1). Four years later, the state of Hawaiʻi negotiated a sixty-five-year lease with the University of Hawaiʻi for the establishment of the Mauna Kea Science Reserve. Under the terms of the lease, the university pays a mere $1 per year to the state ("Mauna Kea Comprehensive Management Plan," 25). Since 1968, thirteen telescopes have been constructed on the mountaintop, and the Association

of Canadian Universities for Research in Astronomy, the California Institute of Technology, and the University of California have proposed the Thirty-Meter Telescope despite ongoing resistance.

19. "He Kanaenae no ka hanau ana o Kauikeaouli," *Ka Na'i Aupuni*. Translation by author, based on translation by Mary Kawena Pukui in Pukui and Korn, *The Echo of Our Song*, 23–24.

20. Kanahele et al., "Kukulu Ke Ea a Kanaloa," 97.

21. Maly and Maly, "Mauna Kea," 155.

22. Kalani Ka'apuni-Phillips, interviewed by Larry Kimura, January 30, 1967, cited in Maly and Maly, "Mauna Kea," 161. Piko o Wākea means "the navel of Wākea," a reference to the summit of Maunakea made in "Hau kahiaka nui 'o Kalani," and hena o nā kuahiwi is "mons pubis of the mountain"; Nogelmeier, *He Lei No 'Emalani*, 112.

23. "A Maunakea o Kalani," HI.M. 71:29, Bishop Museum Archives; translation by author, based on translation by Kīhei de Silva in de Silva and de Silva, "A Maunakea 'o Kalani."

24. De Silva and de Silva, "A Maunakea 'o Kalani."

25. Kanahele, *Ka Honua Ola: 'Eli'eli Kau Mai*, 25.

26. De Silva and de Silva, "A Maunakea 'o Kalani"; Osorio, *Dismembering Lahui*, 151–157.

27. De Silva and de Silva, "A Maunakea 'o Kalani"; Osorio, *Dismembering Lahui*, 151–157.

28. Osorio, *Dismembering Lahui*, 152.

29. De Silva and de Silva, "A Maunakea 'o Kalani," n. 17.

30. "A Maunakea o Kalani," HI.M. 71:29, Bishop Museum Archives; translation by author, based on translation by Kīhei de Silva in de Silva and de Silva, "A Maunakea 'o Kalani."

31. Mole means taproot, ancestral root, foundation, source. Pukui and Elbert, *Hawaiian Dictionary*. Kemole is a pu'u on the northwestern slope of Maunakea.

32. Nogelmeier, *He Lei No 'Emalani*, 112.

33. In an article published in *West Hawai'i Today* on April 1, 2012, the governor of the state of Hawai'i, Neil Abercrombie, is quoted as boldly saying, "The Thirty Meter Telescope project atop Mauna Kea 'will move forward. There will be no more obstruction from someone who found their cultural roots six minutes ago.'" Flickinger, "A Measured Look at Gov. Abercrombie."

34. KAHEA, "Fact Sheet."

35. Deloria, *God Is Red*, 285.

36. Fornander, "No Ke Kaiakahinalii Ma Hawaii Nei," 525.

37. "The Kalakaua Text. The Pule Ho'ola'a Ali'i. He Kumulipo no Ka-'I-'I-Mamao a ia Alapai Wahine," in Beckwith, *The Kumulipo*, 226; Kepelino, *Kepelino's Traditions of Hawai'i*, 34–37; Kekuewa Kikiloi, personal communication, February 2012.

38. Lines 1546–1561 of the Kumulipo list the kāne, Opu'upu'u, Opu'upe, Opu'umauna, Opu'uhaha, Opu'ukalaua, Opu'uhanahana, Opu'uhamahamau, Opu'ukalauli, Opu'ukalakea, Opu'ukalahiwa, Opu'ukalalele, Maunanui, Maunane'e, Maunapapapa, Maunaha'aha'a, and Maunahiolo. Beckwith, *The Kumulipo*.

PART III *Sovereignty*

Kīhei "Soli" Niheu stands on top of a trailer that served as a checkpoint entrance into Kalama Valley, as residents and Kōkua Hawaiʻi supporters hold their ground before the settler-state court ordered evictions and arrests, May 1971.

Aunty Nani Rogers sits at the beach on her island, Kaua'i. Photograph used with permission of the photographer, Bryna Rose Storch.

Portrait. Puanani Rogers

Micky Huihui

Spellbound, I watched as flames engulfed the hundreds of pages of the 1991 environmental impact statement for the Pacific Missile Range Facility on the steps of the Līhu'e Civic Center on Kaua'i. Fresh out of high school, I was ignorant of the idea of focused resistance and simply could not comprehend that adults had lit a fire in a public place. And it was burning in broad daylight. The pillar of smoke billowing from the oddly placed fire brushed the quickly gathering crowd, and the mass of burning paper seemed relieved, somehow liberated from the heavy rhetoric riddling its pages. The group came to demand protection of the sand dune burials at Nohili, threatened by the war games being orchestrated in Mānā by the U.S. military. The demonstration that day would presage their arrest the following year: seventeen Kānaka, camped out at Polihale to protest the disturbance of iwi kupuna in the sand of Nohili, were taken into custody after storming the gates to the military compound.

THIS IS MY VERY FIRST MEMORY of civil disobedience. Among the kūpuna I accompanied to Līhu'e that day was my Aunty Nani Rogers, a beautiful silver-haired product of Kaua'i with a lifetime of careful observation and experiences that justified her protest that day, and every day after.

In Aunty Nani we are reminded of the grace of Lili'uokalani as she stared into the faces of conspirators, who plotted against the very fabric of Hawai'i, and consciously decided not to send them directly to their Maker. Her incredible restraint in the face of a political coup against the Crown and her people serves as an illuminated beacon in our time. We too holomua (move forward) with steady patience, treading lightly in the presence of those who seek to usurp our inalienable right to ea and the homeland we hold so dear. Aunty Nani is an example of this kind of steadfast persistence.

Growing up in a generation born in the wake of Lili'uokalani's death, Nani endured a life similar to the thousands of Hawaiian kūpuna born and raised during the regime of wartime Territorial Hawai'i. The lāhui (nation, people) was forced into national submission by policies and economic aspirations from foreign shores—the United States of America. Like so many who followed the example of our Beloved Queen, she moved through the disorienting time of "progress" toward the unknown, doing the best she could with limited control over her own and her people's destiny. Despite participating during her early life in the charade presented to our people as the only path to salvation in a modern world, Nani eventually regained her footing ma ke ala pono o ko mākou mau kūpuna, along the righteous and just path of our ancestors and elders.

Born on September 8, 1939, to Anacleto Ribuca Battad and Eleanor Puanani White in a neighborhood in Kapa'a affectionately called Kealoha Heights, Angie Puanani is known affectionately as Aunty Nani to all who have been blessed by her sweet 'ano (nature). She continues in the footsteps of her ancestors from the very 'āina where she came into this world.

From the verdant and lush valleys of Manōkalanipō (Kaua'i), Aunty Nani found her way to the epicenter of the changing tide in the heart of downtown Honolulu. The youngest of five children born to Anacleto and Eleanor, Nani was accepted as a day student in the Kamehameha Schools at Kapālama, an island away on O'ahu. Like so many Kanaka Maoli kissed by the benevolence of Pauahi (ali'i founder of the Kamehameha Schools), Aunty Nani was raised in and around Kapālama until her graduation in 1957. Limited beds in the school's dormitories required that she live with her aunt, Pearl Ka'opio, and her family on Kukui Street in downtown Honolulu. Aunty Nani remembers the Vineyard Boulevard neighborhood as a virtual shantytown, in contrast to the Kamehameha campus, densely populated by Kānaka Maoli and other working-class folks. Middle-class residents had been cleared out, as the Territorial government began making way for a new era of businesses and skyscrapers that would soon infest the area. But the endless aloha of her 'ohana (extended family)—a trademark of the family to this day—saw her safely through her first year away from her one hānau (birthplace) in Kealoha Heights. Yet her 'ohana, along with hundreds of Kānaka who called Honolulu home for generations, was being squeezed out.

The path of coming to understand one's surroundings and one's place in them can be a long and winding road, beset by unseen factors shaping the political and social landscape. For Indigenous communities, the journey can be riddled with misconceptions of truth, impending threats to the safety of the nation, and constant pressures to submit to the "lesser of two evils." Perhaps none can relate to this abyss of the unfathomable unknown more than the kūpuna born and raised in Territorial Hawai'i. Having been witness to ill-conceived schemes of political domination, new developments in the capitalistic hijacking of world economies, a complete overhaul of O'ahu's skyline in a matter of two decades, and all of the temptations of modernization that followed, many were left in a state of shock and awe, unable to articulate their degree of loss, and too entrenched in a capitalist lifestyle to notice a treasured way of life was rapidly slipping away. Can we fault our grandparents, our great-grandparents, for their inaction during the 1940s and 1950s? Can we blame them for not taking torches to the buildings that infested the skylines and development encroaching on native settlements? 'A'ole.

Like many in her time, Aunty Nani actively participated in her culture by excelling in hula. After high school, Aunty Nani attended Church College (now known as Brigham Young University, Hawai'i) in Lā'ie, O'ahu. She continued to live and work on the other side of the island in Kalihi and began seeking out hālau hula close to her work in town. She happened upon the school of legendary Kumu Hula Maiki Aiu. At the time, the hālau was actively recruiting dancers to travel to Germany in a hula show, a happenstance that set her on a course away from her beloved pae 'āina (archipelago).

As it turned out, the hui (group) never made it to Germany. Instead, delayed by a recording session in Chicago with the troupe's musical ensemble, the Hilo Hawaiians, they toured the American Midwest for two years, entertaining in supper clubs and hotels as a part of the vigorous campaign to make Hawai'i America's favorite tourist destination. This commodification of culture abroad—an exploitation of a once-sacred dance, now being used to lure shivering Midwesterners to balmy shores—was a path shared by many Hawaiians of her time and even many young entertainers today. Youthful, full of adventure, and with a striking beauty and sway reminiscent of Hawai'i itself, Nani spent two long years in the continental United States dancing with the hālau.

With the impending arrival of her first child, she made her way back to Kealoha Heights, and with this move, Aunty Nani's life again changed. Today—six keiki (children), fifteen mo'opuna (grandchildren), and a lifetime of careful observation later—she continues to share her gift of dance when called upon, yet she has become an ambassador of a message quite different from her days with the Hilo Hawaiians.

He Alaka'i 'O ia: She Is a Leader

For the past five decades, Aunty Nani has brought incredible strength and grace to even the most contentious of Indigenous struggles. In 1991, back in the days when self-determination was considered a pipe dream by many Kānaka, she answered a call in the newspaper summoning Native Hawaiians to come together and engage with the Hawai'i state legislature on issues affecting Native Hawaiian rights and land. The call had been put out by Ka Lāhui Hawai'i (KLH), the largest and most organized group advocating for Hawaiian sovereignty in the 1990s. Nani soon became a KLH citizen. Ka Lāhui Hawai'i was, in many ways, responsible for bringing the notion of sovereignty to the forefront of Hawaiian consciousness, and they found a champion in her. Shortly thereafter, Nani assumed the role of Po'o (head) of KLH's Kaua'i Island contingent.

Armed with a newfound political awareness and an understanding of the history and inner working of Hawai'i government, Nani served tirelessly with KLH, traveling to O'ahu often and rallying kūpuna on Kaua'i to become politically involved. Her role as Po'o allowed her to find new ways in which to mālama her one hānau. She came to exemplify the struggle of her own island, and when she traveled to KLH meetings around ka pae ʻāina, she always brought the ʻaumākua of her beloved Kauaʻi with her to the table.

Her involvement in organizing with KLH and her fervor to right the historical wrongs suffered by the Hawaiian people propelled Aunty Nani from Kealoha Heights to Oʻahu to Washington, DC, and back. However, after nearly a decade of being immersed in political activism with KLH, Aunty Nani's notion of ea began to shift: "I realized that a nation-within-a-nation model was quasi-sovereignty, and that total independence was the only way to freeing our people and nation," she states. To this day, Aunty Nani is a fierce supporter of the independence movement in Hawaiʻi.

He Wahine Hana ʻUpena ʻO ia: She Is a Woman Who Creates Net(work)s

Aunty Nani has been a mainstay for the uphill climb toward restoring ea in Hawaiʻi, known by friends and allies worldwide as an ambassador of the Hawaiian people. From the seven-acre lot on Mailihuna Road above Keālia, Aunty Nani has exemplified the art of hana ʻupena—networking—reaching across expanses of time and oceans, a humble vanguard and servant to the pulse of the planetary struggle for Indigenous justice. Her sweet leo (voice) broadcasts from sleepy Hanalei, Kauaʻi, each Monday afternoon on KKCR community radio, a volunteer-run, noncommercial station.[1] She casts her net across miles of invisible radio waves.

Aunty Nani's unwavering love for her nation and her persistence in oftentimes impossible battles against injustice set her apart in the quest for ea and truth. For example, she remained a faithful and watchful resident at the three-month vigil to protect nā iwi kupuna in Naue when developer Joseph Brescia began construction of a luxury home on Kauaʻi's north coast. Between April and June 2008, she was always present at the site of disinterment and always mindful of the ʻaumākua whose bones she safeguarded. Over the many years of her activism and community organizing, she has participated as a member of countless hui (groups) designed to spark dialogue and progress toward ea. To these Hawaiian initiatives, she has consistently brought the strength of her ancestors with her to the table.

She also reaches beyond our own Hawaiian struggles to connect with those who engage in similar fights for Indigenous sovereignty. An international networking queen, Aunty Nani has followed the ʻupena to the far corners of the globe—beloved by the Ainu in Japan, communities in Vieques, the Aboriginal peoples of Australia, in Europe, and across the Pacific. To the people she meets, she represents the Hawaiian nation. Our lāhui is truly blessed by her stellar representation to those who share similar struggles to restore and protect ea, life, and sovereignty.

YEARS AFTER THAT DAY on the Līhuʻe Civic Center steps, I joined Aunty Nani in protest of another U.S. military action desecrating Hawaiian lands. The crisp Mākua morning settled in our hearts as our hui advanced across the majestic landscape of this broad valley on Oʻahu's west side. Hand in hand, we walked silently, observing the newly exposed ancient structures revealed by rampant summer wildfires. Like the burning environmental impact statement on the Līhuʻe steps those many years ago, flames had somehow liberated us from the threat of our culture being distanced, taken from us. And here again, this warrior, fortified by the strength of her ancestors, fixed her eyes and heart on the work to be done—walking and defending the ʻāina and our sovereign right to live in harmony with it. This is her gift, to her ʻohana, the lāhui, and to the future of Hawaiʻi.

Note

1. Radio station KKCR streams live online at http://kkcr.org/.

CHAPTER 11. Outside Shangri La

COLONIZATION AND THE U.S. OCCUPATION OF HAWAIʻI

Kūhiō Vogeler

In the swimming cove outside Shangri La, Doris Duke's estate on the slopes of Diamond Head, Kanalu Young, a fifteen-year-old student from Kamehameha Schools, dove deep into four feet of water.[1] His head "hit the sand and continued to plow into it." There was a "horrible sound—a snap"—and his body went limp.[2] As he lay in the water, motionless, his friends thought that he was joking, pretending to have drowned.[3] But Kanalu was not faking. His friends lifted Kanalu's limp body up the wall that jutted out from the cove and laid him on his back.[4] Kanalu, who had loved the ocean as a child, injured his spinal cord and became a quadriplegic that day, August 14, 1969.

Kanalu Young spent fourteen months in rehabilitation. He writes, "One day . . . in 1969, November or December, there was this gnat . . . that landed up on my cheek. And I hadn't moved a muscle, literally, since August 14th and the accident."[5] Young tried to swat the tiny fly and missed. His permanently fisted hand remained at his nose until the nurse came. For Young, that first attempt to swat a gnat was "the shred of humanity I had left to build upon." As Kanalu built his own strength and career, so too a Hawaiian nationalist consciousness was growing.

Over the four decades following Young's accident, details regarding Hawaiʻi's occupation would emerge. This growing awareness of Hawaiʻi's legal status under international law would begin to shift the focus in Hawaiʻi from land protests and colonization to the rights of Indigenous peoples, then toward academic research into the U.S. occupation of Hawaiʻi as the next means of resistance. Where land struggles and discussions of reparations dominated the political discourse in the 1970s, by the 1990s the discourse shifted to the rights of Hawaiians as Indigenous peoples, and after the turn of the century a new generation of scholars would explore Hawaiʻi's legal status under U.S. occupation.

During this political evolution, Kanalu Young's personal struggle to overcome his physical limitations and his desire to find his role in Hawaiʻi's independence movement would mirror the evolution of political discourse in Hawaiʻi. In spring 2007 Dr. Kanalu Young would become the first professor at the University of Hawaiʻi to teach a course focusing on the prolonged occupation of Hawaiʻi, titled History of Hawaiian Kingdom Law.

No Treaty of Annexation

The assertion that the U.S. has occupied the Hawaiian Islands since 1898 is based on legal facts under international law. Many of these facts came to light beginning in 1969, the same year as Kanalu Young's accident, and the full argument developed over decades. On February 1, 1969, the *Honolulu Star-Bulletin* ran the headline "Secret Debate on U.S. Seizure of Hawaii Revealed." The transcript of the classified Senate debate on May 31, 1898, was finally released to the public. According to the newspaper article, "at the request of a historian who noted gaps in the Congressional Record," the U.S. Senate had passed "a resolution authorizing the National Archives to take the wraps off the debate transcript."[6]

This debate offers insight into the imperialist machinations behind the United States' illegal annexation of the Hawaiian Islands. Fifty-five years before this closed-door debate, on November 28, 1843, Britain and France had signed the Anglo-Franco Declaration, recognizing the Hawaiian Islands as "an Independent State," a country under international law.[7] An independent state may be occupied by another state, but under international law an independent state may not be colonized, in any legal sense.[8] By 1898 two attempts to annex Hawai'i to the United States had occurred: one in 1893, as a band of conspirators, aided by U.S. minister John L. Stevens, dethroned Queen Lili'uokalani and took control of the government, and the other in 1897, as U.S. imperialism sought expansion into the Pacific. Both attempts failed, in part because of Queen Lili'uokalani's protests and because 38,000 residents of the Hawaiian Islands signed antiannexation petitions.[9] In the wake of the second failed treaty of annexation, on May 4, 1898, at the height of the Spanish-American War, U.S. Representative Francis G. Newlands of Nevada submitted a joint resolution (the Newlands Resolution) for the annexation of the Hawaiian Islands, a unilateral attempt to subsume the Hawaiian Islands within the U.S. territorial borders.[10] During this secret Senate session on May 31, 1898, what had begun as a dispute over a war revenue bill for the Spanish-American War devolved into a debate on the occupation of Hawai'i for military purposes.

A joint resolution is not a treaty and therefore is not a legal means of acquiring territory under international law or U.S. domestic law.[11] Yet both houses of Congress passed the Newlands Resolution, which U.S. President William McKinley signed on July 7, 1898.[12] The August 12, 1898, headline of the *Hawaiian Star* read, "Hawaii Merged into the US," and four days later two thousand combat troops invaded Honolulu.[13] The U.S. occupation of Hawai'i continues today.

In 1969, ten years after Hawai'i had become "the fiftieth state," no one grasped the significance of the newly released debate transcripts.[14] Over the next decade, as Kanalu Young fought back from his accident and completed high school and college, increased awareness of Queen Lili'uokalani's struggle against treason and annexation in the 1890s would lead to the establishment of the ALOHA Association and the Office of Hawaiian Affairs (OHA) and to the legal assertion that Hawai'i remains under continued foreign occupation.

ALOHA Association

On June 30, 1971, when a "terrific fire" engulfed the taxi of Louisa Kanoeokalani Makaiwi Rice, everything was burned except for her $7 hardcover edition of *Hawaii's Story by Hawaii's Queen*. Rice believed that this was a *hō'ailona*, a sign or omen, that she "must read what's in the book."[15] According to Rice, "There were no seats, no nothing—just black metal. But there inside, on top of all this mess was the book. I couldn't help but be affected. There was this picture of Queen Lili'uokalani looking at me."[16] After reading the autobiography, Rice believed she had been given "a mission" and formed the ALOHA Association (an acronym for Aboriginal Lands of Hawaiian Ancestry). By 1973, the ALOHA Association Inc. would become a nonprofit corporation with 12,744 registered members.[17]

In 1972 Louisa Rice read in a newspaper that Congress had given "$1 billion in money and land in reparations to Alaskan natives" through the Alaskan Native Claims Settlement Act. Rice thought, "They got cash for something that happened 100 years ago, so . . . this might show me how to fix up something that happened only 80 years ago here in Hawaii."[18] As a result of the ALOHA Association's efforts, on June 27, 1974, U.S. Representative Spark Matsunaga submitted the Hawaiian Native Claims Settlement Act (H.R. 15666) to the Ninety-Third Congress of the United States.[19] The act sought to establish a Hawaiian Native Fund of one billion dollars, to "earn interest and be invested and administered by the [U.S.] secretary [of the interior] in the same manner as trust funds of Indian tribes." The act would also have created a Hawaiian Native Corporation "to receive and administer the benefits provided by this Act for the Hawaiian Natives."[20]

On February 11 and 24, 1975, during hearings for the Settlement Act, Kekoa Ka'apu, vice president of the ALOHA Association, asserted, "The Hawaiian Natives are the only group of aboriginal people from whom the United States took a country and an independent and sovereign nationhood, recognized by international law and the community of civilized nations." Ka'apu further maintained that "no other aboriginal group impacted by the United States" was an "autonomous, sovereign nation within the community of nations at the time it was wronged." Yet Ka'apu accepted that the United States had gained Hawai'i's territory through the "annexation of the Hawaiian Islands in 1898."[21]

The ALOHA Association continued to seek passage of the Hawaiian Native Claims Settlement Act, but it failed to pass the U.S. Congress in 1977. According to Dr. Kekuni Blaisdell, the failure of the ALOHA Association "led in 1978–1980 to the creation of

OHA, Office of Hawaiian Affairs, by the State government, in order to co-opt the sovereignty movement."[22] In 1978, wording from the Hawaiian Native Claims Settlement Act was integrated into the constitution of the state of Hawaiʻi. Article 12, section 5 of the Hawaiʻi state constitution declares that "the Office of Hawaiian Affairs shall hold title to all the real and personal property now and hereafter set aside or conveyed to it which shall be held in trust for native Hawaiians and Hawaiians."[23] The lands held in trust are the 1.8 million acres illegally seized by the U.S. government through the 1898 Newlands Resolution.[24] But even with the creation of OHA, concerns over land remained and a different strategy emerged.

Continued Foreign Occupation

On October 3, 1978, in the case of *Hawaiʻi v. Wilford "Nappy" Pulawa,* Pōkā Laenui (a.k.a. Hayden Burgess) filed a motion to dismiss due to "Continued Foreign Occupation."[25] Laenui had read *Hawaii's Story by Hawaii's Queen,* the same book that had influenced Louisa Rice, back in 1979. According to Laenui, "Very few people knew about this book," which was first published in 1898, reprinted in 1964.[26] "As I read the book, the queen spoke to me about what had happened in Hawaiʻi, disclosing those activities that occurred in 1893 that resulted in the theft of this independent nation."[27]

Only a few years out of law school, Laenui represented "reputed underworld leader" Nappy Pulawa. As Laenui explains, "This case was very pivotal in the movement for Hawaiian sovereignty. When the prosecutor charged my client with the double murder and double kidnap, I said that we refuse to enter a plea of guilty or not guilty. Instead we asked, 'Who are you foreigners to sit in judgment over our Hawaiian citizens, to pass your foreign laws to govern our Hawaiian people? We are not American citizens, we are citizens of the nation of Hawaiʻi, and we refuse to dignify the court by entering a plea.'"[28] Laenui did not cite any case law as precedent for his "Motion to Dismiss for Lack of Jurisdiction."[29] He wanted to raise awareness through this legal motion:

> When I read into the record the speech of Grover Cleveland to the U.S. Congress, the judge shook his head saying, "I can hear your words, but I cannot believe that the president of the United States had said this." . . . It was an opportunity not only to educate the judge, but to educate the general public about the theft of this independent nation. . . . They found the defendant not guilty of the crimes alleged. Although the decision was not based on the fact that we were Hawaiian citizens, it brought home greater attention to the injustices of the Hawaiian people.[30]

Thus, two models emerged for addressing Hawaiian issues. The ALOHA Association, borrowing from the Alaskan Native Claims Settlement Act, had committed itself to the reparations process sought by Native American tribes. In contrast, Kekoa Ka'apu's assertion that the United States had illegally overthrown an "autonomous, sovereign nation," coupled with the 1978 motion to dismiss due to continued foreign occupation, supported the contention that Hawai'i remains an independent state, occupied by the United States. Throughout the 1980s, the distinctions between these models—one emphasizing colonization and the other emphasizing occupation—were not clarified, and aspects of each argument progressed simultaneously. The assertion that Hawai'i is not part of the United States, but rather under international law definitions is occupied, advanced in energetic bursts and spasms, as one attempting to grasp for truth after a long period of immobility.

Internationally, during a global period of decolonization, the concepts of colonization and occupation were linked. As Eyal Benvenisti explains, "During the 1970s, in the context of the wave of de-colonization and assertions on the right of self-determination of peoples, foreign occupation has been likened by several UN General Assembly documents, including the Charter of Economic Rights and Duties of States, to colonization and other forms of foreign aggression preventing the exercise of this right." Benvenisti further clarifies that certain prolonged occupations resemble colonization, where "the occupant abuses its powers and might taint its continuing presence in the occupied territory with illegality."[31] The nature of prolonged occupation, especially when the occupant claims annexation, as with Hawai'i, causes confusion by hiding occupation under the guise of colonization. Yet occupation describes a nuanced understanding of international law as it pertains to Hawai'i.

Hawaiian Studies

In 1988 Kanalu Young returned to the University of Hawai'i to complete his dissertation in history. Young found himself guided by scholars and activists who described Hawai'i's history using postcolonial and Marxist theory. In 1991 when Young was hired to teach in the Hawaiian Studies Department, he learned from "the mentorship and training of Haunani-Kay Trask . . . [and] the cultural grounding of Lilikala Kame'eleihiwa"—as well as from activists such as Moe Moler, "Bumpy" Kanahele, and Mililani Trask. Haunani-Kay Trask would introduce Young to "the Malcolm Xs of the world, to other struggles, to Frantz Fanon, and to the literature on struggle and on oppression."[32] By 1992 Kame'eleihiwa, in *Native Land and Foreign Desires,* would describe the history of Hawai'i as "a case study in the rapid progression of a Native society from Christianity to capitalism to colonialism."[33] And by 1993, Trask, in *From a Native Daughter,* would categorize Native Hawaiians as "Indigenous Peoples" within the United States, stressing that "the international issue of indigenous human rights has only now, with great resistance, been included in the local discussions regarding Hawaiian sovereignty."[34]

During the late 1980s and early 1990s, writings on Hawai'i's occupation continued. In 1988 the U.S. Attorney General's Office, in a report, "Legal Issues Raised by Proposed Presidential Proclamation to Extend the Territorial Sea" from three miles to twelve miles, concluded, "It is therefore unclear which constitutional power Congress exercised when it acquired Hawaii by joint resolution. Accordingly, it is doubtful that the acquisition of Hawaii can serve as an appropriate precedent for a congressional assertion of sovereignty over an extended territorial sea."[35] Two years later in a journal article, "American Annexation of Hawaii: An Example of the Unequal Treaty Doctrine," Bradford Morse and Kazi Hamid determined that the United States has "forcefully occupied the nation of Hawaii for almost a century during which time it has effectively displaced the legitimate government."[36] The journal article did not mention the Newlands Resolution.

In 1990, following a directive from U.S. president George H. W. Bush to stop all bombing on Kaho'olawe, some Hawaiians remained committed to high-profile demonstrations to bring about political change in Hawai'i.[37] On June 11, 1992, Kamehameha Day, a holiday in Hawai'i, thirty "pro-sovereignty demonstrators" were arrested and charged with trespassing during a protest to "take back" 'Iolani Palace.[38] Kanalu Young was one of the protesters. Dennis "Bumpy" Kanahele later explained that the purpose was "to bring forth" Hawaiian "autonomy."[39]

At 5 p.m., according to officials, "demonstrators suddenly rushed up to and nearly broke into" 'Iolani Palace.[40] During the arrests, some protesters gave the officers false names. Though unable to climb the palace steps in his motorized wheelchair, Kanalu Young was also arrested. Kekai Perry remembers Young's arrest:

> In the heat of the arrest, [Young] turned off the charge of his chair and shut it down. The worst thing happened when they pulled me and the others away and he was left alone. They couldn't move him and the sheriffs ended up pulling out his tubes used for his bodily functions, ripped him from the chair and threw him in the paddy wagon on the floor. I was put into a police car and didn't see what happened until we were waiting for the paddy wagon at the District Court cell. When they pulled in we saw him lying on the floor with the brothers trying to hold him up. . . . Even now, when I relive that memory and see the image in my mind it pains me. At the same time, those were one [*sic*] of the key moments in my life that taught me what real courage was. . . . He taught me then what it means to give yourself fully to the nation.[41]

Pōkā Laenui described the sheriffs' actions as "a reflection of a police state."[42] Within days, Governor John Waihe'e, a Hawaiian, ordered his attorney general "not to prosecute and no charges were filed."[43]

Kanalu Young, flanked by Ka Lāhui Hawaiʻi leaders Mililani Trask (left) and Haunani-Kay Trask (right), proceeds to ʻIolani Palace on January 17, 1993, to remember and protest one hundred years of U.S. occupation of Hawaiʻi.

ʻOnipaʻa

In January 1993, approximately fifty thousand people attended the ʻOnipaʻa Centennial Commemoration, reenacting the U.S. invasion of Hawaiʻi in January 1893. Hawaiʻi Public Radio broadcast the events live to forty-eight countries.[44] CBS and the Associated Press reported that Governor Waiheʻe refused to raise the American flag over the buildings near ʻIolani Palace January 14–17.[45]

On Sunday, January 17, fifteen thousand people marched from Aloha Tower to ʻIolani Palace.[46] Kanalu Young participated in this procession, flanked by Haunani-Kay Trask and her sister, Mililani Trask. Following the march, Haunani-Kay Trask famously declared during her speech at the ʻIolani Palace, "I am not an American!" Then, comparing the U.S. invasion of Hawaiʻi to the Soviet occupation of the Baltic States, she added that, "We will never forget, any more than the people of Latvia, Lithuania and Estonia forgot."[47] Following the ʻOnipaʻa Commemoration, the term "sovereignty" became acceptable in public discourse, but not the word "occupation."

On November 23, 1993, President Bill Clinton signed into law the Apology Resolution (Public Law 103-150), which declared, "The indigenous Hawaiian people never directly relinquished their claims to their inherent sovereignty as a people." The Apology Resolution also affirmed that "the Congress . . . apologizes to Native Hawaiians on behalf of the people of the United States for the overthrow of the Kingdom of Hawaii on January 17, 1893, and the deprivation of the rights of Native Hawaiians to self-determination." However, the Apology Resolution further claimed that "Congress, through the Newlands Resolution, ratified the cession, annexed Hawai'i as part of the United States, and vested title to the lands in Hawaii in the United States." The Apology Resolution also had a disclaimer at the end: "Nothing in this Joint Resolution is intended to serve as a settlement of any claims against the United States."[48]

By 1994, phrasing from the Apology Resolution kept scholarship and political activism directed toward Native Hawaiian autonomy through "claims to . . . inherent sovereignty" and "self-determination." Regarding inherent sovereignty, as early as 1832, in *Worcester v. Georgia*, the U.S. Supreme Court had recognized the "pre-existing power" of the Cherokee "nation to govern itself."[49] In 1991 the U.S. Supreme Court, in *Oklahoma Tax Commission v. Citizen Band Potawatomi Indian Tribe*, had further clarified the meaning of inherent sovereignty for Native Americans: "Indian tribes are 'domestic dependent nations' that exercise inherent sovereign authority over their members and territories."[50] The wording from the Apology Resolution, "indigenous Hawaiian . . . claims to their inherent sovereignty," implies that Native Hawaiians are a "domestic dependent nation" within the United States.

Conversely, "self-determination" is a concept of modern international law. Self-determination has origins in the writings of Vladimir Lenin and Woodrow Wilson and is found in the United Nations Charter. Article 1(2) of the charter promises "to develop friendly relations among nations based on respect for the principle of equal rights and self-determination of peoples."[51] The 1993 "Draft Declaration on the Rights of Indigenous Peoples" asserts that "indigenous peoples have the right freely to determine their relationship with the States in which they live" (the current United Nations Declaration on the Rights of Indigenous Peoples is even more specific regarding state sovereignty and Indigenous peoples).[52] Thus, rights to self-determination assume that Indigenous people are not in a country of their own and that these Indigenous peoples are attempting to gain international recognition as an independent state. "Rights of Native Hawaiians to self-determination," described in the Apology Resolution, presume that aboriginal Hawaiians are Indigenous people within the United States, rather than the citizenry of an occupied state. Though, as Eyal Benvenisti stresses, "the international law of occupation is not incompatible with the right to self-determination," he also clarifies that occupation "is not a violation of the right to self-determination" but "a violation of the ousted government's sovereignty."[53] As with inherent sovereignty, the term "self-determination" inaccurately places Native Hawaiians within U.S. domestic law, implying that the Hawaiian Islands were never an independent state.

Shortly after the passage of the Apology Resolution, on January 16, 1994, Iaukea Bright of the ʻOhana Council issued a Proclamation of the Restoration of the Independence of the Sovereign Nation of Hawaiʻi. Standing at the ʻIolani Palace pavilion and wearing a T-shirt that read, "Last Star On, First Star Off," Bright declared, to a gathering of about four hundred people, "Today, We, the *Kanaka Maoli*, proclaim our Right of self-determination as a People in accordance with Article 1(2) of the United Nations Charter, and join the World Community of States as an Independent and Sovereign Nation. We hereby reestablish our Independent and Sovereign Nation of Hawaiʻi, that was illegally taken from the Kanaka Maoli on January 17, 1893."[54] By grouping Kanaka Maoli (aboriginal Hawaiians) and "self-determination" with the intent to "reestablish our Independent and Sovereign Nation of Hawaiʻi," the proclamation reveals the deep confusion that persisted regarding Hawaiʻi's political status. The distinctions between an occupied state and a colonized people remained muddled. While the proclamation was a bold move, in 1994 Hawaiians were barely closer to ending the U.S. occupation than they had been during the late 1960s.

Rethinking the Native Hawaiian Past

In the wake of the 1993 Apology Resolution, some sought new answers for addressing Hawaiʻi's independence issues and found explanations in the still evolving discourse on occupation. At about this time, Kanalu Young also went through his own transformation.

On August 14, 1994, twenty-five years after the accident, Young revisited the swimming cove where his injury had occurred. Young believed that he "remained an angry man," who "channeled [his] anger into political activism."[55] A year earlier, his wife of twenty years had died of cancer. Surrounded by a "flotilla of friends adorned with lei," the pilgrimage to the swimming cove was, for Young, "an act of forgiving the ocean and myself and starting a journey towards peace."[56] In 1995 Young completed his dissertation, "Rethinking the Native Hawaiian Past," and he soon found a new inspiration for his subsequent scholarship and politics—what would be described as "occupation theory."

In a 1995 *University of Hawaiʻi Law Review* article, Jennifer M. L. Chock was the first to argue that "the U.S. Senate failed to ratify the [annexation] treaty of 1897" and that "the Newlands Resolution would not be operative in Hawaiʻi since a resolution cannot bind people residing outside of the United States' jurisdiction." Chock concluded, "The United States is an alien colonial power that has occupied the Hawaiian nation for over a century." Chock also proposed that reparations may be sought "through the international Court of Justice."[57]

As early as 1996, Kanalu Young began discussing with Keanu Sai and others the illegality of the U.S. occupation.[58] And in 1998, the centennial marker for the U.S. occupation, the documentary *We Are Who We Were: From Resistance to Affirmation,* and its accompanying pamphlet, contended that the sovereignty of the Hawaiian Islands had not merged with the United States. Keanu Sai, who had raised awareness of the U.S. occupation of Hawai'i by challenging the legality of land titles issued after the 1893 occupation, edited the 1998 pamphlet *The Events That Prevented Annexation of the Hawaiian Islands.*[59]

As part of the commemoration events on August 12, 1998, 2,000–5,000 people marched from the Royal Mausoleum at Mauna 'Ala, the burial place of Hawai'i's monarchs, to 'Iolani Palace, the seat of Hawaiian governance.[60] An eighteen-hour vigil for "Fallen Warriors" also remembered those who had "made a significant contribution to the contemporary indigenous Hawaiian movement."[61] Recovered from the U.S. National Archives by Noenoe Silva, the 1897 "petitions of Hawaiians against annexation" were on display at 'Iolani Palace.[62] In addition, the reestablished Hawaiian Patriotic League, with the video team Nā Maka o Ka 'Āina, produced the documentary and pamphlet explaining the events of 1898.[63] The pamphlet stated, "For the past one hundred years, it was assumed that Joint Resolution No. 55 [the Newlands Resolution] possessed the power and effect of a treaty of annexation. However, according to International law and practice, that is false. Joint Resolution no. 55, is not a ratification of a treaty of annexation, but just an internal piece of United States Legislation."[64] The pamphlet offered the conclusion that "without a treaty of annexation, American sovereignty does not exist in these islands. *There was no Annexation.*"[65]

By the beginning of the new century, most Hawaiian activists, scholars, and organizations remained committed to the notion of colonization and the assertion of Native Hawaiian rights to self-determination, either through the Akaka Bill (a U.S. domestic law for Native Hawaiians), or internationally through the rights of Indigenous peoples and the UN decolonization process. By this time, Keanu Sai had also served as the "agent for the Hawaiian Kingdom" at the Permanent Court of Arbitration in The Hague during the legal proceedings for *Lance Paul Larsen v. the Hawaiian Kingdom* (1999–2001).[66] In fall 2002, when Sai returned as a graduate student to the University of Hawai'i at Mānoa, Young aided Sai in educating others regarding Hawai'i's occupation.

In 2003 Young became the faculty advisor for the Hawaiian Society of Law and Politics, a student organization at the University of Hawai'i "that applies Public International Law . . . to Hawaiian history" and promotes "the development of curriculum on the subject of Hawaiian statehood under international law."[67] Young would also publish two articles in the society's *Hawaiian Journal of Law and Politics*: "An Interdisciplinary Study of the Term 'Hawaiian'" (2004) and "Kuleana: Toward a Historiography of Hawaiian National Consciousness, 1780–2001" (2006). In his article on the concept "Hawaiian," Young argues, "The term indigenous peoples used in the political context to define aboriginal Hawaiians and their international status as an exclusive group seeking self-determination is, legally speaking, not applicable to central concerns of the Hawaiian State because in our case, aboriginal Hawaiians as Hawaiian nationals are in control of the apparatus for engaging the American occupant State-to-State *i ka manawa ku pono.*"[68] And in his "Kuleana" article, Young contends, "History based in Hawaiian national consciousness requires continuous, thoughtful academic presentations in a variety of texts and contexts, including journals of published scholarship, monographs, and surveys." He adds, "Hawaiian nationals cannot be ostriches whose heads remain buried in the same historical sand as the purveyors of the occupying forces here."[69]

In 2005 the Center for Hawaiian Studies began a master of arts degree program. As curriculum developed, Young proposed a seminar course, History of Hawaiian Kingdom Law, concentrating on "domestic and international law as it relates to the history of the Hawaiian Kingdom."[70] The content of Young's course remained outside the prevailing postcolonial discourse, such as Merry's *Colonizing Hawai'i*, Osorio's *Dismembering Lāhui*, and Silva's *Aloha Betrayed.* According to Jon Osorio, director of the Center for Hawaiian Studies at the time, the main reason a class on "occupation theory" happened was because of Young's determination:

> He designed the course. This is called academic freedom. Kanalu pushed for the course. He had tenure. . . . The bigger question is, Why were there so many students in the class? What is it that's happening in the university and in Hawai'i today, where there's more and more interest in that kind of analysis? . . . There are a couple of the people here in the department who were not happy with what Kanalu was teaching. But I was the director, and I wasn't one of them. And nobody would have dared try to stop him from teaching something like this. Not for a minute.[71]

Young's course offered a means for the discussion of Hawai'i's occupation to enter mainstream academics at the University of Hawai'i.

On January 8, 2003, Kaleikoa Ka'eo surmised the thoughts of many Hawaiians when he wrote, "Some people say the sovereignty movement is dead, but I think the thing that is dying is the old discourse about nation-within-a-nation. That's where the movement was 10 years ago."[72] Haunani-Kay Trask had similarly announced to the *Hawai'i Island Journal* in August 2003, "The sovereignty movement for all intents and purposes is dead."[73] Occupation theory appears to have gained interest because the perception existed, for some, that the colonization narrative had run its course. And by 2005, the discourse began shifting toward occupation theory.

Since Young's initial class in 2007, one student from the course has completed an MA and two others a PhD, describing Hawai'i as an "occupied state."[74] In addition,

Hawaiian studies professor, musician, composer, and author Kanalu Young at a demonstration at the Hawai'i State Legislature on January 17, 2001.

one student from the class has helped to create a new course at Kapi'olani Community College: Introduction to the Hawaiian State.[75] The initial course of seventeen students was first taught in spring 2008.

Today the future of Young's seminar History of Hawaiian Kingdom Law is uncertain. On August 31, 2008, due to complications from his disability, Kanalu Young passed into spirit. After months of suffering, at Young's own request, doctors removed the tube that had allowed him to breathe. That day, as Jon Osorio sang "Hawaiian Soul," originally composed for George Helm, Young leaned toward the nurse and nodded, smiling, knowing that he was making his final decision. "How about after this song" he mouthed, unable to speak with the tube still inserted in his lungs. Then he whispered, "Wait, in about an hour." When the doctors removed the tube and began the morphine drip, Young, surrounded by family, friends, and students, slipped gently into sleep.

In his long struggle, Dr. Kanalu Young had found peace through his efforts to bring occupation theory into mainstream academics at the University of Hawai'i. Yet the people of Hawai'i, the U.S. government, and the world have not yet fully acknowledged the U.S. occupation of Hawai'i. For now, that peace lingers somewhere outside Shangri La.

Notes

1. George Terry Kanalu Young, PhD, was my mentor and friend. Cardwell, "Hawaiian Superman."
2. Young, "August on My Mind," 329.
3. As I was one of his primary caretakers during the final years of his life, much of this information comes from personal conversations with Dr. Kanalu Young.
4. Young, "August on My Mind," 329–330.
5. Young, "August on my Mind," 329–330.
6. U.S. Senate, "Secret Debate on Seizure of the Hawaiian Islands."
7. "Anglo-Franco Declaration, November 28, 1843," 114.
8. Oppenheim, *International Law*, 287–289, 294–295.
9. Lili'uokalani, "Queen Liliuokalani's Protest of Annexation"; see also Silva, *Aloha Betrayed*, 151.
10. Russ, *The Hawaiian Republic, and Its Struggle to Win Annexation*, 296.
11. Hawai'i is often compared to Texas, but Texas entered the Union as a state, as stipulated in article 4, section 3 of the U.S. Constitution; see also Oppenheim, *International Law*, 266–270.
12. U.S. Congress and Senate, *Joint Resolution to Provide for Annexing the Hawaiian Islands to the United States.*
13. "Hawaii Merged with the Union"; Addleman, *History of the United States Army in Hawaii 1849 to 1939*, 81.
14. Out of "roughly 381,859 eligible voters." Edward E. Johnston to Honorable William F. Quinn, Governor of Hawaii, "July 2, 1959, Memorandum," Statehood Hawaii: Probing a New Statehood History, http://www.statehoodhawaii.org/hist/pleb_results.html (accessed June 11, 2010).
15. Pukui, Haertig, and Lee, *Nānā i ke Kumu*, 53–54.
16. Oliveira, "ALOHA Association, Inc.," 5.
17. Bone, "Aboriginal Lands of Hawaiian Ancestry."
18. Bone, "Aboriginal Lands of Hawaiian Ancestry," A4.
19. Complete bill found in Oliveira, "ALOHA Association."
20. Oliveira, "ALOHA Association," 4–5 of H.R. 15666.
21. Ka'apu, "Statement of Kekoa D. Kaapu."
22. Blaisdell, "Kekuni Blaisdell," 371.
23. The terminology is confusing: "native" is not capitalized. Constitution of the State of Hawaii (1978), article 12, section 5, Hawaii Legislative Reference Bureau, http://hawaii.gov/lrb/con/conart12.html (accessed June 11, 2010).
24. Constitution of the State of Hawaii (1978), article 12, section 5; cf. Office of Hawaiian Affairs, "History."
25. *State of Hawaii v. Wilford K. Pulawa*, Motion to Dismiss, 58 HI 377, 569 P.2d 900, 8 (1st Cir., 1978).
26. Lili'uokalani, *Hawaii's Story by Hawaii's Queen.*
27. Pōkā Laenui, "Hayden Burgess," in Mast and Mast, *Autobiography of Protest in Hawai'i*, 409–410.
28. Laenui, "Hayden Burgess," 410.
29. *State of Hawaii v. Wilford K. Pulawa*, Motion to Dismiss.
30. Laenui, "Hayden Burgess," 410–411.

31. Benvenisti, *The International Law of Occupation*, 17.
32. Cardwell, "Hawaiian Superman."
33. Kame'eleihiwa, *Native Land and Foreign Desires*, 317.
34. Trask, *From a Native Daughter*, 47–49.
35. U.S. Department of Justice, "Legal Issues Raised by Proposed Presidential Proclamation" (1988), 237, 252.
36. Morse and Hamid, "American Annexation of Hawaii," 447, 449.
37. Conrow, "Rebuilding Kaho'olawe."
38. Oshiro, "Arrests Anger Hawaiians."
39. Mariani and Ohira, "Sovereignty Seekers under Vigil."
40. Mariani and Ohira, "Sovereignty Seekers under Vigil."
41. Kekailoa Perry, e-mail message to author, November 8, 2008.
42. Oshiro, "Arrests Anger Hawaiians."
43. Perry, e-mail, November 8, 2008.
44. I was in charge of security for the event. Hawai'i Public Radio broadcast Pōkā Laenui's interviews live.
45. Mitchell, "Hawaii to Remove US Flag during Centennial Commemoration," CBS *Morning News*, January 14, 1993 (LexisNexis); Bruce Dunford, "Hawaii Governor Bans American Flag from State Buildings," Associated Press, January 13, 1993 (LexisNexis).
46. Office of Hawaiian Affairs, *'Onipa'a*, 106.
47. Trask, "January 17, 1993, Speech." Niklaus Schweizer has also been talking about the similarities between Hawai'i and the Baltic States since the late 1980s.
48. Office of Hawaiian Affairs, *'Onipa'a*, 154–155.
49. C. J. Marshall, *Samuel A. Worcester v. the State of Georgia*, 31 U.S. 515; 8 L. Ed. 483; 1832 U.S. LEXIS 489 (1832).
50. William Rehnquist, *Oklahoma Tax Commission v. Citizen Band Potawatomi Indian Tribe of Oklahoma*, 498 U.S. 505; 111 S. Ct. 905; 112 L. Ed. 2d 1112; 1991 U.S. LEXIS 1298; 59 U.S.L.W. 4137; 91 Cal. Daily Op. Service 1504; 91 Daily Journal dar 2376 (1991).
51. See article 1, section 2, of United Nations, "Charter of the United Nations," http://www.un.org/en/documents/charter/index.shtml (accessed June 11, 2010).
52. Reprinted in Trask, *From a Native Daughter*. The September 7, 2007, United Nations Declaration on the Rights of Indigenous Peoples (article 46, section 1) states, "Nothing in this Declaration may be interpreted as implying for any State, people, group or person any right to engage in any activity or to perform any act contrary to the Charter of the United Nations or construed as authorizing or encouraging any action which would dismember or impair, totally or in part, the territorial integrity or political unity of sovereign and independent States." Trask, *From a Native Daughter*, 199–210; cf. United Nations, "United Nations Declaration on the Rights of Indigenous Peoples, Adopted by General Assembly Resolution 61/295 on 13 September 2007," http://www.un.org/esa/socdev/unpfii/en/drip.html.
53. Benvenisti, *The International Law of Occupation*, 17.
54. "Hawaii's Search for Sovereignty"; see also Nation of Hawai'i, "Proclamation of the Restoration of the Independence of the Sovereign Nation of Hawai'i."
55. Young, "August on My Mind," 330.
56. Young, "August on My Mind," 332.
57. Chock, "One Hundred Years of Illegitimacy," 492–511.
58. Jonathan Kamakawiwo'ole Osorio, interview by author, Honolulu, Hawai'i, January 2009.

59. Perez, "State Won't Step into Perfect Title Deed Disputes."

60. The *Honolulu Star-Bulletin* placed the size of the march at two thousand. Eyewitness accounts place the number at five thousand. Altonn, "Ceremonies 'Make Things Right.'"

61. Dallas Kealiihooneiaina Mossman Vogeler (who died on February 28, 1996) was among those honored. Altonn, "Ceremonies 'Make Things Right'"; Omandam, "Fallen Warriors."

62. Altonn, "Ceremonies 'Make Things Right'"; see also Silva, *Aloha Betrayed.*

63. For more information on the Hui Aloha ʻĀina Hawaiian Patriotic League, see Silva, *Aloha Betrayed*, 150–159.

64. Hawaiian Patriotic League, Nā Maka o ka ʻĀina, and Hawaiʻi Loa Kūlike Kākou Committee, *An Historical Overview of the Events That Prevented Annexation*, 20.

65. Hawaiian Patriotic League, Nā Maka o ka ʻĀina, and Hawaiʻi Loa Kūlike Kākou Committee, *An Historical Overview of the Events That Prevented Annexation*, 20, emphasis in original.

66. Crawford, Griffith, and Greenwood, "In the Permanent Court of Arbitration."

67. Hawaiian Society of Law and Politics, "Constitution and By-Laws: Constitution," 2004, http://www2.hawaii.edu/~hslp/constitution.html.

68. Young, "An Interdisciplinary Study of the Term Hawaiian."

69. Young, "Kuleana."

70. Kanalu Young, Hawaiian Studies 691 syllabus, Kamakakūokalani Center for Hawaiian Studies, University of Hawaiʻi at Mānoa, 2007.

71. Osorio, interview.

72. Kelly, "Kūkākūkā," 3.

73. Calizar, "Haunani-Kay Trask . . . in Her Own Voice," 3.

74. Gonschor, "Law as a Tool of Oppression and Liberation"; Beamer, "Na Wai Ka Mana?"; Stephen Kūhiō Vogeler, "'For Your Freedom and Ours.'"

75. Palani H. Kelly and Steve Laudig, Hawaiian Studies 691, syllabus, Kapiʻolani Community College, 2008.

CHAPTER 12. Make'e Pono Lāhui Hawai'i

A STUDENT LIBERATION MOMENT

Kekailoa Perry

> Ua pau ke ao i hala, 'O kēia ke ao e ala
>
> —'ALOHILANI KUALA ROGERS, 1990

The first line of 'Alohilani Rogers's 'ōlelo no'eau (proverb) cautions that the era of U.S. occupation that enabled the perpetuation of myths depicting Hawaiian people and culture as ill suited to live in a modern, civil society has no place in this present space. The second line reflects hope and resilience for a restored Hawaiian nation. This line also calls on us to kū'ē (stand against) U.S. imperialism. It can be read as a pointed gesture for all Hawaiians to wake up to their humanity, embrace their national identity, and courageously carry the enormous weight of the nation on their backs. In fact, the 'ōlelo is all of the above.

Rogers's verse describes a student organization born from struggle on the University of Hawai'i at Mānoa (UHM) campus. The 'ōlelo no'eau reminds us that life is cyclical and filled with valuable lessons. The phrase is also code for a mini student uprising that took root in 1990. The organization born from the uprising was called Make'e Pono Lāhui Hawai'i, or the Hawaiian Student Liberation Union (HSLU).

A Preamble of Sorts

> The aim of the Hawaiian Student Liberation Union is to eliminate from the University of Hawai'i at Mānoa any and all forms of colonialism and vestiges of oppression and exploitation being suffered by all native Hawaiian students.
>
> —STRUCTURE OF THE HAWAIIAN STUDENT LIBERATION UNION, DECEMBER 18, 1990

This chapter presents a short mo'olelo (story) of the origins of Make'e Pono Lāhui Hawai'i (Make'e) or the HSLU and the deeds and actions of its collective membership. The organization held a nationalistic political agenda influenced by Malcolm X, Frantz Fanon, Kwame Ture, the Black Panther Party, and Native Hawaiian organizations such as the Nuclear Free and Independent Pacific–Hawai'i, Ka Lāhui Hawai'i, Hui Mālama i nā Kūpuna o Hawai'i Nei, and Hawaiians United for Liberation and Independence.

The tale is told through the weary eyes of one member. Initially, the story may appear to carry nostalgia. But that is not the purpose of this telling. The intent is to contribute in a small way to the genealogy of native resistance. Make'e's story tells of an organic student awakening during the development of the Center for Hawaiian Studies and Operation Kua'ana. We found guidance from former student activists turned professional organizers, who were engaged in community action. Through those relationships the fire of a previous generation became a vital part of the Make'e identity.

The Make'e story highlights the struggles that we as students either initiated or supported. The story also speaks to some of the internal struggles that ultimately caused our group to disband. It tracks the members generally and highlights the music and politics developed during their short-lived student uprising. The story shows how community organizing can influence decision makers as well as demand a commitment from the organization's members. The essay celebrates a time of student uprising but avoids the temptation to essentialize this small moment of young Hawaiian resistance. It is what it is: students, young Hawaiians, taking the privilege of the ivory tower and turning it, in the best way they knew how, upside down.

Uniting under the Banner for Resistance

The HSLU was an organization whose lofty goals were motivated by a nationalist agenda that gained momentum in the mid-1980s. The decade of 1980–1990 saw tremendous political action and might even be considered a logical result of the cultural renaissance of the late 1970s in Hawai'i. In 1990 the HSLU formally organized by adopting our structural document or manifesto for action at the University of Hawai'i. The HSLU gave itself a Hawaiian name, Make'e Pono Lāhui Hawai'i, which, loosely translated, means the yearning for a balanced continuum for the Hawaiian nation. For a few short years, Make'e became synonymous with a series of student-led boycotts, campus-wide soapbox forums, and involvement in community actions or programs for social justice.

The membership of the organization included undergraduate and graduate students from the University of Hawai'i. The founding members were (in alphabetical order) Makahiapo Cashman, Kaleimomi'olani Decker, Kaheleonalani Dukelow, Miki Eff, Konia Freitas, Kaleikoa Ka'eo, Momi Kamahele, 'Alohilani Kuala, Renee Lewis, Nahua Patrinos, Kekailoa Perry, Nohealani Wallace, and Terry Kanalu Young.

Make'e's ideology was influenced by the Center for Hawaiian Studies and its iconic professor Haunani-Kay Trask. By 1988 Trask had authored several courses that challenged students to critically analyze history and present situations through an anti-colonial lens. The courses became the reawakening of students who supported Hawaiian resistance to U.S. occupation and hegemony.

Trask's classes stoked the political flames and exposed the university as a purveyor of contested information. More importantly, Trask showed students that the university was a potential space for organizing revolutionary thinking. Trask also exposed students to the larger community, and that connection solidified our resolve to rise up. Make'e grew from an intellectual demand for change and an intimate desire to make change from ground zero—inside the Hawaiian communities.

Make'e declared several purposes in our guiding document or manifesto that addressed issues in the university and the Hawaiian community. The language was abrasive and direct, and purposely challenged people to oppose the racist and oppressive structures of colonialism at the university and in Hawai'i's larger community. Our opposition was manifest in an educational strategy that was activist in nature.

Borrowing from Malcolm X's now infamous resistance phrase, Make'e members resolved to oppose all functions of U.S. colonialism "by any means necessary." And we meant it. In practice, Make'e's philosophical approach was a naive attempt at radically attacking segments of the intellectual community in order to alter the prevailing mindset that condoned, supported, and accepted U.S. occupation in Hawai'i.

Our members were young and operated independently of the varying political identities that existed in the Hawaiian community. Our radical agenda and approach caused us to gravitate toward the more vanguard or fringe activist organizations beyond UHM. These relationships broadened our political awareness beyond the confines of the university.

Make'e's eagerness to support Hawaiian issues led us to the forefront of various political struggles. As young people, our involvement was considered refreshing and chaotic at the same time. We were eager to learn from the activists who helped shape the modern Hawaiian movement. We responded well and aggressively to the ideas and tactics of seasoned activists such as Kīhei Soli Niheu, Lei'ānuenue Niheu, Kawaipuna Prejean, Kekuni Blaisdell, Marion Kelly, Mililani and Haunani-Kay Trask, Ho'oipo DeCambra, Skippy Ioane, Walter Ritte, Terri Keko'olani, Palikapu Dedman, Pua and Ed Kanahele, Walter Paulo, Nani Rogers, Emmet Aluli, Julie Ann Cachola, and many others.

Make'e helped to organize protests on various hot issues impacting the Hawaiian community including the state's abuses of Hawaiian Home Lands, the development of golf courses on Moloka'i, the printing of the Hawaiian language in the daily newspapers, challenging the Global Congress of Heritage Interpretation International, and generally advocating for greater rights for underrepresented minorities.[1]

Make'e also made efforts to infiltrate institutional bodies through the introduction of resolutions in the state legislature and the Association of Students at the University

Make'e Pono members, including Kahele Dukelow (far right), Nohea Wallace, and Kekailoa Perry, stand on King Street across from the 'Iolani Palace. Kawaipuna Prejean, a mentor and the visionary behind the 1993 Ka Ho'okolokolo Nui Kānaka Maoli, holds the "No More Uncle Tom" sign.

of Hawai'i, running Hawaiian nationalist slates for student elections at the university (and winning), running weekly columns in the student newspaper *Ka Leo O Hawai'i*, hosting a weekly Hawaiian talk radio program on 90.3 FM KTUH, and composing songs recorded and played on local radio stations with large listening audiences.

Finding a Space

In 1989, UH administrator Amy Agbayani prepared a report titled "Teaching and Learning" for the Office of Faculty Development and Academic Support at UHM. In the study, Agbayani found that 70 percent of the tenured faculty at UHM were Caucasian (a majority of which were identified as men). People of color made up only 26 percent of the tenured faculty. Hawaiian tenured faculty made up only 1.5 percent of the 26 percent minority tenured positions. By contrast, the UHM student body had a minority, student of color population of 67.5 percent, demonstrating a marked difference between those who held teaching powers in the university and the students being mentored by them.

Agbayani's research added to a larger study relating to the development of a stronger Hawaiian presence at the university: the *Ka'ū University of Hawai'i Hawaiian Studies*

Task Force Report.[2] Completed in December 1986 by the University of Hawai'i Hawaiian Studies Task Force, the report recommended that the UH develop a center for Hawaiian studies and a student services division that would address the abysmal representation of Hawaiians at the undergraduate and graduate levels.[3]

The Center for Hawaiian Studies was created as a direct response to the disparity of the times, and the institution's subsequent growth was no coincidence. The professors and administrators found that the creation of a center focusing on the study of all things Hawaiian would be the catalyst for positive changes to the university's poor record of supporting Hawaiians and minorities on campus. Abraham Pi'ianai'a was the director of the Hawaiian Studies certificate in liberal studies. Kekuni Blaisdell became the Center for Hawaiian Studies' first director, followed by Haunani-Kay Trask. When Trask was director she had a staff of two: office manager and secretary "Aunty Marv" Marvlee Naukana-Guilding and assistant professor Lilikala Kame'eleihiwa. The two professors were public icons of the new department. Aunty Marv was the foundation and her behind-the-scenes work empowered the entire department.

The creation of the Center for Hawaiian Studies was followed by a new Hawaiian student services center. In 1988 the newly created Hawaiian student services program hired 'Ekela Kanī'aupi'o to be its director. The program was aptly named Operation Kua'ana (Kua'ana), modeled after the Filipino student services program, Operation Manong. Kanī'aupi'o was tasked with three major goals: increase Hawaiian student admissions, retain Hawaiian students through the duration of their education, and create Hawaiian student placement opportunities in the private and public sectors. Kanī'aupi'o's remarkable skill and charisma helped build strong awareness in students and brought them together as they struggled with UH's institutional racism.

Students were eager to participate in the new Hawaiian-focused program and soon Kua'ana became a focal point for the university's Hawaiian community. With the Center for Hawaiian Studies and Kua'ana student services programs underway, the university climate seemed ripe for action. However, student apathy and fear made many reluctant to speak out in an uninviting, non-Hawaiian arena. In fact, student fears and apathy reinforced Agbayani's assertion that institutional racism (however subtle) was an endemic part of the University of Hawai'i.

By September 1990, students were pushed into action when Professor Trask responded to a haole student in an op-ed piece in the *Ka Leo O Hawai'i* newspaper. Joey Carter, a UH philosophy student, bemoaned the fact that, as a haole in Hawai'i, he was the member of a minority group subjected to local racism. Carter argued that what he experienced from locals amounted to unjustified racism brought about by a historical distrust of haoles dating from the early nineteenth century in Hawai'i. In essence, Carter was saying that the historic wrongs committed against Hawaiians by haoles and the U.S. government were not his fault.[4]

Trask responded that U.S. white privilege could not be sidestepped or disavowed with the passing of time. White privilege and settler notions of equal rights to land and capital in Hawai'i come at the expense of the native population, she said. More directly, Trask used Carter's editorial to illustrate the practice of political and social amnesia that relieves U.S. settlers from recognizing their role in the destruction of the present Hawaiian nation. In the end, Trask told Carter (and all those who subscribed to his amnesia politics) to leave Hawai'i.

In one fell swoop, after a decades-long slumber, racism in the islands burst into the university scene with a fever pitch of emotions and actions. Trask was accused of using her power as a professor to intimidate Carter. In response, students and faculty argued that Carter's editorial and Trask's response letter were conducted in a public forum—the UHM newspaper—which was an appropriate venue to debate political and social issues.

Numerous professors—notably those from the philosophy department, where Carter was a major—attacked Trask, calling for her resignation or termination. The fact that many of her detractors were among the 70 percent of tenured faculty that were Caucasian brought the statistical evidence in Agbayani's study into full relief.

Worse was the nonresponse of other faculty and staff. Some appeared to quietly agree with the white attackers while others sheepishly followed the status quo of the university for fear of retribution. To be on Trask's side meant a greater chance of experiencing the same vile and racially motivated hate both in and outside the university community. Though many came forth to openly support Trask, the level of negativity was overwhelming even for the bravest faculty member.

Student mobilization in support of Trask and against the larger institutional racism of the university was swift and in many ways organic. The result was a series of impromptu demonstrations throughout the university campus, beginning with a large antiracism and counter anti-Hawaiian demonstration at Sakamaki Hall, where the philosophy department was housed.

Make'e members Hiapo Cashman and Kaleikoa Ka'eo recalled to me the grave and potentially life-threatening situation that they and Trask were in. Cashman remembered, "It was serious. Once we got to Sakamaki, Haunani-Kay was surrounded by supporters and haters. There had to be over a thousand people outside and on the streets, many of them angry with HK and yelling at her. She was strong and defiant but the security and cops had no way of managing the crowd. So we made sure we were there with her." Ka'eo further explained, "We realized at that moment that we had to protect Haunani and ourselves and formed a wall between her and the larger crowd. We were ready to go." For Make'e, the rally at Sakamaki was our initiation into direct action.

In essence, students are the principal stakeholders in the university and carry tremendous power due to their educational privilege in society and economic investment

Kaleikoa Ka'eo, Nohea Wallace, and other members of Make'e Pono stand behind Professor Haunani-Kay Trask at the University of Hawai'i Philosophy Department on November 2, 1990.

in the institution. As a result, Hawaiian students armed with Trask's anticolonialism and critical analysis organized to address racism at the university as well as the broader colonial system that had a stranglehold on the islands. Hawaiian Studies and Kua'ana became the two institutional bodies that provided the space to mobilize a more organized student action.

By December 1990, Make'e determined that a home base was needed on the UH campus. The rationale was simple: land is a determining factor for the exercise of sovereignty. Therefore, Make'e made it a goal to establish pu'uhonua, or native sanctuaries, in the university. Make'e believed that by creating safe places to gather, Hawaiians would be able to build a stronger foothold in the university and ultimately reorganize the structure for the benefit of Hawaiian decolonization and independence.

Again, Make'e drew on their experiences and developed an ideological framework to empower Hawaiians on campus. The manifesto was our guidepost and constitution for action and UH became our land base. We proposed systematically taking over UH lands through various forms of occupation and claimed ownership of the entire UH campus. The motto "Keep Hawaiian lands in Hawaiian hands" was a mainstay and our presence in and around campus was meant to do just that.

Moore Hall became the first puʻuhonua for Hawaiians who needed a place to call home. Four offices that housed Hawaiian Studies and Operation Kuaʻana and a hallway became the safe house for student organizing and socializing. Students occupied the area and found solace in the fact that there was a small space in the university that was uncontested by the institution.

Thus, the first major lesson for the group was to establish a space where we could be self-determining, a space to govern ourselves from a position of power.

I Ka ʻŌlelo No Ke Ola

Hawaiian language advocacy became one of Makeʻe's more focused campaigns. All of the students in our organization enrolled in Hawaiian language classes and maintained a strong relationship to the Hawaiian language community. While we all made attempts to speak out on Hawaiian language issues, some of our strongest advocates were Kaleikoa Kaʻeo, Nohealani Wallace, and ʻAlohilani Kuala. Hawaiian language had an established network of nontenured faculty and instructors who provided significant support behind the scenes, enabling us to be the voice of our student movement. However, one of the more empowering moments in our language campaign occurred when native speaker Tuti Kanahele and others came to our rallies holding signs and joining in the demonstrations. The support of Tuti and the broader community gave us the confidence to speak and organize.

Makeʻe emphasized ʻōlelo in our functions and pushed for stronger language revitalization efforts at the university. Makeʻe's language campaign started with the university's student-run newspaper, *Ka Leo O Hawaiʻi*. The goal was simple: provide a venue for the weekly use and exploration of ideas in Hawaiian through heavily accessed print media. Makeʻe believed language revitalization required normalized use in everyday social settings like the newspaper. Exposing language enthusiasts and nonspeakers to the written word would create awareness and generate curiosity to pursue Hawaiian language. The public printing and display of Hawaiian would also provide a more functional space for its use and practice. Such an arena would help release the Hawaiian language from its less active classroom role and eliminate the stigma that Hawaiian is a novel, cute, yet dying language.

Makeʻe's strategy was a basic negotiated approach with an activist twist. The first step was to develop a platform for the campaign. Makeʻe demanded that *Ka Leo* print Hawaiian language stand-alone articles as part of their regular weekly publication. We based the demands on Makeʻe's nationalist agenda and the legal principles of the Hawaiʻi state constitution, establishing the Hawaiian language as an official state language in 1978.[5]

We then generated a list of all *Ka Leo* funders and advertisers. We developed important fact-finding methods including identifying *Ka Leo*'s distribution and delivery locations, and identifying the printing process and equipment suppliers needed for daily operations. We coordinated a phone and mail list to all student, faculty, and community resources associated with *Ka Leo*'s operations.

Initially, *Ka Leo*'s editorial board denied Make'e's demand to print the Hawaiian language, arguing that Hawaiian is a foreign language and *Ka Leo* is an English-medium paper. Make'e reiterated the legal status of the Hawaiian language and pointed out the obvious flaw in the editorial board's argument: the newspaper's name is Hawaiian.

Ka Leo editors raised equal protection concerns arguing that privileging the Hawaiian language would discriminate against others. This rationale was equally flawed, as Make'e did not object to other languages being printed. Instead, the key issue was that privileging English over Hawaiian was discriminatory and unconstitutional under state law. Though our intentions were nationalistic, we asserted that the use of Hawaiian language was constitutionally protected regardless of race. Arguments became circular, with *Ka Leo* staff balking at any real effort to resolve the issue in favor of printing in Hawaiian.

In the second stage of the campaign, Make'e began a series of soapbox forums near or around the *Ka Leo* offices calling student and community attention to three issues: (1) the state constitution identifies Hawaiian as an official language of the state; (2) the Hawaiian language is a living language; and (3) *Ka Leo* editors' refusal to print the Hawaiian language in the paper was unjustified and represented a form of institutional racism applied under the direction of a misinformed or malicious editorial board.

Frustrated by the forums, *Ka Leo* writers and publishers countered with negative articles reporting on our actions. *Ka Leo* published unflattering and awkward pictures of Make'e members as a tool of repression. *Ka Leo*'s strategy backfired as public support waned due to the irrational and vengeful acts of the editorial staff. Make'e used *Ka Leo*'s knee-jerk responses to show how institutional power can become structural forms of discrimination against Hawaiians.

In phase three, we allied with the UH community and the rank and file of the paper. The pressure to print stand-alone Hawaiian articles from within the *Ka Leo* and larger UH communities mounted. *Ka Leo* showed some initial signs of concession when they proposed that a Hawaiian article be printed side by side with an English translation. This compromise, from the editors' point of view, was considerable because it provided two times the amount of column space in their publication. However, it also meant that the goal of a stand-alone Hawaiian language article would not occur.

Make'e ramped up the political pressure by organizing a blockade that would impact *Ka Leo*'s distribution operations. Make'e tracked the *Ka Leo* distribution trucks, removed all of the newspapers from the stands, and left notes that said *Ka Leo* would not be delivered due to its discriminatory practices against Hawaiians. A demonstration followed the blockade at the UH campus center. *Ka Leo* newspapers were placed in trash bags and piled on the campus center steps. Students were informed of the issues and encouraged to take the bagged *Ka Leo* papers and dump them in the metaphorical trash bin that printed them, the *Ka Leo* offices. By the end of the demonstration, the *Ka Leo* office entrance was blocked shut with newspapers and no deliveries were made that week.

Ka Leo editors then offered to print stand-alone Hawaiian language articles provided that a synopsis in English ran alongside the article. Make'e responded, "no."

Make'e initiated phase four of the campaign with an advertiser boycott. Letters were mass distributed to all the *Ka Leo* advertisers. The following week, Make'e members posted notices at the front door of each major business advertising in *Ka Leo*. The notices warned that their business would be the subject of a student boycott if they continued to support *Ka Leo*'s policy against printing a stand-alone Hawaiian language article in the paper.

Responses from the businesses were mixed. Some businesses threatened to sue Make'e. Others made shallow assurances that they did not advertise for any political reasons. The fact that many businesses felt compelled to respond at all signaled that Make'e generated leverage in our boycott.

Several larger demonstrations were held at the *Ka Leo* offices. The demonstrations and continued push for a boycott provided considerable negotiating pressure but *Ka Leo* would not move from its original position. Make'e members then made one final push and moved the negotiations into the community.

Specifically, members tracked the location of *Ka Leo*'s editor in chief, interrupted his daily routine, and demanded a favorable negotiated settlement. The UH administration was also being pressured by Make'e through their various allies in the faculty and administration. Seven months into the campaign, several West Coast newspapers picked up the story and ran the news. It appeared that the news of the struggle to save and perpetuate the native language was getting attention in other parts of the United States. While it was not completely clear then, the pressure to concede was mounting for the *Ka Leo* editors.

In the end, the editors and Make'e agreed to two major points. First, the Hawaiian language would be printed in *Ka Leo* beginning with a permanent weekly column. The column was named Ka Leo 'Ōiwi and its first editor was 'Alohilani Kuala. As a concession, Make'e agreed to have an English synopsis available upon request. The author would provide a hard copy of the English synopsis for *Ka Leo* editors but it would not be a part of the publication.

Second, an unrelated English column would also be published weekly, addressing the major political issues that impact the Hawaiian community. The column, named Kūho'one'enu'u, was a more direct political commentary on Hawaiian nationalist issues. The editors writing for the English column were Nahua Patrinos, 'Olani Decker, and myself. Every member of the community played a role in writing articles and developing the ideas for the columns. It was, at all times, a group effort, and the column provided a significant forum for ideas to be shared and reviewed by peers in the UH community.

The Hawaiian language campaign lasted for about one year and was the longest, most successful of Make'e's student-initiated actions. Hawaiian language and politics finally became a regular part of the *Ka Leo O Hawai'i* student newspaper. Later, Make'e worked with Hawaiian language advocates to successfully encourage the *Honolulu Advertiser,* a daily statewide newspaper, to incorporate Hawaiian standardized diacritical marks in their text.

The issue of Hawaiian language normalization and revitalization continues to gain tremendous momentum in the UH and broader community. Today, the *Honolulu Star-Bulletin* prints a regular weekly stand-alone column called Kauakūkalahale. The inaugural printing occurred in October 2002, and its readership remains consistent and strong. Editors Laiana Wong and Kekeha Solis continue to push the envelope with the daily paper by introducing critical pieces, all in Hawaiian, challenging (and encouraging) many to learn and, more importantly, use the language. Though Make'e had folded by the time Kauakūkalahale was born, many in the organization feel encouraged that they had a small role in the growing genealogy of Hawaiian advocates who make culture a real part of the modern Hawaiian world.

Independence: Not Just from the United States but from Us

Make'e's position relating to governance and politics focused on Hawaiian independence. Our manifesto defined sovereignty as having "complete independence and self government. No sub-status or affiliation with the United States." We believed anything less than independence was a compromise of Hawaiian culture, social structure, and nationality. Our members understood the need to transition from U.S. control to independence, and we recognized that the road would be long and arduous. Yet we knew the goal of independence was necessary to ensure that the well-being of the lāhui Hawai'i was not compromised.[6] To that end, we openly advocated for a proactive, confrontational approach that utilized a quasi-nonviolent, self-defense posture. In fact, the manifesto states, "in order for Hawaiians to unite and decolonize together they must do so from the strongest and most radical position since it is true that the process of colonization has been a very violent phenomenon itself. Radicalism is necessary to combat this violence of colonial oppression and eliminate it."

More important than its public persona was Make'e's internal critique of its membership. Members read various analyses of revolutionary and activist writers like George

Helm, Walter Ritte, Frantz Fanon, Albert Memmi, Edward Said, Kwame Ture, and Assata Shakur and spent a considerable time listening to the stories of Hawaiian activists in the community. We borrowed from the actions of past revolutionaries and made a conscious effort to improve our own group's work. As a result, our members understood that the organization was not immune from internal strife and struggle.

Our membership developed several provisions in the structural framework to proactively address the potential hazards of political dysfunction in activist organizations. The provisions were by no means foolproof and in hindsight the language appears more idealistic than functional. Regarding treatment of members and actions within the organization, Make'e's manifesto states that the membership "will put aside all personal differences and be aware of all forms of our colonial mentality so as to bring forth the positive aspects of self-determination which will benefit the whole of the Hawaiian people."

Other provisions relating to the internal function of membership include references to members' commitment to one another and to reject various vices such as substance abuse. Our code of conduct also addressed appearance and attitude. Under the code, members were "responsible for all their actions in any and all settings public or private" and therefore, "no members are allowed to participate in Make'e functions . . . under the influence of foreign drug substances."

Some of the more influential persons regarding the reflective and self-critical approach were people like Edward Said and Malcolm X. For UH students in the 1980s, authors like Said and Malcolm X were not part of a typical course's required reading. Haunani-Kay Trask introduced us to these thinkers. In many ways, Haunani-Kay was not a typical university professor. And her courses inspired us to read more activist writers beyond the classroom setting. We recognized that the activism of the 1960s and 1970s was an effective way to bring the theory of revolution to the people. We gravitated to these writers because they had a plan and were committed to carrying it into existence by whatever means necessary.

Said argues that the closer one is to power, the greater one's sacrifice will be to maintain that proximity.[7] He cautions that, in struggle, the importance of the organization lies in the hope it provides to the oppressed people it serves. But along with that hope comes the price of submission that the individual must pay to the organization. Organizations need individual members to maintain a critical distance from the center so that they can push it to advance and improve on its delivery of political and social issues for their people. However, submission means that the individual must give up the critical distance necessary to openly and effectively critique the organization. It is a double-edged sword. The lack of critical distance creates a mass support network but tends to obscure the critique and lessen the organization's ability to advance or improve.

Said also comments on the danger that lies within the leadership of an organization. Allowing the organization to operate unchecked, without regular critique, is dangerous and influences many people in leadership to mask their shortcomings and use the group's allegiances "to insulate themselves from their mistakes."[8] Thus, it's not enough to just belong to an organization designed to assist Hawaiians. Part of the group representation is the willingness to reexamine the actions of the group and make changes necessary to secure native Hawaiian self-governance and not replicate unhealthy or destructive methods. Looking back at Make'e, Said's call for reexamination was an integral part of the organization's overall function. Our manifesto actually forced us to internalize our actions and make very difficult choices regarding actions and relationships.

Malcolm X makes similar calls for internal critiques. Members of Make'e gravitated to his practical approach to dealing with issues that impact the organization. One of the more poignant remarks from Malcolm X comes from a 1964 interview with Les Crane.[9] In that interview, Crane asked Malcolm to explain how he dealt with the criticisms leveled against his political approach by other "negro leaders." Malcolm's response helped Make'e guide its own approach to group management and dynamics. Malcolm stated, "All of us should be critics of each other. Whenever you can't stand criticism you can never grow. I don't think that it serves any purpose for the leaders of our people to waste their time fighting each other needlessly. I think that we accomplish more when we sit down in private and iron out whatever difference that may exist and try and then do something constructive for the benefit of our people. But on the other hand, I don't think we should be above criticism. I don't think that anyone should be above criticism."[10]

Make'e focused intently on the notion that no one should be above criticism. As a practical matter, our members spent more time criticizing identified political adversaries. Though not perfect, Make'e worked hard to keep our thinking fresh by establishing an environment that would allow criticism to exist within the ranks.

Toward the end, however, not all members followed the methods outlined in the manifesto. The group splintered and later dissolved due to political differences and graduation. However, many who did follow the approach found stronger ways to fit the idealism into very real forms and methods. In the end, Make'e members essentially lost their critical distance to improve the overall function of the organization.

Ha'ina Ka Puana

The story of Make'e Pono Lāhui Hawai'i is a microcosm of many similar student uprisings in Hawai'i. We filled a space in the history of Hawaiian advocacy during a time when many students and faculty were too entrenched in the daily routine of surviving

U.S. hegemony. The apathy that held students down for years was replaced, if only for a moment, by the naive and brash actions of a handful of Hawaiians.

Still, the story is not about "us" Hawaiian students. The importance of the story is the lessons we learned by our actions and inaction. In our own way, Make'e found remedies for injustice and tools for organizing against institutional racism. Some tools were useless, others effective. Make'e's actions are lessons on how to develop staying power in struggle and how to manage a political campaign that has no immediate signs of success.

Interestingly, all of the members of Make'e are currently working in education. Many started families and are now developing the next generation of fighters. The Make'e experience teaches us that actions of the present moment will be judged and valued by their impact on the next generation. It's too early to judge whether our organization actually provided a valuable stepping stone for our keiki to combat U.S. hegemony and rebuild the nation. Yet from my perspective, the future looks hopeful.

Recall the 'ōlelo no'eau by 'Alohilani Kuala at the top of this essay: "ua pau ke ao i hala, o kēia ke ao e ala." This chapter takes us back to a time when students were invincible and then brings us forward to the present when the children of those students are now exhibiting signs that they are ready to stand up for their people. The 'ōlelo no'eau is not just an "out with the old in with the new" frame of thinking. It is a recognition that life is cyclical and if the lessons are taught well, the young ones will do much better the next time around.

Finally, this chapter acknowledges the passing of a torch. One of Make'e's founding members, Terry Kanalupilikokoama'ihu'i Young, left this realm much too soon. Yet he blessed us with a myriad of memories and wise counsel along the way.[11] For Make'e, Kanalu modeled the behavior we hope to achieve. And his lasting gift will be his love for his people and for the friendships he cultivated. More specifically, Kanalu composed a song for Make'e and recorded it with singer-songwriter Sam Kapu III.[12] The song speaks volumes and is a reminder that revolution is possible if one should dare to stand up and try.

Ua hānau 'ia e ka 'ōpio pono ea
    Ua hānau 'ia e ka 'eha kūpuna ea
        Ua hānau 'ie e ka po'e mākua ea, ea.
    Ua hānau 'ia no ka pua likoliko ea.
        Make'e Pono
        Make'e Pono
        Make'e Pono Lāhui Hawai'i
        Ea.
        Eo e nā kupa maoli

E kū i ke ala hou
Ho'āla ka 'āina nei
E Kōlea, Mai hana 'ino
Wiwo'ole
Wiwo'ole
Wiwo'ole nā koa a'o Pelelohipu'a.

Kanalu's mele is forward thinking and lays an important foundation for what will come. Though the song was written for, and inspired by, Kanalu's activism with Make'e, the words speak to every succeeding generation of young and old advocates of justice.

Kanalu calls on all Hawaiians to "make'e pono" or cherish with great affection and dignity the independence of the Hawaiian nation. The song calls on all Hawaiians to stand tall and reenlist their connection to their lands in a balanced form of service that Kanalu names "Pelelohipu'a," or the formative gathering of those who possess the power and awe of Pele, the compassion of Lohi'au, and the steadfastness of Kamapua'a. Finally, the song encourages everyone to be courageous because the path toward the positive advancement of the nation will test the theoretical and functional foundation on which each community struggle is built.

Perhaps courage in the face of so much change is the greatest lesson for Make'e and the most telling part of the song. All of our membership experienced significant challenges to our personal attitudes and political understandings of what nationalism and nationality mean in the context of the Hawaiian nation. The nationalist approach adopted in 1990 is no longer considered the most important or critical approach in this changing political environment. However, the goal to be a study of the political and cultural evolution of the Hawaiian nation makes the journey fresh and fulfilling.

As with all seasons, Make'e grew quickly from a need to carry on the hard work of the previous generation of student activists and slowly matured and matriculated into the larger community with the passing of time. The Make'e students graduated, left the university, or simply entered other community social justice arenas. People assert that we grew up and grew out of our radical ways. Others suggest that we simply lost the innocence of young revolutionary thinking.

Make'e was the product of our time, a time not determined by an era of the late 1980s and 1990s. Instead, Make'e's time was part of a larger spatial event. In that space, we faced the challenge of every generation, to make good on the promise: to be a part of Hawai'i's history of resistance and lay the next brick on the foundation of independence.

Therefore, Make'e is not an end. The momentum of the ethnic studies students, Hui Aloha 'Āina Tuahine, Ho'okahe Wai Ho'oulu 'Āina, and Hawaiians United for Liberation and Independence set a solid foundation for us, as students, to act. Organizations like Kālai Pō and Kūikalāhiki also took their place in the university and built upon the power of the Hawaiian student movements well after we disbanded. From this author's point of view, Make'e's contribution to student activism serves as an incubator for action and change and a springboard for community leadership and service. E mau i ke ao e ala ana.

Notes

1. The first stand-alone article in the Hawaiian language was printed by *Ka Leo O Hawai'i* student newspaper at UHM in 1991.

2. University of Hawai'i Hawaiian Studies Task Force, *Ka'ū: University of Hawai'i Hawaiian Studies Task Force Report,* December 1986. In the Ka'ū Report, the task force recommended that Hawaiian studies combine instruction, research, student services, and community outreach. The Kamakakūokalani Center for Hawaiian Studies and Operation Kua'ana represent the Hawaiian Studies Center and student services component of that report. See pp. 7–10.

3. Task force members include Isabella Abbott, Jean Ilei Beniamina, Kekuni Blaisdell, Lilikala Dorton, Lucy Gay, Alberta Pua Hopkins, Kauanoe Kamanā, Edward Kanahele, Pualani Kanahele, Larry Kimura, Davianna Pomaikai McGregor, Edith McKinzie, Richard "Dutch" Mossman, Midge Oler, Abaham Pi'ianai'a, David Sing, Haunani-Kay Trask, and 'Ilima Williams.

4. For more on this incident, see Trask, *From a Native Daughter*; Rohrer, *Haoles in Hawai'i,* 60–61.

5. Hawaiian Constitution, article 15, section 4 [added Constitutional Convention 1978 and election November 7, 1978]. The article states, "English and Hawaiian shall be the official languages of Hawaii, except that Hawaiian shall be required for public acts and transactions only as provided by law."

6. In more recent times, scholars of Hawaiian politics and history revisited the application of colonial and postcolonial theory in Hawai'i. Keanu Sai and Kamana Beamer in particular developed strong and persuasive arguments that point to the Hawaiian Kingdom's agency in adopting Western models of governance and crafting an internationally recognized Hawaiian nation-state by 1843. These scholars are now developing tremendous works that assert Hawai'i's rights, under international law, to end the U.S. occupation of the existing, independent nation-state of the Hawaiian Kingdom. Obviously, Make'e's position in 1990 was focused on the colonial model of analysis. Had Make'e continued to the present day, our definitions and analyses would reflect the theoretical shifts now occurring via Sai and Beamer's work. See generally Sai, "A Slippery Path towards Hawaiian Indigeneity"; Beamer, "Na Wai Ka Mana?"

7. Said, "In Conversation with Neeladri Bhattacharya, Suvir Kaul, and Ania Loomba."

8. Said, "In Conversation with Neeladri Bhattacharya, Suvir Kaul, and Ania Loomba," 13.

9. Perry, *Malcolm X: The Last Speeches,* 83.

10. Perry, *Malcolm X: The Last Speeches.*

11. Kūhiō Vogeler expands beautifully on Kanalu's tremendous heart and contribution to the rebuilding of the Hawaiian nation-state in chapter 11, dedicated to our beloved brother.

12. Terry Kanalu Young and Sam Kapu III, *Pelelohipu'a,* recorded September 1997, Bluewater Label, audiocassette. Kanalu wrote the "Pelelohipu'a" song in 1991 with Sam Kapu III while participating as a student member in Make'e. The song was recorded by Sam Kapu III in his first cassette recorded album.

CHAPTER 13. Ka Hoʻokolokolonui Kānaka Maoli, 1993

THE PEOPLES' INTERNATIONAL TRIBUNAL, HAWAIʻI

Kekuni Blaisdell, Nālani Minton, and Ulla Hasager

> There is still time to save our heritage. . . . Never cease to act because you fear you may fail. . . . The voice of the people is the voice of God.
>
> —QUEEN LILIʻUOKALANI

A daring and historic world event occurred in Hawaiʻi on August 12–21, 1993. For the first time, the United States was brought to trial and found guilty before a tribunal of distinguished international human rights experts and advocates for its violations against Kanaka Maoli (KM), the Indigenous Hawaiian people and nation. Ka Hoʻokolokolonui Kānaka Maoli, the first Peoples' International Tribunal to be held in the Pacific, and the first to include traditional KM law in its deliberation and findings, was convened during the centennial of the U.S. armed invasion of the once independent nation of Hawaiʻi. That year, 1993, was also the United Nations International Year of the World's Indigenous Peoples within the first UN Decade of Indigenous Peoples (1992–2002). This chapter features excerpts from the Tribunal testimonies, which span six volumes and are an invaluable record of Hawaiian resistance, intelligence, and persistence.[1] They are a manifestation of ea. Ua mau ke ea o ka ʻāina i ka pono; the life, breath, spirit, and sovereignty of the land is protected by the right intentions and the right actions of the people.

The Tribunal Moʻolelo

Ka Hoʻokolokolonui Kānaka Maoli was convened by physician and activist Dr. Kekuni Blaisdell. Kawaipuna Prejean, roving international envoy for sovereignty organizations, first proposed the Tribunal in March 1992. Kawaipuna passed away before his vision manifested, but the Kānaka Maoli Tribunal Kōmike fulfilled it by organizing with more than five hundred people and sixty sponsors on five islands of Ka Pae ʻĀina. The Hawaiian case was led by three internationally renowned, Indigenous prosecutor-advocates.[2] A panel of nine judges reviewed both oral and written testimonies from KM and other expert witnesses.

At the opening ceremonies, Kumu hula John Kaʻimikaua led his hālau (school) in performing a chant of prophecy from the priests of Pākuʻi Heiau on Molokaʻi. This

Convener of the 1993 Ka Hoʻokolokolonui Kānaka Maoli, Peoples' International Tribunal, Kekuni Akana Blaisdell. In addition to his leadership in the Hawaiian independence movement, Dr. Blaisdell is a highly respected physician and former director of the John A. Burns School of Medicine at the University of Hawaiʻi at Mānoa. A consummate researcher, he has also documented decades' worth of events and meetings for the Hawaiian movement. This photo was taken on May 3, 1993, a few months before the Tribunal.

chant was given as the hoʻokupu (offering) for the Tribunal to convene. Kaʻimikaua explained the central line of the prophecy, "Hōʻaleʻale ka lepo pōpolo," which is a poetic reference to the time when the makaʻāinana (people of the land) shall rise. Half of this prophecy has been fulfilled, he explained, and Hawaiians of today are still searching for sovereignty, searching back to our kūpuna, feeling the pride, looking and building and coming together. The Tribunal was a part of the fulfillment of this prophecy.

Over the course of ten days, the Tribunal judges heard 147 testimonies on five islands, in addition to written and video testimonies. Kānaka Maoli insisted that Tribunal sessions be held at sites of land struggles. This was a unique and important aspect of the Tribunal, as it allowed the judges personally to meet with KM who had taken a stand on the land and who, in some cases, were facing eviction and arrest.

The damage done to KM by the United States and its subordinate, the state of Hawaiʻi, was extensively outlined through the words and personal experiences of hundreds of Kānaka. In addition, historians and other specialists gave well-researched insights into the workings of colonialism, capitalism, militarism, and racism throughout the Hawaiian Islands. At the end of the Tribunal, an international panel of jurists, consisting of recognized experts in international, constitutional, and Indigenous law, wrote an interim report that confirmed that the rights of KM and their inherent sovereignty have never been extinguished.

In addition to the testimonies offered by KM and other Hawaiʻi residents, compelling accounts of the United States' long and continued subjugation of native peoples were given by Indigenous people from Turtle Island (North America), the Pacific, and the Caribbean, members of island nations that have been exploited by U.S. imperialism ever since the Spanish-American War of 1898 propelled the United States to global power. Thus, representatives from the Philippines, Guam, American Sāmoa, the Virgin Islands, Cuba, and Puerto Rico joined the proceedings.

While the Tribunal convenors had invited U.S. and state representatives to attend, a reserved chair labeled "US Representative" remained empty.

Nine charges were brought against the United States at the Tribunal:

1. Impermissible interference in the internal affairs of a sovereign people and nation.
2. Aiding and abetting a foreign coup d'état against the government of a sovereign people and nation.
3. Annexation of a sovereign people, their nation and territory, without their free and informed consent.
4. Imposition of statehood on a people, their nation and territory, without their free and informed consent.
5. Illegal appropriation of the lands, waters, and resources of the Kānaka Maoli.
6. Economic colonization and dispossession of the Kānaka Maoli.
7. Acts of genocide and ethnocide against the Kānaka Maoli.
8. Destruction, pollution, contamination and desecration of the environment of Ka Pae ʻĀina [the Hawaiian Archipelago].
9. Violations by the United States and its subsidiaries of their own established trust responsibilities and other obligations toward the Kānaka Maoli.[3]

As the nine-day proceedings closed, the judges issued the following recognitions and findings:

1. The United States violated nā kānāwai (Kānaka Maoli law) and elements of customary international law, as well as its own Declaration of Independence.
2. The United States accelerated its interventions in the internal affairs of Ka

Lāhui Kānaka Maoli, abridging and impairing its sovereign functioning and right to self-determination. The U.S. also violated the terms of at least three ratified and binding treaties: the 1826 Convention between Commodore A.P. Catesby Jones of the U.S. and Kauikeaouli (Kamehameha III); the 1850 Treaty of Friendship, Commerce and Navigation between Kamehameha III and the U.S.; and the 1875 Treaty of Reciprocity between the Hawaiian Islands and the U.S.

3. In 1893, the U.S. openly supported a coup d'état conducted by [foreign settlers] against the legitimate government of Ka Lāhui Kānaka Maoli. Thereafter, for a period of five years, the U.S. openly supported the usurping regime by use of armed force against the Indigenous population of Hawai'i. In 1898, the U.S. annexed Ka Pae 'āina (the Hawaiian Archipelago), neither obtaining the consent nor consulting the Kānaka Maoli.
4. Following annexation, the United States forcibly subordinated, degraded and systematically dispossessed the Kānaka Maoli and incorporated Hawai'i into the Union as a State.
5. Under provision of Article 20 of the Charter of the Organization of American States, all U.S. assertions of jurisdiction and property title in the Hawaiian Islands are legally invalid.
6. Kānaka Maoli sovereignty has not been extinguished by the illegal actions of the United States. The overthrow of 1893 and purported annexation of 1898 merely changed the nature of the operative state but did not remove the inherent right of the people to sovereignty.
7. The Kānaka Maoli are morally and legally entitled to reassert their right to self-determination under provision of UN General Assembly Resolution 1514.
8. Blood quantum is ethnocidal and is contrary to the virtual entirety of the International Convention on the Elimination of All Forms of Racial Discrimination.
9. The Kānaka Maoli have been subjected to ongoing processes of genocide, both physical and cultural, at the hands of the U.S. government and the government of the State of Hawai'i, which violates nā kānāwai as well as the 1948 Convention for Prevention and Punishment of the Crime of Genocide.
10. The Kānaka Maoli have exhausted all existing peaceful avenues for rectifying the multiplicity of wrongs done to them. Consequently, they are entitled on an urgent basis, to explore potentially more productive approaches, such as mediated negotiations with the U.S. Department of State [nation to nation].[4]

Additionally, the Tribunal concluded with the following recommendations:

1. The U.S. and the world recognize the sovereignty and right to self-determination of Lāhui Kānaka Maoli under provision of the International Covenant on Civil and Political Rights and the International Covenant on Economic, Social and Cultural Rights, among other elements of international law.
2. The U.S. and the world should acknowledge the right of Lāhui Kānaka Maoli to decolonization under provision of United Nations Resolution 1514.
3. Kānaka Maoli lands, including all ceded lands, Hawaiian Home lands, and all other lands to which they have a claim, should be returned to the control of Lāhui Kānaka Maoli without delay. Land restoration should be construed as including restoration of water rights.
4. Jurisdiction over restored lands should be transferred to Lāhui Kānaka Maoli at the time of restoration.
5. Blood quantum standards of identification should be immediately suspended. Lāhui Kānaka Maoli itself should determine the composition of its citizenry, free from external interference.
6. All other wrongs suffered by the Kānaka Maoli at the hands of the United States and its subsidiaries should be rectified in a manner deemed satisfactory to the people themselves.
7. The United States, in negotiations and other interactions with Lāhui Kānaka Maoli, should observe the provisions of the United Nations Declaration on the Rights of Indigenous Peoples as the minimum standards to be followed.
8. The United States should immediately effect a valid ratification of and adherence to the 1948 Convention on Punishment and Prevention of the Crime of Genocide.[5]

The judges' recommendations called for two main actions: (1) the return by the United States of all stolen KM lands without delay to the KM people and nation; and (2) the start of talks between the United States and the KM people, observing the UN Declaration of the Rights of Indigenous Peoples as the minimum standard, and recognizing the right to decolonization and the subsequent withdrawal by the United States from its illegal occupation of Hawai'i *nei.*[6]

As powerful as this strong verdict are the testimonies of the people themselves. George Helm once wrote, "The defense of the nation is in the spirit of the people." What follows is only a small sampling of the extensive testimonies given.[7] In the spirit of aloha by which these testimonies were given, it has been agreed that they belong to the KM people and cannot be owned by an individual or group, because that would violate the collective intellectual and cultural rights that these testimonies represent.

Excerpts from the Tribunal Testimonies

ON CULTURAL FOUNDATIONS

Ku'umeaaloha Gomes

With the Kanaka Maoli, food and proper nutrients are very important. Papa, our earth mother, gives us the food that springs from her bosom. Wākea, our sky father, gives nutrients to us through the power of the sun, the wind, and the rain. Hāloa, the elder sibling of the Kanaka Maoli, who was buried in the ground and sprouted up as the first kalo plant, is sacred as our staple food, poi. It is this Hāloa with the earth mother and the sky father, who nurture our people. In a true sense of 'ohana and ha'aha'a, or humility, the Kanaka Maoli have over the years treasured the lo'i kalo and respected it as the giver of life for all generations of the nation of Hawai'i.

Lilikalā Kame'eleihiwa

There was no ownership of land in traditional Hawai'i. . . . We are the stewards. We have the opportunity and responsibility to take care of the land and to take care of the water and the ocean. But you can't own it. It doesn't make sense [in our traditions] to own creation. When Kamehameha IV came to the throne in 1854, he said foreigners were welcome so long as they respected the laws of the land and the people. If they came to take away the land, if they came to exploit the people, then they were not welcome.

Marion Kelly

The ahupua'a land system is a [designation of land and watershed areas] that goes from the top of the mountains, down through the valley, to the ocean and beyond. It gives use rights and resource rights to all the people there. It provides access to all the various things that grow at these different elevations and to ocean resources. And so the people share back and forth. This is the body of the social, cultural dimension of Hawaiian life.

ON DELIBERATE VIOLATIONS

Stephen Boggs

Congress decided that a vote on annexation by the people of Hawai'i was not required by the U.S. Constitution and would undoubtedly undo the overthrow of the monarchy, and, therefore, could not be allowed.

Jon Osorio

Hawaiians have always been under suspicion [by dominant society] of being not up to self-rule, despite the fact that we ruled ourselves more than adequately for over two thousand years. By the time of the overthrow [in 1893], 80 to 85 percent of all the lands were either owned or leased by foreigners.

John Kelly

The Ala Wai canal, which was dredged two-and-a-half miles long, 250 feet wide, and 28 feet deep by Dillingham, destroyed six square miles of highly fertile land, 38 major fishponds, and evicted thousands. This is the all too familiar story of development. In 1993, of the 1.1 million residents in Hawaiʻi, just 80 major landowners control 95 percent of all the land.

Mililani Trask

There are three classes of Americans not allowed access to the Federal courts: children, retarded adults, and Native Hawaiians. The[se] three classes of American citizens are not allowed into the U.S. Federal courts to bring breach of trust suits for collective entitlement.

The 1990 Hawaiian Judicial Relief Act was the State's response to seven years of our efforts to obtain legislation for our right to sue in State court. The Act allows Hawaiians the right to go into the State court to sue to protect their assets but it prevents us from winning. It provides that any successful plaintiff cannot receive an award of either money or land. And the court is specifically directed to return their winning proceeds to their trustee, the state of Hawaiʻi. This is the kind of outrage that has occurred. When Talk Radio asked the Governor to comment, his response was, "I told them I would give them the right to sue, but I never told them I would give them the right to win."

In the Māhele there is clear language: "subject to the right, of the native tenant." The Kuleana Act, which gives out little house lots, doesn't extinguish aboriginal title, collective title, or title of native tenants. Through the Newlands Resolution and Organic Act, the land laws continue. So not only do the inherent rights to land remain, the native title remains.

A pattern of resistance emerges immediately after the overthrow. The rights and sovereignty of the native people of Hawaiʻi were ignored. *Pono* is right relationship. You know if you live righteously, if you walk on the earth righteously. In Western ways you talk justice, you go to court for justice. But people live all kinds of ways that are hurtful to others and the earth. They don't see that they're doing something that is unjust [as long as it is defined as legal].

Donna Wong

Can't get agricultural lands redesignated to urban? Pass a state law allowing golf courses on agricultural lands. Can't build your corporate retreats or industrial strip mines on conservation lands? Pass state regulations allowing subzones. Can't build a Federal pork-barrel highway because of national environmental or cultural laws? Get your Congressional delegation to pass a law to break that law.

At the heights of the golf-course frenzy, 102 golf courses were proposed in addition to those 65 already existing. Each 18-hole golf course requires 100 to 250 acres. Golf courses use between 500,000 and one million gallons of water a day. The idea that Hawai'i can surround itself by a sea of sewage, [pesticides,] and pollution and escape any consequence is preposterous.

Bill Dougherty

Our Board of Water Supply has been testing 14 wells for 6 pesticides for at least 5 years, and that's all. Yet we have more than 100 wells and more than 40 pesticides that have been detected. Although the use of DBCP and EDS has stopped, the levels are still growing because the pesticides on the top filter down through the earth to where we pick up our ground water. The half life of DBCP and EDS, according to our Department of Health, is 120 years. This means that in 120 years, that level is only half gone.

Erik Seitz

The U.S. military always has done whatever it needed to dominate and exploit these islands for its larger purposes. Need a Naval base? Take an important fishing area. Need a place for bombing practice? Take a whole island. Need to practice artillery fire? Take one, two or three valleys. No environmental impact studies, of course. No concerns about dislocating the native peoples or about dropping artillery shells on people's farms and houses. By the 1960s, the military controlled more land in Hawai'i than any other landowner (other than the State). Over 24 percent of the land on O'ahu was either owned outright or controlled on long-term leases by the military.

Raymond Kamaka

[Taro farmer Raymond Kamaka and his 'ohana are from Waikāne, O'ahu, a place full of cultural, religious, and historical significance. Its lo'i kalo (taro fields) are on the National Register of Historic Sites. From 1942 to 1976, the U.S. government leased 1,061 acres in Waikāne Valley, 187.4 of those acres from the Kamaka family, for military training. The U.S. government promised to restore the land to its original condition and remove all ammunition and unexploded ordinance. However, the United States disavowed this commitment to clean up, stating that the $7 million would be too expensive. A federal court awarded the military the right to condemn all 187.4 acres of the Kamaka land for a mere $735,000, a ridiculously low sum considering real estate prices in Hawai'i. Forced to give up their ancestral homelands, Raymond Kamaka listed the United States and state of Hawai'i on his IRS forms and was found guilty of tax fraud. On September 8, 1993, two weeks after the Tribunal, Kamaka was taken to Pleasanton Prison in Northern California.]

Today I stand alone with my family, one person against the feds, against the government here. They lock me up for two years as a political prisoner. They used my land for bombing so that they could take the land away from another Kanaka Maoli.

CULTURAL PRACTICES, CULTURAL LAWS

John Ka'imikaua

Our people have lived on these islands for 2,000 years. And for the first thousand that our people have lived upon these lands there was no ali'i system.

When the kapu system was abolished, it was the national religion, the religion of the chiefs, that was abolished. The 'aumākua and the religion of the maka'āinana, the family religion, the religion of the ancestors, still prevailed.

Before the time of the ali'i, there was only the maka'āinana. And the maka'āinana lived upon the land, the maka'āinana worked upon the land. They were born, they planted, and they died upon the land. It is important for us to reflect the original attitudes of our people from even before the time of the ali'i.

Colette Machado

The reason behind the strength and energy of the people that come from this land is the fact that we are still rural [cultural] practitioners. And we have to struggle to even keep this for ourselves.

Noa Emmett Aluli

The Protect Kaho'olawe 'Ohana wants Kaho'olawe to set a precedent for a sovereign land base that would eventually come under the jurisdiction of a re-established Hawaiian nation.

William Kalipi

[Fishpond builder William Kalipi Sr. testified at ʻUalapuʻe, Molokaʻi. He explained the necessity in the present-day world to respect the KM concept of mālama ʻāina, to take care of the land, never to take more than you need, give back what you take and be grateful. Later, during the Tribunal session at Mālama Cultural Park, he made it clear how the right to practice sovereignty, to live it out in everyday life, is closely connected to these and other important KM concepts, which are still being taught.]

Whenever we go mauka to the mountains for gathering, we take what God has planted. But we never take what somebody planted [out] of hardship. We respect the next man's [work]. And yet Western culture comes to us with private property and "No trespassing," put fences up, so that we cannot go and gather—a necessity for our lives. Today you no can be buried on your own property. Why? Because they no can sell the land. Nobody like buy one land with graveyards. It is our tradition. I'm going to be buried on my land.

Everything I do, I live in pono with myself, my God, my family, my community and the ecosystem of the environment I live in. The government harassed me and everything becomes a genocide to my lifestyle. I never did take an oath to become one American citizen. If you ask the immigration how does one become an American citizen, they have to go through school and say one oath. I have never taken an oath. And my great-grandparents never take an oath. So as far as I'm concerned, I'm a Hawaiian national, sovereign heir to the Kingdom of Hawaiʻi.

They have stolen many of the lands that belong to our forefathers. The land was undivided interest to every Hawaiian Kanaka Maoli that lives in the Kingdom of Hawaiʻi. They broke the land system, they put the land under fee simple so they can steal it away from you. Our way of life was simplicity. We mālama the ʻāina, the ʻāina feed us. We take care of our land.

In our traditional system, as we raise our children we take in hānai. All the children become hānai, will be raised by Grandma or Grandpa, Uncle or Aunt, and if anything should happen to me, my children could automatic [be] with one of the family by tradition. Within the State of Hawaiʻi, if anything happens to you, your children become ward of the State and that's against our traditional culture.

CARETAKERS OF THE LAND

Nani Rogers

Three governors of the Territory of Hawaiʻi turned over 548.57 acres of Hawaiian Home Lands to the U.S. Government for the Mānā Airport Military Reservation, without the knowledge and consent of us, the beneficiaries of these sacred, cultural Nohili burial dunes. We should be left alone to promulgate our life purpose, which is to mālama ʻāina, care for the land. Not be the wards of the State, but caretakers of the land. Why were we ignored?

I speak with aloha, compassion and pain when I say, admit your wrongs, apologize for the pain and destruction of our people, and get Congress to sign that document that will return *all* the lands stolen from us. Then *peace* can be restored, all *healing* of the wounds and pain inflicted can commence, and *aloha pono* can flourish.

Attwood Makanani

All of the ʻāina was very sacred. Life itself was very sacred in the use of the land. A conflict [exists] over the use of the resources just to survive. Families are dependent upon their fishing, their gathering, their mountain resources. And without that they will be forced economically [to] change, the family begins to break up, they begin to move out, they begin to be dependent upon a different resource. It is not by their choice. Those who choose to follow the [cultural] traditions usually end up in a court of law being arrested, evicted, their homes broken down.

Kealohikina

Our kūpuna taught that a life was all about potential. Society was molded over hundreds of years to fit into subtleties of nature. Like a tree, people were rooted to the earth, and yet to the open sky. We receive and we give. This was what was given to us as Kanaka Maoli. We were self-monitoring. All of us had a practical mastery immortalized in our myths and stories, handed down over generations. We are a part of the physics, nuclear sciences, sky sciences, psychology, theology of mastery of self. We are a people of hidden knowledge. We live by a common traditional knowledge.

What we are sharing with the judges today is the theft of our breath of life, our hā, our inherited birthright as Native Hawaiians is so important. It's something that words cannot describe. As Native Hawaiians, when we are born, we have inherited the soul of our ancestor.

Jeff Chandler

I live the ahupuaʻa concept. My ancestors lived it, my uncles, my aunties, my kūpuna, they all live 'em. I want to pass that on. We are the way of life. This is our life. This is it. That's the Hawaiian concept of life.

ON STOLEN LANDS

Sharon Pomroy

Over 500 acres of our stolen Hawaiian Homelands was given to the U.S. military for bombing runs and practices during World War II. Today, they have almost 2,000 acres of stolen ceded trust lands [to] launch their missiles. They've turned Hawaiian Homelands into a hazardous materials and munitions storage area.

The Federal government pays one dollar rent for a sixty-year lease. They paid the Philippine government billions of dollars. They paid the Japanese government billions of dollars to put their bases on their soil. Yet, for our land, which they claim as American, they will not even pay us a fair market value for rent. . . . For me, the bottom line is independence. No military, no federal government, just Kanaka Maoli making decisions for ourselves on our own land.

Sondra Field Grace

We have consistently argued that these are stolen lands, the state does not have title. My husband [as] an Indigenous Hawaiian has interest in these lands, inalienable and inherent interest. Genocide "subjects the group to conditions of life that are intended to cause physical destruction of the group in whole or in part." That applies to our situation here.

We've been thrown in jail nearly a dozen times. We've had our homes destroyed. We have warrants out for us. We never know if they're gonna arrest us or not. They're trying to get a permanent injunction to keep us off this land. And we tell them every time, "No matter what you do to us, we're coming back." As an international tribunal, we call on you to help us make these powers stand by their obligations to respect our self-determination.

Michael Grace

The state and the US has no jurisdiction over us. We keep asking the judges, "Do you have the jurisdiction?" They say no. They stole the land [but] the land is not stolen. You cannot lift up the land and take it away. The land is here. But we gotta use and exercise our rights to these lands. Stay on them and use them.

Ginger Kahapea

Adverse possession and quiet title action appear daily in the newspapers. The blatant misuse of the legal system completes quiet title actions against Native Hawaiians, the true genealogical heirs of these lands. Who speaks out for the Native Hawaiian? Where are the agencies of the State to protect these claims? Where is OHA and the Native Hawaiian Legal Corporation? Let sugar repay its moral debt to Native Hawaiians. Give Hāmākua lands to those Native Hawaiians that need it for taro, culture and lifestyles.

The Native Hawaiian[s] who now go to the mountains or the ocean to gather food, or practice their religion and culture are finding the fences are up. The security guards roam these lands and the "No Trespassing" signs stop them. It is not Native Hawaiians' intention to destroy these lands, but to be allowed to continue to cross these lands for subsistence and cultural purposes.

Skippy Keliʻikanakaʻole Ioane

We don't call Hawaiians homeless because we, the Hawaiian people, are home. We are just houseless. So we changed that. What you see out here [tents and tarps] is affordable housing. Nature is not our enemy. Nature is our mother.

ON FORMS OF GENOCIDE AND ETHNOCIDE

Bernice Hokoana

We have the worst health record in the entire nation—diabetes, high blood pressure, heart problems, you name it. One form of genocide is when the white man came here and took all our rights and food away from us and made us unhealthy. A lot of our Hawaiians died because of all the disease brought in—gonorrhea, syphilis, measles. For instance, my husband's family lost nine of their children from measles here in Kīpahulu. Is there anything out there that you can teach us to defend ourselves?

Mahealani Cypher

US Interstate H-3 has a 30-year history of destruction of our land, water, and cultural resources. At $100 million per mile, it is the most costly highway project in the history of the United States. As a result of this project and the actions of the United States and the State of Hawaiʻi, the following rights have been denied or seriously undermined: the right to worship ancestral gods, to visit our *heiau* and other sacred places; the right to protect and preserve the *iwi* and burial places of our ancestors; the right to free-running water in our streams for cultural use, for fishponds and needed irrigation, because they have diverted the water from the stream for the construction of this road; the right to gather greens, medicinal plants, and other products from our forests and uplands; the right to educate our people about our history and sacred places through their denial of our access and the destruction of our cultural, historical, and sacred sites. It is ethnocide.

Dana Naone Hall

It's a simple human value we all share, the protection of our ancestral burials. We're trying here at Waiheʻe to prevent the further loss of what is really the foundation of our culture. So my plea to this Tribunal is that unless we have and are able to exercise sovereign decision-making over our cultural, sacred sites, we will always be at the mercy of exactly the forces that have been decimating us and destroying the land.

Kaleikoa Kaʻeo

The state courts decided to force the sale of land and to force our families to accept the cash amounts. This is genocide when they force the dispossession of people from their ancestral lands.

Donya Minoʻaka Fitzsimmons

The Hawaiian movement doesn't make us anti-haole, it makes us anti-exploitation, anti-oppression, and anti-subjugation. If they don't want us to be anti-American, then stop oppressing us, exploiting us and subjugating us.

The tourist industry thrives on the exploitation of our cultural ways. These racist attitudes forced many Kanaka Maoli to want to forget about being Kanaka Maoli. The Federal government stipulated a blood quantum percentage of who is Hawaiian and who is not. Their way, you must be 50 percent blood quantum to be Hawaiian. Think about this. In a few years, given our poor health rate, there will be no more Kanaka Maoli.

This is a clear violation of our human rights. This is also blatantly contributing to the genocide of the Kanaka Maoli. We know today that when the United States government says "and justice for all," we know that they mean "justice for some." THEM.

Larry Kauanoe Lindsey Kimura

When our independent Hawaiian government was wrongfully overthrown, the door was opened to those who would destroy one of the few remaining aspects of our way of life that had remained strong since the beginning of time. It was opened to those who would snatch Hawaiʻi's native language from the mouths of Hawaiian children, to ensure that the language of our people would be the same as that of the plunderers, who were establishing their new government. If Hawaiian thinking were to change, such change would be hastened in government schools where minds were molded, and where the cord of language attaching the child to his own people would be severed, so that his entire way of thinking would reflect that found in English, thereby completely destroying the life, wholeness, and sovereignty of the Hawaiian people [translation from the original testimony, given in the Hawaiian language].

Melissa Moniz

Anything Hawaiian was forbidden. I was taught that, in order to get anywhere in this world, I had to behave as a white. My Hawaiianness would always be second. Most of my life I was ashamed to be Hawaiian.

Abel Simeona Lui

I got arrested twenty-three times for simple trespassing on my tutu man's 'āina. Twenty-two times I went before the court and I was found not guilty. . . . They send a DLNR down there to tear down my house. One night I wen go fishing. I came home three o'clock in the morning and I had no house. . . . Over 80 percent of the people in prison is Kānaka Maoli. I did 18 years over there. We got to stop all this.

Pele Hanoa

My culture is a living culture that depends upon the land and ocean base. We need to educate the world of the injustice and encroachment of the US upon our fertile and viable land base, of and for our people. We need to stop the desecration of historic sites, the theft of the sacred land. The rip-off by the US is endless. The time has come. We must stand together and fight for our rights as Kanaka Maoli. Injustice must stop. We must be self-determined and self-governing for sovereignty.

Walter Paulo

In 1980, Brother Puhipau, Brother Bobby, and I were arrested on Sand Island for, they claim, "squatting." I went to court and pled "not guilty." I denounced my American citizenship. We all did. I like to die as a Hawaiian. No way as an American.

Palikapu Dedman

Our religion starts from the top of the mountain to the sea, not around a church. The resources and the elements that surround these islands are our gods. The forest and all its species are related to us. [It is] our responsibility to carry on for thousands more years to come. Industrial development cannot be in these islands. It will be the end of everything. Geothermal, rockets, ocean mining, radiation plants. They don't fit here.

Let's set our priorities. We have to destine our own future. We have to run our own government. We have to take care of our resources. . . . Crimes that we see everyday. Pilau ships with toxics to dump. Over-commercialization of fishing to foreign people to rip us off way inside the 200-mile limit. The gross neglect of Hawaiian Homes still falls in the hands of the Feds and the State. The crimes are daily crimes. We have to tell the world of these crimes. The hardest thing to be in Hawai'i is one Hawaiian.

Holding on to the remains of our fragile island ecosystem however we can, we are indeed a most endangered human species. We will continue to do whatever we can do as Hawaiian[s] to bring world awareness to our position as a distinct people with a unique and valuable culture to be appreciated, nurtured and perpetuated.

Mahealani Pai

In 1988, the Greenwell family came and told us to sign a palapala for them to sell the land to the Federal government for a national park. We have a verbal agreement that we would remain here to practice our cultural heritage. Today, we are threatened by the National Park Service. We are struggling. This is our plight.

Hank Fergerstrom

The destruction of the religious system, the destruction of the native language, the illegal taking of land and alienation from that land, the claiming of mineral rights, and the imposing of laws and a judicial system that ensures dominance over the Indigenous People of these islands. These acts are genocidal in intent and purpose. Flour costs $1.97 for five pounds. Rice costs 1.99. A five-pound bag of poi costs $13.68. The reason why it costs so much more is because to grow *taro* from which *poi* is made, it takes considerable land, which Hawaiians no longer have. It takes water. The State illegally controls water. The State has determined that better use of this water is for indoor plumbing, for resorts, for public fountains and golf courses, and for waste industry, such as sugar cane. The wastewater and all the other pollutants are then pumped into our oceans, destroying our other major source of food, the reef fish.

Clarence Medeiros

Our state government misuses our state lands. While our people is on the beach, homeless, some in jail, some jobless, there are thousands of acres in Kona which they have put in reserve for the birds and the plants. I say that's okay, but the Hawaiians are also endangered species. They should be allowed to use those lands.

Lehua Lopez

Cultural appropriation and cultural cannibalism may be defined as the buying, the selling and the consuming of other peoples' cultural artifacts, images, values and beliefs as well as sacred sites without permission of the culture being used. Cultural cannibalism is an insidious and hideous part of colonialism as it is part of the process of assimilation, what I would call a deliberate attempt to eradicate those beliefs, values, attitudes, behaviors, language, religion and practices of a [native] culture that are in contradiction or in conflict with the dominant [society].

Mary Ann Bennett

My grandfather always told me to keep my mind and my heart strong with much aloha, because our ancestors believe in the tide changing. Because so much has been taken away, I know one day the tide will change and all that was wrong will be made right.

Ma mua, Ma hope: In Defense of the Nation—Mana'o by Nālani Minton

Through the Tribunal process, the resounding voices of the people spoke truth to power and mandated a return to nationhood. This is consistent with UN General Assembly Resolution 1514, Declaration on the Granting of Independence to Colonial Countries and Peoples: "The subjection of peoples to alien subjugation, domination and exploitation constitutes a denial of fundamental human rights, is contrary to the Charter of the United Nations and is an impediment to the promotion of world peace and co-operation." Rights of self-determination have two intrinsic aspects: that the people themselves determine their own destiny and that the nation they embody is recognized as inherently sovereign. The United States recognizes both aspects in Public Law 103-150, the Apology Resolution, which acknowledges the disruption of Kanaka Maoli rights of self-determination. Therefore, it is imperative that Kanaka Maoli continue to exercise their rights of self-determination, such as decolonization and independence.

The formal UN decolonization process requires that other nations support reinscription or reenlistment on the decolonization list for non-self-governing territories.[8] The UN Decolonization Committee must then be directed to proceed with the process. The failure to have the option of decolonization at the time of the 1959 U.S. statehood elections must be exposed, as well as the forced annexation of Hawai'i against the expressed will of KM people in the massive Kū'ē petitions of 1897–1898.[9]

The UN process of decolonization includes the right to educate the peoples of non-self-governing territories about all options regarding their rights of self-determination. These options may include full independence as a sovereign nation-state, as well as free association with or incorporation into another nation-state: "All peoples have the right to self-determination; by virtue of that right they freely determine their political status and freely pursue their economic, social and cultural development."[10] The right, choice, and option of independence were denied in the 1959 statehood process, resulting in the illegal incorporation of Hawai'i by the United States. Hawai'i expresses the dual rights of self-determination as both a nation-state and as an Indigenous people.

Within its apology, Public Law 103-150 begs the development of a cultural process of self-determination. Ka Ho'okolokolonui Kānaka Maoli has enduring significance in this regard. Furthermore, the Tribunal connects with the global Indigenous peoples' movements that are gaining recognition and standing. Indigenous peoples, cultures, and nations are acknowledged as having laws, customs, languages, protocols, systems of knowledge, and practices uniquely arising from our special and diverse origins as expressed in ancestral cosmologies. As the global movement to restore the languages and true identities of Indigenous peoples surges forward, we will someday be known by our own names and more than seven thousand realities, languages, cultures, peoples, nations, and places of origin that we represent.

Cosmologies express the practical wisdom of interrelationships between all life forms as family. Indigenous laws and practices that arise from a cosmic and natural organization of life, life support, and life renewal, express accumulated wisdom gained over thousands of years prior to colonial laws, practices, and governments that have enslaved, contaminated, and dominated the earth and its peoples, life forms, waters, oceans, life sources, and natural resources. As an urgent remedy, each culture and community must effectively implement self-correcting actions to recover and protect the biological and cultural diversity that sustains life in all the regions of the world.

As the prophecy predicts, as the oceans rise, so will the power of the people to right the wrongs of the past and set into place the pono of the future. With access to the global networks of communication and visibility, the voices of the people of the world are demanding and creating social change to end poverty, hunger, inequality, exploitation, and oppression. Power to the peoples to create peace and mutual respect for a thriving new world—region by region, nation by nation, community by community, people by people—"interrelated, interdependent and complementary, which share a common destiny."[11]

Ma mua, ma hope . . . the past is forever before us, as the future comes with us. We create it with the guidance of our ancestors, whose spirits reside as kino lau; within all life forms of creation and within all dimensions of the cosmos, they light our way.

Notes

1. The Tribunal materials are available at http://hookolokolonui.wix.com/hookolokolonui.

2. The Tribunal judges include the following individuals, listed with their professional affiliations at the time of the event: Milner S. Ball, Caldwell Professor of Constitutional Law at the University of Georgia; Hyun-Kyung Chung, assistant professor of theology from Ewha Women's University, Seoul; Ward Churchill (Creek Cherokee Métis), associate professor of American Indian studies at the University of Colorado at Boulder; Richard Falk, Albert G. Milbank Professor of International Law and Practice, Princeton University; Lennox Hinds, professor of law at Rutgers University, past director of the National Conference of Black Lawyers, and counsel to the African National Congress; Te Moana Nui a Kiwa Jackson (Ngati Kahungunu and Ngati Porou Maori), director of Maori Legal Service, Wellington, New Zealand; Asma Khader, attorney, educator, journalist, and member of the Palestinian Rights Society and the National Committee for the Protection of Children in Amman, Jordan; Oda Makoto, novelist, literary critic, and visiting professor of comparative studies at the State University of New York at Stony Brook, member of the Permanent Peoples' Tribunal; and Sharon Venne (Cree), lawyer, UN human rights advocate, and Rockefeller fellow on Indigenous legal systems. The advocate-prosecutor team consisted of Glenn Morris (Shawnee), attorney and director of the Fourth World Center for the Study of Indigenous Law and Politics, University of Colorado at Denver, and director, American Indian Movement, Denver Chapter; Maivan Clech Lam, professor of law at City University of New York and Rockefeller Fellow at University of Colorado at Boulder; and José Morin (Puerto Rico), attorney and executive director of the North Star Foundation in New York, previously with the Center for Constitutional Rights. These international jurists, lawyers, and educators provided unique points of view and brought to the proceedings a familiarity with conventions and agreements that were changing the dynamics and the language of international law at the time (Tribunal Kōmike, *Ka Ho'okolokolonui Kānaka Maoli 1993, Peoples' International Tribunal Hawai'i—Mānoa*, 7–9). Special commendations go to Alejandro Molina, as lead advocate, adviser, and organizer for the Tribunal, and to Joan Lander and Puhipau from Nā Maka o ka 'Āina for documenting the Tribunal in film and text.

3. Ka Ho'okolokolonui Kānaka Maoli, Introduction to the Verdict of the International Peoples' Tribunal Hawai'i, 1–2.

4. Tribunal Kōmike, "Interim Report"; Tribunal Kōmike, *Ka Ho'okolokolonui Kanaka Maoli* Tribunal, 10–11. The Tribunal's findings and recommendations were prepared for wide distribution as an official report to the United Nations, the International Court of Justice, the Organization of American States, the Nuclear Free and Independent Pacific, other international bodies, the United States, other nation-states, and the state of Hawai'i.

5. Tribunal Kōmike, "Interim Report," 11–12. Additional information on the International Covenant on Civil and Social and Cultural Rights of Indigenous Peoples and the Convention on the Prevention and Punishment of the Crime of Genocide can be found at the United Nations Department of Economic and Social Affairs website, www.un.org/en/development/desa/index.html.

6. The United Nations General Assembly adopted the Declaration on the Rights of Indigenous Peoples on September 13, 2007. The text is available online at www.un.org/esa/socdev/unpfii/documents/DRIPS_en.pdf.

7. The following excerpts of testimonies are taken from Tribunal Kōmike, "Mana'o," 10–19, which is based on an early version of Nā Maka o ka 'Āina's transcripts, now revised and published in Nā Maka o ka 'Āina, *Proceedings of Ka Ho'okolokolonui Kānaka Maoli, Peoples' International Tribunal Hawai'i 1993*.

8. United Nations, Declaration on the Granting of Independence to Colonial Countries and Peo-

ples, Resolution 1514 (XV), adopted by the United Nations General Assembly, December 14, 1960. This "Decolonization Declaration" can be found at www.un.org/en/decolonization/declaration.shtml.

9. Minton and Silva, "Kūʻē."

10. United Nations General Assembly Resolution 1514.

11. This phrase comes from Law Number 300: "Framework Law for Mother Earth and Integrated Development to Live Well" passed by the Bolivian government in October 2012. For more information, see "Bolivia: Ley Nº 300, 15 de octubre de 2012," www.lexivox.org/norms/BO-L-N300.xhtml; and Shahriari, "Bolivia Enacts New Law for Mother Earth."

CHAPTER 14. Ke Kūʻē Kūpaʻa Loa Nei K/Mākou (We Most Solemnly Protest)

A MEMOIR OF 1998

Noenoe K. Silva

My research into the annexation period began in 1995. I had just completed a seminar on postcolonial theory, taught by Sankaran Krishna. Edward Said's *Culture and Imperialism* struck me—especially his observations on how history constructs the idea of the native as always primitive, savage, and incomprehensible.[1] The class also covered the subaltern studies collective, which is a group of mostly South Asian scholars theorizing and rewriting the history of India based on their own sources. It was incredible to learn, for example, that a six-volume history of India had been written in Oxbridge by an English scholar who prided himself on never having gone to India.[2] This made me wonder about how Hawaiian history had been written. At that time I had only read histories of Hawaiʻi like Kamakau's, the original of which was written in Hawaiian; I had read it in translation as well as some of it in the original. So for my seminar paper in that class, I did an analysis of Gavan Daws's *Shoal of Time.*

In that paper, I was looking for whether or not Daws had used any of the wealth of historical information contained in Hawaiian-language newspapers or Hawaiian-language archives. Like Kuykendall and others before him, he didn't. I was also able to see a familiar construction of the image of the native in Daws, as the aliʻi are always portrayed as too something: too big, too drunk, too uncontrollable, and Hawaiians other than aliʻi nui in positions of power are virtually nonexistent in the book.

The following summer I learned about the work that Nancy Morris, librarian in the Hawaiian collection, had done on a Hawaiian-language newspaper, *Ka Loea Kalaiaina.* She read and indexed the newspaper for the year 1899. Her thesis, written in 1975, reinforced everything I had learned in Krishna's class: it argued forcefully that no history of Hawaiʻi had yet been written that drew upon the perspectives of Hawaiians as reflected in the Hawaiian newspapers.[3] Since then, Lilikalā Kameʻeleihiwa had published *Native Land and Foreign Desires* on the change in Hawaiian land tenure to private property.[4] This was virtually the only work that drew on Hawaiian sources and analyzed the behavior of aliʻi according to Hawaiian cultural traditions. I chose to mimic Morris's methodology and read all the issues of one year of a newspaper in Hawaiian, and also following her, I chose a year in the same era, 1895. The newspaper was *Ke Aloha Aina*, founded by Joseph Nāwahī following his release from prison after the 1895 civil war.[5]

All my suspicions were immediately realized. The Kānaka had fought the overthrow and annexation with everything they had, and especially with discourse. They wrote and published their opposition to the usurping business class and the predominantly haole government, even after many had been imprisoned for trying to overthrow the illegitimate government with arms.

The research in the newspaper led me to the riches in the Hawaiʻi State Archives. One day I went to the reference desk there and the archivist showed me a catalog from an exhibit at the U.S. National Archives in Washington, DC, titled *The Ties That Bind: Communities in American History*.[6] Hawaiʻi was represented by two documents: one a photograph of surfers on Kauaʻi and the other a page from the anti-annexation petitions of 1897. I hadn't yet read that far into *Ke Aloha Aina* so I didn't yet know about these petitions. But I saw that the women's Hui Aloha ʻĀina had organized the petition drive, and I was already familiar with them. When I presented my research in a class, Nālani Minton was in attendance and told me afterward that she and others knew about the petitions and had searched for them previously but unsuccessfully. She hoped that I would be able to go to Washington and find them.

Shortly thereafter, I had an opportunity to travel to Washington, DC, for the first time. I suspect this was the first in a series of interventions by kūpuna o ka pō in support of my research. Our kūpuna o ka pō are our ancestors who have passed on and now live in the realm known as the pō: where we come from and where we go when we die, and also where the whole universe came from. When I got to the National Archives, I purchased a copy of the exhibit catalog and took it to the archivists. After a time, they located the file and brought me the box containing the petitions. I was astonished to see that there were over 550 pages of the petition, some organized by Hui Aloha ʻĀina o nā Kāne and some by the wāhine. I saw signatures of men, women, and children from five islands, page after page—and at the end, Lorrin Thurston's attempt to discredit them. I photocopied just a few pages.

At home I continued to read in *Ke Aloha Aina*. I read it in chronological order, seeing what the two Hui had done, day by day. People's concerns and personalities emerged through the pages. Joseph Nāwahī always stood out. When the Republic government harassed community leaders, for example, he put himself at risk. When an epidemic raged through Honolulu and killed perhaps a hundred people, the government ordered certain neighborhoods quarantined, focusing on heavily Hawaiian areas like Kalihi. Then police went in and arrested some parents for violation of truancy laws because they complied with the quarantine order. Nāwahī stood up for the couple in a meeting with the authorities, pointing out the obvious harassment. The authorities ordered him to be silent or face arrest but he did not stop speaking.

Nāwahī's editorials and speeches were inspiring, and he was a natural leader on whom people in our community relied for guidance in fighting the impending annexation. When I read in the paper that he had died in San Francisco after traveling there to try to improve his health after contracting tuberculosis in Oʻahu prison, I was devastated. Alone in my room, reading papers printed from microfilm, I couldn't believe he had been taken from us at that moment. I knew the outcome of the struggle but I was caught up in the struggle, reading the paper day by day—it was like I was there. Through Kahikina Kelekona's eulogistic biography, I knew that Nāwahī had died and that many mele had been written for him, but I hadn't known it was right then, in the middle of the struggle our kūpuna had a reasonable chance of winning.

I was also inspired by so many of the others who stepped up: Emma Aima Nāwahī, ke aliʻi nui Kuaihelani Campbell, and all the other women who traveled from Honolulu to four other islands to garner signatures on the petition and who led the younger male leaders to make the right decisions. Sam Kamakaia was another, the leader of the Bana Lāhui Hawaiʻi who composed mele and traveled around the United States with their musical message of aloha ʻāina.

During the same time, I was introduced to Tom Coffman, a local haole historian and documentary film maker, who was looking for someone who could read Hawaiian to assist him with his book and film about the annexation. He planned to have the two ready to release a week before the centennial of the annexation ceremony. I hadn't yet thought about the serendipity of what I was discovering. I agreed to meet with him and then agreed to work with him—not to assist him but so that we could mutually assist each other. He was experienced and motivated to seek out grants from the Office of Hawaiian Affairs and Pacific Islanders in Communication to fund his projects and I was a graduate student. He was interested in tracking down the story of what happened in the United States and in the relationships between the leaders of the overthrow and annexation drive in Hawaiʻi with the U.S. expansionists. My business was to tell the story of our kūpuna whose voices had been buried in the post-annexation colonial erasure avalanche. It was mutually beneficial, and I am grateful to our kūpuna for bringing him to me. Tom brought me a research grant from Pacific Islanders in Communication, and he is a photographer. He took the photo of the McKinley statue with the treaty of annexation in its hand that stands in front of McKinley High School. This was very important because I was able to use it to explain my analysis of the erasure of our people's moʻolelo by the occupying forces. It is a physical manifestation of the attempt to lie about our kūpuna's' fight—an attempt that was successful for many decades. He also generously shared his many photographs with me for my presentations and for the book *Aloha Betrayed.*

I began to realize that I needed a complete copy of what have come to be known as the kūʻē petitions. I contacted the U.S. National Archives and ordered a complete copy.

When they finally arrived three months later, my (then) partner Dore Minatodani and I photocopied them, organized them into regions, and then on Sovereign Sunday in January 1997, set up a card table on the ʻIolani Palace grounds, with a big sign saying "Anti-Annexation Petitions." A few very important people stopped by the table that day. Puʻuhonua (Bumpy) Kanahele came up to the table, looked over the pages, turned around, and stomped away without saying a word. A few days later, he called me and explained that he had become enraged that knowledge of this petition had been kept from us our whole lives. He had walked away and released his rage by punching a wall of the palace. He called because he wanted to help in any way he could to make the petitions known in our communities.

Soon after, Nālani Minton organized a meeting with the education department of the Bishop Museum to persuade them to exhibit the petitions during the summer of 1998, the centennial commemoration of the illegitimate annexation. She brought Dr. Kekuni Blaisdell, her uncle, and Maile Meyer of Native Books. We met with Tom Cummings and Guy Hīnano Kaulukukui. At first they explained to us that the museum had no plans to commemorate the centennial and had allocated no funds to their department for any centennial event. Maile then articulated her vision, illustrating with her hands the expansiveness of the possible exhibit: "I see walls covered with page after page after page of our kūpuna's signatures and people searching for their own kūpuna's names." I watched Tom and Hīnano following her hands with their eyes and understanding how powerful such an exhibit could be. They then promised to see what they could do. They managed to get some funding and they ordered their own full copy of the petition from the U.S. National Archives.

Nālani also had the idea to photocopy all the pages into a book that anyone could buy from a copy shop. Hīnano arranged for Nālani and me to be able to copy a master from the museum's much better copy of the petition. We arranged the pages by region and by women and men, just as the kūpuna had collected them. I wrote an essay contextualizing the petition, and we added some illustrations of the petition drive meeting that had been published in the *San Francisco Call*. We got in touch with Puʻuhonua, who arranged for the initial copies to be printed at a copy shop in Kāneʻohe at a discount. These first copies were printed on beautiful parchment-like paper with a clear vinyl cover in front and black vinyl on the back. Nālani then traveled to various other islands with masters and deposited them with cooperating copy shops so that our communities outside Oʻahu might have access. Many, many people bought these copy shop books.

Around this time, I had written a short account of the petitions. I had run into my old friend Tuti Kanahele, who was working with Keanu Sai mā at Perfect Title. She asked for more information and so I dropped off a copy of the essay at the Perfect Title office, leaving it with Keanu, whom I did not yet know. I was a bit stunned a few days later at a protest at the state capitol where Tuti was passing out hundreds of copies of my essay.

The next day my cousin Haunani Kauka came to my home (for another reason) with a copy of the essay and exclaimed, "We've been lied to our whole lives!"

Also around this time, the American Friends Service Committee invited me to give my first public lecture. My mom, Betty (née Decker) Williams, happened to be on Oʻahu for our family reunion. I told her that I would drop her off at the reunion, go do my lecture, and come back. But she wanted to hear it. A not-very-large room in Kaumakapili Church was the venue; it was filled to overflowing. Nālani Minton came with a box of copies of the petition, which I had not thought myself to bring. With my mom by my side, I told the story of the Hui Aloha ʻĀina and Hui Kālaiʻāina, with photographic slides. Afterward my mom said very angrily, "I never knew any of this!" She was enraged and also very proud of me.

As August 12, 1998—the centennial of the annexation ceremony—approached, Hīnano Kaulukukui was arranging for the exhibit at the Bishop Museum. The U.S. National Archives decided to treat the document as a treasure even though in Washington they had stored it carelessly, stuffing it into a box that was too short so the last half inch of each page was bent over and many pages' bottoms had broken off. They wouldn't let the museum exhibit the originals, except for a few pages on the top of stacks. They did allow Hīnano to order color facsimiles of about five pages, which they selected at random. When the pages arrived, one of them had the signature of Hīnano's kūpuna on it. I understood this as a communication of approval from his kūpuna.

In June 1998, Rev. Tom Van Culin of St. Matthew's Episcopal Church called me to ask if I could speak to the Waimānalo community at his church. Because I was on a Ford Foundation dissertation fellowship, I felt that it was my job to write the dissertation and not spend time doing anything else. I said no. But just as I hung up the phone I felt a whack on my head. I was alone in the house so it was obviously a kupuna o ka pō letting me know I had made the wrong decision. I immediately called Rev. Tom back and agreed.

That turned out to be one of the most beautiful events of my life. I spoke in the chapel, with a slide projector set up. Puʻuhonua brought a film crew to tape the lecture. The church overflowed with Kānaka from Waimānalo. I was surprised to see Professor Rubellite Kawena Johnson and Jim Bartels, curator of ʻIolani Palace, walk in. These were people much more knowledgeable than me, so I was honored by their presence. After the lecture, some people announced that their kūpuna were in the photos of the Hui Aloha ʻĀina, and others said their kūpuna had worked on Queen Liliʻuokalani's imprisonment quilt. Jim Bartels stood up and told the crowd that he thought the kūʻē petitions were the most significant discovery of the twentieth century for Kanaka Hawaiʻi.

Because of the Bishop Museum's public relations, the *Honolulu Advertiser* did a story about the petitions and put my photo in front of ʻIolani Palace on the front page. It was crazy for me, a usually very quiet person, but I was grateful for the attention to the

PALAPALA HOOPII KUE HOOHUIAINA.

I ka Mea Mahaloia WILLIAM McKINLEY, Peresidena, a me ka Aha Senate, o Amerika Huipuia.

ME KA MAHALO :—

NO KA MEA, na waihoia aku imua o ka Aha Senate o Amerika Huipuia he Kuikahi no ka Hoohui aku ia Hawaii nei ia Amerika Huipuia i oleloia, no ka noonooia ma kona kau mau iloko o Dekemaba, M. H. 1897; nolaila,

O MAKOU, na poe no lakou na inoa malalo iho, na wahine Hawaii oiwi, he poe makaainana a poe noho hoi no ka Apana o Puna, Mokupuni o Hawaii, he poe lala no ka AHAHUI ALOHA AINA HAWAII O NA WAHINE O KO HAWAII PAEAINA, a me na wahine e ae i like ka manao makee me ko ka Ahahui i oleloia, ke kue aku nei me ka manao ikaika loa i ka hoohuiia aku o ko Hawaii Paeaina i oleloia ia Amerika Huipuia i oleloia ma kekahi ano a loina paha.

PETITION AGAINST ANNEXATION.

To His Excellency WILLIAM McKINLEY, President, and the Senate, of the United States of America.

GREETING :—

WHEREAS, there has been submitted to the Senate of the United States of America a Treaty for the Annexation of the Hawaiian Islands to the said United States of America, for consideration at its regular session in December, A. D. 1897; therefore,

WE, the undersigned, native Hawaiian women, citizens and residents of the District of Puna, Island of Hawaii, who are members of the WOMEN'S HAWAIIAN PATRIOTIC LEAGUE OF THE HAWAIIAN ISLANDS, and other women who are in sympathy with the said League, earnestly protest against the annexation of the said Hawaiian Islands to the said United States of America in any form or shape.

IKEA—ATTEST: Mrs Lilia Aholo, Kakauolelo—Secretary. Mrs Kuaihelani Campbell, Peresidena—President.

	INOA—NAME.	AGE.		INOA—NAME.	AGE.
	Mrs Kapua Pea	29		Mrs Kalaukia	46
	Hiiaka	17		Miss Kaini	19
	Kanaimahoe	14		Mrs. Kahanulu	18
	Pepe	14		Nanui	46
	Keaho	35		Miss Kahi	23
	Hauka	15		Miss Lili	21
	Mrs Mele	20		Mrs Kawaimaka	51
	Kehukai	35		Miss Kawaimaka	15
	Ahi	13		Kaanaana	19
10	Wiliama	16		Mrs Keaupuni	64
	Kahaikamoku	36		Mrs Mele	36
	Kaleikahua	40		Kaiealani	80
	Mabeka	16		Mrs Keapuni	16
	Kaaukai	61		Ululani	14
	Paakaula	57		Loahiwa	42
	Lii aloha	21	41	Kamala Kauhi	18
	Mrs Kahupu	60		Kealohe	48
	Miss Naomi	18		Kauhi Lehulua	58
	Miss. Malao	19		Kaunu	28
	Mrs. Kaomiloula	27		Nupuaikaina	22
	K. Ellen Keakiki	19		Kapuaokahikina	25
	E. Kaike Kahoomana	43		Kalii	19
	Mrs Kaainoa	61		Kamuhahiki	20
	Miss Kahikina	16		Kaliipupohaku	48
	Mrs Haka	80		Miss Keakamahana	18

Noenoe Silva sits with copies of the antiannexation petitions that her research helped to recover for the lāhui Hawaiʻi, January 2013. After their rediscovery in the late 1990s, they came to be known as the Kūʻē petitions.

(opposite) One page of the 1897 antiannexation petitions, organized by the Hui Aloha ʻĀina and Hui Kālaiʻāina. These petitions were instrumental in ensuring that the U.S. Congress never approved a treaty of annexation of Hawaiʻi. Courtesy of Noenoe Silva.

petition. That was an extremely effective way for Kanaka everywhere to learn about it. When I got home that evening, there was a record number of calls on my voice mail, most of them from strangers. One woman left a message telling me that the petition was a window into the world of her kūpuna. It was apparent that these petitions were not seen by people as just historical or political documents. They were and are seen as ways that our kūpuna are also speaking directly to us. I heard stories about people coming in and lovingly touching the names of their kūpuna on the petitions, as though they were stroking their faces, or touching the hands that were reaching out to them across the century.

On August 12, I was with Leandra Wai and others who collaborated on a community education exhibit located on the ʻIolani Palace grounds.[7] Early in the day, a woman approached me, clutching her petition book to her chest. She said, "Now we will never forget again." I participated in the march from Maunaʻala, the Royal Mausoleum, to the palace. The march was led by ali'i societies. I was in back with Keanu Sai, Didi Lee Kwai, and other activists. Sai had a big banner made that referred to maka'āinana society and the kū'ē petitions. We stopped at O'ahu cemetery to leave flowers to honor the great leader, Kuaihelani Campbell. We stopped at Washington Place to honor Mō'īwahine Lili'uokalani, then to 'Iolani Palace to enjoy the day and, for me, to answer questions at our exhibit.

That afternoon I spoke at Rev. Tom Van Culin's family reunion at St. Andrew's Church, across the street from the palace. This family included Uncle David Kahelemauna and Mikahala Roy, Gard Kealoha, and members of the Thompson family. There I failed to identify myself properly (genealogically), so afterward these highly knowledgeable Hawaiians asked me who my parents and grandparents were. When I told them my mother was Betty Decker and her parents were Kathleen Kauhili'ili'iopuna Jay Decker and Theodore Decker of Kailua, I heard a loudly whispered comment from the back of the room: "Do you think she knows?" Then someone said, "You are family to us. Your mother married our cousin, Liko Johnson." I laughed with delight. Uncle Liko was indeed my mother's first husband. He was a kumu hula and an entertainer. He was also a very accomplished māhū who participated in female impersonation contests (as they were called in those days). My mom had been a butch eighteen-year-old when the two decided to get married and live their lives their own way. They truly loved each other but not in the conventional way. When my grandparents realized what they had done, they insisted on an annulment. My mother still cried about this in her last years. At the end, I was given a family reunion T-shirt.

In February 1999, in the middle of my dissertation writing my mother passed into the pō. I miss her every day and still, at age fifty-eight, wish I were not a motherless child. I am grateful that she was able to experience with me the ways that the kūpuna facilitated getting the knowledge out about their fight to prevent annexation through me. I was blessed at birth with an unusual capacity to learn languages and I never knew at all that it had a purpose until these events came to pass. Auē ka nui o ke aloha i ka makua a me nā kūpuna.

One of the most important things I learned through these experiences was that our kūpuna o ka pō are always with us. When we do research with the intention of bringing their stories forward, they intervene and help us. Sometimes research is handed to us by people we don't yet know. Sometimes descendants call or e-mail us out of the blue (as has happened to me twice in the last year as I work on a new project). Sometimes they speak to us in dreams, daydreams, or sudden realizations (or even slap our heads!) while we are awake. We are connected to them not only through family ties and mo'okū'auhau, but we share our connection to this 'āina aloha with them. Their struggle to retain sovereignty—e mau i ke ea—is our struggle. As James Kaulia said, "E kū'ē loa aku i ka ho'ohui 'ia o Hawai'i me Amerika a hiki i ke aloha 'āina hope loa" ([We will] protest the annexation of Hawaiʻi to America until the very last aloha ʻāina). We are the contemporary aloha ʻāina and thus we will continue to protest, organize, and otherwise work for the ea of our ʻāina aloha until a state of pono for Hawaiʻi is reached.

Notes

1. Said, *Culture and Imperialism.*
2. Mill, *The History of British India.*
3. Morris, "Ka Loea Kalaiaina."
4. Kameʻeleihiwa, *Native Land and Foreign Desires.*
5. See Spencer, *Ka Hoʻokahuli Aupuni Kaulana o 1893*; and Loomis, *For Whom Are the Stars?*
6. Auel, *Ties That Bind.*
7. Leandra Wai and Sparky Rodrigues were stalwart activists in the Mākua Valley struggle (see chapter 7, this volume).

CHAPTER 15. Resisting the Akaka Bill

J. Kēhaulani Kauanui

On Wednesday, July 6, 2011, Hawai'i governor Neil Abercrombie signed Senate Bill 1520 into law—legislation with a long genealogy stemming from efforts to undercut the restoration of the Hawaiian nation under international law. Act 195—the First Nation Government Bill—provides U.S. state authorization of a process for the creation of a "Native Hawaiian governing entity."[1] It gave the governor the power to appoint a five-member Native Hawaiian Roll Commission that lays the foundation for participation in a newly domesticated governing body. Abercrombie declared, "This is an important step for the future of Native Hawaiian self-determination and the ability for Native Hawaiians to decide their own future. . . . This Commission will put together the roll of qualified and interested Native Hawaiians who want to help determine the course of Hawai'i's indigenous people."[2] Adding insult to great injury, this ceremonial event took place at Washington Place in Honolulu, the residence of former Hawaiian monarch Queen Lili'uokalani, who was overthrown in 1893 with backing from the U.S. Marines.

This legislation is the state version of federal legislation known as the Native Hawaiian Government Reorganization Act, which had been repeatedly proposed and consistently defeated in Congress throughout the prior decade. From the start it was dubbed the Akaka Bill—named after its sponsor, Democratic U.S. Senator Daniel Akaka. In the midst of the early period when the legislation was first conceived, the Council for Native Hawaiian Advancement was formed to become a key driving force in support of the federal bill (and much later its state version) along with the two primary Hawai'i state agencies, the Office of Hawaiian Affairs (OHA) and the Department of Hawaiian Home Lands. All claimed that the entity that would be formed through the legislation would represent self-determination for Native Hawaiians, but this assertion is called into question when one considers the structural framework, which is inherently limiting.

From the start, Hawai'i's congressional delegates attempted to push through the bill despite massive opposition to it among Kanaka Maoli, whom it affects first and foremost. The delegation has held just one five-day hearing, back in 2000, on the bill since its inception. Although there was overwhelming opposition to the bill—from two distinct camps: pro-independence Hawaiian nationals and pro-American conservatives—the delegation reported quite the opposite to Congress. The federal version of the legislation proposed that the U.S. government recognize a "Native Hawaiian governing entity" that was to be certified by the U.S. Department of the Interior in conformity with U.S. federal law and practice regarding Native American tribal nations. For independence activists and other supporters who advocate for the restoration of a Hawaiian nation under international law, the entire bill is seen as a farce since the historical harm the United States first committed in Hawai'i in the 1893 overthrow brought down not a "Native Hawaiian governing entity" but the Hawaiian Kingdom government, an independent state comprising Kanaka Maoli and nonindigenous subjects.[3] Consequently, the Kanaka Maoli people and other descendants of Hawaiian Kingdom citizens have, since that time, accumulated fundamental political and other claims against the United States under international law. Although the state version is modeled after the Akaka Bill, it does not authorize a nation-to-nation relationship between the U.S. federal government and a Native Hawaiian governing entity. Instead, it authorizes a First Nation–to-state relationship.[4]

At the event where Abercrombie signed the bill into law, activists protested the supposed surrender of the Hawaiian nation to the U.S. government, as the trustees of OHA and other state agents poised for transition to the new "First Nation." Representatives of various ali'i (chiefly) societies and trusts, OHA trustees, Native Hawaiian civic clubs, and state lawmakers were among those who attended the signing ceremony. Those Kānaka Maoli and other Hawaiian nationals who protested the event held signs with declarations such as "Hawaiian Independence," "'A'ole Pono, 'A'ole Pau," "Our Nation, Not Your State," and "Hell no, we won't enroll"—punctuated by "and neither would the Queen." In many ways, that historical moment marked the depressed culmination of a decade of resistance to the Akaka Bill and state co-optation of the Hawaiian sovereignty struggle.

This essay offers an overview of the politics of the controversial proposal for U.S. federal recognition for Native Hawaiians. I document its origins and the rationales advanced in support of it, as well as the community resistance against it. The federally driven bill was continuously introduced in each U.S. Congress since 2000 but has a history of being summarily defeated by conservatives in the U.S. Senate. Conservatives' refusal to support the measure became more pronounced when the George W. Bush administration took a position against the legislation, which lasted throughout Bush's administration. Throughout that period the legislation gained committee approval in both the House and Senate, yet it stalled when it came to a floor debate. Despite multiple revisions and reintroductions of new drafts aimed at satisfying Department of Interior concerns and appeasing Republican critics who called the proposal a plan for "race-based government," the legislation never progressed to a Senate vote.[5] With the new leadership of President Barack Obama in 2008, the administration provided firm support; however, the bill—which continues to be revised and reintroduced—still serves as a political football between Republicans and Democrats.

Conservatives were not the only ones opposed to the legislation; many Kānaka Maoli committed to the broader national claim actively opposed the legislation. Continuing from the oppositional testimony at the hearings in 2000, throughout the decade that followed, there were numerous protests and petitions, as well as online organizing to stop the legislation. As a comprehensive account of a decade's worth of resistance is beyond the scope of this essay, I selectively document the emergence of Hui Pū, an activist group that was formed in July 2005 specifically to defeat the bill.[6] For several years, Hui Pū was the most persistent, vocal, and visible group organized to expose the role of the state in containing the full Hawaiian national claim. And although the founders of Hui Pū explicitly insist that it is not an independence group per se, the work of the prominent activists who drove the multiple forms of resistance certainly had the effect of keeping the outstanding claim of independent statehood on the table within the broader Hawaiʻi community.

Given the fact that the state's Act 195 explicitly supports efforts in Congress to gain federal recognition for Hawaiians, an examination of critical resistance during the 2000s is instructive.[7] In July 2011, Hawaiʻi governor Abercrombie appointed former governor John Waiheʻe to lead a new commission to prepare and maintain a roll of qualified Native Hawaiians who would work toward the reorganization.[8] By July 20, 2012, the effort was named Kanaʻiolowalu and would entail an online registry to create a base roll of Native Hawaiians—individuals who would then be eligible to participate in the formation of a governing entity.[9] This process arguably would create the first documented evidence of collective acquiescence to the U.S. government or its subsidiaries. Hence, the question of whether there will be sustained opposition to this state-driven initiative in order to protect the outstanding Hawaiian sovereignty claim is pressing.

Purported Rationales for the Akaka Bill

Proponents of the Akaka Bill have continuously advanced three key legal developments for their argument in support of federal recognition for Native Hawaiians: (1) the ruling in the U.S. Supreme Court case *Rice v. Cayetano*, which was repeatedly misconstrued by proponents of the bill; (2) the lawsuits that followed in the aftermath of the ruling in *Rice*; and (3) a long line of legislation passed by the U.S. Congress that already recognizes Native Hawaiians as an indigenous people—notably including the 1993 Apology Resolution (Public Law 103-150), which calls for reconciliation. The bill originated in March 2000 when Senator Akaka and the rest of the Hawaiʻi congressional delegation formed the Task Force on Native Hawaiian Issues. This was just one month after *Rice v. Cayetano,* the U.S. Supreme Court ruling that struck down Native Hawaiian–only voting for OHA trustee elections as unconstitutional. As its immediate stated goal, the task force aimed to clarify the political relationship between Hawaiians and the United States through the U.S. Congress.

During the 106th U.S. Congress, Senator Akaka introduced federal legislation that proposed to recognize Hawaiians as indigenous people who have a special relationship with the United States and thus a right to self-determination under federal law acknowledging tribal governance. The entity would be formed by a commission of nine members appointed by the secretary of the interior whose duty first and foremost would be to report to the secretary. The legislation allowed only for the recognition of a Native Hawaiian governing entity and not the rights of that entity, which would be subject to later negotiation between the U.S. federal government, the Native Hawaiian entity, and the Hawaiʻi state government. Federal protection was now being sold to Native Hawaiians as a defense against average citizens who challenge the Hawaiian trusts that the United States never upheld in the first place.

At stake in the *Rice* case were restricted elections for OHA trustees, along with the very existence of the Office of Hawaiian Affairs. Prior to the court ruling, participation in OHA elections was restricted to Native Hawaiians, of any Hawaiian ancestry, who resided in Hawaiʻi. Harold Rice, a fourth-generation white resident of Hawaiʻi, was denied the right to vote because he is not Hawaiian by any statutory definition (he is neither "native Hawaiian" nor "Native Hawaiian").[10]

As plaintiff in the case, Rice claimed that both the trust managed by the office and the OHA voting provisions were racially discriminatory and violated the Fourteenth and Fifteenth Amendments to the U.S. Constitution, which, respectively, are meant to provide equal protection and to guarantee that the right of citizens to vote shall not be denied or abridged on account of race, color, or previous condition of servitude. But even though the trust itself is, according to the state, for the benefit of "native Hawaiians" (defined by a 50 percent blood quantum rule) the U.S. Supreme Court's majority opinion decreed that the state's electoral restriction enacted race-based voting qualifications and thereby violated the Fifteenth Amendment.

Because the U.S. federal government does not recognize Hawaiians collectively as a sovereign entity, the state of Hawaiʻi maintained that the voting classification was rationally tied to its requirement to uphold a congressional requirement—in other words, because the United States has a special relationship with and obligation to native Hawaiians stemming from the Hawaiian Homes Commission Act of 1920.[11] Thus the state's defense in the *Rice* case rested on the claim that Congress has the power to enter into special trust relationships with indigenous peoples—a power that is not confined to treatment of tribal Indians—and that the state stood in for the United States with regard to land claims and related entitlements.

Although, in the end, the majority opinion in *Rice v. Cayetano* did not rule on the Fourteenth Amendment, and thus did not affect the trust that OHA is meant to manage, the ruling laid the essential groundwork for further assaults on Hawaiian lands and people through a rash of lawsuits throughout the 2000s.[12] These new cases threatened the existence of all Hawaiian-specific funding sources and institutions, including OHA; all federal funds for Hawaiian health, education, and housing; and the state Department of Hawaiian Home Lands. Plaintiffs charged that these institutions are racially discriminatory. Within the broader context of these legal assaults, which deem any indigenous-specific program racist, many Native Hawaiians and their allies support Senator Akaka's proposal for federal recognition, especially since he pitched the legislation as a protective measure against such lawsuits.

Critics of the bill suggested throughout the course of the decade that those primarily worried about protecting these funds should be urged to consider what they would forfeit in exchange for supporting the bill. It seemed that Kanaka Maoli might have a better chance at de facto self-determination by remaining under the state situation (prior to the passage of Act 195) while pressing forward on international claims and resisting any U.S. federal recognition that would foreclose the legitimate claims to independence. In other words, why not protect the claim even if it cannot be realized at the current political moment? This seemed especially poignant given that federal funding could be cut at any time for any reason, and this proved to be true throughout the course of the 2000s as federal expenditures were largely diverted to the prolonged U.S. imperial wars of aggression in Iraq and Afghanistan after 9/11, and later during the economic crisis of 2008. However, even at their highest dollar total of an estimated $70 million per year, that amount came to only 0.7 percent of the state's entire annual budget at the time.[13] Furthermore, since one of the main leveraging points that has historically enabled the Hawai'i congressional delegation to secure funding earmarked for Native Hawaiians was that there was no parity for self-governance like federally recognized tribal nations, it seemed highly likely that if the Akaka Bill were to pass, federal funds would be cut anyhow in the name of self-determination and since there would be little justification left in the logic of the previous justification.

Supporters also cite a long line of legislation in which the U.S. government recognized Native Hawaiians as an indigenous people similar to American Indians (and sometimes Alaska Natives). As early as 1903, the U.S. federal government passed legislation acknowledging the indigenous people of Hawai'i, and currently over 160 federal statutes address the conditions of Native Hawaiians. Since the 1970s, in the midst of a thriving Hawaiian rights movement, the U.S. Congress has enacted numerous special provisions of law for the benefit of Native Hawaiians in the areas of health, education, labor, and housing such as the Native Hawaiian Health Care Act and the Native Hawaiian Education Act.[14] Thus, some suggested it could be argued that the U.S. Congress has already recognized that a special relationship—that is, a political one, not a racial one—exists between the United States and the Native Hawaiian people.

Proponents of the Akaka Bill also cite the Hawaiian Homes Commission Act of 1920, which allotted approximately 200,000 acres of land, with ninety-nine-year lease provisions, to those who qualify as "native Hawaiians," defined as "descendants with at least one-half blood quantum of individuals inhabiting the Hawaiian Islands prior to 1778."[15] These allotted lands comprise the Crown and Government Lands of the kingdom. The Hawaiian Homes Commission Act was originally conceived as a Native rehabilitation project for the Hawaiian population, which had been experiencing dramatic reductions linked to colonial urbanization. Advocates for the Akaka Bill—namely OHA trustees and leaders with the Council for Native Hawaiian Advancement—continue to argue that the act institutionalized a trust agreement, and therefore constitutes a special legal relationship similar to that between the U.S. government and Indian tribes.

But it was the 1993 U.S. Apology Resolution that Senator Akaka himself cited most as a basis for the Akaka Bill. After all, he was the one who introduced the legislation that led to the congressional apology in the first place. The Apology Resolution acknowledges U.S. participation in the overthrow of Queen Liliʻuokalani and the constitutional monarchy. Besides accounting for the events that led to the U.S.-backed coup, the resolution also acknowledges that "the indigenous Hawaiian people never directly relinquished their claims to their inherent sovereignty as a people or over their national lands to the United States, either through their monarchy or through a plebiscite or referendum."[16] It also expresses a "commitment to acknowledge the ramifications of the overthrow of the Kingdom of Hawaii, in order to provide a proper foundation for reconciliation between the United States and the Native Hawaiian people" and "urges the President of the United States to also acknowledge the ramifications of the overthrow of the Kingdom of Hawaiʻi and to support reconciliation efforts between the United States and the Native Hawaiian people." In the post-*Rice* climate, he suggested that the apology provided the foundation for reconciliation and that the Akaka Bill was the means by which a resolution was best served.

Parity as Farce, Parity as Problem

Throughout the decade, in all versions, proponents claimed that passage of the bill would lay the foundation for a nation-within-a-nation model of self-governance that would offer Native Hawaiians parity with American Indians and Alaska Natives when it comes to federal recognition. But this was never the case until the most recent draft of the legislation amended by the Senate Committee on Indian Affairs on September 13, 2012, which (in section 5) "recognizes the Native Hawaiian right to reorganize under Section 16 of the Indian Reorganization Act."[17]

But even in that version—while providing for the recognition of a Native Hawaiian governing entity that would have "the inherent powers and privileges of self-government of an Indian Tribe"—the unresolved questions about territory and the attendant issue of civil and criminal jurisdiction in the Hawaiian case remain unresolved, such as whether the secretary of the U.S. Department of the Interior would be allowed to take land into trust for the Native Hawaiian governing entity. This is significant because only land held by the federal government on behalf of Native nations is allowed to be used by Indian tribes as part of their sovereign land base where they can assert jurisdiction. U.S. federal Indian policy defines tribal sovereigns as "domestic dependent nations" that have a limited right to self-government, including the right to assert jurisdiction over their people and their respective land bases legally classified as "Indian Country" to be held in trust by the U.S. government; define their own tribal membership criteria; create tribal legislation, a measure of law enforcement, and court systems; and tax their own citizens. Most versions of the Akaka Bill, on the other hand, have exempted any future Native Hawaiian governing entity from "Applicability of Certain Federal Laws"—laws pertaining to federally recognized Indian tribes that happen to greatly benefit them. It should also be noted that Alaska Native villages have a different status than federally recognized tribes in the lower forty-eight states, so asserting that a Native Hawaiian governing entity afforded by the Akaka Bill would be the same as both them and American Indians is problematic in that regard as well.

The distinct status of Alaska Natives was affirmed in the 1998 U.S. Supreme Court case of *Alaska v. Native Village of Venetie Tribal Government*, in which the high court ruled that Venetie's land base did not count as Indian Country in the legal sense since Indian Country is legally defined to include all dependent Indian communities in the United States. Venetie Village did not qualify, because their lands are not held in trust by the U.S. federal government. Thus, they cannot assess tax, enforce their own laws, or assert their jurisdiction over these lands as American Indian governments do on reservations. Moreover, the Alaska Native villages are subject to Alaska state laws. Despite these crucial distinctions, ever since the federal recognition proposal was first introduced in 2000, Senator Akaka continuously asserted that his measure seeks to establish equality in the federal policies extended toward American Indians and Alaska Natives for Native Hawaiians, and the media have unquestioningly reproduced that claim.[18]

But even if the legislation was to set forth a proposal for meaningful parity, that is still problematic for the national claim under international law. The legislation would limit Hawaiian self-determination due to the fundamental legal distinction between Indian tribes and foreign nations under the U.S. Constitution. Because of the limits on independent national sovereignty under the proposed plan for federal recognition, dozens of Hawaiian sovereignty groups have persistently and consistently rejected the application of U.S. federal Indian law that would recognize a Hawaiian domestic dependent nation—as ward to guardian—under the plenary power of Congress. It is for this reason, among numerous others, that pro-independence Hawaiians oppose this model of self-governance.

Yet federal and state agents consistently insist that federal recognition would not compromise Hawaiʻi's national claims under international law. The senator himself held the same line throughout the decade, which he articulated through press statements. From the start, the senator asserted, "This measure does not preclude Native Hawaiians from seeking alternatives in the international arena," and "Let me be clear—It is not my intention, nor the intention of the delegation, to preclude efforts of Native Hawaiians at the international level. The scope of this bill is limited to federal law."[19] Akaka's contention that passage of the bill would not preclude Kanaka Maoli from seeking "alternatives in the international arena" has been a standard response to challenges posed to him by those individuals and organizations opposed to the legislation because they favor Hawaiian independence from the United States—that is, the restoration of an independent state under international law. Akaka's response, however, only speaks to the rights of indigenous peoples. But because his mention of "alternatives in the international arena" here and elsewhere are ill defined, they have led many to infer that Kanaka Maoli could pursue full independence in a post–federal recognition political scenario if they should so desire. What few proponents of federal recognition acknowledge is that this structure differs from the outset, and that the U.S. government prohibits Native governing entities from securing international legal status as independent states. Akaka's vague assurances have been echoed repeatedly by Hawaiʻi's state and federal officials over the last decade.[20] For example, OHA administrator Clyde Namuʻo said trustees' support of the Akaka Bill does not mean opposition to independence from the United States. He noted the concerns among those in the independence movement that once federal recognition is achieved, a drive for independence may be diminished. "But that remains to be seen," Namuʻo said. "If, truly, the Hawaiian community feels independence is the noblest of goals, regardless of whether federal recognition comes about, it could still be pursued."[21]

Of the many proponents, one of the few to put forth a clear and compelling rationale was Davianna Pōmaikaʻi McGregor. Rather than perpetuating the myth that federal recognition could be a first step to Hawaiian independence, she made the case for nation-within-a-nation status by asserting that even within a restored Hawaiian nation (independent from the United States), Kanaka Maoli would still be an indigenous minority (unlike during the time of the Hawaiian Kingdom) and therefore vulnerable in any national setting due to being numerically overwhelmed by settlers and other nonindigenous people. Hence, she suggests that internal self-determination under the auspices of the U.S. government would afford more opportunity to protect Hawaiian cultural practices.[22]

However, U.S. jurisdiction over Kanaka Maoli is illegal and unjust. Therefore, to have a Native Hawaiian governing entity formed by U.S. legislation and contained by U.S. jurisdiction is structurally limiting. Given that Hawaiian Kingdom sovereignty was not lost via conquest, cession, or adjudication, those rights to independent statehood are still in place under international law. Unilateral political force prohibited the ability to be self-determining, but at no time did that amount to a legal termination of sovereignty. It is this bottom line that the Hui Pū has asserted continuously since its founding.

Hui Pū: Coming Together

The group Hui Pū was founded in June 2005 with the sole purpose of defeating the Akaka Bill.[23] Members—made up of "leaders in the areas of Hawaiian-rights activism, cultural practice and protocol, farming, academics and other fields, as well as sovereignty groups"[24]—have engaged in direct action protests and interventions, tracking the legislation and power players, sharing information and advancing critical analysis—all of which was undergirded with the mature historical perspective of the veteran warriors who are able to contextualize the social and political positions of the major actors. Hui Pū first convened at the hālau at Kamakakūokalani (the Center for Hawaiian Studies at the University of Hawaiʻi at Mānoa) in July 2005. Andre Perez organized the meeting with help from Terri Kekoʻolani and Ikaika Hussey in response to word from Kale Gumupac a month prior that Keliʻi "Skippy" Ioane and Palikapu Dedman were interested in doing something about the Akaka Bill and were soon to travel from Hawaiʻi Island to Oʻahu to pull people together to fight the bill. Andre made a flyer announcement for the meeting with help from Kaleikoa Kaʻeo: "He kāhea maiā Skippy. A call from Skippy." Perez notes that Ioane "knew most everyone, had their respect and was the glue that brought everyone together."[25] The media reported that approximately seventy-five people attended the founding meeting.[26]

At that first gathering, Hui Pū issued a "Declaration Rejecting and Condemning the Native Hawaiian Government Reorganization Act."[27] The declaration was purposefully designed after the 1897 kūʻē petitions uncovered by Noenoe K. Silva (see chapter 14, this volume). The petitions, as documented Hawaiian opposition to becoming part of the United States "in any shape or form," brought to light a powerful history of broad-based Hawaiian resistance to U.S. annexation.[28] In fact, Kanaka Maoli successfully defeated a proposed treaty of annexation in 1897. Hence, Hui Pū drew on this legacy by continuing in the footsteps of the ancestors in order to protest against what was seen as another

Hawaiian independence supporters say "No to Akaka Bill" in front of ʻIolani Palace, January 11, 2011.

type of annexation. In the declaration, Hui Pū asserted the legislation would serve the interests of the U.S. government against Hawaiians. Those who signed include Kīhei "Soli" Niheu of Nuclear Free Independent Pacific, Keoni Choy of Na Kupuna Moku o Keawe, Keliʻi "Skippy" Ioane of King's Landing Village, Palikapu Dedman of the Pele Defense Fund, Moanikeʻala Akaka of the Aloha ʻAina Education Center, Puʻuhonua "Bumpy" Kanahele of the Independent and Sovereign Nation State of Hawaiʻi (Nation of Hawaiʻi), Henry Noa of the Reinstated Hawaiian Kingdom, Kekuni Blaisdell of the Kanaka Maoli Tribunal Komike and Ka Pākaukau, Kaleikoa Kaʻeo of Not of Hawaiʻi, and Mililani Trask, former kiaʻāina of Ka Lāhui Hawaiʻi.[29] The declaration addressed the version of the bill active at the time, S. 147, and was put forth weeks before the bill was expected to get a vote on the Senate floor.[30] It was addressed to President George W. Bush and the U.S. Congress and was also immediately sent to media outlets within Hawaiʻi and beyond. It reads as follows:

> WHEREAS, there has been submitted to the Congress of the United States of America(n) a Bill S.147, further referred to as the Native Hawaiian Government Reorganization Act (NHGRA), also known as the Akaka Bill, for imminent consideration, therefore, We, the undersigned, he poʻe makaʻāinana (native Hawaiian citizens) and poʻe noho ʻōiwi Hawaiʻi (residents) who are mamo (descen-

dants) of the members of the Hawaiian Patriotic League of the Hawaiian Islands 1897, and others who are in sympathy with the said League members and their mamo (descendants), categorically and adamantly reject and condemn S.147, NHGRA, a.k.a. the Akaka Bill in any shape or form, as it purports to legislate the political status of a people who have never yielded their sovereignty to the United States.

HUI PŪ POSITION POINTS:

1. The Native Hawaiian Reorganization Act (NHGRA), a.k.a. the Akaka bill, debases our sovereign heritage and our right to self-determination.
2. Hawaiian people have never acquiesced to the illegal, US backed overthrow of our queen and country in 1893.
3. Furthermore, 38,000 of our kūpuna opposed and defeated US annexation in 1897. We must heed the legacy of our ancestors.
4. Passage of the bill would be a disaster. It would mark the first time in history that we acquiesced to the illegal US backed overthrow in 1893.
5. If Hawaiians agree to federal recognition they are consenting to give all power over their rights, lands and self-determination to the US federal government and whomever the US President appoints as the Secretary of the Interior. Under the bill, the Secretary of the Interior would become the sovereign of the Hawaiian people. Even more power and control over our lands and our rights would be exported from Hawaiʻi to Washington, D.C.
6. Federal recognition puts money and instant gratification before what is pono for our people.
7. The Akaka bill sets up a negotiation process for what? Based on our past experiences—Kahoʻolawe, Mākua, Waikāne, etc. why should we trust and believe the US this time around?
8. The Akaka bill derails our path towards justice and healing as a people and as a Nation.
9. Versions of the Akaka bill contain a clause that says claims must be submitted within 20 years—after that point, all claims are silenced.
10. Federal recognition is already a risky proposition with attacks aimed on Native American Indian rights by the same people who are attacking Hawaiian rights.
11. The Akaka bill does not protect Kanaka Maoli from future attacks and lawsuits by groups like the Society for Colorblind America, Americans Against Discrimination and Preferences and the Center for Equal Opportunity.
12. US government officials cannot represent Kanaka Maoli because we are a separate and equal people.
13. The Akaka Bill is being rubber stamped and pushed by the very people we

know have not been friends to us without hearings, without full public education and open workshops and without a consensus of the people.

14. The bill is nothing more than a US mechanism to create a puppet "Native Hawaiian" government under the US Department of Interior.
15. The bill deprives Kanaka Maoli of our inherent sovereignty and right to full self-determination by establishing our Kanaka Maoli status as indigenous native peoples of the US which we are not.
16. This is a continuation of all that has happened in the past and it is our kuleana to stop it now and for the future.
17. The bill would attempt to label us with an identity as Native Americans that is not and will never be who we are as a people.
18. The bill puts a guise of legality over a history of illegality.
19. By accepting the Akaka bill, we are not only selling out ourselves, we are selling out our ʻāina, our resources, our keiki and a multitude of generations to come, leaving them an empty, broken legacy. We do not have the right to sell out our keiki.
20. The Akaka bill relies on Congress' identification of Native Hawaiians as "a distinct group of indigenous, native people of the United States within the scope of its authority under the Constitution."[31]

Along with pointing out the illegality of the 1893 overthrow, this declaration clearly draws on the cultural, political, and legal legacy of the kūʻē petitions with a renewed refusal to acquiesce. This is clear too in the signatories' assertion that Kanaka Maoli are not part of the United States.

It is also important to note that the statement asserts guiding indigenous principles of ea—those of kuleana (right and responsibility), pono (right, just), and the tradition of resistance bequeathed by kūpuna (grandparents, elders, ancestors). Furthermore, as the authors of the declaration point out, there is a major contradiction: the means by which the legislation was proposed allows for no self-determination within a process promising self-determination. In other words, given that the bill would be decided by congressional representatives and not the Kanaka Maoli people, it preempted the exercise of self-determination by its very form. It should be noted that Hui Pū members also called for hearings in Hawaiʻi before any vote in Congress, and pointed to the farce of self-determination when Hawaiians have no actual voice in the matter of the bill.[32] And even if there was an internal referendum, the mechanism, as noted in the statement, would only afford a new governing body (a puppet government) self-determination with the approval of the U.S. Department of the Interior. As the declaration suggests in point 4, passage of the legislation could be used against Hawaiians to show that claims that exceed the domestic sphere have been forfeited. This containment draws attention away from demands for Hawai'i's independence from the United States, based on international law.

That same month, about twenty members of Hui Pū showed up at a July 7, 2005, regularly scheduled meeting of OHA in Honolulu and demanded that OHA spend money to explain the positions of those against the controversial measure.[33] Hui Pū members suggested that OHA use some of its resources to enable public debate that would include oppositional voices rather than marshaling trust revenues to lobby for the bill. They noted that by that time, OHA had already spent millions promoting the legislation through an advertising campaign, hiring a Washington-based lobbying group, and other efforts. Media reports suggest that as early as May 2003, OHA paid the lobbying group Patton Boggs about $650,000 to push congressional members for passage of the legislation.

Hui Pū argued that those most in support of federal recognition do not represent the Hawaiian people. Instead, those who work for OHA, the Department of Hawaiian Home Lands, the Native Hawaiian Health Project, and other agencies represent the state, federal, and nonprofit organizations—the same institutions that receive the funding being challenged in the courts. Therefore, supporting the proposal for federal recognition ensures their continued employment and they have a fiduciary duty to advocate for it. Furthermore, one cannot expect state and federal employees, at least, to publicly advocate for Hawai'i's independence from the United States, even though numerous individuals in these positions do so in private.

Also in July 2005, Hui Pū held a press conference on the steps of the 'Iolani Palace to publicize their strongly opposing stance. Hui Pū spokesperson Andre Perez reportedly told the media, "The Akaka Bill is being crammed down our throats with power and money. But they forget, there is a gag reflex."[34] Members placed a chair on the front porch of 'Iolani Palace with a sign on the seat marked "Department of the Interior." Perez pointed to it, suggesting, "That symbolizes our throne in our palace being occupied again by the United States government. . . . We do not want to be with the Department of Interior," referring to the bill's language that would pull any federally recognized Native Hawaiian governing entity under its authority. He went on to assert on behalf of the group, "This seat here is something that we are soon to reclaim." Perez presented the group's declaration statement—which by then had already acquired more than one thousand names in support in just five days from its issue—as a unified position among Maoli groups that have differing views on the specifics of achieving independence.

Hui Pū eventually dispersed and by late 2010 seemed more or less disbanded. As a group founded for the purpose of opposing the Akaka Bill, the five years of resistance oscillated with the legislation itself. Not only would the bill seem close to passage and in turn stir energy among those opposing it as a threat to self-determination, to be opposed in the Senate by Republicans who succeeded time and again in preventing it from gaining traction; it would be redrafted after each dead end in order to appease conservatives. Some members have suggested that over the years, activists tired of responding to it time after time when it seemed like the threat of its passage was being stalled by other forces. But also, Hui Pū never had organized leadership, which may (in part) account for the group's demise. However, the horizontal form of organizing can be seen as a strong point since it enabled different forms of resistance and direct action. And while there was intense diversity among members in terms of broader political commitments and various ideas about sovereignty, nationhood, and self-determination, as mentioned earlier, its primary goal was to stop the legislation. This meant that while internal tensions were often discussed among members, the focal point of the group's purpose was kept at the forefront.

Conclusion: Back to the State, the Fiftieth State

On March 30, 2011, three months prior to the passage of the First Nation Government Bill, Senator Akaka introduced S. 675 to the Senate Committee on Indian Affairs.[35] On April 7, 2011, the bill was ordered by the Senate committee to be favorably reported without amendment, but on September 13, 2012, the bill was ordered by the committee to be reported favorably with an amendment in the nature of a substitute. The amendments are substantial (reducing the bill from sixty to fifteen pages) and reflect the passage of Act 195 in the Hawai'i state legislature. Its shortened title is now the Native Hawaiian Government Reorganization Act of 2012, with the full title, "A bill to express the policy of the United States regarding the United States relationship with Native Hawaiians and to provide parity and a process for the recognition by the United States of the Native Hawaiian governing entity."[36] The structural framework of the proposal subordinates Hawai'i's rightful status as an independent nation by admitting only the right of limited self-determination: "Congress possesses and exercises the constitutional authority to address Native Hawaiian conditions; the Native Hawaiian people have the right to autonomy in internal affairs." Section 5 "recognizes the Native Hawaiian right to reorganize under Section 16 of the Indian Reorganization Act; defines the membership of the Native Hawaiian people for the purposes of reorganization as those people appearing on the roll certified by the State of Hawaii Native Hawaiian Roll Commission authorized under Act 195; provides for the establishment of an Interim Governing Council, tasked with preparing the Constitution and By-Laws and submitting them for Secretarial approval; and requires the Interim Governing Council, with assistance from the Secretary, to conduct the election of officers of the Native Hawaiian governing entity, then terminates the Council." Section 6 "provides the following: the Native Hawaiian Governing Entity has the inherent powers and privileges of self-government of an Indian Tribe."

These amendments now look as if the proposal finally allows for parity with federally recognized tribal nations. However, the question of territory and jurisdiction remains unclear, especially given the fact that the counterpart to the political status question is that of territory. Central to discussions among Kanaka Maoli activists was the portion of the kingdom Crown and Government Lands that the fiftieth state considers public lands, delineated in section 5(f) of the state constitution. While on the one hand, past legislation specifically precluded land being held in trust for the Native Hawaiian governing entity, on the other, the state of Hawai'i made clear what their plans were for these lands: to sell them. The state administration that moved to sell them in 1994 was prevented by a lawsuit initiated by Jonathan Kamakawiwo'ole Osorio, later joined by three other Kanaka Maoli plaintiffs and eventually OHA.

Hence, for most of the decade, struggles over the bill centered on the contestation of these 1.8 million acres—the same lands over which the Apology Resolution acknowledged Native Hawaiians had never directly relinquished sovereignty. The bill looked like a sure way for the state to settle outstanding land claims laid out in the apology that the state wanted for itself. Most immediately, it seemed federal recognition would set up a process for extinguishing most claims to land title—except for whatever the state of Hawai'i and the U.S. federal government may be willing to relinquish in exchange for that recognition—and even then the U.S. federal government would not hold it in trust, so it could not be considered the sovereign territory of any Native Hawaiian governing entity within the U.S. system. However, the terms of the struggle to reclaim these lands were sorely diminished by the 2009 U.S. Supreme Court ruling in *State of Hawaii v. Office of Hawaiian Affairs, et al.*, which stated that the apology does not change the legal landscape or restructure the rights and obligations of the state. In other words, according to the high court, the state has "perfect title."[37]

On December 17, 2012, an amended version of the infamous Akaka Bill (S. 675) was placed on the Senate Legislative Calendar under General Orders. Passed by the Senate Committee on Indian Affairs on September 13, the bill was radically revised from the sixty-page version introduced March 30, 2011, to fifteen pages. It now reflects passage of the First Nation Government Bill signed into Hawai'i state law on July 6, 2011, as Act 195. As the 113th Congress opens, Democrats control the Senate, but Republicans control the House—and the House Committee on Natural Resources (to date) has yet to pass the bill and move it further.

Meanwhile, the Kana'iolowalu initiative moves along full steam to develop a base roll of Native Hawaiians—a registry of individuals to sign on to take part in the formation of the First Nation within the state process. According to the Native Hawaiian Roll Commission, they would "then be eligible to participate in the formation of a sovereign government, and also gather signatures from Hawaiians and non-Hawaiians on petitions declaring support for the reunification of Native Hawaiians and recognition of Native Hawaiians' un-relinquished sovereignty."[38] The goal of those driving the initiative is to register 200,000 Native Hawaiians. Kana'iolowalu was to run through

January 19, 2014, with certification of the roll to follow. But as of March 17, 2014, the Native Hawaiian Roll Commission reopened the registry to May 1, 2014, in the hopes of securing more names. Once the roll is finished, the Commission is required to publish the registry to start the process of holding a convention to organize a Hawaiian governing entity and then the Commission will be dissolved.[39]

Many defenders of the Kana'iolowalu process continue to insist that the creation of a Native Hawaiian roll does not preclude a bid for restoring independence, and that they are committed to an inclusive process. But what they refuse to account for is the fact that the fiftieth state is not in the business of passing laws that enable anything outside of the U.S. federal government. Act 195 is not about crafting a process that allows for anything other than a state-recognized First Nation that will form in anticipation of passage of the Akaka Bill. This is a structural problem; it is a state process in the service of federal recognition.

Time will tell whether pro-independence Kanaka Maoli will mobilize people to reject the process. Perhaps some original members of Hui Pū who are still committed to the original purpose of the group will organize. At this writing, a newer hui, Makawalu—composed of Kanaka Maoli 'ōpio (youth)—are actively countering this state-driven development with both searing critique and humor. At stake is evidence of collective acquiescence to the U.S. government or its subsidiaries; that is, the perception that the will of the people will seem to have been expressed—as a form of self-determination in support of federal recognition—in a way that would make international intervention much more far-fetched given the likelihood that the world community would see the Hawaiian question as even more of a U.S. domestic issue than it does today. In any case, it entrenches the Hawaiian sovereignty claim further within the U.S. government.

Notes

Mahalo nui loa to the editors of this volume for their willingness to bring this project together, the anonymous reviewers for their productive critical feedback, and to Andre Perez for his editorial input on the section about Hui Pū.

1. For text of the bill, see Hawaii State Legislature, http://www.capitol.hawaii.gov/session2011/bills/SB1520_CD1_.pdf. For a legislative history of the bill, see http://legiscan.com/HI/text/SB1520/id/180990.

2. "Governor Enacts Bill to Further Self-Determination for Native Hawaiians," http://www.hawaii247.com/2011/07/07/governor-enacts-bill-to-further-self-determination-for-native-hawaiians/.

3. Those who support Hawai'i's independence from the United States include, but are not limited to, those who are part of the Hawaiian Independence Action Alliance: the Pro-Kanaka Maoli Independence Working Group, Ka Pakaukau, Komike Tribunal, HONI (Hui o Na Ike), Ka Lei Maile Ali'i Hawaiian Civic Club, Koani Foundation, 'Ohana Koa, NFIP–Hawai'i, Spiritual Nation of Kū–Hui Ea Council of Sovereigns, Living Nation, Settlers for Hawaiian Independence, MANA (Movement for Aloha No Ka 'Āina), as well as the Hawai'i Institute for Human Rights.

4. The political term "First Nation" itself is curious in this context, given that it typically refers to the indigenous peoples of the Americas located in what is now Canada, except for the Arctic-situated Inuit, and the Métis.

5. For a critical analysis of the neoconservative forces on-island that organized against the legislation because they regarded it as a proposal for race-based government, see Kauanui, "Colonialism in Equality."

6. I joined the group within weeks of its formation and participated as a long-distance member starting in July 2005 with active engagement on the closed listserv and through meetings with individual members during my regular visits to Kaua'i and O'ahu to connect with family and for academic purposes including research. Because the protocol of the listserv set by the group required that discussions be kept confidential, my account in this essay is based on published media coverage. I should note that although I have never officially left the group, I withdrew from the listserv in November 2010 when the focus among a core group of active members seemed to shift substantially away from organized opposition to the proposed legislation for federal recognition to the formation of a civic club.

7. See the text of the bill itself at http://legiscan.com/HI/text/SB1520/id/180990.

8. Other members of the Native Hawaiian Roll Commission are Nā'ālehu Anthony, chief executive director of 'Ōiwi TV and the principal of Palikū Documentary Films; Lei Kihoi, former staff attorney for Judge Walter Heen; Mahealani Perez-Wendt, former executive director of the Native Hawaiian Legal Corporation; and Robin Puanani Danner, president and chief executive officer of the Council for Native Hawaiian Advancement.

9. The commission is funded by OHA and authorized to prepare and maintain a roll of qualified Native Hawaiians who meet specific criteria; each person must be at least eighteen years old, be able to trace ancestry back to 1778, show that he or she has maintained the indigenous culture, and be willing to participate. *Native Hawaiian Roll Commission,* "Kana'iolowalu Launches Online Registry for Native Hawaiians."

10. For a detailed historical account of the legal definition of each term, see Kauanui, *Hawaiian Blood.*

11. For a critical analysis of the Hawaiian Homes Commission Act and how it was evoked in *Rice,* see Kauanui, *Hawaiian Blood.*

12. The role that OHA played in lobbying in support of the Akaka Bill deserves a chapter unto itself and is beyond the limited spaced allotted here. In short, the OHA trustees and administration pushed for the legislation on questionable grounds in the first place by misconstruing the ruling in *Rice* to suggest the court ruled on the Fourteenth Amendment when it actually struck down racially exclusive voting conducted by the state on grounds of the Fifteenth Amendment. Furthermore, it is precisely because of the ruling in *Rice* that the trustees of OHA can no longer claim to even remotely represent the vote of the Native Hawaiian people because all state residents can vote for OHA, and non-Kanaka can run for trustee.

13. The $70 million figure is a high-end estimate put forth by the Council for Native Hawaiian Advancement—a pro–federal recognition consortium. The state of Hawai'i budget figures were accessed at the state budget website (http://www.state.hi.us/budget/), July 17, 2004.

14. In all of these acts, Hawaiians are defined by the most inclusive definition: "any individual who is a descendent of the aboriginal people who, prior to 1778, occupied and exercised sovereignty in the area that now constitutes the State of Hawai'i."

15. For an analysis of what led to the 50 percent blood criterion, see Kauanui, *Hawaiian Blood.*

16. Captain Cook first arrived in the island archipelago in 1778; thus that year marks a time prior to which it is assumed that no one other than Hawaiians was present. Silva, in *Aloha Betrayed*, questions

whether Cook was the first European to land in Hawai'i. In any case, the apology was not extended to non-Hawaiians who also endured the legacy of the overthrow—that is, those nonindigenous descendants of citizens of the Kingdom of Hawai'i.

17. United States Senate Committee on Indian Affairs, "Section-by-Section Analysis of S. 675, as Amended": http://www.indian.senate.gov/issues/2011-03-30.cfm.

18. There are numerous examples of the Honolulu dailies asserting the same. For example, Pang reported that the Akaka Bill "sets up a process that would lead to the U.S. government's recognition of the nation's 400,000 Native Hawaiians in the same way that it recognizes American Indians and Alaska Natives"—a statement that repeatedly was included in his numerous articles covering the legislation during that period. See Pang, "Hawaiian Independence Groups Send 'No' Message." Akaka reasserted this claim that the measure would provide parity in a speech on the Senate floor on December 20, 2009, in his capacity as chairman of the Senate Committee on Indian Affairs soon after the death of Senator Inouye. Senator Akaka, "Akaka Calls for Passage of Native Hawaiian Government Reorganization Act in Honor of Senator Inouye," YouTube, December 20, 2012, http://www.youtube.com/watch?v=GK_Qn1noRzk&feature=youtu.be.

19. Akaka, "Native Hawaiian Federal Recognition Bill Introduced."

20. See Namuo, "Misinformation Abounds on Revisions to Akaka Bill."

21. Pang, "Hawaiian Independence Groups Send 'No' Message."

22. See McGregor, "Proper Recognition"; McGregor, "Statehood."

23. The group has been referred to in the media alternately as a "confederation" (TenBruggencate, "Sovereignty Movement Has Many Turning Points"), a "coalition" (Kelly, "Hui Pū"), and an "alliance" (Kelly, "Hui Pū").

24. Kelly, "Hui Pū."

25. Andre Perez, e-mail, August 29, 2011.

26. Pang, "Opponents Ask OHA's Aid to Derail Akaka Bill."

27. Hawai'i Nation Info, "Hui Pū Declaration and Position Points against Akaka Bill," July 8, 2005, Yahoo! Groups, http://groups.yahoo.com/group/hawaii-nation/message/741.

28. See Silva, *Aloha Betrayed.*

29. Pang, "Opponents Ask OHA's Aid to Derail Akaka Bill."

30. Pang, "Opponents Ask OHA's Aid to Derail Akaka Bill."

31. Document in the author's possession. The Hui Pū's position points were reprinted in Honolulu newspapers. The points can also be found at http://hawaiialoha.tribe.net/thread/312a5dea-c652-41ad-a052-615f18d4932c, and with related articles at http://www.islandbreath.org/2005Year/a05-16-sovereign/0516-01StopAkakaBill.html.

32. Pang, "Opponents Ask OHA's Aid to Derail Akaka Bill."

33. Pang, "Opponents Ask OHA's Aid to Derail Akaka Bill."

34. Pang, "For Some, Akaka Bill Falls Far Short."

35. A House companion measure to S. 675, H.R. 1250, was introduced to the Committee on Natural Resources on the same day. At this writing, no action has been taken on it. Prior to the 2011 proposals, at the start of the 111th Congress (January 3, 2009), three sets of proposals made their way to the table, all titled the Native Hawaiian Government Reorganization Act of 2009.

36. Senate Report 112-251, "To Express the Policy of the United States Regarding the United States Relationship with Native Hawaiians and to Provide Parity and a Process for the Recognition by the United States of the Native Hawaiian Governing Entity," http://thomas.loc.gov/cgi-bin/cpquery/?&sid=cp112foXTh&r_n=sr251.112&dbname=cp112&&sel=TOC_178474&.

37. The state of Hawai'i asked the high court whether or not the state has the authority to sell, ex-

change, or transfer 1.2 million acres of land formerly held by the Hawaiian monarchy as Crown and Government Lands. Prior to the state's appeal to the SCOTUS, the State Supreme Court unanimously ruled that the state should keep the land trust intact until Hawaiian claims to these lands are settled, and prohibited the state from selling or otherwise disposing of the properties to private parties; it did so based on the 1993 Apology Resolution issued by Congress to the Hawaiian people. The SCOTUS reversed the judgment of the Hawai'i Supreme Court and remanded the case for further proceedings with the stipulation that the outcome not be inconsistent with the U.S. Supreme Court's opinion. The contested land base constitutes 29 percent of the total land area of what is now known as the state of Hawai'i and almost all the land claimed by the state as public lands. Once the case was remanded back to the state, the Hawai'i Supreme Court threw it out after some of the original plaintiffs brokered a deal with the governor and attorney general to have the case dismissed due to new legislation that had passed in the state legislature to provide for the sale of these lands through resolutions in piecemeal fashion. Although Osorio refused to take part in the sellout, the Supreme Court dismissed the case by saying it was no longer "ripe for adjudication." The case reveals just how enduring U.S. imperial dispossession persists into the twenty-first century.

38. Native Hawaiian Roll Commission, "Kana'iolowalu Launches Online Registry for Native Hawaiians."

39. Native Hawaiian Roll Commission, "Moving the Hawaiian Nation Forward."

CHAPTER 16. Kū'ē Mana Māhele

THE HAWAIIAN MOVEMENT TO RESIST BIOCOLONIALISM

Le'a Malia Kanehe

As Kanaka Maoli today, we live in an era of biotechnology and biocolonialism—the extension of the process of colonization to genetic material and traditional knowledge of Indigenous peoples. Genes, the building blocks of life, are a valuable commodity in Western science and industry. The use and trade of genes has become the new gold rush of our times. In this era, scientists seek Indigenous peoples' DNA for anthropological, behavioral, medical, and genetics mapping studies.[1] Bioprospectors are keen to access biodiversity-rich Indigenous territories to find plant, animal, and microbial organisms to develop for pharmaceutical, cosmetic, chemical, and industrial uses. Genetic engineering (GE) also poses special threats to Indigenous peoples' traditional food sources, agricultural systems, health, food sovereignty, and the environment.

Biocolonialism in Hawai'i is an extension of the U.S. invasion of our kingdom in 1893. Today, the genetic resources that underlie the immense biodiversity of our archipelago are the subject of a new theft as gene hunters commit biopiracy—the theft of genetic resources and associated traditional knowledge. Furthermore, just as Hawai'i has been and continues to be used as an American military testing and practice ground, our lands and people are now being sacrificed for the development and release of genetically modified organisms. In fact, Hawai'i has had more plantings of experimental biotech crops than anywhere in the United States or the world, truly making our islands an international and national sacrifice zone.[2]

As Kanaka Maoli activists began to learn more about the context of these types of genetic research and biotechnologies, it did not take long to make the obvious comparison to other Euro-American efforts to undermine ea and take or misuse 'āina. Longtime sovereignty activist and Moloka'i community organizer Walter Ritte coined the name Mana Māhele to refer to this age of biocolonialism in Hawai'i. Uncle Walter has explained, "They have taken our lands and now they come to take our mana, our very soul."

Recalling the 1848 Māhele and resulting privatization of land in Hawai'i, this chapter examines Kanaka Maoli activism to kū'ē (resist or protest) new threats posed by a foreign legal system—Euro-American intellectual property rights—which legitimates claims to ownership over genes and traditional knowledge and which supports a foreign economic system, globalized capitalism, that encourages the commercialization of the sacred. This chapter reveals that the heart of the movement to resist biocolonialism in Hawai'i is aloha 'āina (love for the land)—a core value and practice underlying all Hawaiian movements. Aloha 'āina was the impetus for the movement to stop the bombing of Kaho'olawe—an earthly embodiment of the god Kanaloa—in the 1970s and 1980s. And aloha 'āina is the core demand to stop the bombardment of foreign genes into kalo, the embodiment of Hāloa, today.

An Era of Biocolonialism: Mana Māhele

There are several categories of projects that involve the utilization and manipulation of genetic material and the study of genetics (including human population genetic research, bioprospecting, GE, and patenting) that have occurred in Hawai'i. Each of these genetic technologies falls under a broad agenda that Indigenous peoples often refer to as biocolonialism—the extension of the forces of colonization to biological processes, genetic material, and traditional knowledge of Indigenous peoples. One Indigenous commentator describes biocolonialism as follows: "If colonialism encompasses the interlocking array of policies and practices (economic, social, political and legal) that a dominant culture draws on to maintain and extend its control over other peoples and lands, biocolonialism emphasizes the role of science policy and of scientific practice within that array."[3]

Like all other struggles to protect 'āina and ea, Kānaka Maoli at the forefront of this struggle have had to come to understand the historical and legal context of biocolonialism. This section briefly examines the so-called genetic revolution and the area of Euro-American law known as intellectual property rights, particularly patent law, that bolsters genetic research and the resulting technologies. I then apply this understanding of biocolonialism to Hawai'i and examine what Kanaka Maoli activists have come to call Mana Māhele.

THE GENETIC REVOLUTION AND PATENTS ON LIFE

As Andrew Kimbrell has noted, "When scientists James Watson and Francis Crick first described the double helix of DNA in 1953 it was considered a historic 'discovery,' which has been called 'the greatest achievement of science in the twentieth century' and 'one of the epic discoveries in the history of scientific thought.'"[4] From a critical Indigenous perspective, Watson and Crick were to genes what Columbus was to the Americas or Captain Cook was to Hawai'i. Once Westerners discover and name a creation of akua, whether it be land or genes, they begin to utilize and develop it, and eventually they must devise ways to legally claim it as their own property.

Patents are the means by which derivatives and products developed from genetic material receive legal protection. A patent is a form of intellectual property created to award exclusive ownership to the inventor of a new product. Patents were designed to reward inventors for their contributions by guaranteeing them a market monopoly and exclusive market return for a period of seventeen to twenty years.

A basic tenet of patent law has always been that "phenomena of nature" are not by themselves patentable. However, in 1980, the U.S. Supreme Court departed from this line of reasoning in the landmark case of *Diamond v. Chakrabarty*. The Court held that a genetically engineered bacteria was patentable by reasoning that the microorganism was "a nonnaturally occuring manufacture or composition of matter—a product of human ingenuity."[5]

This decision threw open the legal door for the patenting of DNA, ushering in what has been called "the genetic revolution" and "the biotech century."[6] All genes or gene segments isolated by humans are now considered inventions and are therefore patentable. The Supreme Court provided the legal protection and the corresponding economic incentive that comes through the exclusive monopoly of patents that the budding biotech industry needed to bring pharmaceutical, agricultural, and chemical applications of genes to market.[7]

Patents also undergird an international system of free trade in genes and commercialization of Indigenous knowledge. The ultimate beneficiaries of this biocolonial system are the multinational biotech corporations, many of which we have come to know all too well in Hawai'i. "It's all about patents," states Kamuela Enos of MA'O Farms. "We understand the market drivers behind the research. A lot of this research is being underwritten by these multinational corporations that want to own the patent to the basic building blocks of life."[8]

Accordingly, the intellectual property system is one that many Indigenous peoples have criticized as a legalized means for misappropriation of cultural property. Kanaka Maoli law professor Hōkūlei Lindsey comments, "The latest frontier of colonialism, intellectual property perpetrates an injustice and pointed reality in Hawai'i amounting to the ultimate debasement and disenfranchisement of an indigenous, native people—the theft of culture and identity, physically, and spiritually."[9]

MANA MĀHELE

In traditional Hawaiian thinking, land comes from the gods and was traditionally managed by the ali'i (chiefs) for the collective benefit of all the people. However, that changed in 1848 when the concept of private property was introduced by Western business interests seeking to secure fee simple land title. The time when the traditional land tenure system was supplanted by private land ownership was called the Māhele. The Māhele had the dual effect of dispossessing Kanaka Maoli from their land in Hawai'i and facilitated the expansion of an agricultural industry where sugar became king. To protect their interest in importing Hawai'i-grown sugar tariff free in the United States, sugar plantation owners colluded in the 1893 overthrow, which would eventually lead to Hawai'i's purported annexation to the United States.

The efforts of many Kānaka Maoli to kū'ē (resist) genetic modification and patenting of our kalo, Hāloa, has become the symbol of a second Māhele, now called the Mana Māhele. The term originated with activists on Moloka'i to describe owning and selling of our mana or life force. An aspect of mana is the spiritual force Hawaiians have, stemming from our familial relationship with nature. Walter Ritte has remarked, "Biotechnology is here in Hawai'i. . . . Taro is the example and the red flag. They tried to change its genes and patent it for 'ownership.' Biotechnology is the second Māhele . . . the Mana Māhele. Hawaiians need to maka'ala and wake up!"[10]

A new generation of activists, such as Hanohano Nā'ehu, mentored by Walter Ritte, understands the colonial context of GE in Hawai'i, stating, "They took our land; they took our Kingdom; they took our confidence, our pride, everything. Now they like take our mana."[11] Applying the Māhele metaphor further, we can see that the biotech barons have become Hawai'i's new Big Five, with the goal of impacting Hawai'i's agricultural future in much the same way that the old Big Five sugar barons once controlled the political, economic, and social path of Hawai'i.

Genetic Technology and Kanaka Maoli Activism

Kanaka Maoli have witnessed biocolonial activities coming to our shores in multiple forms, including interest in our ancestral bloodlines for both medical and anthropological ends; prospecting our unique biodiversity for commercially viable chemical and industrial compounds; patents on kalo hybridized by the University of Hawai'i (UH); genetic modification of kalo; and the use of thousands of acres of prime agricultural lands to grow genetically engineered crops treated with toxic pesticides. This section provides an overview of these various forms of biocolonialism in Hawai'i.

HUMAN POPULATION GENETIC RESEARCH

Indigenous peoples' DNA is seen as a resource for use in medical, behavioral, anthropological, and genetic variation studies. Kanaka Maoli DNA has been sought for research at UH. For example, Dr. Charles Boyd, who was a researcher at UH's Pacific Biomedical Research Center, drafted a proposal for a Hawaiian Genome Project seeking $5–10 million to produce an annotated map of the entire genetic makeup of the Hawaiian people. Boyd stated, "There are many communities now with their own unique genetic history imprinted into their genomes and these include Asians, Europeans and the peoples of Oceania. The Hawaiian genome represents an important example of one of these communities of the Oceania people."[12] Boyd was hoping to target residents of the

Hawaiian Homestead communities because they are seen as being the most purebred native Hawaiians. He hoped to find a genetic basis for the high rate of obesity, diabetes, renal disease, and hypertension in Kanaka Maoli.[13] This type of research essentializes the role of genes, while devaluing key environmental and lifestyle factors, including the role dispossession of land has had in traditional diet and activities.

Another type of research, known as anthropological genetics, studies the history of human populations, often using Indigenous peoples' DNA to develop theories of ancient human migrations. The proposed Hawaiian Genome Project also anticipated an anthropological genetic research component. In 2003, an Association of Hawaiian Civic Clubs resolution called for a cease to the project or any other patenting or licensing of genetic material of the Hawaiian peoples.[14]

This resolution led to a response from Dr. Boyd, wherein he asserted that a map of the Hawaiian genome would be a cultural icon for Kanaka Maoli because it would tell us about our migratory history through the Pacific region. When faced with the prospect of a genetic study that was claiming to tell Kanaka Maoli where we come from, we very sternly responded that we know where we come from—Kumulipo, referring to a cosmogonic genealogy chant that traces the lineage of the Hawaiian people back to the beginning of time.[15] Conceding to Kanaka Maoli opposition to the project, the UH Mānoa campus chancellor put an end to the proposed project.[16]

BIOPROSPECTING AND BIOPIRACY

Biodiversity prospecting, or bioprospecting for short, is "the exploration, extraction and screening of biological diversity and Indigenous knowledge for commercially valuable genetic and biochemical resources."[17] Bioprospecting involves genetic screening and isolation of interesting genes that could be used in pharmaceutical, agricultural, chemical, or industrial products. Bioprospectors often use traditional knowledge of Indigenous peoples as a lead to identify plants with medicinal or other potentially useful compounds, often without their prior informed consent. This misappropriation of knowledge and resulting commercial benefit has come to be known as "biopiracy." Indigenous African legal scholar Ikechi Mgbeogi explains that biopiracy may be defined as "the unauthorized commercial use of biological resources and/or associated traditional knowledge, or the patenting of spurious inventions based on such knowledge, without compensation."[18] Because of Hawai'i's unique and diverse array of species, many of them still unknown to the commercial world, our islands are a hotspot for bioprospecting and inevitably biopiracy.

In June 2002, UH's Marine Bioproducts Engineering Center (MarBEC) entered into an agreement with Diversa Corporation for biodiversity access and collaboration.[19] The UH/Diversa Material Transfer Agreement gave Diversa the exclusive right to discover genes from existing UH material collections and from environmental samples collected by university researchers, with the intent of commercializing the resulting products. The agreement did not mention any rights of Kanaka Maoli in the subject material. Therefore, the UH/Diversa activities became a prime example of biopiracy—the taking of genetic material without the free, prior, informed consent of the Indigenous peoples who have rights over the lands or waters where such material originates and who are the keepers of the knowledge of the useful applications of the plants within their territories.

As a result of these concerns, Kanaka Maoli organizations began lobbying the state legislature to adopt legislation to regulate bioprospecting. Several bills were introduced from 2003 to 2009 and a Hawai'i State Temporary Advisory Commission was formed under the auspices of the Office of Hawaiian Affairs. However, no regulatory legislation has been forthcoming, largely due to a protective veil over the biotech industry by policymakers hoping this industry will be a savior to Hawai'i's struggling economy.

PLANT PATENTS: OWNERSHIP OVER HĀLOA

In 2005, it came to light that UH took out three U.S. plant patents on varieties derived from the Hawaiian variety Maui Lehua.[20] Plant patents are a specific type of patent typically used to claim rights to hybridized plants. Kanaka Maoli were faced with answering the question, "Is it okay to own our ancestor?" The answer was a firm 'a'ole (no) based on mo'olelo that teach that Hāloanakalaukapalili, the first kalo, is the elder sibling of the Hawaiian people. The kalo will feed the people as long as the people care for the kalo, which includes the 'āina it depends upon.[21] As such, we, as Kanaka, have a kuleana to care for the kalo.[22]

In 1999, the university applied for three plant patents claiming invention of Pauakea, Pa'akala, and Palehua, which the U.S. Patent and Trademark Office granted in 2002. Each of these were hybridized by cross-pollinating the Micronesian male Ngeruuch variety from Palau, which is resistant to taro leaf blight disease, with the Hawaiian female Maui Lehua, which is known for its desirable agronomic properties (such as taste) but is also highly susceptible to leaf blight.[23]

Some university researchers have claimed that their hybridization of kalo is the same as what Kanaka Maoli have always done by doing selective cross-breeding of kalo varieties. The distinction is that Kanaka Maoli have never claimed an exclusive, monopolistic ownership over kalo through patenting. Respected Kanaka Maoli activist Alapa'i Hanapī explained that "ownership of taro is 'like slavery.' . . . 'It is as if someone owns your relatives.'"[24]

In 2006, taro farmers, Kanaka Maoli students and faculty, Hawaiian-focused charter school students, and other supporters held several protests demanding that UH withdraw the patents.[25] When officials tried to ignore their demands, protesters chained the doors to a board of regents meeting. Video footage on the public-access TV program

Jesse Ikaika Jones and Kaleo Manuel at a 2007 rally at the University of Hawai'i's central administration building, Bachman Hall.

Da Hemowai Bros. reveals a new generation of warriors, Kalaniua Ritte and Hanohano Nā'ehu, stepping up to secure the locks.[26]

The protesters' overwhelming political message, "No patents on kalo," was brought to life through cultural means. Organizers erected an ahu (altar) and carved wooden statue of Hāloa, and participants offered hula, chants, and ho'okupu in honor of Hāloa. In response, UH offered to assign the patents to a Hawaiian organization, but that proposal was rejected. Kānaka Maoli made clear that we object to anyone patenting kalo, even ourselves.[27] As a result of protests, discussions, and negotiations, UH officials finally agreed to terminate the patents.[28] Kānaka Maoli celebrated their victory with a ceremony and by tearing up the patent documents.[29] Walter Ritte explains that ripping the patents was a signal to the biotech industry: "You cannot own our ancestors; you cannot own our eldest brother, Hāloa."

Hinaleimoana Wong Kalu hands Hanohano Naehu a pohaku, as students from Hālau Lōkahi stand watching, 2007.

Students from Hālau Lōkahi public charter school rearrange stones from the garden outside Bachman into the shape of an ahu. More students stand in the background prepared to offer a hula, 2007.

GENETIC ENGINEERING

Genetic engineering is another type of genetic technology that has caused great concern for Kanaka Maoli, as well as the general population. Often used for agricultural or biopharmaceutical purposes, the result of GE is a genetically modified organism or GMO.[30] These GMOs are produced through the isolation of genes from one species that are considered to carry a particular desirable trait, which are then forced into a different host species using a gene gun.[31] Thus GE allows humans "to cross natural boundaries and force together DNA from any different species, such as jellyfish genes with corn plants or human genes with rice," as well as spider-goat, fish-strawberry, and corn-human combinations.[32] Kanaka Maoli faced genetic modification of kalo, again by UH scientists.

Mālama Hāloa: Protecting Kalo from Genetic Manipulation

> I feel like I can hear the taro crying, crying to be heard.
> [Genetic engineering] is crossing sacred barriers.
> —CHRIS KOBAYASHI, WAI'OLI, KAUA'I KALO FARMER (SPEAKING IN NĀ MAKA O KA 'ĀINA'S FILM *ISLANDS AT RISK: GENETIC ENGINEERING IN HAWAI'I*)

In general, the Hawaiian community was not that involved in opposing genetic manipulation and biotechnology until word spread in early 2005 that UH tried to genetically modify kalo.[33] Again, based on our traditional familial relationship with and kuleana to protect Hāloa, Kānaka Maoli immediately demanded that the university sign a moratorium against any GE of Hawaiian kalo. In May 2005, UH's College of Tropical Agriculture and Human Resources, the entity responsible for doing the genetic modification, signed a memorandum of understanding in which the university agreed to a moratorium on genetically modifying Hawaiian varieties of kalo.

Kanaka Maoli and non-Native support organizations and individuals have also worked with legislators to introduce bills in the state legislature to ban any genetic engineering of kalo; however, no measures have passed at that level. During a rally for the bills, scores of Kānaka Maoli and supporters filled the capitol rotunda with the sound of pōhaku ku'i 'ai (kalo pounding stones) while convening the largest poi-making gathering in history.[34] More success has been had at the county level, including a 2008 Hawai'i County Council measure banning the growth of GMO kalo on Hawai'i Island.[35]

Beyond Kalo: Becoming Aware of the GMO State

Concerns over the GE of kalo served as an impetus for our community to become aware of the extensive and varied types of GMOs in Hawai'i. Due to a lack of broad-based education and a "culture of secrecy" promoted by government, our islands became a GMO state without most of us even really knowing it. For example, most of us did not even know that half of papaya grown on Hawai'i Island is genetically modified.[36] In 2004, when more than half of 20,000 organic and wild seeds on the Big Island tested positive for GMO contamination, organic farmers were outraged, fearing a loss of their organic certification, the end of the natural papaya industry, and lawsuits for unintended patent infringement.[37]

Hosting over 2,230 GE field trials (as of 2008), Hawai'i has earned the dubious title of GE capital of the world.[38] The reasons for the prominence of GMOs in Hawai'i include a year-round growing climate not available on the U.S. continent, geographic isolation, a favorable political climate, biotech-friendly business laws, and, until recent years, relatively little organized opposition to GMOs. The state has also facilitated the production of GMOs, including lease of state lands for seed corn operations.[39] Because of such factors, sovereignty leader and attorney Mililani Trask has accurately characterized Hawai'i as an "international and national sacrifice area for biotech and genetic modification."[40]

Starting in the 1990s, under Governor Cayetano, the state attracted biotech corporations to Hawai'i with laws that encourage investment capital, exclude royalties from gross income, and provide tax subsidies, tax credits for research, and tax exemptions.[41] As a result of this "collusion between multinational seed companies and the State," the world's largest agrochemical corporations, including Monsanto, Pioneer (owned by DuPont), Dow Agrosciences, Syngenta, and BASF—the new Big Five—are all doing business in our islands.[42] Approximately 25,000 acres of land on O'ahu, Kaua'i, Maui, and Moloka'i support a $250 million per year GE seed industry.[43] The favorable political and legal environment has spurred the GE seed corn industry to become both the largest agricultural crop in the state and the largest industry in Hawai'i, producing 10 million pounds of seed per year, which is distributed worldwide.[44]

In the 2012 legislative session, the Hawai'i GMO Justice Coalition, including Kānaka Maoli, lobbied for the passage of GMO labeling bills based on consumers' rights to know what they are eating. However, the responsible legislative committees did not hear the bills.[45] Reflecting on his experience in the lobbying efforts, Uncle Walter Ritte also notes the stance of government officials to protect the GMO industry. "Our government officials really believe that the future of the state is based on the success of these GMO companies—that in order for agriculture to survive in Hawai'i, GMO companies are gonna have to be the foundation. . . . So they were not willing to threaten these GMO companies in any way, shape, or form."[46] Nevertheless, he remains optimistic that the community at large is becoming more educated about their right to know what they are buying and is learning that GMO-laden products really are unhealthy.[47]

Failure to pass legislation at the state level fueled more local efforts to pass laws at the county level on both Hawai'i Island and Kaua'i. On November 19, 2013, the Hawai'i County Council passed Bill 113, which provides that "No person shall knowingly engage in the open air cultivation, propagation, development, or testing of genetically engineered crops or plants."[48] The bill specifically exempts the papaya industry, because papaya is already established largely as a GMO crop on the island. When Mayor Kenoi signed the bill into law he noted, "With this new ordinance we are conveying that instead of global agribusiness corporations, we want to encourage and support community-based farming and ranching."[49]

Unlike Hawai'i Island, Kaua'i has four of the big ag corporations, which collectively own several thousand acres, and at least two of them (or their predecesors) have been in business on the island for over four decades. But only recently, through community-based educational efforts, have anti-GMO advocates raised awareness about the intensive use of pesticides with GMO crops and the resulting human and environmental risks. Eighteen tons of regulated pesticides were sprayed on Kaua'i, along with many other general-use pesticides that have gone unreported. Educator and kalo farmer Kaina Makua explains that he is concerned by the approximately 1,000 acres of Dupont Pioneer's research and test fields that line the ridge just east of his home in Waimea valley: "When the company sprays pesticides on their crop, the wind blows the dust and pesticides downwind over Waimea valley and into residents' houses as well as on to his lo'i."[50]

When West Kaua'i residents became aware of the prevalent use of pesticides on GMO-producing fields in their communities and reports of cancer clusters became publicized, concerned citizens organized a rally in September 2013 that drew more than three thousand people. The "Mana March" in support of a bill to regulate GMOs on the island was the largest rally in Kaua'i history.[51] The rally galvanized support for the hearing on the bill, and more than a thousand people showed up to testify.

Heeding the call of their constituents' concerns over human and environmental health risks, the Kaua'i County Council passed Bill 2491 amid much controversy on an island where the GE seed industry represents $80 million per year and more than five hundred jobs.[52] The original bill sought to implement a moratorium on GMOs on the island; however, this aspect of the bill was dropped in order to save the remainder of the ordinance, which mandates disclosure of regulated pesticides and locations of GMO crops; establishes buffer zones around schools, child and adult care facilities, hospitals, and waterways leading to the ocean; and requires an environmental impact study.[53] The mayor vetoed the bill in October 2013; however, the county council overrode that veto by a 5–2 margin in November. The law does not go into effect for nine months, and in the meantime the biotech companies are expected to file a lawsuit to challenge the ordinance.[54]

Noting that the discontent with GMOs in Hawai'i has been brewing for a decade, the *Honolulu Star-Advertiser* credits the recent successes to three primary factors. First, the U.S.-mainland environmentalists' philanthropic donations to local nonprofit organizations have boosted their ability to educate and advocate; for example, Uncle Walter acknowledges that these funds have helped provide travel funds to neighbor island advocates. Second, anti-GMO activists effectively utilized social media platforms like Facebook and Twitter to keep more people aware and involved. And finally, new political leaders are activists' allies capable of introducing and shepherding the bills through the legislative processes.[55] Despite the much more significant monetary resources available to the biotech industry, Uncle Walter has predicted that the more the biotech companies resist disclosure, the bigger will be the grassroots wave to demand stricter regulations.[56]

"Not for Human Consumption": Biopharming, Not Farming

Kanaka Maoli have also partnered with other citizens of Hawai'i to raise concerns about another form of GE thriving in our islands known as "biopharm" (short for biopharmaceuticals). This particularly dangerous form of technology involves GE of plants or animals to function as factories to produce pharmaceutical drugs and industrial compounds. Signs on some test fields that read "Experimental Crop—Not for Human Consumption Nor Animal Feed" reveal that biopharming is not true farming.[57] Biopharmaceutical crops grown in Hawai'i include corn that generates a blood-clotting protein that causes pancreatic disease in lab animals and also harms many insects, including honeybees, corn containing part of the ape version of HIV, and sugarcane that produces a potent human hormone.[58]

Lack of regulation by the state Department of Agriculture as well as federal agencies responsible for oversight, namely the Food and Drug Administration, U.S. Department of Agriculture (USDA), and the Environmental Protection Agency, raised great concerns within Hawai'i regarding the environmental and human health risks that biopharmaceuticals pose. For example, the Hawai'i Agriculture Research Center conducted experiments on corn and sugarcane plants genetically modified to produce human hormones, drugs, and ingredients for vaccines against AIDS and hepatitis B, which have the potential to taint corn grown for food.[59]

From 1999 to 2002, the USDA issued fourteen permits for biopharming in Hawai'i. However, the permits did not specify the location of test sites, which genes were undergoing alteration, or what kind of substance was being produced.[60] In 2003, when the state Department of Agriculture refused to produce information about the ongoing open air field tests, the public interest law firm Earthjustice, representing citizen groups Center for Food Safety, Friends of the Earth, Pesticide Action Network North America, and KAHEA: The Hawaiian-Environmental Alliance, filed a lawsuit to compel the government to review the environmental and public health impacts of such activities.[61] Against the biotech industry's wishes, the federal court compelled the defendants to hand over documents revealing test site locations to the plaintiffs' attorneys, but not to the public.[62] Considering Hawaiʻi's high number of endangered species, the federal court also held that the USDA violated environmental protection laws when it issued four permits without evaluating the environmental impact of biopharming.[63]

The state has also threatened our fragile marine environment by issuing permits for producing biopharm algae.[64] In 2005, ʻOhana Pale Ke Ao, Kohanaiki ʻOhana, GMO Free Hawaiʻi, and Sierra Club–Hawaiʻi, again represented by Earthjustice, challenged the state Board of Agriculture's approval of a project to mass-produce potentially dangerous GE algae at the Natural Energy Laboratory of Hawaiʻi on state lands on the Kona coast of the island of Hawaiʻi.[65] Mera Pharmaceuticals, a marine biotechnology firm and tenant at Natural Energy Laboratory, applied to the state for a permit to import biopharm algae containing human monoclonal antibody proteins with a potential capacity to fight a variant of the herpes simplex virus.[66] Despite public concern about the importation, storage, production of the GE strains of algae and urging to undertake an environmental assessment, the agency approved Mera's application without conducting any environmental review.[67] Again the courts found in favor of the community organizations and required an environmental assessment.[68]

This protracted biopharmaceutical-related litigation in Hawaiʻi indicates both a continued need for strong regulation and community involvement to hold government agencies accountable to protect Hawaiʻi's unique biosystem. Perhaps most importantly, it has highlighted that prime agricultural lands that could be producing food are being sacrificed for experimental pharmaceutical drug development.

In sum, Kanaka Maoli have opposed the various types of biocolonial projects in our islands because they conflict with aloha ʻāina—a cultural value and practice underlying all of the Hawaiian movement. Mililani Trask notes, "The concepts underlying genetic manipulation of life forms [are] offensive and contrary to the cultural values of aloha ʻāina (love for the land). . . . To modify, patent and commercialize life forms [is] hewa (a wrongful act, an act of desecration of the sacred) which will bring imbalance and negativity into our lives and our environment."[69] To gain deeper insight into the wide-ranging impacts of GE corporations in Hawaiʻi, the next section examines the experience of Molokaʻi with Monsanto, the world's largest GE corporation.

Walter Ritte, a longtime community organizer and activist for aloha ʻāina, has become a vocal opponent of GMOs across Ka Pae ʻĀina (the Hawaiian archipelago). Photo taken 2007.

Threats to ʻĀina Mōmona: Monsanto's Impacts on Molokaʻi

Walter Ritte tells a story of how GE giant Monsanto has had significant negative impacts on Molokaʻi, an island known for her ability to produce abundant food such as kalo, sweet potato, and fish. The island has, in fact, long been known as Molokaʻi ʻĀina Mōmona (the Fat Land).

After researching Monsanto's background, Molokaʻi community leaders realized the company was a threat to the island and "a threat to the future that we all believe in, which is the production of food for not only this island, but the rest of this state. The things that they produce have labels on their bags that say 'not fit for human consumption.' They are producing things that we cannot eat."[70]

Under Uncle Walter's leadership, community members began an educational campaign to raise awareness about Monsanto and the impacts their activities were having on Molokaʻi, where more than 50 percent of the population is Kanaka Maoli and where both Native and non-Native residents engage in subsistence ways of life. Reflecting on this educational process, Uncle Walter comments:

> Ten years ago, nobody would say anything against Monsanto because nobody knew anything. Now if you go into the community and mention Monsanto the words that will come out are all negative words. The famous word for us is pilau. It means bad, dirty, no good. So people now have this overall view that these chemical companies in our farm lands are no good, they're pilau. We haven't really tried to get them off of the island or anything really heavy duty like that. But we have made sure that people understand that the products they are producing are having bad effects on our island.[71]

Molokaʻi residents now have grave concerns about the human health impacts caused by the significant amounts of chemical-laden soil that blows through their main town of Kaunakakai from Monsanto's cornfields growing adjacent to housing areas and school facilities. They are also concerned about future water quality if these chemicals seep into the water table.

There is further concern over Monsanto's acquisition of 1,600 acres of prime agricultural lands on the slopes of Hoʻolehua, which is where most of the island's Hawaiian homesteaders reside. Uncle Walter observes that Hoʻolehua, famous for her winds, is now a dustbowl because Monsanto's farming method of plowing the land several times per year leaves the soil exposed. Additionally, when the rainy season arrives, the exposed soil on Hoʻolehua washes downslope, thereby negatively impacting the reefs, habitat for Molokaʻi's abundant marine life.

Another significant issue raised by Monsanto's presence on the island is water quantity. Uncle Walter explains that because Molokaʻi's agricultural water system was built to accommodate Hawaiian homesteaders, the law ensures that two-thirds of all the water in the reservoir belongs to homesteaders. However, 80 percent of the water in the reservoir is now being used by nonhomesteaders, mostly the GMO companies. Uncle Walter forecasts that the water issue is going to come to a head because GMO companies are buying water systems all over the world. "People are worried that sooner or later they are going to try and buy the water systems on this island to ensure having water for them in the future."[72]

We learn from this story of struggle that threats of the GMO industry are not just the science of GE itself. We see parallels with other Hawaiian struggles to protect human health, to prevent degradation of land and reef ecosystems, and to conserve water for community-based farming. Other communities impacted by the GMO companies have taken up the fight. In December 2011, 150 Kauaʻi farmers filed suit against Pioneer for pesticide use, including contamination of the Waimea River.[73] Currently, this lawsuit is still ongoing. In a separate action, Poʻai Wai Ola / West Kauaʻi Watershed Alliance is seeking to restore stream flows to the Waimea River in a case before the State of Hawaiʻi's Commission on Water Resource Management.[74] The group asserts that the state-run Agribusiness Development Corporation and its tenant, the Kekaha Agricultural Association, which operate the old sugar plantation ditch systems diverting Waimea River, are excessively draining the river and even dumping the water, rather than letting the river flow for the environment and public uses.

Kū'ē: Reflecting on Our Resistance and Strategies

Reflecting on the various reasons and forms of resistance to genetic research over more than a decade, we see kū'ē based on the assertion of land rights and kuleana to protect ancestral relationships. The movement needs to broaden and protect all the kūpuna named within our Kumulipo genealogy. In addition to rallies and demonstrations, our kū'ē must include living the alternative to GE by ensuring 'āina is reserved for true food sovereignty.

ASSERTING RIGHTS TO LAND AND NATURAL RESOURCES

When I asked Kamuela Enos to reflect on commonalities in the sovereignty movement and the movement to resist genetic engineering, he responded, "It's about articulating our right over resources. It's about being able to control the resources that allow us to survive in place whether it is the political will of the land or the mea 'ai that feeds us."[75]

Similarly, when Kānaka Maoli were raising concerns about the university's bioprospecting contract with Diversa, opposition centered on undermining our recognized rights to Hawaiian Kingdom Crown and Government Lands (a.k.a. ceded lands). In 2002, the Association of Hawaiian Civic Clubs passed a resolution that called for a moratorium on bioprospecting, in part stating, "The public lands, submerged lands, and natural resources include vast biological and genetic resources, which are also trust assets subject to the public trust."[76]

In October 2003, the 'Īlio'ulaokalani Coalition organized the first Ka 'Aha Pono, which brought together kūpuna, kumu hula, mākua, and 'ōpio from all islands on the lands of Queen Lili'uokalani to address matters of intellectual and cultural property, including use of genetic material. The key organizers of the event, Kumu Hula Victoria Holt-Takamine and the late Kumu Hula Wayne Kaho'onei Panoke, believed that it was important to make a clear statement of Kanaka Maoli kuleana on these issues. So the 'Aha issued the Paoakalani Declaration, which included several rights-based assertions.[77] For example, the declaration states, in part: "Although biological and genetic samples have been transferred, sold, patented or licensed, Kanaka Maoli never relinquished our rights to our biological and genetic materials and, therefore, call for the rightful repatriation of such samples and due compensation."[78] The declaration has been utilized by Kanaka Maoli to advocate for recognition of our rights at multiple levels including with UH officials, the state legislature, and internationally at United

Nations forums. However, the foundation of the Paoakalani Declaration, as well as the movement to resist Mana Māhele, is a spiritual one invoking our genealogical responsibility to mālama all life forms in a pono (just and balanced) way.

KULEANA TO PROTECT THE ANCESTORS AND FAMILIAL RELATIONSHIPS

In the Kanaka Maoli worldview, we recognize our common ancestry with all the flora and fauna of our islands. A recurring theme in the movement has been kuleana to protect all life forms. The Paoakalani Declaration explains that the Papa (foundation) of the document is a Kanaka Maoli worldview based on the Kumulipo, a cosmogonic genealogical chant of creation. The Papa states, in part,

- According to the Kumulipo, a genealogical chant of creation, Pō gave birth to the world. From this female potency was born Kumulipo and Pōʻele. And from these two, the rest of the world unfolded in genealogical order. That genealogy teaches us the land is the elder sibling and the people are the younger sibling meant to care for each other in a reciprocal, interdependent relationship. Humanity is reminded of [its] place within the order of genealogical descent. The foundational principle of the Kumulipo is that all facets of the world are related by birth. And thus, the Hawaiian concept of the world descends from one ancestral genealogy.
- From time immemorial, Kanaka Maoli have understood the evolution of the world, its life forms, and our cultural place within the cosmic worldview. All life forms of the honua, arising first from the kai with counterparts on the ʻāina, the naming of our ʻohana and the identification of our moʻokūʻauhau in the Kumulipo, impress upon our peoples the obligation to act as the kiaʻi of the honua and its life forms. Through pono behavior, we perpetuate the life of our lands and our peoples.[79]

The Paoakalani Declaration expressed the cultural and spiritual grounds for our rights-based approaches to kūʻē against biocolonialism.

In an interview with educator Kū Kahakalau about her reflections on the anti-GMO movement, she explained another culturally and linguistically based way of analyzing our kuleana:

> When we talk about "plants," we use the word poʻe, "kēlā poʻe kalo, kēlā poʻe maiʻa." And "poʻe" means "people." So the plant people, the taro people, the banana people. . . . All of those poʻe have mana and are part of our extended ʻohana. So . . . we need to protect one another. They impact us in a positive way, not in a negative way. So it is our kuleana to reciprocate that and impact them in a positive way and that would be protecting them from changes that could be their end

> literally and physically or a change that is so dramatic that we can't recognize the original species. I feel very strongly that to mess with any of those parts is not our kuleana. It is not our right or our responsibility.[80]

Knowing our kuleana also means respecting the kuleana of Kāne to create life. During the interview, Kū shared the ʻōlelo noʻeau (proverb) "Kapu ke ola iā Kāne; life is sacred to Kāne." She explained this traditional teaching's applicability to our present-day struggle with GE that it is not human responsibility to create life. Rather, it is Kāne, as Creator, who has that kuleana.[81]

Strong Kanaka Maoli participation in the movement to oppose GE did not ignite until more people understood that Hāloa, our kalo ancestor, was in harm's way. Facing the reality of GE kalo forced Kanaka Maoli to ask the question, "Is genetic engineering consistent with our cultural values?" The answer has been "ʻaʻole (no)!"

Reflecting on why she got involved in the movement against GMOs, Kū explains that the critical analysis of her haumana at the Kanu o Ka ʻĀina Hawaiian Charter School spurred her to be a voice for the poʻe who could not speak.

> When we first heard of the concept of GMO it was a very, very disturbing concept. . . . It is not a voluntary coming together to create a new thing. When we first analyzed it, the kids came up saying, "Aunty, this is like rape." It really hit home. Just like we wouldn't condone this to happen to our children, we can't let this happen to the plants that have no voices, and especially Hāloa, who is our elder sibling. When that word "rape" came out . . . it was clear to us to at least be a voice in this movement.[82]

The spiritual relationship of Kanaka Maoli to kalo has been reasserted in contemporary times through rallies and demonstrations and on signs reading, "Mālama Hāloa." In so doing, Kanaka Maoli have made the link between other movements centered on mālama ʻāina and aloha ʻāina. Hāloa, the kalo, has now become the rallying point for efforts to control or stop the advancement of biotechnology beyond kalo. For example, the carving depicting Hāloa that was first created to stop UH's genetic engineering of kalo and plant patents was again erected in 2012 by advocates lobbying for enactment of GMO labeling laws. Activists gathered around the ʻahu for Hāloa while ʻōpio performed oli and hula on the capitol grounds.[83] Through video and social media, the message to kūʻē GMOs is spreading, utilizing Hāloa as a symbol for more than just kalo.

REMEMBERING AND PROTECTING KALO'S MOʻOKŪʻAUHAU

Through our experience with protecting Hāloa and kalo, it is clear that a fundamental conflict of interest exists between the biotechnology industry and Kanaka Maoli. The biotech industry demands manipulation and ownership of sacred things. Although kalo rallied us, this issue goes beyond kalo. There will be other plants, animals, fish, and microorganisms that the industry will seek to patent or manipulate.

When interviewing Kamuela Enos, I asked him whether he thought that all life forms in the Kumulipo should be protected. He agreed, recommending a broader framework of analysis as the movement moves forward:

> If it's in the Kumulipo, then it is older than us and we have kuleana to preserve it. . . . We can't say this is just a kalo issue. . . . The way to frame it all up is that we have to use the word "ʻāina." ʻĀina doesn't mean land. ʻĀina means "that which feeds" and ʻāina means relationship. All of these different things had a part to play in the system, the ecology, in which Hawaiians survived. Yes, kalo is very prominent and is reflected in its standing in our cosmology. But [it doesn't exist] without all the other parts, like the flora and fauna that was within the ʻauwai that flowed down to the muliwai that created this life. You didn't just have kalo and Hawaiians. . . . If you only talk about kalo, then you are neglecting all of the other kūpuna that were part of kalo's moʻokūʻauhau.[84]

Thus, as we face other acts of biocolonialism in the future we must remember kalo's genealogy and assert our kuleana to protect all the kūpuna of Pō as recalled in the Kumulipo.

A SOLUTION FOR THE FUTURE: EA ʻĀINA (FOOD SOVEREIGNTY)

It has been crucial to the movement to kūʻē the actions of biotech corporations or UH through multiple means, including community-based education, organizing rallies and demonstrations, bringing lawsuits, lobbying for policy changes, and working in coalition with non-Native supporters. The activism against GE demonstrates a strong commitment to fulfill our duty as Kanaka to ensure that ʻāina is able to fulfill her role as "that which feeds." It has been important for the movement to develop a solution—an alternative to corporate-controlled food. As the anti-GMO movement has grown, so has the food sovereignty movement grown in Kanaka Maoli communities and beyond. Hawaiʻi's people have awakened to the reality that approximately 90 percent of what we consume is imported to the islands.

Kamuela Enos of MAʻO Organic Farms comments, "To me, the GMO piece is the corporatization of food. [This is] taking away the ability of communities to articulate their own food destiny and putting it in the hands of some remote boardroom." He further explains, "The food sovereignty piece is about creating a vibrant food system that allows us to be resilient on islands. It pushes us toward the kind of system our kūpuna were able to create uninterrupted for thousands of years."[85]

Thus, the proactive, solution-oriented activism against Mana Māhele has been to reconnect ʻāina and ea. The food sovereignty movement, like other movements for self-determination, restores Kanaka to our appropriate role as servants to ʻāina and restores ea to ʻāina so that all our ancestors continue to live as part of "that which feeds." Kamuela explained that while this has a spiritual basis, it is also practical. During our interview, he chuckled and asked, "What happened to the sugar and pineapple plantations?" and then went on to forecast that the new Big Five biotech corporations will meet the same demise as the old Big Five sugar companies. When oil prices soar and it becomes too expensive to ship their chemicals and seeds in and out of Hawaiʻi, they will leave because they have no vested interest here. "It's really bad, short-term economic forecasting to think they are going to be here forever." So it will be "up to this generation to create the building blocks for a food system to grow farms, farmers, and the system of a localized food economy." It will be up to this generation to follow the advice of mahiʻai (farmer) Uncle Jerry Konanui of Puna to "just kanu [plant]."[86] He has taken up the kuleana as a kupuna to share his knowledge of numerous kalo varieties uniquely adapted to thrive in different environs of Hawaiʻi. It is all of our kuleana to plant and mālama them for future generations of kalo and Kanaka.

Hāʻina

The movement against Mana Māhele is intrinsically related to the broader Hawaiian movement. At the heart of this and other movements for ʻāina and ea are Kanaka Maoli asserting our rights and responsibilities inherent in our relationship to this ʻāina and understanding our kuleana to Hawaiʻi. To kūʻē biocolonialism in all of its forms is aloha ʻāina. To love the land includes protecting that which feeds us from genetic manipulation. Our activism is based on respect for our genealogy, gifts of nature, and traditional knowledge that our ancestors have passed down to us, and for which we have kuleana to protect and perpetuate for the benefit of future generations. E mau ke ea o ka ʻāina i ka pono.

Notes

1. The term "Indigenous peoples'" (not people's) is consistent with international law and distinguishes us from ethnic minorities. In international law only peoples (with the "s") have the right of self-determination. At the heart of this struggle for recognition as a peoples is the fight for the right of self-determination, a right of *peoples* (not merely a group of individual people). The UN Declaration on the Rights of Indigenous Peoples recognizes in article 3 that "Indigenous peoples have the right to self-determination. By virtue of that right they freely determine their political status and freely pursue their economic, social and cultural development." (See http://www.un.org/esa/socdev/unpfii/documents/DRIPS_en.pdf.) The United Nations Declaration on the Rights of Indigenous Peoples was adopted in 2007 by 144 member states and represents the culmination of more than two decades of Indigenous advocacy to enshrine accepted international legal norms relevant to the rights of In-

digenous peoples. While no formal, official definition exists, the term "Indigenous peoples" is now accepted in international law as the appropriate terminology. The working definition provided in the UN *Study on the Problem of Discrimination against Indigenous Populations*, by José Marinez Cobo (http://www.un.org/esa/socdev/unpfii/documents/MCS_v_en.pdf), is useful to consider: "Indigenous communities, peoples and nations are those which, having a historical continuity with pre-invasion and pre-colonial societies that developed on their territories, consider themselves distinct from other sectors of the societies now prevailing on those territories, or parts of them. They form at present non-dominant sectors of society and are determined to preserve, develop and transmit to future generations their ancestral territories, and their ethnic identity, as the basis of their continued existence as peoples, in accordance with their own cultural patterns, social institutions and legal system."

2. Freese, "Biotech Not Hawai'i's Answer."
3. Whitt, "Indigenous Peoples, Intellectual Property and Imperial Science," 50.
4. Kimbrell, *The Human Body Shop*, 136.
5. Kimbrell, *The Human Body Shop*, 318, 309.
6. Rifkin, *The Biotech Century*.
7. Rifkin, *The Biotech Century*, 43–44.
8. Kamuela Enos, interview with the author, Honolulu, Hawai'i, April 6, 2012.
9. Lindsey, "Responsibility with Accountability," 765.
10. Hawai'i SEED, *Facing Hawai'i's Future*, 18.
11. Da Hemowai Bros., "Put Up or Shut Up!"
12. Boyd, "Hawai'i Genome Project Proposal."
13. Altonn, "UH Makes Gene Patent History."
14. Association of Hawaiian Civic Clubs, "Resolution 03-14."
15. Kanehe, "From Kumulipo," 114.
16. Kanehe, "From Kumulipo," 114.
17. Latin American Alliance, "Bioprospecting/Biopiracy and Indigenous Peoples."
18. Mgbeogi, *Global Biopiracy*, 13.
19. Diversa was a U.S. corporation trying to find enzymes within microorganisms from extreme environments such as geysers and coral reefs. By 2005, Diversa had collected genes for over 3 million microorganisms, had patented 192, and had 500 patents pending. GRAIN, "Diversa Dominates Global Search for Blockbuster Microbes." In June 2007, Diversa merged with Celunol to create Verenium. Verenium Corporation, "Diversa and Celunol Complete Merger to Create Verenium Corporation."
20. This section is adapted from Ritte and Kanehe, "Kuleana No Hāloa (Responsibility for Taro)."
21. Kame'eleihiwa, *Native Land and Foreign Desires*, 19–32.
22. Kame'eleihiwa, *Native Land and Foreign Desires*.
23. Trujillo, "Taro Cultivar Named 'Pauakea.'"
24. Gima, "Protestors Block Medical School."
25. Gima, "Protestors Block Medical School."
26. Da Hemowai Bros., "Put Up or Shut Up!"
27. Da Silva, "Lab Work on Taro Opposed."
28. Essoyan, "Activists Tear Up 3 UH Patents for Taro."
29. Essoyan, "Activists Tear Up 3 UH Patents for Taro."
30. Howard, "Life, Lineage and Sustenance," 8.
31. Howard, "Life, Lineage and Sustenance," 9.
32. Anderson, "What Is Genetic Engineering?," 11–12.
33. This section is adapted from Ritte and Kanehe, "Kuleana No Hāloa (Responsibility for Taro)."

34. Nā Maka o Ka 'Āina, *Mālama Hāloa*.
35. Boyd, "Genetically Modified Hawaii."
36. Bondera, "Papaya and Coffee," 44.
37. Lo, "Patents on Life."
38. Boyd, "Genetically Modified Hawaii."
39. Dawson, "Agribusiness Corporation Gives Tenants Control over Most State Land at Kekaha," 6.
40. Nā Maka o Ka 'Āina, *Islands at Risk*.
41. Redfeather, "GMOs in Hawai'i," 21.
42. Quote from Enos, interview.
43. Hervey, "Boss GMO"; "The GMO Debate, Food for Thought."
44. Hervey, "Boss GMO."
45. Hervey, "Boss GMO."
46. Walter Ritte Jr., interview with the author, Kaunakakai, Hawai'i, March 25, 2012.
47. Ritte, interview.
48. Hawai'i County Council, Bill 113, draft 3, http://www.biofortified.org/wp-content/uploads/2013/11/Bill-113-Draft-03-2012-2014.pdf.
49. "Mayor Signs GMO Bill 113 into Law," http://www.bigislandvideonews.com/2013/12/05/mayor-signs-gmo-bill-113-into-law/.
50. Yap, "An Island Divided," 49.
51. Yap, "An Island Divided," 47.
52. Hurley, "Bouncing Back," 17.
53. Hurley, "Bouncing Back," 17.
54. D'Angelo, "Overrode."
55. DePledge, "Mainland Cash Fuels the Fight," A10.
56. DePledge, "Mainland Cash Fuels the Fight," A10.
57. Nā Maka o Ka 'Āina, *Islands at Risk*.
58. Freese, "Biotech Not Hawai'i's Answer."
59. Weiss, "Gene-Altered Crops Denounced."
60. Choi, "No Paradise for Pharming."
61. Earthjustice, "Government Forced to Disclose Locations."
62. Earthjustice, "Government Forced to Disclose Locations."
63. *Center for Food Safety, et al. v. Johanns*, 451 F. Supp.2d 1165, 1181–1186 (D. Haw. 2006), 451:1181–1186.
64. Earthjustice, "Citizens Sue for Environmental Review of Biopharm Algae in Hawaii."
65. Earthjustice, "Citizens Sue for Environmental Review of Biopharm Algae in Hawaii."
66. *'Ohana Pale Ke Ao et al. v. Board of Agriculture, State of Hawai'i*, 188 P.3d 761, 763–764 (Haw. Intermediate Court of Appeals 2008), 188:763–764.
67. *'Ohana Pale Ke Ao et al. v. Board of Agriculture, State of Hawai'i*, 188:766.
68. *'Ohana Pale Ke Ao et al. v. Board of Agriculture, State of Hawai'i*, 188:767–770.
69. Trask, "Hawaiian Perspectives on GMOs," 27.
70. Ritte, interview.
71. Ritte, interview.
72. Ritte, interview.
73. "The GMO Debate, Food for Thought."
74. Earthjustice, "Citizens Demand Restoration of River in 'Grand Canyon of the Pacific' on Kaua'i."
75. Enos, interview.
76. Association of Hawaiian Civic Clubs, "Resolution 02-08."

77. Lindsey, "Responsibility with Accountability."
78. 'Īlio'ulaokalani Coalition, "Paoakalani Declaration," para. 19.
79. 'Īlio'ulaokalani Coalition, "Paoakalani Declaration," paras. 5, 6.
80. Kū Kahakalau, interview with the author, Honoka'a, Hawai'i, March 28, 2012.
81. Kahakalau, interview.
82. Kahakalau, interview.
83. Ritte, interview; "GMO RALLY Hawai'i State Capitol 2012," YouTube video, 10:00, posted by "bergdraft," February 23, 2012, http://www.youtube.com/watch?v=mfKq6AiXmSE.
84. Enos, interview.
85. Enos, interview.
86. Nā Maka o Ka 'Āina, *Mālama Hāloa*.

Puanani Burgess talks with Dr. Kekuni Blaisdell and news reporter Paula Akana at a 1985 rally against the construction of the H-3 freeway. Protesters had gathered at the Bishop Museum because museum staff were believed to be covering up or undervaluing the importance of Hawaiian sacred sites in the path of the planned construction.

Portrait. Puanani Burgess

HE ALO A HE ALO

Mehana Blaich Vaughan

Aunty Puanani Burgess is a poet, community development consultant, grassroots activist, and facilitator from the Wai'anae Coast of O'ahu. She has been involved in a number of sovereignty and 'āina-based struggles throughout Hawai'i, including Kaho'olawe, Sand Island, and the process to renegotiate taro farming leases in Waipi'o Valley. Aunty Pua finds it difficult to discuss her role separately from that of her husband of forty years, Pōkā Laenui (Pōkā) Hayden Burgess, because he has always provided thoughtful and intellectual grounding for her work. His research to unearth the history of Hawai'i's illegal overthrow provides a foundation of many efforts for Hawaiian independence.

This portrait is a transcribed interview with Aunty Pua, in which she reflects on how her own role evolved to focus on community building and translation, helping different parties to understand each other's perspectives.[1] She recalls her engagement in opposing the West Beach development on the Leeward Coast of O'ahu in the 1980s as a turning point in her life. The West Beach proposal included 4,000 rooms in eight separate hotels, 5,200 residential units, a marina, golf course, shopping center, and four lagoons, making it the largest proposed resort development on the island of O'ahu outside of Waikīkī. Aunty Pua helped to negotiate the West Beach settlement to substantially reduce the allowable development size (at the present day site of Ko Olina resort). The settlement also funded growth of two fledgling Wai'anae community programs teaching the relationship between ma uka and ma kai, Ka'ala Farms and the 'Ōpelu Project.[2] Both became models for ahupua'a-based cultural education and community-based economic development throughout the state. Aunty Pua connects lessons learned from the West Beach experience to her current work with Hawaiian women prisoners at O'ahu Community Correctional Center (OCCC).

IN 1982, I was in law school and I decided to go home [to Wai'anae]. I was pregnant and people thought that was the reason I quit. It was a very convenient excuse, but that wasn't the reason. I just knew I didn't want to be a lawyer. [In law school I worked on the Kaho'olawe negotiations.] I helped to give Protect Kaho'olawe 'Ohana a voice that sounded reasonable. I did press releases and strategized about how to build a campaign, bring different kinds of people . . . not just the bruddah action, but bringing in legislators, folks that make decisions. And during that process I changed from a really loud aggressive activist into something more like what I am right now.

When I went home Eric (Enos) saw me as a resource. He knew that I had done that kind of strategic work with Protect Kahoʻolawe ʻOhana and was interested to have me come in and see what was possible as a way of defeating the development of West Beach. [At the time,] Eric was running a youth development program, the ʻŌpelu Project, using the fishing and the canoe [with two uncles from Miloliʻi fishing village on the Big Island], Uncle Walter Paulo and Uncle Eddie Kaanana. They would take teens and young adults to go out and learn how to fish ʻōpelu in the old way, to weave net and prepare the palu and of all the things that [go] with being a fisherman. The ʻōpelu fishing grounds off the [proposed development were] one of the major places where Uncle Walter taught and so all of that was going to change with West Beach.

The West Beach development was going to change how life was lived on the [leeward] coast by changing the coastline. Their plan called for building lagoons because there was no natural beach that they could use for their resort. They were going to change the landscape of the ocean and the ability for the fishermen to fish, families who relied on fishing. [There were] petroglyphs and sinkholes that were very important archaeological sites to our people and small heiau, small shrine areas that were not mapped but would be destroyed.

And then the issue came up, where is the water going to come from? That is where the farmers came in. Already water was scarce and expensive and there was a lot of it [needed] to water the golf courses, provide drinking water for the resort. What was going to happen to the farms in Waiʻanae?

Part of the West Beach developer's strategy was to promise jobs to the people in Waiʻanae. But people didn't think that really was going to happen because of the literacy and graduation rate being so low. Lots of things had to be done in order to have people be employable at those places and they weren't talking about that. There was worry about displacement of more local people and more new people coming in. Those were the complex issues that we were beginning to understand how deep they were. And people in downtown were worried because we were beginning to touch on issues that made the development very vulnerable to challenge.

We were going to have a hearing before the Land Use Commission and usually we would bring the farmers and the fishermen. But you know it's like bringing fish out of water and to a meeting. They don't look too healthy. People don't look powerful when they come in their slippers and not too nice T-shirt and still smell of the ocean, plenty dirt under their fingernails and they speak in broken sentences and they cry. So what I suggested, and got the Land Use Commission to allow, was to videotape the farmers and the fishermen on their sites. On their sites they're brilliant. We played the videotape, about a half an hour long, and got all of that tape introduced into the records

[As] our movement got stronger, the concern by West Beach [developers] increased. There was a lot of activity wondering how could they bring us to the table. Before I got into the fracas, they had offered money but no modification of the development. It was always a transactional situation: "How much do you want to go away?" It wasn't money that we were after. We wanted the development to go away. That thing was so huge, a $6 billion resort, not a million, billion. So a lot of power, and lot of other people's survivals relied on it.

We also didn't understand how much the unions were going to be involved. A lot of union jobs were dependent upon that development. A lot of folks in Wai'anae are in those unions; construction workers, electricians, heavy machine operators. So us keeping the development from going forward meant they weren't working. And you had a lot of pressure family to family and within families.

At the same time we were in the Supreme Court [represented by Native Hawaiian Legal Corporation]. We were worried if the court ruled against us that would set a negative precedent for other communities who were going to be challenging developers. So there were all these complex issues bearing down at the same time. And while we were doing all of this protest and administrative hearings, you know, nobody was home taking care of the programs.

[One friend and business leader proposed that our group and the West Beach developers, including the owners, sit down to mediation] with Tanouye Roshi [founder and head of Chozenji Zen temple in Kalihi]. When they mentioned Tanouye versus going to a court-based mediator we decided to try that. . . . Our group agreed that Eric and I would be the lead negotiators for the discussions.

[During negotiations,] friends in the activist field were calling us sellouts and turncoats and all kinds of things because we were engaged in the conversations that would settle these issues in our community. I could understand the criticisms. I probably had done that too before. But when it was being done to you and you know the clarity and purity of why you're doing it, because you just cannot take the fighting and fighting and fighting and nobody's tending to the taro and nobody's watching the shore, and you know you cannot live that life.

When we were doing the mediation around West Beach, I started to get threatening telephone calls. Men would call and say, "We know where you are and we know where you're going." And, "We are going to hurt your children." So, you know when you choose force against force? They were carrying weapons they were willing to use against me. So my solution was to carry a weapon and be willing and able to use it against them. A friend got his father to loan me his registered pistol, and taught me how to shoot the gun.

So here we are, [after eighteen months of mediation,] signing the mutual agreement between West Beach and our community organization, settling issues we had been fighting over for fourteen years. I am carrying the gun in my bag when we sign the documents at Governor Waihe'e's office. Afterwards [the members of our community group] all go to Zippy's to eat and celebrate a moment of peace. After our meal, we get into the van, and start to make our way back to Wai'anae. I forget my bag at the restaurant.

So I call and I ask if they found my bag. "Oh yes, we're holding it for you." [When we went back], there were about ten police officers waiting at Zippy's to arrest me for carrying a weapon. Now, fortunately for me, the gun was wrapped in a diaper, and the bullets were wrapped in another diaper. In the police car, me in the backseat, the lieutenant asks what I was thinking. I tell him that I was getting threatened, that I was scared. Then he said, "But you know, if the gun is all wrapped up and the bullets was all wrapped up, how you was going hurt anybody?"

"Yeah, that's the problem. I didn't want to load it. It might go off. It might hit innocent people. So I just kept it separate."

"Yeah, would be funny, you telling them, 'Try wait, let me load the bullet inside the gun and then shoot you.'"

They took me to the police station and they fingerprinted me, booked me, and put me in a cell all by myself. I sat there. I was singing. [My husband] Hayden came in the cell. He shook his head and said, "This is not surprising."

He got me out of jail, and for some reason I never got charged. I wasn't arraigned. I wasn't anything. I just got let go. Except that arrest followed me and I could not go into the prison, OCCC, because I have that thing on my record. All these years later, getting me into prison for the women's project, I couldn't have done it if the warden wasn't there to vouch for me. So that was my crime, and people end up in jail for less. There were circumstances that kept me out of prison because other people intervened on my behalf who had power. I didn't know it, but I knew it long after the interventions happened. These women didn't have that circle around them, so I could've been one of them, still in prison after fifteen years, for carrying a weapon.

A prison can become a place of refuge. [In my work at OCCC,] I am doing my piece in transforming an experience that can be so debilitating into part of a healing process, part of returning the life of the land back to people. I am given the opportunity to work with women, most of whom are Hawaiian, a few of whom are from Nānākuli or Wai'anae where I live. Some are in there for life, or have spent half of a very young life, at say twenty-four years old, in prison. These are women who have done things that are really hard for people on the outside to think of as making them redeemable.

I was asked to come in to begin to examine the trauma of the women which resulted in them choosing crime. [The idea] was that in order for them to heal and be whole again, they need to process that trauma, understand it, and walk their way away from it. I thought, "No, that's not my job." That people have suffered and that they choose not to talk about it publicly, that's their right to choose, even though we are "trying to help them."

I saw that my real work was to help design a process through which people, the women first, could have trust in other women that they live with. Our project tries to [make prison] not just healthy and safe physically, but healthy and safe spiritually; a place that appreciates their intelligence, in which those things that usually get separated from them when they come into prison are restored. And my role is not to help them. My role is to create a safe place in which they and other people who work in the prison can come together and figure out a different way to run a prison.

The process was about creating a level playing field—from the psychologist, to the women, to the head of their work release program, everybody had to do something hard. Tell you my name, how I got it, how I feel about it, about my community, and finally to tell you the story of my gift. Most of the people, women in prison and the people in the professional roles who work in their circle, they never talk about that stuff. So just about everyone there experienced something about being human in a deep way for the first time in prison.

I was very sure that there would be women I met there that would amaze me. I knew that there would be women I met there who would scare or even disgust me. I was not prepared for the level of thoughtfulness, the level of care, and the level of hurt in the things they've had to go through. And I wasn't ready for their ability to bring outsiders to their circle. The thoughtfulness they have, having gone through the prison system: the way this particular prison is run, what it did to them to be in prison, how it has created problems with their children. They were able to tell the story of how they got to where they are as a way of hoping, giving hope to other young girls and women not to follow their footsteps, that it's preventable. They do more thoughtful consideration of their lives than a lot of us who are wandering around the streets daily.

I talk to them about my life . . . that I am who I am, and I am amazed that they are who they are and where they are. I don't know why I'm not where they are. [When the threats during the West Beach mediation started], all I could think was, "I going [to] find you and hunt you down and curse you and your family"—that's where I was. When someone threatened my children, I thought I could kill. But when that situation happened, and having a gun and taking it apart in a way that I could never use it to do harm, I understood something fundamental about who I was. It was that moment that changed my approach to work. I started to look at reclaiming words like "development" or "economics." How do we create a parallel economic system in our community, which we manage and control and govern?

I can tell you about my regrets. Once the door was open to West Beach, then it's open to Walt Disney.[3] I'm still struggling with being angry about the Disney people having so many resources to create a message that may be appealing to more people than the West Beach developers, which looked just like exploitation of land and people. The question I always ask, but never get an answer to, "Where is the water [for the Disney resort] coming from? What lo'i? What patch of land? What MA'O Farms?[4] Where is that water coming from?" So in some ways, I'm still in the hard questioning place but not closing my heart off to the people who are struggling to answer that.

AUNTY PUANANI is newly a grandmother. I ended this interview by asking her what she wanted her seven-month-old granddaughter to know. Here is her response:

> I want her to always know what it's like to have mango growing in her yard.
> I want her to know what it's like
> to have taro and fish growing in her yard.
> I want her to be able to go to Kaho'olawe
> without having to get permission,
> to stand at the top of Moa'ula
> and see the course her ancestors took to go back to Kahiki,
> to be able to swim in those waters.
> I want her to experience an estuary
> in the community she comes from
> which hasn't been taken apart.
> I want her to be able to go into any library
> and take out the documents signed by her queen,
> to touch them and to smell them,
> To run her fingers on the pen signature of the queen,
> of all of our ancestors who held the line in one way or another for us.
> I want her to hear the story of how the queen would welcome people
> who had come and walked for miles and days
> to bring her a gift of fish.
> And the fish was spoiled.
> And she would open the wrapping,
> she would take the fish,
> and she would eat it.
> I want her to know that queen also.
> The one who understood what a real gift is.
> I don't want her to grow up in a world
> in which things are in museums,
> But to know that history is alive

and she has a responsibility to keep it alive.
I want her to know she has cousins beyond blood.
That is what I want for her.

Notes

1. Puanani Burgess is my aunty and mentor. We met in the summer of 1997, which I spent shadowing her through an internship with the Wai'anae Coast Community Alternative Development Center. I admire the way she brings people together, illuminates others' gifts, and speaks underlying truths with gentleness and humor. Because Aunty Pua is a natural storyteller, I chose to transmit her words directly. Any additions [in brackets] are intended only to provide context and clarity, allowing the reader to experience her story in her voice for themselves.

2. See Ka'ala Farm, http://www.kaalafarm.org. The 'Ōpelu Project evolved into the Wai'anae Coast Community Alternative Development Corporation.

3. West Beach, known today as Ko'olina, is now the site of Disney's Aulani resort, opened in late summer of 2011.

4. MA'O Farms (http://www.maoorganicfarms.org) is a Wai'anae organic farming project that grows youth and community by teaching farming, business, and leadership skills while helping to provide a bridge to tertiary education.

Bibliography

"Activist's Choice: Jail, Not Bail." *Honolulu Advertiser,* May 12, 1977.

Addleman, William C. *History of the United States Army in Hawaii 1849 to 1939.* Honolulu: Hawaii War Records Depository, University of Hawai'i at Mānoa Library, 1939.

"Agreement Prohibits Camping at Mākua." *Leeward Coaster* (Wai'anae, HI), July 1996.

Akaka, D. K. "Native Hawaiian Federal Recognition Bill Introduced." Press release from the office of U.S. senator Daniel Akaka, January 22, 2001.

———. "Statement of Senator Daniel K. Akaka on Revisions to the Native Hawaiian Federal Recognition Bill, April 16." Accessed August 11, 2009. http://www.senate.gov/~akaka/speeches/2001427548.html.

Alegado, Dean. *Sinking Roots: Filipino American Legacy in Hawai'i.* Honolulu: Philippine Centennial Committee, 1998.

Alfred, Taiaiake. *Peace, Power, Righteousness: An Indigenous Manifesto.* Ontario: Oxford University Press, 1999.

———. *Wasáse: Indigenous Pathways of Action and Freedom.* Toronto: Broadview, 2005.

Allen, Chadwick. *Blood Narrative: Indigenous Identity in American Indian and Maori Literary and Activist Texts.* Durham, NC: Duke University Press, 2002.

Altonn, Helen. "Ceremonies 'Make Things Right': Rites at Royal Mausoleum Honor Hawaiian Ancestors, Bring 'a Rebirth' on the Centennial of U.S. Annexation." *Honolulu Star-Bulletin,* August 12, 1998.

———. "UH Makes Gene Patent History." *Honolulu Star-Bulletin,* December 23, 2002. http://starbulletin.com/2002/12/23/news/story7.html.

Altonn, Helen, and Christine Donnelly. "Top Court Backs Rice in OHA Vote Challenge. Hawai'i's Law Restricting OHA Trustee Selection to Hawaiians Is Struck Down." *Honolulu Star-Bulletin,* February 23, 2000.

Amalu, Samuel Crowningburg. "Sing a Song of Love for Hawaii Soil." *Honolulu Advertiser,* Sunday edition, January 11, 1976.

American Friends Service Committee, Hawai'i Area Office. *He Alo ā He Alo: Face to Face.* Honolulu: American Friends Service Committee, Hawai'i Area Office, 1993.

Anderson, Luke. "What Is Genetic Engineering?" In *Facing Hawai'i's Future: Harvesting Essential Information about GMOs,* 11–16. Hilo: Hawai'i SEED, 2006.

Andrade, Carlos. *Hā'ena: Through the Eyes of the Ancestors.* Honolulu: University of Hawai'i Press, 2008.

Andrews, Lorrin. *A Dictionary of the Hawaiian Language.* Waipahu, HI: Island Heritage, 2003.

"Anglo-Franco Declaration, November 28, 1843." *Hawaiian Journal of Law and Politics* 1 (summer 2004): 114.

Aoudé, Ibrahim, ed. "Ethnic Studies Story: Politics and Social Movements in Hawai'i—Essays in Honor of Marion Kelly." *Social Process in Hawai'i* 39 (1999).
———. "The Political Economy of Hawai'i, 1980–1994: The State of Research." Unpublished working paper, 1994.
———. "Public Policy and Globalization in Hawai'i." *Social Process in Hawai'i* 40 (2001).
Arakawa, Lynda. "Bush Support Needed for Akaka Bill." *Honolulu Advertiser*, August 13, 2003.
"Army's Application for EPA Permit Is Long, but Not Informative." *Environment Hawai'i*, November 1992.
Association of Hawaiian Civic Clubs. "Resolution 02-08, Urging the State of Hawai'i to Place a Moratorium on All Bioprospecting Expeditions Currently Being Undertaken on Public Lands, Submerged Lands, and Natural Resources under the State's Jurisdiction until Such Time as an Appropriate Legislation Can Be Enacted." Honolulu, 2002.
———. "Resolution 03-14, Urging the University of Hawai'i to Cease Development of the Hawaiian Genome Project." Honolulu, 2003.
Auel, Lisa B. *Ties That Bind: Communities in American History*. Washington, DC: National Archives, 1992.
Bacchilega, Cristina. *Legendary Hawai'i and the Politics of Place: Tradition, Translation, and Tourism*. Philadelphia: University of Pennsylvania Press, 2007.
Barker, Joanne, ed. *Sovereignty Matters: Locations of Contestation and Possibility in Indigenous Struggles for Self-Determination*. Lincoln: University of Nebraska Press, 2005.
Barrère, Dorothy B., and Marion Kelly. *Background History of the Kona Area, Island of Hawai'i*. Honolulu: Department of Anthropology, Bernice P. Bishop Museum, 1980.
Barrère, Dorothy B., Marion Kelly, and Barry Nakamura. *Hilo Bay, a Chronological History: Land and Water Use in the Hilo Bay Area, Island of Hawai'i*. Honolulu: Department of Anthropology, Bernice P. Bishop Museum, 1981.
Basham, Leilani. "Ka Lāhui Hawai'i: He Mo'olelo, He 'Āina, He Loina, a He Ea Kākou." *Hūlili: Multidisciplinary Research on Hawaiian Well-Being* 6 (2010): 37–72.
———. "Mele Lāhui: The Importance of Pono in Hawaiian Poetry." *Te Kaharoa* 1 (2008): 152–164.
Basso, Keith H. *Wisdom Sits in Places: Landscape and Language among the Western Apache*. Albuquerque: University of New Mexico Press, 1996.
Beamer, B. Kamanamaikalani. "Living Ahupua'a: Challenges in Research, Agency and Land Tenure." University of Hawai'i at Mānoa, February 10, 2012.
———. "Na Wai Ka Mana? 'Ōiwi Agency and European Imperialism in the Hawaiian Kingdom." PhD diss., University of Hawai'i at Mānoa, 2008.
Beamer, Kamanamaikalani, and Kaeo Duarte. "I Palapala No Ia Aina—Documenting the Hawaiian Kingdom: A Colonial Venture?" *Journal of Historical Geography* 35 (2009): 66–86.
Beckwith, Martha Warren. *Hawaiian Mythology*. Honolulu: University of Hawai'i Press, 1970.
———. *The Kumulipo: A Hawaiian Creation Chant*. Honolulu: University of Hawai'i Press, 1951.
Benvenisti, Eyal. *The International Law of Occupation*, 2nd ed. Oxford: Oxford University Press, 2012.
Blaisdell, R. K. "The Meaning of Health." *Asian American Pacific Island Journal of Health* 4 (winter 1996): 232.
Blaisdell, Richard Kekuni. "Kekuni Blaisdell." In *Autobiography of Protest in Hawai'i*, edited by Robert H. Mast and Anne B. Mast. Honolulu: University of Hawai'i Press, 1996.
Bondera, Melanie. "Papaya and Coffee: GMO 'Solutions' Spell Market Disaster." In *Facing Hawai'i's Future: Harvesting Essential Information about GMOs*, 44–46. Hilo: Hawai'i SEED, 2006.

Bone, Robert. "Aboriginal Lands of Hawaiian Ancestry, the Billion-Dollar Hope: Message from an Alii Gave Birth to Movement." *Sunday Honolulu Advertiser and Star-Bulletin*, August 4, 1974.

Bowman, Pierre. "The Valley That Was, and Is." *Honolulu Star-Bulletin*, March 1, 1977.

Boyd, Charles. "Hawai'i Genome Project Proposal." Pacific Biomedical Research Center, University of Hawai'i at Mānoa, March 25, 2004.

Boyd, Robynne. "Genetically Modified Hawaii." *Scientific American*, December 8, 2008. http://www.scientificamerican.com/article.cfm?id=genetically-modified-hawaii.

"Breach of Trust? Native Hawaiian Homelands." Prepared for the Hawai'i Advisory Committee to the U.S. Commission of Civil Rights, 1980. http://www.law.umaryland.edu/marshall/usccr/documents/cr12h312.pdf.

Calizar, Yvonne Mokihana. "Haunani-Kay Trask . . . in Her Own Voice." *Hawaii Island Journal*, August 2003.

Cardwell, Ehu Kekahu. "Hawaiian Superman—a Visit with Dr. Kanalu Young." YouTube video, 28:34. Posted by Voices of Truth, February 26, 2007. http://www.youtube.com/watch?v=nCqrHoihSqQ.

"Cayetano Meets with Squatters' Sympathizer." *Honolulu Star-Bulletin*, March 19, 1996.

Chock, Jennifer M. L. "One Hundred Years of Illegitimacy: International Legal Analysis of the Illegal Overthrow of the Hawaiian Monarchy, Hawai'i's Annexation, and Possible Reparations." *University of Hawai'i Law Review* 17 (1995): 492.

Choi, Charles Q. "No Paradise for Pharming: Lawsuit Seeking Information on Hawaii Test Fields Is Just the Beginning, Activists Say." *Scientist*, July 30, 2003. http://www.the-scientist.com/?articles.view/articleNo/22360/title/No-paradise-for-pharming/.

Cobo, José R. Marinez. *Study on the Problem of Discrimination against Indigenous Populations, Final Report (Supplementary Part)*. June 20, 1982, E/CN.4/Sub.2/1982/2/Add.6. http://www.un.org/esa/socdev/unpfii/documents/MCS_v_en.pdf.

Coffman, Tom. *Nation Within: The History of the American Occupation of Hawai'i*, rev. ed. Kīhei: Koa Books, 2009.

Commission on Water Resource Management. "Findings of Fact, Conclusions of Law, and Decision and Order." Contested Case Hearing, no. CCH-MA06-01, June 10, 2010. http://www.state.hi.us/dlnr/cwrm/cch_CCHMA0601.htm.

Conrow, Joan. "Rebuilding Kaho'olawe: PKO Saved the Island, but Has the Group Lost Its Way?" *Honolulu Weekly*, February 8, 2006.

Cooper, George, and Gavan Daws. *Land and Power in Hawaii: The Democratic Years*. Honolulu: University of Hawai'i Press, 1990.

Crawford, James, Gavan Griffith, and Christopher Greenwood. "In the Permanent Court of Arbitration: Case No. 99001, Lance Paul Larsen vs. the Hawaiian Kingdom." The Hague, Netherlands, December 11, 2000. http://alohaquest.com/arbitration/transcript_001211.htm.

Da Hemowai Bros. "Put Up or Shut Up!" Streaming video, 52:38. Moloka'i, HI: Ali'i Essence Productions. http://hawaiicommunitytelevision.blogspot.com/2008_01_01_archive.html.

D'Angelo, Chris. "Overrode: Dying 2491 Revived by New Council Member Was Voted into Law." *Garden Island*, November 17, 2013. http://thegardenisland.com/news/local/overrode/article_0d7f22fc-4f52-11e3-9b90-001a4bcf887a.html.

"Dan Raps Navy on Kaho'olawe." *Honolulu Advertiser*, January 7, 1970.

Da Silva, Alexandre. "Lab Work on Taro Opposed." *Honolulu Star-Bulletin*, June 6, 2006. http://archives.starbulletin.com/2006/06/06/news/story09.html.

Dawson, Teresa. "Agribusiness Corporation Gives Tenants Control over Most State Land at

Kekaha." *Environment Hawai'i* 14, no. 10 (April 2004). http://www.environment-hawaii.org/archives_summary.php?id=210_0_20_0_M.

Daysog, Rick, and Debra Barayuga. "Federal Judge Upholds Hawaiians-Only School." *Honolulu Star-Bulletin*, November 18, 2003.

Dedman, Palikapuokamohoalii, and Noa Emmett Aluli. "Pele Ha." In *Mālama Hawaiian Land and Water*, edited by Dana Naone Hall. Honolulu: Bamboo Ridge Press, 1985.

Deloria, Vine, Jr. *God Is Red: A Native View of Religion*. Golden, CO: Fulcrum, 2003.

———. *The World We Used to Live In: Remembering the Powers of the Medicine Men*. Golden, CO: Fulcrum, 2006.

DePledge, Derrick. "Mainland Cash Fuels the Fight." *Honolulu Star-Advertiser*, September 29, 2013.

de Silva, Kihei, and Mapuana de Silva. "A Maunakea 'o Kalani." Hālau Mohala 'Ilima, 2006.

Devaney, Dennis M., Marion Kelly, Polly Jae Lee, and Lee S. Motteler. *Kāne'ohe: A History of Change*. Honolulu: Bess Press, 1982.

Dudley, Michael Kioni, and Keoni Kealoha Agard. *A Call for Hawaiian Sovereignty*. Honolulu: Nā Kāne O Ka Malo Press, 1993.

Earthjustice. "Citizens Demand Restoration of River in 'Grand Canyon of the Pacific' on Kaua'i." Press release, July 24, 2013. http://earthjustice.org.

———. "Citizens Sue for Environmental Review of Biopharm Algae in Hawaii." Press release, August 2, 2005. http://earthjustice.org.

———. "Court Orders Public Oversight of 'Biopharm' Experiment in Hawai'i." Press release, October 5, 2005. http://earthjustice.org.

———. "Government Forced to Disclose Locations of Test Sites of Biopharmaceutical Crops." Press release, February 8, 2005. http://earthjustice.org.

———. "Kaulana Nā Wai 'Ehā: Restoring Maui's Famous Streams." YouTube video, 7:56. Posted by "nawaieha," August 20, 2007. http://www.youtube.com/watch?v=NZ2BmMcRBuo.

———. "Restore Stream Flow." Accessed February 19, 2012. http://earthjustice.org/our_work/campaigns/restore-stream-flow.

Enomoto, Catherine Kekoa. "Dance of the Red Dog." *Honolulu Star-Bulletin*, December 29, 1997. http://archives.starbulletin.com/1997/12/29/features/index.html.

"Environmentalists Enraged by These Military Practices." *Leeward Coaster* (Wai'anae, HI), January 1996.

Essoyan, Susan. "Activists Tear Up 3 UH Patents for Taro." *Honolulu Star-Bulletin*, June 21, 2006. http://archives.starbulletin.com/2006/06/21/news/story03.html.

Fanon, Frantz. *The Wretched of the Earth*. New York: Grove, 1965.

Fernandes, K. "UH Tries to Cut 14 Classes." *Ka Leo o Hawai'i*, May 1, 1995.

Finney, Ben. *Sailing in the Wake of the Ancestors: Reviving Polynesian Voyaging*. Honolulu: Bishop Museum Press, 2003.

"First the Cattle, Then the Bombs Oust Hawaiians from Mākua Valley." *Environment Hawai'i*, November 1992.

Flickinger, Reed. "A Measured Look at Gov. Abercrombie: Who Have We Got Here?" *West Hawai'i Today*, April 1, 2012.

Fornander, Abraham. *Fornander's Ancient History of the Hawaiian People*. Honolulu: Mutual, 1996.

———. "No Ke Kaiakahinalii Ma Hawaii Nei." In *Fornander's Collection of Hawaiian Antiquities and Folk-Lore*, edited by Thomas Thrum. Honolulu: Bishop Museum Press, 1998.

Freese, Bill. "Biotech Not Hawai'i's Answer." *Honolulu Advertiser*, May 10, 2004.

Frickel, Scott, and Neil Gross. "A General Theory of Scientific/Intellectual Movements." *American Sociological Review* 70, no. 2 (2005): 209.
Fujikane, Candace. "Introduction: Asian Settler Colonialism in the U.S. Colony of Hawai'i." In *Asian Settler Colonialism: From Local Governance to the Habits of Everyday Life in Hawai'i*, edited by Candace Fujikane and Jonathan Okamura. Honolulu: University of Hawai'i Press, 2008.
Fujikane, Candace, and Jonathan Okamura, eds. *Asian Settler Colonialism: From Local Governance to the Habits of Everyday Life in Hawai'i*. Honolulu: University of Hawai'i Press, 2008.
Garcia, M., comp. "Summary of Eruption Episodes." Hawaii Center for Volcanology, 1999. http://www.soest.hawaii.edu.
Geschwender, James A. "Lessons from Waiahole-Waikane." *Social Process in Hawai'i* 28 (1980–1981): 121–135.
———. "The Social Context of Strategic Success: A Land-Use Struggle in Hawai'i." In *Social Movements in the Sixties and Seventies*, edited by J. Freeman. New York: Longman, 1982.
Gima, Craig. "Protestors Block Medical School." *Honolulu Star-Bulletin*, May 19, 2006. http://archives.starbulletin.com/2006/05/19/news/story06.html.
"The GMO Debate, Food for Thought: Part 3—Critics Question Lawmakers? GMO Labeling Bill Killing Move." Transcript. *KITV4 News*. Honolulu: KITV4, February 24, 2012. http://www.kitv.com/The-GMO-Debate-Food-For-Thought-Part-3/-/8906042/9658312/-/4tji4y/-/index.html.
Gonschor, Lorenz. "Law as a Tool of Oppression and Liberation: Institutional Histories and Perspectives on Political Independence in Hawai'i, Tahiti Nui/French Polynesia and Rapa Nui." MA thesis, University of Hawai'i at Mānoa, 2008.
Gordon, Mike. "Protest Held at Kamehameha Schools." *Honolulu Advertiser*, August 21, 2003.
"Governor Enacts Bill to Further Self-Determination for Native Hawaiians." Media release, Hawaii 24/7, July 7, 2011. http://www.hawaii247.com/2011/07/07/governor-enacts-bill-to-further-self-determination-for-native-hawaiians/.
GRAIN. "Diversa Dominates Global Search for Blockbuster Microbes." *Seedling*, January 2005. http://www.grain.org/es/article/entries/448-diversa-dominates-global-search-for-blockbuster-microbes.
Griffen, P. Bion, and Dorothy Pyle. *The Archaeology of Koolau-Poko, O'ahu from the Ahupua'a of Waiahole to the Ahupua'a of Waikane: Archaeological Reconnaissance and Historical Investigation of the Makai 2.5 Square Miles of Waiahole and Waikane*. Honolulu: Environmental Communications (Archaeological Research Center Hawaii), 1974.
Hālau O Kekuhi. *Holo Mai Pele*. Film. Honolulu: Pacific Islanders in Communications, International Cultural Programming and Thirteen/WNET New York, 2004.
Hamilton, Chris. "Na Wai Eha: HC&S Speaks." *Maui News*, 2009. http://www.mauinews.com/page/content.detail/id/524576.html.
Handy, Craighill, Elisabeth Green Handy, and Mary Kawena Pukui. *Native Planters in Old Hawai'i: Their Life, Lore, and Environment*. Honolulu: Bishop Museum Press, 1991.
Harris, Aroha. *Hīkoi: Forty Years of Māori Protest*. Wellington: Huia Press, 2006.
Hasager, Ulla, and Jonathan Friedman, eds. *Return to Nationhood*. Copenhagen: IWGIA, 1994. http://www.iwgia.org/publications/search-pubs?publication_id=151.
"Hawaiian Activist Invades Kaho'olawe Again." *Honolulu Star-Bulletin*, January 13, 1976.
Hawaiian Patriotic League, Nā Maka o ka 'Āina, and Hawai'i Loa Kūlike Kākou Committee (Hawaii). *An Historical Overview of the Events That Prevented Annexation of the Hawaiian Islands to the United States*. Honolulu: Hawaiian Patriotic League, 1998.

Hawai'i County Council. Bill 113, draft 3, An Ordinance Amending Chapter 14 of the Hawaii County Code 1983 (2005 edition, as amended), by adding a new article relating to genetically engineered crops and plants. http://www.biofortified.org/wp-content/uploads/2013/11/Bill-113-Draft-03-2012-2014.pdf.

Hawai'i SEED, ed. *Facing Hawai'i's Future: Harvesting Essential Information about GMOs.* Hilo: Hawai'i SEED, 2006.

Hawai'i Sovereignty Advisory Council. *Preliminary Report of the Sovereignty Advisory Council of the State of Hawai'i to the Sixteenth Legislature, the State of Hawai'i.* Honolulu: HSAC, 1992.

"Hawaii's Search for Sovereignty." *Christian Science Monitor,* October 17, 1994.

Hervey, Tiffany. "Boss GMO." *Honolulu Weekly,* January 4, 2012.

Hinton, Leanne, and Ken Hale. *The Green Book of Language Revitalization in Practice.* San Diego: Brill Academic Press, 2001.

"Homeless Beach Person Criticizes State Tactics." *Honolulu Star-Bulletin,* March 8, 1996.

Ho'omanawanui, Sherilyn Ku'ualoha. "Pele's Appeal: Mo'olelo, Kaona and Hulihia in 'Pele and Hi'iaka' Literature (1860–1928)." PhD diss., University of Hawai'i at Mānoa, 2007.

Howard, Stephanie. "Life, Lineage and Sustenance: Indigenous Peoples and Genetic Engineering: Threats to Food, Agriculture, and the Environment." A Primer and Resource Guide, September 2001. Wadsworth: Indigenous Peoples Council on Biocolonialism. http://www.ipcb.org/pdf_files/LifeLineageandSustenance.pdf.

Hurley, Timothy. "Bouncing Back: Outside Interests Sustain and Challenge Kaua'i Two Decades after Hurricane Iniki." *Honolulu Star-Advertiser,* December 15, 2013.

Iaukea, Sydney L. *The Queen and I: A Story of Dispossession and Reconnections in Hawai'i.* Los Angeles: University of California Press, 2011.

'Īlio'ulaokalani Coalition. "Paoakalani Declaration." Ka 'Aha Pono, 2003. http://kaahapono.com/PaoakalaniDeclaration05.pdf.

Johnson, Rubellite. "The Hawaiian Language and Hawaiian Studies." In *Mālamalama: A History of the University of Hawai'i,* edited by Robert M. Kamins and Robert E. Potter, 137–143. Honolulu: University of Hawai'i Press, 1998.

Ka'apu, Kekoa. "Statement of Kekoa D. Kaapu, Vice-President, A.L.O.H.A. Association: On H.R. 1944 to Settle the Historic Claims of Hawaiian Natives, before the Sub-committee on Indian Affairs of the House Committee on Interior and Insular Affairs." In Carmen E. Oliviera, "ALOHA Association, Inc.: A Nativistic Millenarian Movement." Unpublished manuscript, Hamilton Library, University of Hawai'i, 1975, p. 8. Photocopy.

KAHEA. "Fact Sheet: New Massive 18-Story Telescope Complex Proposed for Mauna Kea." Honolulu: KAHEA: The Hawaiian-Environmental Alliance, 2011.

Ka Ho'okolokolonui Kānaka Maoli. "Introduction to the Verdict of the International Peoples' Tribunal Hawai'i, August 1993." Unpublished manuscript, 1995.

Kamahele, Momiala. "'Īlio'ulaokalani: Defending Native Hawaiian Culture." In *Asian Settler Colonialism: From Local Governance to the Habits of Everyday Life in Hawai'i,* edited by Candace Fujikane and Jonathan Okamura, 76–98. Honolulu: University of Hawai'i Press, 2008.

Kame'eleihiwa, Lilikalā. *Native Land and Foreign Desires: How Shall We Live in Harmony / Ko Hawai'i 'Āina a Me Nā Koi Pu'umake a Ka Po'e Haole: Pehea Lā E Pono Ai?* Honolulu: Bishop Museum Press, 1992.

Kamehameha III, King of the Hawaiian Islands. "Buke Kakau Paa No Ka Mahele Aina I Hooholoia Iwaena O Kamehameha III a Me Na Lii a Me Na Konohiki Ana." Hale Alii Honolulu: Hawai'i State Archives, 1848.

"Kamehameha-Maui Grad Is First Non-Hawaiian." *Honolulu Star Bulletin*, May 20, 2007.

Kanahele, Pualani Kanaka'ole. *Ka Honua Ola: 'Eli'eli Kau Mai / The Living Earth: Descend, Deepen the Revelation*. Honolulu: Kamehameha, 2011.

———. *Ka Honua Ola (The Living Earth)*. Honolulu: State Foundation on Culture and the Arts, 1992.

Kanahele, Pualani Kanaka'ole, Huihui Kanahele-Mossman, Kalei Nu'uhiwa, and Kaumakaiwapo'ohalahi'ipaka Keali'ikanaka'ole. "Kūkulu Ke Ea a Kanaloa: The Culture Plan for Kanaloa Kaho'olawe." Edith Kanaka'ole Foundation, 2009.

Kana'iaupuni, Shawn, Nolan Malone, and Koren Ishibashi. *Ka Huaka'i: 2005 Native Hawaiian Educational Assessment*. Honolulu: Pauahi Publications, Kamehameha Schools, 2005.

Kanehe, Le'a Malia. "From Kumulipo: I Know Where I Come From—an Indigenous Pacific Critique of the Genographic Project." In *Pacific Dialogue on Ownership of Genes: Pacific Indigenous Experiences and Analysis of the Commodification and Ownership of Life*, edited by Aroha Te Pareakae Mead and Steven Ratuva, 114–129. Wellington: Call of the Earth Llamado de la Tierra and the United Nations, University Institute of Advanced Studies, 2007. http://www.ias.unu.edu/sub_page.aspx?catID=97&ddlID=229.

Kauanui, J. Kēhaulani. "Colonialism in Equality." Special issue, *South Atlantic Quarterly* (SAQ) 107, no. 4 (2008).

———. *Hawaiian Blood: Colonialism and the Politics of Sovereignty and Indigeneity*. Durham, NC: Duke University Press, 2008.

———. "Hawaiian Nationhood, Self-Determination, and International Law." In *Transforming the Tools of the Colonizer: Collaboration, Knowledge, and Language in Native Narratives*, edited by Florencia E. Mallon. Durham, NC: Duke University Press, 2011.

———. "Precarious Positions: Native Hawaiians and U.S. Federal Recognition." *Contemporary Pacific* 17, no. 1 (2005): 1–27.

Kawai'ae'a, Keiki K. C., Alohalani Kaluhiokalani (Kaina) Housman, and Makalapua (Ka'awa) Alencastre. "Pū'ā i ka 'Ōlelo, Ola ka 'Ohana: Three Generations of Hawaiian Language Revitalization." In *Hūlili: Multidisiplinary Research on Hawaiian Well-Being* 4, no. 1 (2007): 183–237.

Keith, Victoria, and Jerry Rochford. *The Sand Island Story*. Honolulu: Windward Video, 1981.

Kelly, Anne Keala. "Kūkākūkā." *Honolulu Weekly*, January 8, 2003.

Kelly, Gretchen. "Hui Pū: Hawaiians Unifying for Independence?" *SPASIFIK*, September–October 2005. http://www.hawaiiankingdom.info/C1126750129/E20050922123842/index.html.

Kelly, Marion. "Changes in Land Tenure in Hawaii, 1778–1850." MA thesis, University of Hawai'i, Pacific Islands Studies, 1956.

———. *Historical Study of Kawainui Marsh Area Island of O'ahu*. Honolulu: Department of Anthropology, Bernice P. Bishop Museum, 1985.

———. *Loko I'a o He'eia: Heeia Fishpond*. Honolulu: Department of Anthropology, Bernice P. Bishop Museum, 2000.

———. *Majestic Ka'u: Mo'olelo of Nine Ahupua'a*. Honolulu: Department of Anthropology, Bernice P. Bishop Museum, 1980.

———. *Nā Mala o Kona—Gardens of Kona: A History of Land Use in Kona, Hawai'i*. Honolulu: Department of Anthropology, Bernice P. Bishop Museum, 1983.

Kelly, Marion, and Sidney Michael Quintal. *Cultural History Report of Makua Military Reservation and Vicinity, Makua Valley, Oahu, Hawaii*. Honolulu: Department of Anthropology, Bernice P. Bishop Museum, 1977.

Kent, Noel. *America in 1900*. Armonk, NY: M. E. Sharpe, 2000.

———. *Hawaii: Islands under the Influence*. Honolulu: University of Hawai'i Press, 1983.

Kepelino. *Kepelino's Traditions of Hawai'i*. Edited by Martha W. Beckwith. Honolulu: Bishop Museum Press, 2007.

Kido, Pamela S. "Becoming Local: Social Movement and Literary Production in Late-Twentieth Century Hawai'i." PhD diss., University of California, Santa Cruz, 2008.

Kikiloi, Kekuewa. "Rebirth of an Archipelago: Sustaining a Hawaiian Cultural Identity for People and Homeland." *Hūlili* 6 (2010): 73–115.

Kimbrell, Andrew. *The Human Body Shop: The Engineering and Marketing of Life*. San Francisco: Harper, 1993.

Kimura, Larry. "The Hawaiian Language." In *Native Hawaiians Study Commission Report*. Washington: U.S. Department of Interior, June 1983, 173–203.

KITV. *Mo'olelo o ka 'Āina: Story of the Land, a three-part series*. Video. Honolulu: Western Telestations, KITV, 1984. University of Hawai'i library system, http://library.manoa.hawaii.edu/.

"The KS Impact: Increasing Access to Quality Educational Experiences." Policy Analysis and System Evaluation (PASE) Report #03–04:10. Information Brief, October 2003. Honolulu: Kamehameha Schools.

Kua'āina Associates. "The Lifework and Collective Song of Sam Kaha'i Ka'ai." Exhibit brochure, Maui Arts and Cultural Center, Wailuku, December 1–30, 2006.

Kubota, Gary. "Panel Hears Pleas to Both Increase, Reduce Water Flow." *Maui News*, April 28, 1988.

Kuykendall, R. S. *The Hawaiian Kingdom*, vol. 1, *1778–1854*. Honolulu: University of Hawai'i Press, 1938.

Lâm, Maivân Clech. *At the Edge of the State: Indigenous Peoples and Self-Determination*. Ardsley, NY: Transnational, 2000.

Lasky, Jacqueline. "Community Struggles, Struggling Communities: Land, Water and Self-Determination in Waiāhole-Waikāne, Hawai'i." PhD diss., University of Hawai'i at Mānoa, 2010.

Latin American Alliance. "Bioprospecting/Biopiracy and Indigenous Peoples." Ottawa: Rural Advancement Foundation International, 2002. http://enviro.lclark.edu:8002/rid=1162267760943_253495562_1464/bioprospecting_people.pdf.

"Legislators Impressed by Their Trip to Island." *Honolulu Star-Bulletin*, February 13, 1976.

Lili'uokalani, Lydia Dominis. *Hawaii's Story by Hawaii's Queen*. Boston: Lee and Shepard, 1898.

———. *The Kumulipo: An Hawaiian Creation Myth*. Preface by K. Campbell. Boston: Lee and Shepard, 1897. Reprint, Kentfield: Pueo Press, 1978.

———. "Queen Liliuokalani's Protest of Annexation, June 17, 1897." *Hawaiian Journal of Law and Politics* 1 (summer 2004). http://www2.hawaii.edu/~hslp/journal/vol1/1897_Protest_(HJLP).pdf.

Lindsey, R. Hokulei. "Responsibility with Accountability: The Birth of a Strategy to Protect Kanaka Maoli Traditional Knowledge." *Howard Law Journal* 48 (2005): 763.

Lo, Catherine. "Patents on Life: The Whole World in Whose Hands?" *Honolulu Weekly*, April 5, 2006.

Loomis, Albertine. *For Whom Are the Stars?* Honolulu: University of Hawai'i Press, 1976.

Lucas, Paul F. Nahoa. "E Ola Mau Kākou I Ka 'Ōlelo Makuahine: Hawaiian Language Policy and the Courts." *Hawaiian Journal of History* 34 (2000): 1–28.

MacDonald, Peter. "Fixed in Time: A Brief History of Kaho'olawe." *Hawaiian Journal of History* 6 (1972).

MacKenzie, Melody Kapilialoha. *Native Hawaiian Rights Handbook*. Honolulu: Native Hawaiian Legal Corporation, 1991.

"Makua Valley Ideal Training Area for Soldiers to Fine-Tune Skills." *Honolulu Star-Bulletin*, April 26, 1996.

Malo, David. *Hawaiian Antiquities*. Honolulu: Hawaiian Gazette, 1903.

Maly, Kepā, and Onaona Maly. "Mauna Kea—Ka Piko Kaulana O Ka ʻĀina: A Collection of Native Traditions, Historic Accounts, and Oral History Interviews For: Mauna Kea, the Land of Kaʻohe, Humuʻula, and the ʻĀina Mauna on the Island of Hawaiʻi." Hilo: Kumu Pono Associates, 2005.

Marcos, Subcomandante Insurgente. *Our Word Is Our Weapon*. Edited by Juana Ponce de Leon. New York: Seven Stories Press, 2002.

———. *Ya Basta! Ten Years of the Zapatista Uprising*. Oakland: AK Press, 2004.

Mariani, Jeanne, and Rod Ohira. "Sovereignty Seekers under Vigil." *Honolulu Star-Bulletin*, June 11, 1992.

"Marines Cancel Mākua Exercise." *Honolulu Advertiser*, March 20, 1997.

Martin, Liko. "Waimanalo Blues." Recorded by Country Comfort, on *We Are the Children*. Tom Moffat Productions, 1972.

Mast, Robert H., and Anne B. Mast, eds. *Autobiography of Protest in Hawaiʻi*. Honolulu: University of Hawaiʻi Press, 1996.

Matsuoka, Jon K., Davianna McGregor, and Luciano Minerbi; Cultural Action Network for Developing Options (CANDO). "Native Hawaiian Ethnographic Study for the Hawaiʻi Geothermal Project Proposed for Puna and Southeast Maui." Environmental Impact Study prepared for U.S. Department of Energy, Oak Ridge Operations Office. Oak Ridge: Oak Ridge National Laboratory, 1996.

"Mauna Kea Comprehensive Management Plan: UH Management Areas." Honolulu: Kuʻiwalu Consulting, January 2009.

"Mayor Signs GMO Bill 113 into Law: Genetically Modified Organisms Banned!" *Big Island Video News*, December 5, 2013. http://www.bigislandvideonews.com/2013/12/05/mayor-signs-gmo-bill-113-into-law/.

McGregor, Davianna. *Nā Kuaʻaina: Living Hawaiian Culture*. Honolulu: University of Hawaiʻi Press, 2007.

———. "Proper Recognition: Is the Akaka Bill the Best Prescription for Hawaiians? Yes: Independence Does Not Offer Same Guaranteed Protection of Native Rights." *Honolulu Advertiser*, Sunday editorial section, April 25, 2004.

———. "Statehood: Catalyst of the Twentieth Century Kanaka ʻŌiwi Cultural Renaissance and Sovereignty Movement." *Journal of Asian American Studies* 13, no. 3 (2010): 311–326.

McGregor, Davianna, and Linda Revilla, eds. *Our History, Our Way: An Ethnic Studies Anthology*. Dubuque, IA: Kendall/Hunt, 1996.

McGregor-Alegado, Davianna. "Hawaiians: Organizing in the 1970s." *Amerasia Journal* 7, no. 2 (1980): 29–55.

McMillen, Georgia. "Social Organization in Waiahole-Waikane: The Impact of an Eviction Struggle." Unpublished manuscript, University of Hawaiʻi at Mānoa, 1978.

Merry, Sally E. *Colonizing Hawaiʻi: The Cultural Power of Law*. Princeton, NJ: Princeton University Press, 2000.

Meyer, Meleanna Aluli, dir. and prod. *Hoʻokuʻikahi: To Unify as One*. Video recording. Honolulu: Native Books and Beautiful Things, 1998.

Mgbeogi, Ikechi. *Global Biopiracy: Patents, Plants and Indigenous Knowledge*. Ithaca, NY: Cornell University Press, 2006.

Mill, James. *The History of British India*. Classics of British Historical Literature. Chicago: University of Chicago Press, 1975.

Minerbi, Luciano. "Sustainability versus Growth in Hawai'i." *Social Process in Hawai'i* 35 (1994).

Minton, Nālani, and Noenoe Silva, comps. and eds. "Kū'ē: The Hui Aloha 'Āina Anti-Annexation Petitions, 1897–1898." University of Hawai'i at Mānoa Special Collections, 1998. http://libweb.hawaii.edu/digicoll/annexation/petition.html.

Modavi, Neghin. "Land, Environment and Power: State, Capital and Community Forces in Environmental Disputes in Hawaii." PhD diss., University of Hawai'i at Mānoa, 1992.

Mokuau, N. "Culturally Based Interventions for Substance Use and Child Abuse among Native Hawaiians." U.S. Department of Health and Human Services, *Public Health Reports* 117 (2002): S82–S87.

Morales, Rodney, ed. *Ho'iho'i Hou: A Tribute to George Helm and Kimo Mitchell*. Honolulu: Bamboo Ridge, 1984.

Moreton-Robinson, Aileen M. "I Still Call Australia Home: Indigenous Belonging and Place in a White Postcolonising Society." In *Uprootings/Regroundings: Questions of Home and Migration*, edited by Sarah Ahmed, 23–40. Oxford: Berg, 2003.

———, ed. *Sovereign Subjects: Indigenous Sovereignty Matters*. Crows Nest, Australia: Allen and Unwin, 2008.

Morgensen, Gretchen. "A Mortgage Tornado Warning, Unheeded." *New York Times*, February 4, 2012.

Morris, Nancy Jane. "Ka Loea Kalaiaina, 1898: A Study of a Hawaiian Language Newspaper as a Historical Reference Source." MA thesis, University of Hawai'i at Mānoa, 1975.

Morse, Bradford W., and Kazi A. Hamid. "American Annexation of Hawaii: An Example of the Unequal Treaty Doctrine." *Connecticut Journal of International Law* 5, no. 2 (1990): 447, 449.

Nakata, Bob. "The Struggles of the Waiahole-Waikane Community Association." *Social Process in Hawai'i* 39 (1999): 60–73.

Nā Maka o ka 'Āina. *Act of War: The Overthrow of the Hawaiian Nation*. Film. Honolulu: Nā Maka o ka 'Āina in association with Center for Hawaiian Studies, University of Hawai'i at Mānoa, 1993.

———. *Hui Na'auao: A Community Education Project*. Film. Honolulu: Nā Maka o ka 'Āina, 1992.

———. *Islands at Risk: Genetic Engineering in Hawai'i*. Film. Honolulu: Nā Maka o ka 'Āina, 2006. https://www.youtube.com/watch?v=P29nhSR1l30.

———. *Kalo Pa'a o Waiāhole—Hard Taro of Waiāhole*. Film. Honolulu: Nā Maka o ka 'Āina, 1995.

———. *Mākua: To Heal the Nation*. Film. Honolulu: Nā Maka o ka 'Āina, 1996.

———. *Mālama Hāloa: Protecting the Taro*. Film. Honolulu: Nā Maka o ka 'Āina, 2010.

———. *Mauna Kea—Temple under Siege*. Film. Honolulu: Nā Maka o ka 'Āina, 2006.

———. *Pele's Appeal*. Film. Honolulu: Nā Maka o ka 'Āina, 1989.

———. *A Presentation by Sam Ka'ai*. Video recording. Honolulu: Nā Maka o ka 'Āina, 1991.

———. *Proceedings of Ka Ho'okolokolonui Kānaka Maoli Peoples' International Tribunal Hawai'i 1993*. Transcribed from the audio portion of videotapes recorded by Nā Maka o ka 'Āina during August 12–20, 1993. 6 vols. Nā'ālehu, HI: Nā Maka o ka 'Āina, 2010. http://www.namaka.com/transcripts/tribunal.html.

———. *The Tribunal: Ka Ho'okolokolonui Kānaka Maoli—Peoples' International Tribunal Hawai'i 1993*. Film. Honolulu: Nā Maka o ka 'Āina, 1994.

———. Video Catalog. Honolulu: Nā Maka o ka 'Āina. http://www.hawaiianvoice.com.

———. *We Are Who We Were: From Resistance to Affirmation*. Film. Honolulu: Nā Maka o ka 'Āina and Hawaiian Patriotic League, 1998.

Namuo, Clyde. "Misinformation Abounds on Revisions to Akaka Bill." *Honolulu Advertiser,* May 2, 2004. http://the.honoluluadvertiser.com/article/2004/May/02/op/op10a.html.

Nation of Hawai'i. "Proclamation of the Restoration of the Independence of the Sovereign Nation State of Hawai'i, January 16, 1994, 'Iolani Palace, Honolulu, O'ahu, Hawai'i [Official English Version]." Hawaiian Independence. http://www.hawaii-nation.org/proclamall.html.

Native American Rights Fund. "A Move toward Sovereignty: Interior Publishes Alaska Tribe List." NARF *Legal Review* 19, no. 1 (1994).

Native Hawaiian Roll Commission. "Kana'iolowalu Launches Online Registry for Native Hawaiians." Press release, July 20, 2012. http://www.oha.org/page/native-hawaiian-roll-commission.

———. "Moving the Hawaiian Nation Forward." Kana'iolowalu, March 17, 2014. http://www.kanaiolowalu.org/news/story/?id=47.

"Native Hawaiian Roll Commission to Be Led by Former Gov. Waihee." *Star-Advertiser,* September 8, 2011. http://www.staradvertiser.com.

"Native Hawaiians Will Not Benefit by Bill, Say Some Sovereignty Groups." *Honolulu Star-Bulletin,* February 25, 2003.

NeSmith, Keao. "Tutu's Hawaiian and the Emergence of a Neo-Hawaiian Language." *'Ōiwi: A Native Hawaiian Journal* 3 (2003): 135–152.

Niheu, Soli Kiheu. "Huli: Community Struggles and Ethnic Studies." *Social Process in Hawai'i* 39 (1999): 43–59.

Nimmo, H. Arlo. "Pele, Ancient Goddess of Contemporary Hawaii." *Pacific Studies* 9, no. 2 (1986).

Nogelmeier, M. Puakea, ed. *He Lei No 'Emalani: Chants for Queen Emma Kaleleonālani.* Honolulu: Bishop Museum Press, 2001.

"No Kalani Kauikeaouli Kamehameha III." *Ka Nupepa Kuokoa* 5, no. 12 (March 24, 1866). Available at the Papakilo Database, http://www.papakilodatabase.com/main/main.php.

Oda, Dennis. "All Pau; Aloha!" *Honolulu Star-Bulletin,* February 17, 1997.

Odo, Franklin. *No Sword to Bury: Japanese Americans in Hawai'i during World War II.* Philadelphia: Temple University Press, 2004.

Odo, Franklin, and Kazuko Sinoto. *Pictorial History of the Japanese in Hawai'i, 1885–1924.* Honolulu: Hawai'i Immigrant Heritage Preservation Center, Department of Anthropology, Bernice P. Bishop Museum, 1985.

Office of Hawaiian Affairs. "History: Establishment of OHA." Office of Hawaiian Affairs. http://www.oha.org/about/history.

———. *'Onipa'a: Five Days in the History of the Hawaiian Nation: Centennial Observance of the Overthrow of the Hawaiian Monarchy.* Honolulu: Office of Hawaiian Affairs, 1994.

'Ohana Pale Ke Ao, et al. v. Board of Agriculture, State of Hawai'i. 188 P.3d 761 (Haw. Intermediate Court of Appeals, 2008).

Okamura, Jonathan. *Ethnicity and Inequality in Hawai'i.* Philadelphia: Temple University Press, 2008.

———. *Filipino American History, Identity and Community in Hawai'i.* Honolulu: Department of Sociology, University of Hawai'i at Mānoa, 1996.

———. *Imagining the Filipino American Diaspora: Transnational Relations, Identities, and Communities.* New York: Garland, 1998.

———. *The Japanese American Contemporary Experience in Hawai'i.* Honolulu: Department of Sociology, University of Hawai'i at Mānoa, 2002.

———. *The Japanese American Historical Experience in Hawai'i.* Dubuque, IA: Kendall/Hunt, 2001.

"Olelo Hawaii." *Ka Puuhonua o na Hawaii,* January 26, 1917.

Oliveira, Carmen Ewalaniki'eki'e. "ALOHA Association, Inc.: A Nativistic Millenarian Movement." Unpublished manuscript. Hamilton Library, University of Hawai'i at Mānoa, 1975.
Omandam, Pat. "Fallen Warriors: An 18-Hour Vigil at Iolani Palace Will Honor Those Now Dead Who Significantly Helped Hawaiian Movement." *Honolulu Star-Bulletin*, August 11, 1998.
Oppenheim, Lassa. *International Law: A Treatise. Vol. 1: Peace*. New York: Longmans, Green, 1905.
Oshiro, David. "Arrests Anger Hawaiians." *Honolulu Star-Bulletin*, June 12, 1992.
Osorio, Jonathan Kamakawiwo'ole. *Dismembering Lāhui: A History of the Hawaiian Nation to 1887*. Honolulu: University of Hawai'i Press, 2002.
———. "Unpublished Journal of Huaka'i to Kaho'olawe." 1988.
Pang, Gordon Y. K. "For Some, Akaka Bill Falls Far Short." *Honolulu Advertiser*, July 21, 2005.
———. "Hawaiian Independence Groups Send 'No' Message." *Honolulu Advertiser*, July 1, 2005.
———. "Opponents Ask OHA's Aid to Derail Akaka Bill." *Honolulu Advertiser*, July 8, 2005.
Paoa Productions. *Wahine Mākua Speak*. Video recording. Honolulu: Paoa Productions, 1996.
Parker, Barry. *Stairway to the Stars: The Story of the World's Largest Observatory*. New York: Plenum, 1994.
Perez, Rob. "State Won't Step into Perfect Title Deed Disputes: The Attorney General's Office Say Bills before the Legislature Already Address the Issue." *Honolulu Star-Bulletin*, January 29, 1997.
Perry, Antonio. "Hawaiian Water Rights." In *Hawaiian Almanac and Annual for 1913*, edited by Thomas G. Thrum et al. Honolulu, 1912.
Perry, Bruce, ed. *Malcolm X: The Last Speeches*. New York: Pathfinder, 1989.
Poepoe, Joseph Mokuohai. "Ka Moolelo Hawaii Kahiko." *Ka Na'i Aupuni*, February 9–12, 1906.
Protect Kaho'olawe 'Ohana. "Kaho'olawe Island: History." 2013. http://www.protectkahoolaweohana.org/history.html.
"Protesters Besiege Bachman Hall." *Ka Leo o Hawai'i*, May 1, 1995.
Pukui, Mary Kawena. *'Ōlelo No'eau: Hawaiian Proverbs and Poetical Sayings*. New York: Bishop Museum Press, 1983.
Pukui, Mary Kawena, and Samuel H. Elbert. *Hawaiian Dictionary*, rev. and enlarged ed. Honolulu: University of Hawai'i Press, 1986.
Pukui, Mary K., Samuel H. Elbert, and Esther T. Mookini. *Place Names of Hawai'i*. Honolulu: University of Hawai'i Press, 1974.
Pukui, Mary Kawena, E. W. Haertig, and Catherine A. Lee. *Nānā i ke Kumu: Look to the Source*, vol. 1, 7th ed. 1972. Reprint, Honolulu: Hui Hānai, 1983.
———. *Nānā i ke Kumu: Look to the Source*, vol. 2. Honolulu: Hui Hānai, 1972.
Pukui, Mary Kawena, and Alfons L. Korn. *The Echo of Our Song: Chants and Poems of the Hawaiians*. Honolulu: University of Hawai'i Press, 1979.
Redfeather, Nancy. "GMOs in Hawai'i: The Big Picture." In *Facing Hawai'i's Future: Harvesting Essential Information about GMOs*, 20–23. Hilo: Hawai'i SEED, 2006.
Richardson, William S. *Ka Lama Kū O Ka No'eau: The Standing Torch of Wisdom: Selected Opinions of William S. Richardson, Chief Justice, Hawai'i Supreme Court, 1966–1982*. Mānoa: University of Hawai'i, William S. Richardson School of Law, 2009.
Rifkin, Jeremy. *The Biotech Century: Harnessing the Gene and Remaking the World*. New York: Tarcher/Putnam, 1998.
Ritte, Walter, Jr., and Le'a Malia Kanehe. "Kuleana No Hāloa (Responsibility for Taro): Protecting the Sacred Ancestor from Ownership and Genetic Modification." In *Pacific Genes and Life Patents: Pacific Indigenous Experiences and Analysis of the Commodification and Ownership of Life*, edited by Aroha Te Pareakae Mead and Steven Ratuva, 130–137. Wellington: Call of the Earth and the

United Nations University Institute of Advanced Studies, 2007. http://www.ias.unu.edu/sub_page.aspx?catID=97&ddlID=229.

Ritte, Walter, Jr., and Richard Sawyer. "Nā Mana'o Aloha o Kaho'olawe." Honolulu: Aloha 'Āina o Nā Kupuna, 1978.

Rohrer, Judy. *Haoles in Hawai'i.* Honolulu: University of Hawai'i Press, 2010.

Rosa, Henry "David." "Letter to the Editor from Henry 'David' Rosa, Chairperson, Makua Council." *Honolulu Advertiser,* March 13, 1996.

Russ, William Adam. *The Hawaiian Republic, and Its Struggle to Win Annexation, 1894–98.* Selinsgrove, PA: Susquehanna University Press, 1961.

Sai, David Keanu. "The American Occupation of the Hawaiian Kingdom: Beginning the Transition from Occupied to Restored State." PhD diss., University of Hawai'i at Mānoa, 2008.

———. "American Occupation of the Hawaiian State: A Century Unchecked." *Hawaiian Journal of Law and Politics* 1 (2004): 46–81.

———. "A Slippery Path towards Hawaiian Indigeneity: An Analysis and Comparison between Hawaiian State Sovereignty and Hawaiian Indigeneity and Its Use and Practice in Hawai'i Today." *Journal of Law and Social Challenges* 10 (2008): 101–166.

———. *Ua Mau Ke Ea, Sovereignty Endures: An Overview of the Political and Legal History of the Hawaiian Islands.* Honolulu: Pu'a Foundation, 2011.

Said, Edward. *Culture and Imperialism.* New York: Knopf, 1993.

———. "In Conversation with Neeladri Bhattacharya, Suvir Kaul, and Ania Loomba." "Ideologies of the Postcolonial," special issue of *Interventions: International Journal of Postcolonial Studies* 1, no. 1 (1998): 81–96.

Santos, Jerry. "Me ke Aloha ku'u Home o Kahalu'u." Recorded by Olomana on *Seabird.* 1975.

Scheuer, Jonathan Likeke. "Water and Power in Hawai'i: The Waiāhole-Waikāne Case and the Future of the Islands." PhD diss., University of California, Santa Cruz, 2002.

Shahriari, Sara. "Bolivia Enacts New Law for Mother Earth." *Indian Country,* October 26, 2012. http://indiancountrytodaymedianetwork.com/gallery/photo/bolivia-enacts-new-law-mother-earth-141899.

Shimabukuro, Jimmy. "Kahoolawe: A Different Meaning." *Hawaii Observer,* March 10, 1977.

Shintani, T., S. Beckham, H. K. O'Conner, C. Hughes, and A. Sato. "Waianae Diet Program: A Culturally Sensitive, Community-Based Obesity and Clinical Intervention Program for the Native Hawaiian Population." *Hawaii Medical Journal* 53, no. 5 (1994): 136–141.

Siddall, John William. *Men of Hawaii: A Biographical Reference Library, Complete and Authentic, of the Men of Note and Substantial Achievement in the Hawaiian Islands,* vol. 1. Honolulu: Honolulu Star-Bulletin, 1921.

Silva, Noenoe K. *Aloha Betrayed: Native Hawaiian Resistance to American Colonialism.* Durham, NC: Duke University Press, 2004.

———. "Early Hawaiian Newspapers and Kanaka Maoli Intellectual History, 1834–1855." *Hawaiian Journal of History* (2008): 42.

———. "Kanaka Maoli Resistance to Annexation." *'Ōiwi: A Native Hawaiian Journal* 1 (1998): 40–80.

"Six in Kahoolawe Trial Found Guilty of Trespass." *Honolulu Advertiser,* June 24, 1977.

Smith, Pam. "Kaho'olawe: Hawaiians on Trial." *Hawaii Observer,* July 28, 1977.

———. "The Ohana: Birth of a Nation or Band-Aid Brigade?" *Hawaii Observer,* May 19, 1977.

Smith, Paul Chaat, and Robert Allen Warrior. *Like a Hurricane: The Indian Movement from Alcatraz to Wounded Knee.* New York: New Press, 1996.

Somerville, Alice Te Punga. *Once Were Pacific: Maori Connections to Oceania*. Minneapolis: University of Minnesota Press, 2012.

"Sovereign in Hawaii." Sovereign Stories, Pacific Islanders in Communication, Honolulu, 2004. http://www.sovereignstories.org.

Spencer, Thomas P. *Ka Hoʻokahuli Aupuni Kaulana o 1893: Kaua Kūloko ma Honolulu, Ianuari 7, 1895: Ka Hoʻāʻo ʻana e Hoʻokahuli i ka Repubalika Hawaiʻi, Aupuni Hou ko Hawaiʻi Pae ʻĀina: Hoʻohiwahiwa ʻia me nā Kiʻi* [The Famous Overthrow of 1893: Civil War in Honolulu, January 7, 1895: The Attempt to Overthrow the Hawaiian Government: The New Government of the Hawaiian Islands: Beautifully Illustrated with Pictures]. Bishop Museum Classical Reprints in Hawaiian Language. Honolulu: Bishop Museum Press, 2000.

Sproat, D. Kapuaʻala. "The Backlash against PASH: Legislative Attempts to Restrict Native Hawaiian Rights." *University of Hawaiʻi Law Review* 20 (summer–fall 1998): 321.

———. "Water." In *The Value of Hawaiʻi: Knowing the Past, Shaping the Future*, 187–194. Honolulu: University of Hawaiʻi Press, 2010.

Sproat, D. Kapuaʻala, and Isaac H. Moriwake. "Ke Kalo Paʻa o Waiāhole: Use of the Public Trust as a Tool for Environmental Advocacy." In *Creative Common Law Strategies for Protecting the Environment*, 247–284. Washington, DC: Environmental Law Institute, 2007.

Stack, Carol B. *All Our Kin: Strategies for Survival in a Black Community*. New Brunswick, NJ: Rutgers University Press, 1985.

Stannard, David. "Disease and Infertility: A New Look at the Demographic Collapse of Native Populations in the Wake of Western Contact." *Journal of American Studies* 24 (1990): 325–350.

Stauffer, Robert H. *Kahana: How the Land Was Lost*. Honolulu: University of Hawaiʻi Press, 2004.

Sterling, Elspeth P., and Catherine C. Summers. *Sites of Oʻahu*. Honolulu: Bishop Museum Press, 1978.

"Stryker Brigade in Hawaiʻi." DMZ Hawaiʻi Aloha ʻĀina, 2003. http://www.dmzhawaii.org/dmz-legacy-site/stop_stryker.html.

Suka, Eddie. "Makua ʻOhana Project." Unpublished report to Hawaiʻi Community Action Program, May 1996. On file with Kalama Nīheu.

Suka, Edmond. "Mākua." Report presented to the Waiʻanae Neighborhood Board on behalf of the Mākua Community Council, February 1996.

Swain, Harry. *Oka: A Political Crisis and Its Legacy*. Vancouver: Douglas and McIntyre, 2010.

TenBruggencate, Jan. "Sovereignty Movement Has Many Turning Points: Suits Will Continue without Akaka Bill." *Honolulu Advertiser*, June 11, 2006.

Tengan, Ty P. Kāwika. *Native Men Remade: Gender and Nation in Contemporary Hawaiʻi*. Durham, NC: Duke University Press, 2008.

———. *Report on the Archival, Historical and Archaeological Resources of Nā Wai ʻEhā, Wailuku District, Island of Maui*. With collaboration from J. L. A. Perry and N. Armstrong. Prepared for the Office of Hawaiian Affairs. Honolulu, September 2007.

Thiongʼo, Ngũgĩ wa. *Decolonising the Mind: The Politics of Language in African Literature*. Portsmouth, NH: Heinemann, 1986.

Trask, Haunani-Kay. "The Birth of the Modern Hawaiian Movement: Kalama Valley, Oʻahu." *Hawaiian Journal of History* 21 (1987): 126–153.

———. *From a Native Daughter: Colonialism and Sovereignty in Hawaiʻi*. Monroe, ME: Common Courage Press, 1993.

———. *From a Native Daughter: Colonialism and Sovereignty in Hawaiʻi*, rev. ed. Honolulu: University of Hawaiʻi Press, 1999.

———. "January 17, 1993, Speech." DVD. Los Angeles: In-D Press.
———. "Settlers of Color and 'Immigrant' Hegemony: 'Locals' in Hawai'i." In *Asian Settler Colonialism: From Local Governance to the Habits of Everyday Life in Hawai'i*, edited by Candace Fujikane and Jonathan Y. Okamura, 45–65. Honolulu: University of Hawai'i Press, 2008.
Trask, Haunani-Kay, and Ed Greevy. *Kū'ē: Thirty Years of Land Struggle in Hawai'i*. Honolulu: Mutual, 2004.
Trask, Mililani. "Hawaiian Perspectives on GMOs." In *Facing Hawai'i's Future: Harvesting Essential Information about GMOs*, 24–27. Hilo: Hawai'i SEED, 2006.
Tribunal Kōmike. *Interim Report, Kānaka Maoli Nation, Plaintiff v. United States of America, Defendant, August 12–21, 1993*. Pamphlet. Honolulu: Ka Ho'okolokolonui Kānaka Maoli, 1993.
———. *Ka Ho'okolokolonui Kānaka Maoli, 1993, Peoples' International Tribunal Hawai'i—Mana'o*. Booklet. Honolulu: Ka Ho'okolokolonui Kānaka Maoli, 1993.
Trujillo, Eduardo E. "Taro Cultivar Named 'Pauakea.'" U.S. Patent 12,342, filed October 22, 1999, and issued January 8, 2002. http://patentscope.wipo.int/search/en/WO2001029181.
Tsosie, Rebecca A. "Engaging the Spirit of Racial Healing within Critical Race Theory: An Exercise in Transformative Thought." *Michigan Journal of Race and Law* 11, no. 21 (2005): 21–49.
Tuggle, Myra. "The Protect Kaho'olawe 'Ohana: Cultural Revitalization in a Contemporary Hawaiian Movement." MA thesis, University of Hawai'i at Mānoa, 1982.
Tuttle, Dan. "Dan Raps Navy on Kaho'olawe." *Honolulu Advertiser*, January 7, 1970.
"2 Claim Isle Desecrated." *Honolulu Advertiser*, January 7, 1989.
U.S. Congress and Senate. *Joint Resolution to Provide for Annexing the Hawaiian Islands to the United States*. 55th Cong., 2nd sess., no. 55. 1898.
U.S. Department of Justice. "Legal Issues Raised by Proposed Presidential Proclamation to Extend the Territorial Sea." In *Opinions of the Office of Legal Counsel*. Washington, DC: U.S. Government Printing Office, 1988.
U.S. Senate. "Secret Debate on Seizure of the Hawaiian Islands." *Hawaiian Journal of Law and Politics* 1 (summer 2004): 230–284. http://www2.hawaii.edu/~hslp/journal/vol1/Secret_Debate_(HJLP).pdf.
Vance, Audrey 'Iwalani. *Hui Na'auao: Education, the Path to Sovereignty and Self-Determination*. Honolulu: A. I. Vance, 1994.
Van Dyke, Jon M. *Who Owns the Crown Lands of Hawai'i?* Honolulu: University of Hawai'i Press, 2008.
Verenium Corporation. "Diversa and Celunol Complete Merger to Create Verenium Corporation, a Leader in the Emerging Biofuels Industry." Press release, June 20, 2007. http://ir.verenium.com.
Vogeler, Stephen Kūhiō. "'For Your Freedom and Ours': The Prolonged Occupations of Hawai'i and the Baltic States." PhD diss., University of Hawai'i at Mānoa, 2009.
Waite, David. "Court Order Due Today in Kamehameha Suit." *Honolulu Advertiser*, August 20, 2003.
Walker, Ranginui. *Ka Whawhai Tonu Matou*. Auckland: Penguin Books, 2004.
Warner, Sam L. No'eau. "*Kuleana*: The Right, Responsibility, and Authority of Indigenous Peoples to Speak and Make Decisions for Themselves in Language and Cultural Revitalization." *Anthropology and Education Quarterly* 30, no. 1 (1999): 68–93.
———. "The Movement to Revitalize Hawaiian Language and Culture." In *The Green Book of Language Revitalization in Practice*, edited by Leanne Hinton and Ken Hale, 133–146. San Diego: Brill Academic Press, 2001.
Weiss, Rick. "Gene-Altered Crops Denounced: Environmental Groups Seek Moratorium on Open-Air Tests." *Washington Post*, August 16, 2006.

"'White' Laws Unacceptable the Court Told." *Star-Bulletin*, September 22, 1971.

Whitt, Laurie Anne. "Indigenous Peoples, Intellectual Property and Imperial Science." *Oklahoma City University Law Review* 23 (1998): 211.

"Why Hawaiians Value Kaho'olawe." *Honolulu Star-Bulletin*, February 2, 1977.

Wilcox, Carol. *Sugar Water: Hawai'i's Plantation Ditches*. Honolulu: University of Hawai'i Press, 1996.

Wilson, William H., and Kamanā, Kauanoe. "Mai Loko Mai O Ka 'I'ini: Proceeding from a Dream: The 'Aha Pūnana Leo Connection in Hawaiian Language Revitalization." In *The Green Book of Language Revitalization in Practice*, edited by Leanne Hinton and Ken Hale, 147–178. San Diego: Brill Academic Press, 2001.

Wong, K. Laiana. "He Hāwa'e Kai Nui a Kau ma Kula." *Educational Perspectives* 37, no. 1 (2004): 31–39.

Yap, Britt. "An Island Divided: Native Hawaiians Stand to Lose the Most in Kaua'i's Raging GMO and Pesticide Debate." *Mana*, January 2014.

Young, Kanalu G. Terry. "August on My Mind." In *Chicken Soup from the Soul of Hawaii: Stories of Aloha to Create Paradise Wherever You Are*, edited by Jack Canfield. Deerfield Beach, FL: Health Communications, 2003.

———. "An Interdisciplinary Study of the Term Hawaiian." *Hawaiian Journal of Law and Politics* 1 (summer 2004): 40. http://www2.hawaii.edu/~hslp/journal_vol1.html.

———. "Kuleana: Toward a Historiography of a Hawaiian National Consciousness, 1780–2001." *Hawaiian Journal of Law and Politics* 2 (summer 2006): 40. http://www2.hawaii.edu/~hslp/journal_vol2.html.

———. *Rethinking the Native Hawaiian Past*. New York: Garland, 1998.

Young, Lum Pui. *The Chinese on Windward Oahu: Waiahole, Waikane and Hakipuu*. Honolulu: Hawaii Chinese History Center, 1975.

Contributors

NOA EMMETT ALULI, MD, is a physician in family practice on the island of Moloka'i and a medical director with Moloka'i General Hospital. He is a founding member of the Protect Kaho'olawe 'Ohana and was vice president of the Pele Defense Fund.

IBRAHIM AOUDÉ is a professor of ethnic studies at the University of Hawai'i at Mānoa and is the author and editor of numerous articles about Hawai'i's political economy and social movements. Aoudé is the editor of *Arab Studies Quarterly* and the *International Journal of Contemporary Iraqi Studies.*

KEKUNI BLAISDELL, MD, convener of the 1993 Peoples' International Tribunal, is one of Hawai'i's most renowned Kanaka Maoli physicians and political leaders. He became politicized by the dire health disparities and inequities of Kanaka Maoli, helping to author the *Native Hawaiian Health Care Act* and becoming an activist for native rights as a key leader in the Hawaiian sovereignty movement.

JOAN CONROW is an award-winning Kaua'i-based independent journalist who has been reporting for regional and national publications for more than twenty-five years.

NOELANI GOODYEAR-KA'ŌPUA is an associate professor of political science at the University of Hawai'i at Mānoa, where she teaches Hawaiian and Indigenous politics. She is the author of *The Seeds We Planted: Portraits of a Native Hawaiian Charter School* and the coeditor of *The Value of Hawai'i*, vol. 2, *Ancestral Roots, Oceanic Visions.*

EDWARD W. GREEVY is a freelance photographer concentrating on social and political documentary work for the last forty years. His documentary photographs have appeared in numerous published books and journals dealing with Hawaiian social and political themes.

ULLA HASAGER is director of civic engagement for the College of Social Sciences at the University of Hawai'i at Mānoa. She organized and archived testimonies from the 1993 Peoples' International Tribunal.

PAUAHI HOʻOKANO is originally from Oʻahu and lives in Wailuanui, Maui. She teaches at Kalama Intermediate in Makawao, and is pursuing her doctorate in curriculum studies through the University of Hawaiʻi at Mānoa, College of Education.

MICKY HUIHUI is a Kanaka Maoli writer, musician, and patriot devoted to community engagement and empowerment in Hawaiʻi.

IKAIKA HUSSEY is the founder and publisher of the *Hawaiʻi Independent*, an award-winning current affairs news magazine. Ikaika has been a community organizer and advocate for Hawaiian independence for fifteen years.

MANU KAʻIAMA is a Hawaiian national with a master's degree in business and a master's degree in Hawaiian studies. For over a decade, she has created and led grant-based programs that have supported over a thousand Hawaiians seeking higher education degrees.

LEʻA MALIA KANEHE is a Kanaka Maoli lawyer from Honolulu. She is a legal analyst with the Indigenous People's Council on Biocolonialism based in Nevada, where she works to address the impacts of genetic technologies on Indigenous peoples and their territories and natural resources.

J. KĒHAULANI KAUANUI is an associate professor of American studies and anthropology at Wesleyan University. She is the author of *Hawaiian Blood: Colonialism and the Politics of Sovereignty and Indigeneity* and a radio producer and host of two public affairs shows: one on Indigenous politics and the other relating to anarchism.

ANNE KEALA KELLY's work as a journalist and filmmaker focuses primarily on Hawaiian political and cultural issues, Indigenous peoples, and the environment. She has filed stories from Hawaii, Kathmandu, and Geneva, and her articles and essays have been published in the *Nation, Indian Country Today, American Indian Quarterly*, the *Honolulu Weekly*, and other journals.

JACQUELINE LASKY has been involved in community organizing and activism for many years in Hawaiʻi, Ohio, Guam, and Germany. She has a PhD in political science and currently teaches in women's studies at the University of Hawaiʻi at Mānoa.

DAVIANNA PŌMAIKAʻI MCGREGOR is a professor and founding member of the University of Hawaiʻi at Mānoa Ethnic Studies Department. She is a coordinator of the Protect Kahoʻolawe ʻOhana and author of *Nā Kuaʻāina: Living Hawaiian Culture*.

NĀLANI MINTON is director of ʻIKE AO PONO at the University of Hawaiʻi at Mānoa. She was designated by Dr. Kekuni Blaisdell as the 1993 Peoples' International Tribunal ʻElele Pono for the United Nations Working Group on Indigenous Populations during the Decade of Indigenous Peoples. At the UN, Nālani wrote many interventions for the Tribunal Kōmike and worked on the Draft Declaration on the Rights of Indigenous Peoples.

KALAMAOKAʻĀINA NIHEU is a Kanaka Maoli physician, warrior, and founding member of ʻOnipaʻa Nā Hui Kalo, a Hawaiʻi-wide kalo farmer association. She practices Family Medicine in Koʻolauloa and is the author of *Reclaiming the Sacred ʻĀina: The Impact of the Military on the Health of Native Hawaiians.*

KATRINA-ANN R. KAPĀʻANAOKALĀOKEOLA NĀKOA OLIVEIRA is an associate professor and the director of Kawaihuelani Center for Hawaiian Language at the University of Hawaiʻi at Mānoa.

JONATHAN KAMAKAWIWOʻOLE OSORIO is a professor of Hawaiian studies, musician, and community leader. He is the author of *Dismembering Lahui: A History of the Hawaiian Nation to 1887.*

LEON NOʻEAU PERALTO was born and raised in Waiākea Uka, Hilo, Hawaiʻi, and is a proud descendant of kūpuna from both Hāmākua, Hawaiʻi, and Kīpahulu, Maui. He holds a master's degree in Hawaiian studies from the University of Hawaiʻi at Mānoa, and is actively engaged in kuleana-based research and activism in his kulāiwi of Hāmākua.

KEKAILOA PERRY is a student of Hawaiian resistance and a teacher of Hawaiian rights, culture, and legal guerilla warfare.

PUHIPAU, as part of Nā Maka o Ka ʻĀina, has documented the Hawaiian movement in sight and sound. Of Palestinian and Hawaiian heritage, he has produced some ninety documentaries that have aired on PBS, public and commercial television stations in Hawaiʻi, and broadcast and cable networks throughout the world.

NOENOE K. SILVA, Kanaka Hawaiʻi from Kailua, Oʻahu, is a professor of political science at the University of Hawaiʻi at Mānoa. She is the author of *Aloha Betrayed: Native Hawaiian Resistance to American Colonialism.*

D. KAPUA'ALA SPROAT is an attorney and professor of law at the University of Hawai'i William S. Richardson School of Law. She has worked to protect water and land rights for more than two decades.

TY P. KĀWIKA TENGAN is an associate professor of ethnic studies and anthropology at the University of Hawai'i at Mānoa. He is the author of *Native Men Remade: Gender and Nation in Contemporary Hawai'i.*

MEHANA BLAICH VAUGHAN is a teacher and writer raised in Namahana, Kaua'i. She is an assistant professor of sustainable watershed and coastal management at the University of Hawai'i, and her work focuses on creating 'āina-based education programs that better prepare Hawai'i's young people to care for their home.

KŪHIŌ VOGELER is a scholar of international law and international relations as they relate to the U.S. occupation of Hawai'i. He teaches at Leeward Community College and the University of Hawai'i at Mānoa. He has participated in Hawai'i's independence movement since 1991.

ERIN KAHUNAWAIKA'ALA WRIGHT is the director of Native Hawaiian Student Services in Hawai'inuiākea School of Hawaiian Knowledge at the University of Hawai'i at Mānoa.

General Index

Index to Hawai'i Place Names

Index to Personal Names